Proletarian Power

Transitions: Asia and Asian America

PROLETARIAN POWER

Shanghai in
the Cultural Revolution

ELIZABETH J. PERRY

AND LI XUN

WestviewPress
A Division of HarperCollins*Publishers*

Transitions: Asia and Asian America

Copyright © 1997 by Westview Press, A Division of HarperCollins Publishers, Inc.

Published in 1997 in the United States of America by Westview Press, 5500 Central Avenue, Boulder,
Colorado 80301-2877, and in the United Kingdom by Westview Press, 12 Hid's Copse Road, Cumnor
Hill, Oxford OX2 9JJ

Library of Congress Cataloging-in-Publication Data
Perry, Elizabeth J.
  Proletarian Power : Shanghai in the Cultural Revolution /
Elizabeth J. Perry and Li Xun.
    p.   cm. — (Transitions—Asia and Asian America)
  Includes bibliographical references and index.
  ISBN 0-8133-2165-4 (hc.) — ISBN 0-8133-2166-2 (pbk.)
    1. Working class—China—Shanghai—Political activity—
History—20th century.   2. China—History—Cultural Revolution,
1966–1969.   I. Li, Xun.   II. Title.   III. Series.
HD8738.P47   1997
322.4′1′0951132—dc20
                                                                              96-42940
                                                                                 CIP

The paper used in this publication meets the requirements of the American National Standard for Per-
manence of Paper for Printed Library Materials Z39.48-1984.

10   9   8   7   6   5   4   3   2   1

Contents

Tables

Acknowledgments

This collaborative project was made possible by financial support from a number of sources. A Luce Foundation grant for the study of modern Shanghai brought Li Xun to Berkeley, while a research grant from the Institute of International Studies of the University of California at Berkeley permitted her to remain long enough to complete her contribution. Grants from the National Endowment for the Humanities, the Guggenheim Foundation, and the Chiang Ching-kuo Foundation enabled Elizabeth Perry's participation.

The research for this book was conducted primarily at the Shanghai Municipal Archives. We are grateful to the staff of that institution, and to the Shanghai Federation of Trade Unions (where Li Xun worked as a researcher for many years), for facilitating access to invaluable source materials.

Insightful readings of the book manuscript (in whole or in part) were undertaken by Lowell Dittmer, Roderick MacFarquhar, Michael Schoenhals, Dorothy Solinger, Wang Shaogang, Jeffery Wasserstrom, Ernest Young, and especially Mark Selden. Research assistance was provided by Susan McCarthy and Douglas Stiffler. Credit for the bibliography and index goes to Martin Beversdorf.

Essential as all this help was in improving the final product, the authors accept full responsibility for any errors in fact or interpretation that may remain.

Elizabeth J. Perry
Li Xun

Acronyms

CLCC	Criticize Lin Biao–Criticize Confucius campaign
CR	Cultural Revolution
CRSG	Cultural Revolution Small Group
CYL	Communist Youth League
KMT	Kuomintang
NPC	National People's Congress
PLA	People's Liberation Army
PRC	People's Republic of China
SFTU	Shanghai Federation of Trade Unions
SPC	Shanghai Party Committee
SRC	Shanghai Revolutionary Committee
WGH	Workers' General Headquarters
WPT	Workers' Propaganda Teams
WTT	Workers' Theory Troops

Introduction

China's Cultural Revolution (CR) looms as one of the most important, yet least understood, milestones of the twentieth century. Its significance derives not simply from its immense impact on subsequent developments within China, but also from what it reveals more generally about patterns of collective action under conditions of extreme politicization. Having built one of the most powerful systems of state domination the world had ever seen, Mao Zedong in 1966 then called upon the revolutionary masses of China to "bombard the headquarters"—that is, to attack the party-state apparatus itself.

In responding to Mao's clarion call, Chinese citizens evidenced a capacity for political activism that startled even the most seasoned observers of Communist systems, reliant as they had been upon a totalitarian model that downplayed the influence of social forces.[1] Analytical lenses had to be hastily refashioned to reflect new realities. As Franz Schurmann wrote in the second edition of his classic *Ideology and Organization in Communist China,*

> That extraordinary event known as the Great Proletarian Cultural Revolution, which came as a surprise to almost everyone in the field, called into question many analyses of China done by the growing corps of scholars of contemporary China. . . . Evidence indicates that the forces of Chinese society are equally as important as those coming from the structure of state power. . . . China's major social classes exert great pressure on the ideology and organization which direct that country. . . . This does not mean that China has ceased to be Communist, but that its communism has undergone a major transformation as the result of the Cultural Revolution.[2]

Schurmann was not alone in drawing attention to the newfound salience of social forces. The CR marked a watershed in the analysis of contemporary Chinese politics. A number of careful monographic studies of the Cultural Revolution highlighted the role of mass participation in shaping this historic event. Facilitated by the emergence of new primary sources, most notably the Red Guard press and refugee interviews, a younger cohort of scholars jettisoned the totalitarian model in favor of alternative approaches designed to explain the political activism of ordinary citizens.[3]

Pathbreaking as this research proved to be, its findings were nonetheless constrained by the limitations of the new sources themselves. The Red Guard materials revealed much about the actions and attitudes of students in Guangzhou and Beijing, but relatively little about the perspectives and political movements of

1

other social groups in other parts of China. The steady stream of Cultural Revolution memoirs that ensued, written for the most part by former Red Guards or intellectuals, only heightened the imbalance.[4]

The Red Guard movement accounted for only a part of the mass activism of the Cultural Revolution—a rather brief part, as it turned out. The Red Guards survived only the initial phase of the CR. In December 1968, their organizations were disbanded on Mao's order, and college and middle school students were assigned jobs or sent "up to the mountains and down to the villages" in a massive resettlement effort to defuse their militancy.[5] By contrast, rebel workers in Shanghai remained politically influential for much longer—and with far greater impact—than the student Red Guards.

Worker participation was a critical ingredient in the social unrest of the Cultural Revolution decade, but the relative dearth of source materials has made it difficult to address labor's involvement with anything approaching the degree of refinement attained in studies of the student movement.[6] In this book we strive to remedy the gap by utilizing a variety of heretofore unavailable archival sources: factory surveys, classified government and party reports, transcripts of worker roundtable discussions, handbills issued by worker organizations, background data on nearly 2,000 rebel-worker leaders, and—most important—Public Security Bureau confessions as well as firsthand interviews with key participants.

The new sources afford an unprecedented entrée to worker activism during the Cultural Revolution. In particular, the confessions provide—in the words of the principals themselves—detailed firsthand accounts of their emotions and experiences. One should, of course, be duly skeptical about testimony given to state authorities under conditions of duress. Despite the stunning breakthroughs in French social history afforded by access to local police archives or the fresh understanding of popular unrest in imperial China based upon rebel confessions from the Ming-Qing archives, obvious questions remain concerning the biases inherent in such sources.[7] Although this is an inescapable dilemma in the use of state (especially police) archives, it is important to point out the special attributes of the Public Security Bureau materials consulted for this study. For most workers, we have access to transcripts of repeated interrogation sessions. In between each such session, the experienced interrogators compared their findings against the confessions of other detainees as well as against evidence garnered in interviews with friends and family members, roundtable discussions with fellow workers, and so forth. At every stage, before making a self-criticism (*jiancha*), detainees were encouraged to confess (*jiaodai*) their inner motives, as well as to offer detailed accounts of their activities. The consistency among confessions from the same person as well as the marked differences in style and substance among different informants lends credence to the reliability of these (highly classified) documents. Whenever possible, we have corroborated the confessional materials with our own interviews, as well as with information contained in handbills, transcripts of meetings, personnel dossiers, memoirs, and the like.

The result, we hope, is to put a more human face on the workers' movement, as well as to facilitate a more comprehensive analysis of the bases of labor activism. The sources permit us to pursue a number of questions: Why were workers motivated to join the Cultural Revolution? What divided the ranks of "rebels," "conservatives," and apolitical members of the workforce? Did workers separate along lines of class origin, ideological inclination, political networks, or other criteria? What was the relationship between the workers' movement and the concurrent activism of students and intellectuals? And what do answers to these questions imply about the wellsprings of discontent and potential for change within the Chinese socialist system?

In pursuing these specific inquiries, we hope to contribute to larger debates about the nature of popular protest. Aside from its influence on China and on the field of Chinese studies, the CR had a far-reaching international impact as well. In the late 1960s, student activists and their allies in France, Japan, and the United States were of course strongly attracted to idealizations of the CR. Major intellects of the day—Herbert Marcuse, Louis Althusser, Georg Lukacs, for example—were also deeply impressed by events in China. And yet, somewhat curiously, the CR has made virtually no impact on general theories of popular protest. One searches in vain in Charles Tilly's *From Mobilization to Revolution* or Sidney Tarrow's *Power in Movement* for any mention of the CR, replete as these books are with references to social movements across time and space.[8] In this book, we try to reexamine the CR with an eye toward its broader theoretical implications.

Social science theories of popular protest might be said to be entering their third generation of scholarship. The first generation, active in the late 1960s and early 1970s, stressed the importance of *grievances* in giving rise to collective violence. In the Marxian tradition, of course, these grievances were rooted in class exploitation; in the political psychology approach of Ted Gurr and James Davies (who brought us "relative deprivation" and the "J-curve" of rebellion) social aggression was born out of personal frustration.[9] Whatever the particular variant, this first generation emphasized negative gripes as the basis for protest.

A second generation, active in the 1970s and 1980s, saw collective action as motivated less by negative grievances and gripes than by positive interests and incentives. Resource Mobilization theory, pioneered by Anthony Oberschall, Charles Tilly, Doug McAdam, and many others—highlighted the *organizational bases* of collective action.[10] This second generation, influenced to some extent by rational choice perspectives, stressed the importance of preexisting social networks and the use of selective incentives in overcoming Mancur Olson's famous freerider problem.[11]

More recently, a third generation has come to the fore. Since the late 1980s we can detect an increasing concern with the role of *cultural identities* in shaping patterns of protest. The New Social Movement theories of Alberto Melucci; studies by historians of France (Francois Furet, Mona Ozouf, Lynn Hunt, Keith Baker, and others) on the political culture of the French Revolution; and work by David

Snow, Robert Benford, and Sidney Tarrow on "collective action framing" or by James Scott on the "hidden transcript" all emphasize the importance of culturally constructed meanings and identities in the development of popular movements. Influenced to varying degrees by postmodernist trends, these approaches highlight the symbolic resistance waged by protesters in the course of their struggles.[12]

These three generations of scholarly fashion, stressing in turn grievances, organizations, and identities, roughly parallel the three explanations of CR activism to be found in the China literature. Scholarly interpretations of mass participation during the Cultural Revolution have fallen into three basic camps. The dominant approach, prefigured in Schurmann's pioneering study and developed by Hong Yung Lee, Stanley Rosen, and others, emphasizes the importance of *socioeconomic groups*—especially class background, but also age, skill level, and the like—in inclining different groups of students and workers to enlist in rival mass organizations.[13] By this account, rebel mass organizations recruited primarily from the social categories in which people had the deepest grudge against the socialist system: those with "bad" class labels, contract and temporary workers, young apprentices, and so on. By contrast, conservative organizations were generally composed of people from "good" family backgrounds, older, skilled workers, model workers, and the like.

A second interpretation, elaborated by Andrew Walder in particular, stresses the role of *political networks* in mobilizing workers along competing lines of patronage and allegiance. According to Walder, vertical party-sponsored networks (which cut across horizontal bases of group affiliation) generated much of the strife that gripped Chinese factories during the Cultural Revolution.[14]

A third explanation highlights the centrality of *psychocultural orientation*. As formulated by Lucian Pye and Richard Solomon, it is the extreme dependence of ordinary Chinese upon higher political authorities that produces periodic outbursts of "disorder" (*luan*), of which the Cultural Revolution was the supreme example. Factionalism was but one expression of a larger psychocultural complex.[15]

Although the three approaches have sometimes been posed as competing interpretations, they might better be seen as complementary. Social groups, party networks, and personalities all played a role in stimulating the militancy of the Cultural Revolution era. They did so, however, in distinctive ways. Thus rather than offer a synthetic, multifactor explanation of labor activism in general, we will argue that different types of Cultural Revolution militancy are best explained by different analytical traditions.

Labor unrest during the CR era was not all of a piece; three distinctive forms were well recognized at the time: "rebellion," "conservatism," and "economism." (Although none of these labels should be taken at face value, we retain the CR terms as representing meaningful distinctions to the participants themselves. It is in explaining, rather than naming, the phenomena that we attempt to make our own analytical contribution.) Rebel organizations (*zaofan pai*) attacked particular party authorities, and conservative outfits (*baoshou pai*) defended them, while during the wind of economism (*jingjizhuyi feng*) workers raised essentially materialistic demands. Each of these three varieties, we suggest, is best captured by a different analytical approach. Although psychocultural orientation (albeit a substantially modified version of the Pye-Solomon brand) has much to tell us about the leadership of the *rebel* workers' movement, party networks are essential for understanding the *conservative* reaction. And in explaining the wind of *economism* that swept the Chinese workforce in the winter of 1966–1967, we seem well served by a conventional emphasis on group characteristics.

General histories of the Cultural Revolution are readily available, so we will not attempt to retrace that ground here.[16] Firsthand accounts and social science analyses of the CR scene in Shanghai have also been produced in abundance, and we refer readers to those useful works for basic background.[17] In lieu of providing a strictly chronological or event-centered treatment, as has been traditional in studies of the Cultural Revolution, we opt instead to structure our presentation by mass organizations. Departing from a common image of Chinese popular protest as amorphous and disorganized in the face of overweening state power,[18] we find that mass politics evidenced considerable associational virtuosity. Although often termed a time of "great chaos" (*da luan*), the CR spawned an impressive amount of bottom-up organization. Maoist state initiatives, rather than stifling the possibility of collective dissent, served to structure mass activism into identifiable patterns of association promoted by different types of local leaders.

Where the sources permit, we focus on the backgrounds and experiences of individual labor leaders. As one might expect in such a politicized setting, followers switched organizational affiliations with alacrity, depending upon the prevailing political winds. Leaders, who had much more invested in a particular course of action, evidenced greater commitment to it. It is thus largely through a consideration of leadership that we seek to unravel distinctions among competing varieties of labor association.

Labor unrest did not occur in a social vacuum, however. Previous accounts have devoted a lopsided degree of attention to the experiences of students and intellectuals; nonetheless, it is undeniable that these groups took the lead in interpreting for mass consumption the initiatives of Mao Zedong and other central leaders. Indeed, one of the defining features of the CR—in contrast to other moments of dissent in the People's Republic of China (PRC)—was the catalytic connection between members of the intelligentsia and labor leaders. Whereas in other mass campaigns the state took pains to separate the activities of workers and intellectuals, during the CR these groups were officially encouraged to ally. Relations between rebel workers and radical intellectuals, fractious and fragile though they proved to be, were a key factor in shaping the trajectory of the Cultural Revolution in Shanghai.

Although our primary concern is the labor movement, we set the stage in Chapter 1 with a brief look at the Red Guard and literati rebel organizations of students and intellectuals. We then proceed in Chapter 2 to examine the formation of the dominant rebel-worker force in Shanghai, the Workers' General Head-quarters (WGH), commanded by Wang Hongwen. In Chapter 3, our attention shifts to the conservative opponents of the WGH—the Scarlet Guards. Chapter 4 explores a type of labor protest distinctive from the politicized activism of either rebels or conservatives: the so-called wind of economism in which hundreds of ad hoc organizations raised a host of demands for higher wages and improved working conditions. In Chapter 5, we look at rival groups within the rebel move-ment: the regiments and Lian Si (United Headquarters). Finally, Chapter 6 traces the institutionalization of gains by rebel workers over the course of the CR decade, concluding with their abrupt demise after the arrest of the Gang of Four in October 1976.

All of these manifestations of labor activism were strongly influenced by the in-tense political climate in which they developed. Groups, networks, and personali-ties—although familiar enough bases of protest in other times and places—as-sumed a peculiarly politicized shape under the unusual imperatives of Maoism. As previous scholarship has established, class labels that divided the populace into "good" and "bad" political categories became, in effect, caste-like brands; clien-telist networks were based largely on access to party-state resources; and rebel personality was measured in terms of Chairman Mao's own restless spirit.[19] Yet, arguably, the truly extraordinary thing about the Cultural Revolution was less the oppressive political atmosphere imposed from on high than the diversity of orga-nized popular responses that exploded from below. It is to these that we now turn.

1

Radical Intellectuals:
Red Guards and Literati Rebels

Shanghai's most distinctive manifestation of the Cultural Revolution lay in the prolonged activism of its working class, but it was among the intelligentsia in educational and cultural circles—rather than among workers in factories—that the movement first gained momentum. Although student Red Guards served as the principal social force in igniting the campaign, they were soon overshadowed by worker rebels. Certain politicized intellectuals, however, remained highly influential throughout the duration of the movement. Links between radical literati and leftist powerholders in Beijing redounded to the advantage of both sides over the course of the Cultural Revolution. Cooperation and conflict between such intellectuals and rebel workers helped to define the contours of the CR in Shanghai.

Protest movements in Communist China have seldom exhibited sustained cooperation between workers and intellectuals. Although both groups were involved in all the major expressions of dissent that have punctuated the history of the PRC (the Hundred Flowers Campaign of 1956–1957, the April Fifth Incident of 1976, the Democracy Wall movement of 1978–1979, and, most notably, the Tiananmen Uprising of 1989), their actions proceeded for the most part along quite separate paths.[1] This was in marked contrast to the Republican period, when a united front involving students, workers, and merchants gave rise to the massive general strikes of the 1920s.[2]

Historically, partnerships between intellectuals and workers have been unusual in China, thanks to a bureaucratic system that rewarded intellectuals for their loyalty and a Confucian ideology that encouraged scholars to think of themselves as superior to manual laborers. Cooperation between the two groups required a *weakened state*, incapable of commanding the fealty of its educated, and a *new ethos* that valorized the status of manual as well as mental labor. In the early Republican era, warlordism effectively paralyzed the state apparatus, and the New Culture movement repudiated Confucian elitism in favor of a populist commitment.

With the consolidation of state power under the PRC, the historic separation between workers and intellectuals was reinstituted. During the Cultural Revolution, however, this rift was bridged—albeit fitfully—by Red Guards and literati rebels. Mao's call to "bombard the headquarters" plunged party and state agencies into chaos, and the initiatives of his wife and other radicals in the cultural arena glorified the status of peasants, workers, and soldiers at the expense of intellectuals. In short, the basic requirements for a partnership—state weakness and a populist ethos—seemed in place. As it turned out, however, the decisive political influence wielded by a core of leaders in Beijing, most notably Chairman Mao and the Cultural Revolution Small Group (CRSG), meant that in fact there remained a powerful central authority. Intellectuals thus continued to show more interest in signals from Beijing than in the demands of restive factory workers. Moreover, the ostensibly "populist" artistic reforms of Chairman Mao's wife, Jiang Qing, were transparently the product of elite engineering, rather than the expression of spontaneous cultural ferment. Interaction between workers and intellectuals was a critical part of the Cultural Revolution story, but the limitations of this engagement reflect the political manipulation that underpinned the entire movement.

Background Connections

In spring 1964, more than two years before the formal launching of the CR, Jiang Qing had accompanied her husband to Shanghai on a two-month excursion to promote a new style of revolutionary opera.[3] The first secretary of the Shanghai Party Committee (SPC) at the time, Ke Qingshi, was known as sympathetic to Jiang's radical brand of cultural experimentation.[4] Ke immediately deputized his trusted subordinate in the SPC, Zhang Chunqiao, to serve as Jiang Qing's assistant during her sojourn in Shanghai. The ambitious Zhang (who directed the SPC Propaganda Department) spared no effort to ingratiate himself with Mao's wife, even listening for hours to phonograph records so as to memorize her favorite opera arias. When Zhang's own wife inquired as to why her husband was so preoccupied with his work for Jiang Qing, Zhang reportedly replied, "Without going through her there's no way I can get close to the Chairman."[5]

The collaboration between Zhang Chunqiao and Jiang Qing blossomed over the ensuing years and helped Zhang to get very close to the chairman, indeed. In February 1966, after Jiang—at the request of Defense Minister Lin Biao—convened a symposium in Shanghai on artistic activities within the military, she was dissatisfied with the transcript of the meeting, so she commissioned Zhang Chunqiao to prepare a revised version. The resulting manuscript, in which Zhang referred to Jiang Qing as a "standard-bearer of the CR," received the endorsement of Chairman Mao and became a key document of the period.[6]

When Jiang Qing began to organize criticism of the historical drama *Hai Rui Dismissed from Office* (widely, if mistakenly, seen as a thinly veiled attack on Chairman Mao's role in the disastrous Great Leap Forward),[7] again it was Shanghai that provided the receptive personnel. Through Zhang Chunqiao's introduction, Jiang was put in touch with Yao Wenyuan, a writer in the internal-circulation publications division of the Shanghai Party Committee.[8] Yao Wenyuan's scathing critique of *Hai Rui Dismissed from Office*, published in November 1965, was hailed in retrospect as the opening salvo of the Cultural Revolution. The preparation and publication of this influential essay brought Zhang and Yao to the special attention of Chairman Mao and propelled them to the vortex of the CR storm then brewing in Beijing.[9] When a nine-person Cultural Revolution Small Group was established in Beijing on May 28, 1966, to direct the new movement, both Zhang Chunqiao and Yao Wenyuan were asked to serve.[10] Five days later, the Shanghai Party Committee announced its own four-person CR Small Group, headed by Zhang Chunqiao.[11]

With the publication in *People's Daily* on June 1, 1966, of Nie Yuanzi's famous big-character-poster criticizing the party leadership at Beijing University, the Cultural Revolution expanded from an intraparty affair into a mass movement. At first, Shanghai's expression of this campaign was little more than a carbon copy of what was occurring in Beijing. Big-character-posters sprouted at campuses and research institutes across the city.[12] At some high schools, the criticisms escalated beyond posters to struggle sessions, at which denounced teachers and administrators were forced to don dunce caps and submit to beatings at the hands of their students.[13] The SPC imitated the Beijing Party Committee in launching public criticisms of "bourgeois reactionary authorities"[14] and in sending work teams to various educational and cultural units in an effort to control the direction of the movement.

The Red Guards

As in Beijing, however, the mass movement soon outstripped the ability of the municipal authorities to contain it. The principal vehicle of this process was the Red Guards, feisty young students who relied on Chairman Mao's personal backing to stage often brutal attacks against academic and political authorities alike. On August 1, 1966, Mao Zedong answered a letter from the Red Guards at Qinghua University's attached middle school in which he expressed his enthusiastic support for their opposition to the CR work team stationed at their campus. Shortly thereafter, Mao criticized Chief of State Liu Shaoqi in an essay entitled "Bombard the Headquarters—My Big-character-poster." The treatise, disseminated across the country via Red Guard handbills, generated a fever of "bombardment" (*paoda*, or *paohong*) directed against party and government cadres and agencies at all levels. Then, to make his endorsement of student behavior perfectly clear, Mao greeted a million Red Guards at Tiananmen Square on August 18, sporting a Red Guard armband.

The Red Guards of Shanghai were not limited to studying their Beijing prototypes from afar. A series of expeditions by Beijing Red Guards, dubbed the "three tours of Jiangnan" (*san xia Jiangnan*), brought firsthand experience to the southern metropolis. On the afternoon of August 26, some 170 Red Guards from fourteen Beijing schools arrived in Shanghai. Prior to this, a few dispersed groups of Red Guards had ventured south, but this was the first major delegation. The visitors were warmly greeted at the train station by the SPC secretary and hailed in the local newspapers as emissaries from the capital. The next day more than nine hundred students from around the country, mostly Beijing, converged on Shanghai. Their numbers increased daily, until by early September several thousand outsider Red Guards had reached the city.[15]

This first contingent of northern Red Guards had been formed hastily and was not well organized. Many of the participants had actually joined up quite spontaneously while on the train. They shared no unified leadership or appellation; their common goal was simply to "light a fire" (*dianhuo*) in Shanghai. Nevertheless, the newcomers proceeded to attack the SPC authorities, charging that their handling of the Cultural Revolution had been altogether too restrained. Taking their words directly from Mao Zedong's "Report of an Investigation of the Hunan Peasant Movement," penned in the mid-1920s at the height of the agrarian revolution, the student emissaries insisted that 1960s Shanghai also needed a "red terror" to deal forcefully with class enemies. Boasting that back in Beijing beatings had become commonplace, the northerners instructed their Shanghai counterparts in techniques of torturing former landlords, school administrators, and fellow students.

A Shanghai middle school student recalled the impact of this northern intrusion:

> When the Beijing Red Guards came south, wearing military uniforms complete with leather belts, they were really awesome. They said to us, "Why are you folks here so civil, without even a bit of revolutionary spirit?" At that time I didn't understand what they meant by "revolutionary spirit." A girl Red Guard from Beijing then took off her leather belt and started to demonstrate how to whip someone. This was my first look at the Beijing Red Guards.[16]

On September 10 a second wave of Red Guards descended from Beijing, this time with tens of thousands of participants and an official name: "Southern Touring Regiment of Capital Universities and Institutes." Organized into divisions and battalions, the delegation was directed by a "general headquarters" stationed at the Shanghai stadium. The command post dispatched large contingents of Red Guards to fan out to the various schools and factories in the city to communicate the northern model of "revolution" to the students and workers of Shanghai. The emissaries then proceeded to investigate the class backgrounds and political experiences of cadres in neighborhoods throughout the city, enjoining residents to engage in violent struggle against so-called class enemies.

The third excursion arrived in early October. Although much smaller than its predecessor, this delegation proved even more influential because most of its participants were under the direct sponsorship of Jiang Qing and Zhang Chunqiao.

In contrast to the first two delegations, its struggle targets were precise and its explicit aim was to topple the SPC. Members of this third contingent founded a liaison post, with branches dotted across the city, which established links to rebel workers at nearby factories.[17]

Inspired by these missionary forays from the north, Shanghai students were quick to found their own Red Guard outfits—despite the opposition of the Shanghai Party Committee. On the night of August 22, when the SPC convened a large meeting of college students and teachers to discuss the Cultural Revolution, a note was passed to Mayor Cao Diqiu requesting permission for Shanghai to establish its own Red Guard units. Sobered by what he had witnessed of Red Guard initiatives to date, the mayor responded unequivocally, "I do not advocate the establishment of Red Guards!"[18] The SPC was unable to stem the tide, however, and students in Shanghai rushed to emulate their Beijing counterparts.

On September 12 the first all-city Red Guard organization in Shanghai was founded, its membership composed of high school students. Around the same time, a headquarters for Red Guards at Shanghai's universities and technical institutes was also established. However, because they advocated keeping the Red Guard movement under Communist party supervision, these early associations were later branded "conservative" by other less subservient Red Guard units; in January 1967 they were entirely disbanded.

In contrast to the so-called conservative Red Guards, which had only two organizations (for high school and college students, respectively), numerous "rebel" Red Guard units, advocating resolute opposition to the SPC, cropped up across the city. The largest and most influential of these outfits were three: "Red Revolutionaries," "Bombard Headquarters," and "Red Third Headquarters." The Red Revolutionaries was founded on October 12, 1966, as the first all-city rebel Red Guard association in Shanghai, with initial strongholds at Fudan University, Shanghai Teachers College, and East China Teachers University. Later, it spread to high schools and claimed a total membership of 50,000. Bombard Headquarters, whose name was of course taken from Chairman Mao's famous big-character-poster, was established on November 3, with main bases at Fudan University, East China Textile Institute, Jiaotong University, Shanghai Number 2 Medical College, and Shanghai Teachers College. Red Third Headquarters, founded on December 20 as a split-off from the Shanghai Red Guard Third Headquarters, was initially strongest at Fudan and Jiaotong Universities. High school students soon composed 80 percent of its membership, however, which grew to number approximately 100,000 youngsters.[19]

As Red Guard units formed in most of the city's schools, the level of violence escalated in tandem. According to incomplete statistics compiled by the SPC, in the single month of September 1966 Shanghai suffered 704 suicides and 354 deaths connected to the Cultural Revolution.[20] Early Red Guard activities in Shanghai were patterned on the Beijing model: renaming stores and streets with revolutionary appellations, raiding temples and churches, burning books, shaving victims' heads into a yin-yang pattern and then parading them through the streets with placards denouncing them as "capitalist roaders," beating up and ransacking the homes of "class enemies" and packing many of them off to the countryside, and the like.[21] With tens of thousands of former capitalists still resident in the city, Shanghai was an especially alluring site for house ransackings. Twenty years later, the research office of the Shanghai Branch of the Bank of China offered the following statistics:

> In August 1966 the Red Guards took to the streets to destroy the "Four Olds" [old customs, habits, culture, and thought] through house ransackings. Some 150,000 homes were raided, netting 65 ounces of gold; 900,000 jin of gold and silver jewelry; 3,340,000 U.S. dollars; 3.3 million yuan in other foreign currencies; 2.4 million silver dollars; 370 million yuan in cash and bonds; 300,000 jin of pearls and jade; and large amounts of all sorts of commercial products.[22]

These figures included only those items turned over to the Bank of China for safekeeping and subsequent redemption, a tiny fraction of the total amount confiscated.

Although the presence of such a large concentration of former capitalists rendered Shanghai an appealing center of "class struggle," comparable activities were being carried out, albeit on a lesser scale, by Red Guards throughout the country. What eventually came to differentiate the Red Guard movement in Shanghai—and, ironically enough, to cut short its life span as well—was its relationship to the burgeoning labor movement.

The most important outcome of the excursions of Red Guards from Beijing, as it turned out, was not the formation of copycat student organizations but the development of a rebel-workers' movement. On November 6, 1966, the student emissaries—eager to extend their rebellion from the school yard into the workplace—convened an organizational meeting, attended by several dozen worker representatives from seventeen Shanghai factories, as well as a number of members of local Red Guard outfits. Participants at this get-together decided to establish an all-city alliance of worker rebels known as the General Headquarters of the Shanghai Workers' Revolutionary Rebels (or, Workers' General Headquarters [WGH]).[23] Under the leadership of Wang Hongwen, the WGH became the decisive mass organization in Shanghai for the duration of the Cultural Revolution. (See Chapters 2 and 6.)

The *Liberation Daily* Incident

Despite the importance of Red Guard initiatives in launching the first formal umbrella organization of worker rebels, cooperation between students and workers was sporadic at best. The first major confrontation of the CR in Shanghai, the Anting Incident—in which workers attempted to hijack a train for Beijing—was (as we shall see in the next chapter) largely undertaken without student involvement. Although the resolution of that incident forged lasting ties between the worker rebels and Zhang Chunqiao, it did not lead to a merger of worker and student movements. The second major confrontation, which erupted at the offices of the Shanghai newpaper *Liberation Daily*, was instigated by students without significant worker participation. Students soon found themselves forced to turn to the workers for assistance, but that very act signaled the imminent demise of the Red Guard movement.[24]

The *Liberation Daily* Incident was precipitated by an argument over the circulation of a publication of the Red Revolutionaries. On November 25, 1966, Red Guards belonging to the Red Revolutionaries and Shanghai Third Headquarters jointly convened a meeting to attack Mayor Cao Diqiu and the "bourgeois reactionary line" of the SPC. After the criticism meeting, Red Revolutionaries dragged the mayor from the rostrum to a back room and demanded that the ninth issue of their *Red Guard Battle News* be distributed as an insert in *Liberation Daily*. Whereas *Red Guard Battle News* was essentially a student handbill, *Liberation Daily* was a "party paper" (*dangbao*) under the jurisdiction of the SPC Propaganda Department. At the time, *Liberation Daily* enjoyed the highest circulation of any newspaper in Shanghai—or for that matter, in the East China region—and was delivered to subscribers by the post office. The Red Revolutionaries hoped to piggyback the established success of *Liberation Daily* to expand the influence of their own publication.

The mayor felt duty bound to refuse the demand of the Red Revolutionaries in light of a recent unhappy experience with their brethren-in-arms, the Shanghai Third Headquarters. Only a few days earlier, the SPC had in fact approved distribution of the Third Headquarters' handbill, *Revolutionary Rebel*, as an insert in *Liberation Daily*. However, the decision had resulted in more than six hundred phone calls to the newspaper office in a single day from irate subscribers protesting the unwelcome delivery. Postal carriers had also complained about their heavier load. The SPC had just made a public self-criticism over this matter when the Red Revolutionaries raised their demand.[25] Although Mayor Cao did not feel at liberty to approve the new request, he did agree to supply enough paper to print up some 650,000 copies of *Red Guard Battle News*—far greater than the circulation of *Liberation Daily* itself.[26]

The Red Revolutionaries were not mollified by Mayor Cao's concession, however. On the evening of November 29, more than three hundred Red Revolutionaries marched to the newspaper distribution office of the Shanghai Post Office to insist that the postal authorities agree to distribute their handbill. Unsuccessful in that effort, they then rushed over to the nearby *Liberation Daily* offices. As night turned into day, more and more Red Guards converged on the scene. By the next morning, the newspaper office had been effectively occupied by students. *Liberation Daily* was forced to shut down operations, and for seven days the city was without its largest newspaper.[27]

The takeover of *Liberation Daily* aroused considerable aversion among the ordinary citizenry of Shanghai. As eyewitness Neale Hunter reported,

> The rebels could not deny that popular opposition to their "revolutionary action" reached overwhelming proportions. The number of defenders inside the [*Liberation Daily*] building never exceeded 5 or 6 thousand, while the streets outside were packed for two or three blocks. By the Rebels' own admission, more than a million people demonstrated outside the building during the 6 days that the siege was at its height. They counted no less than 120 worker, peasant, and student organizations among the crowds.[28]

Finding themselves increasingly isolated, the Red Revolutionaries turned to the worker rebels for aid. On the afternoon of December 2, emissaries were sent to WGH leader Wang Hongwen to request that "worker elder brothers support our revolutionary actions." Wang accordingly directed his chief lieutenants, Pan Guoping and Dai Liqing, to mobilize rebel ranks from all WGH district liaison posts to lend support. From his own Number 17 Cotton Mill, Wang recruited more than four hundred rebel workers to secure the main gate of the newspaper office.[29]

Workers' assistance was crucial in permitting the Red Guards to maintain their siege, but it came with a steep price. At 3 A.M. on December 3, the beleaguered Red Guards at *Liberation Daily* agreed to establish a "frontline command post" headed by the WGH, with Wang Hongwen as commander-in-chief. With this concession, rebel leadership passed at one stroke from the students to the workers.

The central involvement of workers captured the imaginations of radical leaders in Beijing. The Cultural Revolution Small Group quickly issued instructions for resolving the dispute in favor of the rebels, asserting that temporary cessation of *Liberation Daily* was really "no big deal" (*mei shenme liaobuqi*).[30] As a consequence of this intervention by Beijing, the SPC felt compelled to sign resolutions caving in to the demands of Red Guards and workers alike. In addition to approving the circulation of *Red Guard Battle News* to all *Liberation Daily* subscribers, the local authorities agreed to provide full protection for workers who had participated in the confrontation.[31]

Literati Rebels

Just a few days after the resolution of the *Liberation Daily* Incident on December 9, another bombshell exploded in Shanghai: The Writers' Group of the SPC announced its "collective rebellion" (*jiti zaofan*). The early months of the CR had seen a number of so-called rebellions in schools, factories, and even in a few government agencies. But in every case, the "rebels" who declared their independence from higher party authority had been a distinct minority of the unit concerned. The collective rebellion of the Writers' Group, which involved all employees in a sensitive government agency, was unprecedented.

The Shanghai Writers' Group had been established in May 1965 as an outgrowth of the "Ding Xuelei" and "Luo Siding" writers' groups founded the previous year. Both units had been housed at the internal-circulation publications department of the Communist party's East China Bureau, located in Dingxiang Garden in the extreme western part of Shanghai. (The garden, named for its profusion of lilacs (*dingxiang*), had once served as a villa for Qing official Li Hongzhang.) The two groups were formed just at the time that Chairman Mao was calling for "learning from Lei Feng," a young martyred soldier praised after his death as an exemplar of self-sacrifice in the service of Mao Zedong Thought. The "spirit of Lei Feng" was epitomized by one of his famous diary entries in which Lei expressed his willingness to serve as a "screw in the locomotive of revolution." The names of the two writers' groups, drawn from the Lei Feng campaign, signaled their allegiance to Mao's radical agenda. "Ding Xuelei" referred to "studying Lei Feng in Dingxiang Garden," and "Luo Siding" was a homophone for "screw." Whereas the members of Ding Xuelei concentrated on literary criticism, the Luo Siding group focused on historical essays.

Writers in both circles enjoyed close connections to prominent figures within Shanghai's literary/political world, most notably Yao Wenyuan and Zhang Chunqiao. At that time, Yao Wenyuan was working on the editorial committee for internal-circulation publications, whose offices were also housed in Dingxiang Garden, so he came into frequent contact with writers of both groups. When Zhang Chunqiao was appointed secretary for culture and education of the Shanghai Party Committee in spring 1965, he merged Ding Xuelei and Luo Siding into the SPC Writers' Group (*xiezuo ban*). It was members of this group, later known colloquially as "literati rebels" (*xiucai zaofan pai*), to whom he turned for materials on Ming history to facilitate Yao Wenyuan's scathing critique of *Hai Rui Dismissed from Office.*

The Writers' Group was composed of two types of people: older cadres and younger academics. The former did boast a modicum of higher education; some had been sent by their work units to university for a period of study, after which they had returned to their original units to serve as personal secretaries (*mishu*) to leading officials. The latter were regular university graduates who had been assigned to college teaching positions, where they gained a reputation for political activism.

Xu Jingxian, who headed Ding Xuelei before the merger and was named party branch secretary of the Writers' Group after its establishment, exemplified the cadre type. While in high school in the late 1940s, Xu had joined a front organization connected to the Communist party underground. After the Communist victory in 1949, he graduated from high school and entered the Chinese Communist party's (CCP) East China Bureau Propaganda Department as a secretary charged with drafting documents, preparing summary reports, ghostwriting speeches for various leaders, and the like. This experience honed his political skills and afforded Xu access to inside information. In the early 1960s, Xu's biographical account of a revolutionary in the party underground at Jiaotong University, *Child of the Party: Mu Hanxiang*, gained him considerable popularity among Shanghai students. Soon thereafter he coauthored a drama, *Youthful Generation*, which garnered a Ministry of Culture prize in 1964. As a result of these literary successes, Xu was transferred to the Ding Xuelei writing group.

An exemplar of the young academic type was Zhu Yongjia. Politically active as a student, Zhu had served as chair of the student association at Fudan University. After graduation, he remained at Fudan as an instructor in the History Department, specializing in the Ming dynasty. Zhu's exceptional bibliographic and textual command of Ming primary sources resulted in his assignment to Luo Siding. At the start of the CR, he was tapped by Zhang Chunqiao to help Yao Wenyuan develop his inflammatory critique of *Hai Rui Dismissed from Office*.

Xu Jingxian, Zhu Yongjia, and their colleagues in the Writers' Group became the amanuenses of the radical faction during the Cultural Revolution. They explained and elaborated the pronouncements of Chairman Mao and penned many of the proposals that ostensibly emanated from the ranks of the worker rebels. After Zhang Chunqiao and Yao Wenyuan moved to Beijing as members of the Cultural Revolution Small Group, contacts with the Writers' Group continued uninterrupted. In late September 1966, Zhu Yongjia was transferred to Beijing (ostensibly as a newspaper reporter) to serve as a personal liaison with the center of power. Soon thereafter, Zhang and Yao met with Zhu in Beijing for the express purpose of encouraging a rebellion against the SPC, admonishing the Writers' Group "not to write behind closed doors" but to "go to the masses," "be with the masses." Zhu immediately phoned Shanghai to pass the message along to Xu Jingxian.[32] On November 25, Zhu Yongjia's return to Shanghai allowed him to relate Zhang and Yao's suggestions in person to his colleagues in the Writers' Group.

As soon as Zhu Yongjia returned to Shanghai, however, he was kidnapped by Red Revolutionaries. Eager to criticize all teachers of any renown at their campus, the radical students at Fudan University considered Zhu too big a fish to let escape their nets. The Red Guards used Zhu's earlier writings as evidence that he had been in the business of "gilding the face" of the SPC. In self-defense, Zhu pointed out that his essays at the time had all been approved by Zhang Chunqiao; Red Guard attacks on his essays were therefore tantamount to a denuciation of Zhang himself. The students refused to accept this argument, however. On November 27, they raided the history division of the Writers' Group (i.e., the former Luo Siding group) to seize incriminating materials that would force Zhu Yongjia to "thoroughly confess his black connections at the SPC."

Since Zhu was such a central figure in the Writers' Group, an attack on him was a threat to the entire operation. Highly agitated by his younger colleague's predicament, Xu Jingxian phoned Beijing to complain about the recent turn of events and to express his desire to rise up in rebellion against the SPC. The next day, Yao Wenyuan called back to reiterate his enthusiasm for a writers' rebellion. Yao advised Xu to inform the Red Guards that the Writers' Group was under the direct leadership of Zhang Chunqiao and had no connections to other party secretaries at the SPC. Two weeks later, when Xu had still not convinced all of his fellow writers to take the plunge, Yao Wenyuan phoned again to encourage a Writers' Group rebellion. As he put it, "Are you just writing essays or are you taking to the frontlines?" Yao informed Xu that he and Zhang would soon be returning to Shanghai to lead the movement there and that they expected to rely on the Writers' Group as their basic working staff.[33]

The following afternoon, the entire Writers' Group discussed Yao's phone call at length. Xu admonished them, "Zhang Chunqiao and Yao Wenyuan have called on us to rebel. We can no longer delay, no longer serve as slaves of the SPC. We must defend this fortress of the Writers' Group. The battle trenches can extend to the SPC office. We can then join together in rebellion with the staff of the Personnel Committee, [the] Education and Public Health departments, etc." In the end, the Writers' Group opted unanimously for "collective rebellion."[34]

Having proclaimed their independence from the Shanghai Party Committee, Writers' Group members immediately set out to contact rebel cadres at other key agencies: the editorial department of *Party Branch Life*, an internal-circulation publication of the SPC; the clerical office of the SPC; the SPC Propaganda Department; the SPC Party School; and the Shanghai Academy of Social Sciences. Receptive personnel from these various units jointly formed the "SPC Agencies' Revolutionary Rebel Liaison Post," headed by a four-person leadership group, of which three members were from the Writers' Group. During this critical period, Xu Jingxian maintained constant contact with Zhang and Yao in Beijing, reporting his every move to them. With their approval, on December 18 the "SPC Agency Liaison Post" convened a public meeting at Cultural Plaza "to expose the bourgeois revisionist line of the SPC." Thanks to Zhang's prompting, the Workers' General Headquarters dispatched 1,500 rebel workers to lend support; Red Revolutionaries, Red Third Headquarters, Tongji University's "East is Red," and other Red Guard units sent thousands of student sympathizers to the meeting; and Red Flag of the Beijing Aeronautics Academy mobilized hundreds of Red Guards to post notices announcing the historic event.[35]

Although the Writers' Group was numerically small, its insider status, as well as its role in public communication, meant that its rebellion posed a grave threat to the integrity of the Shanghai Party Committee. In essence, this act of defiance destroyed the municipal authorities' effort to control the direction of the CR in Shanghai and plunged the SPC into virtual paralysis—a feat that the much larger and more flamboyant worker and student rebels had been unable to accomplish. The shock of the Writers' Group rebellion reverberated across the ranks of cadres in the city. Initially, many officials had been unsympathetic to the Cultural Revolution. But now that the most politically astute and best educated among them had rebelled, other highly placed cadres (like SPC secretaries Ma Tianshui and Wang Shaoyong) also decided to break with the top leadership of the SPC.

The Writers' Group proved critically important to Zhang Chunqiao during the Cultural Revolution. Although publicly Zhang made much of his reliance on the worker rebels, his most stalwart backers were actually the literati rebels. They were his confidants as well as his brain trust; at times he even turned to them for help in controlling the worker rebels. The importance of the Writers' Group became clear during the "January Revolution" of 1967, which began when rebel organizations took over the offices of *Wenhui Bao*, one of Shanghai's three major newspapers. The next day, January 4, at 10 A.M., Zhang Chunqiao and Yao Wenyuan returned to Shanghai as an "inspection team of the Cultural Revolution Small Group." As they explained their project, "We aren't involved in the work of the Shanghai Party Committee and have no relationship to it; our mission is to help the leftists, to carry out investigations, and to hold meetings to solicit opinions from all sides."[36] At two o'clock that afternoon, Zhang and Yao convened a meeting of the Writers' Group, at which Zhang announced that the literati rebels would "act as our working group, act as the agency to make contact with various mass organizations, and help us gather intelligence."[37] Throughout the entire month of power seizures that followed, the Writers' Group served as the principal support staff for Zhang and Yao, helping them to arrange and prepare transcripts of meetings, guide various mass organizations, and so forth.

On January 5, Zhang and Yao met with representatives of the Workers' General Headquarters to express their wish that rebels assume control of key government offices in Shanghai. The following day, the SPC Agency Liaison Post (which included at its core the Writers' Group) joined with the Workers' General Headquarters and the Red Revolutionaries in staging a "topple-the-SPC meeting." At this gathering it was announced that from that day forth Cao Diqiu would no longer be recognized as mayor of Shanghai and would be put to labor reform under rebel supervision. In addition to a huge gathering at People's Plaza in the center of Shanghai, the denunciation meeting was marked by dozens of branch gatherings (of some 100,000 people) throughout the city. This was the first all-city power seizure in China.[38]

The Pivotal Role of Zhang Chunqiao

Two days after the power seizure, members of the Cultural Revolution Small Group (CRSG) in Beijing called Zhang Chunqiao to relay Mao Zedong's laudatory comments on the Shanghai situation. At a Politburo meeting earlier that day, Mao had exclaimed,

> *Wenhui Bao* has been seized by leftists; this is a good direction. This is one class overthrowing another class; this is a great revolution.

When the revolutionary forces in Shanghai arise, this gives hope to the entire country. It cannot but influence all of East China—influence every city and province across the country.

Don't think that the death of the butcher will mean eating hairy pork.[39]

Mao's cryptic comment at the end referred to a well-known Chinese proverb: "When the butcher dies, people have no choice but to eat pork with the hair still on it." Mao was thus attempting to allay fears that the toppling of the mayor would result in a suspension of government work. The chairman went on to take the extraordinary step of instructing CRSG leader Chen Boda to send a congratulatory telegram to the Shanghai rebels in the names of Party Central, the State Council, the Central Military Commission, and the CRSG.

After the congratulatory cable, a high tide of power seizures swept across Shanghai. Between January 11 and January 13, takeovers occurred at forty-nine municipal, district, bureau, and county-level government units.[40] When rebels seized power at the city personnel committee on January 15, they declared Zhang Chunqiao and Yao Wenyuan the new first party secretary-cum-mayor and second party secretary-cum-vice-mayor, respectively. Late that night, CRSG member Wang Li phoned Shanghai to relay Mao Zedong's assessment of the latest development.

> Today the Politburo held a meeting, and Chairman Mao asked me to tell the mass organizations that he applauds their selection of Zhang Chunqiao as first party secretary and mayor of Shanghai and Yao Wenyuan as second party secretary and vice-mayor. . . . Chairman Mao said, "This Shanghai method is good. This method of mass takeover is good. It is better than the reorganization method of the Beijing Party Committee."
>
> Chairman Mao said, "In our previous revolution, the armies fought for territory, the villages encircled the cities; after entering the cities, the organizations were maintained in place. . . . The war of liberation developed very quickly, and when old party members entered the cities some of them changed character and became very subjective. This current method, in which the masses rise up and seize power, this Shanghai method is good. Let's see, in early November the revolutionary forces in Shanghai were small—only a thousand or so—and after two months they number over a million. The force of the masses cannot be resisted."
>
> Chairman Mao criticized some people for not understanding principle and cursing the masses: "Having carried out revolution for so long, they became conservatives. Some people organized so-called emergency committees, united action committees, etc.—imitating the older generation. Our cadres must quickly awaken and stand on the side of the masses. If they don't change, they'll be set aside and given rice to eat. The masses cannot be repressed. . . . In the past, the military fought the battles; now it is the masses who have risen up in revolution."[41]

Thanks to the personal endorsement of Mao Zedong, Zhang Chunqiao's authority in Shanghai was virtually unassailable. Although anti-Zhang incidents did erupt in January 1967 and April 1968, both failed miserably, thanks to intervention by Beijing. Zhang's preeminent position had major implications for the course of the CR in Shanghai. With Zhang holding de facto command over the

Shanghai Garrison, after the January power seizure the city was not plagued by the competition between civilian radicals (beholden to Jiang Qing) and military radicals (loyal to Lin Biao) that had come to define much of the factional strife of the day.[42] Because of Zhang's ability to control the local situation, Shanghai was spared the military takeovers that occurred in many other parts of China during the Cultural Revolution. The relative lack of military involvement, in turn, meant that when conflicts erupted among mass organizations they seldom escalated into the bloody battles that raged across much of the rest of the country.

Efforts to unseat Zhang Chunqiao, fruitless though they were, did nonetheless serve to alter permanently the balance of power among mass organizations in Shanghai. Whereas the *Liberation Daily* Incident had tipped the scales away from the students in favor of the workers, the January 28 "bombardment" of Zhang Chunqiao definitively sealed the fate of the Red Guards. This attack on Zhang was instigated by the oldest, largest, and most influential Red Guard organizations in the city: Red Revolutionaries, Bombard Headquarters, and Red Third Headquarters. The fact that Zhang Chunqiao had opposed efforts of various Red Guard outfits to seize power during the January Revolution had aroused their enmity toward him. More fundamentally, however, the assault on Zhang Chunqiao represented a student protest against the declining fortunes of the Red Guard movement. Red Third Headquarters leader and Fudan University student An Wenjiang analyzed his own motivations in a later memoir.

> In the newspapers, broadcasts, central documents and leaders' speeches, criticisms of Red Guards were mounting daily. No longer did we see the paeans of praise: "worker-peasant-soldiers firmly support the revolutionary students," "respect our Red Guards," etc. Now the editorials read instead, "We must struggle against selfishness and criticize revisionism," "We must learn from the working class," and other such injunctions. In the lingo of those times, the Red Guards had reached the point of "revolting against themselves" (*ge ziji de ming*).[43]

The January 28 bombardment began when Red Revolutionaries kidnapped Writers' Group leader Xu Jingxian from the SPC Agency Liaison Post and spirited him off to the Fudan University campus in hopes of gathering incriminating evidence about his patron, Zhang Chunqiao. When Zhang learned of this development, he immediately phoned the Shanghai Garrison Command to request a military rescue for Xu. The arrival of troops at Fudan further fanned the flames of opposition to Zhang; that evening Red Guards from Bombard Headquarters and Red Third Headquarters joined the Red Revolutionaries in printing and posting anti-Zhang slogans all over the Fudan campus and throughout the streets of the city.

The following day, Zhang summoned Wang Hongwen and other rebel-worker leaders[44] to his home to inform them of the kidnapping and to remind them: "I fought alongside you in the past. . . . Now the Red Revolutionaries want a 'bombardment.' You think it over: What should your response be?" Without hesitation, Wang Hongwen expressed full support for his benefactor. Before Zhang

Chunqiao had even finished speaking, the worker-rebel commander shouted out, "Damn it! Let's dispatch our forces immediately. We'll level Fudan University this very night!" Zhang cautioned that it was not necessary to raze the university, but recommended that the WGH post its personnel as sentries at all major thoroughfares in the city to prevent any "bombardment" mass meeting from assembling.[45] Wang thereupon phoned all district liaison posts of the Workers' General Headquarters to advise his followers on how to thwart the Red Guards' initiative.[46]

The backing of the WGH solidified Zhang's position and pulled the rug out from under the student rebels. At the same time, the CRSG in Beijing offered Zhang Chunqiao its full support in an urgent telegram, which dubbed the bombardment a "complete mistake" and warned ominously that if the Red Revolutionaries persisted, the CRSG would take all "necessary measures."[47] Thoroughly chastened, the students abandoned their offensive.

It was soon decided that any organization that had taken part in the bombardment against Zhang was thereby ineligible to join the Shanghai Commune. At one stroke, the city's largest, most influential Red Guard outfits were rendered impotent. Wang Hongwen, who had once spurned the armband of his own Workers' General Headquarters in favor of wearing an armband from the student group Bombard Headquarters, had now jettisoned his erstwhile comrades-in-arms. He issued an order expelling from the WGH and its liaison posts all Red Guards who had participated in the bombardment, refusing to make an exception even for those individuals who had a long history of cooperation with him. This meant the loss of many of the top administrative staff of the WGH, from Wang Hongwen's personal secretary to the editor of *Worker Rebel*, the periodical of the WGH.[48]

The second bombardment of April 12, 1968, also involved remnant Red Guards, who now accused Zhang Chunqiao of having betrayed the revolution back in the 1930s. Thanks to the intervention of Jiang Qing, however, the air force was quickly persuaded to suppress the bombardment. Red Guards who participated in this last-ditch offensive suffered severe reprisals. According to official government statistics, 856 students at seven colleges in Shanghai were disciplined for the incident, of whom 368 were incarcerated, twelve were persecuted to death, and twelve were driven mad.[49]

When a nationwide campaign was later launched to eradicate a fictitious "May Sixteenth conspiracy," in Shanghai it led to a three-year witch-hunt against students who had participated in the two bombardments of Zhang Chunqiao. More than 2,500 former Red Guards were targeted in conjunction with this drive.[50]

Literati-Worker Tensions

Red Guard attacks on Zhang Chunqiao helped ensure that students were rapidly eclipsed by workers over the course of the CR, but the demise of the Red Guards did not end all friction between the intelligentsia and the working class. Eventually, members of the Writers' Group, despite their assignment as a mouthpiece for the worker rebels, found themselves in conflict with their proletarian comrades. In their case, however, the special relationship with Zhang Chunqiao guaranteed that they, rather than the workers, would generally prevail.

Despite changes in personnel and nomenclature, the functions of the Writers' Group remained constant throughout the Cultural Revolution: to serve as a secretariat to the Shanghai Revolutionary Committee and, later, to the restored Shanghai Party Committee; to draft documents and resolutions; and, most important, to act as the eyes and ears of Zhang Chunqiao and Yao Wenyuan in Shanghai, using "brief notes," "internal reference materials," and other documentary formats to report on all aspects of the situation in Shanghai, including the worker rebels. As Zhu Yongjia put it, "We listened to Zhang and Yao. As for other people, we could listen or not."[51] With about forty core members and an additional three hundred ancillary personnel, the Writers' Group formed a substantial brain trust for their patrons in Beijing. In the Shanghai Revolutionary Committee (SRC) that eventually replaced the toppled Shanghai Party Committee, Xu Jingxian assumed the post of vice-chair, and other members of the group took charge of the departments of political propaganda, investigation, mass movements, and reception.

Well aware of the value of the Writers' Group to their political fortunes, Zhang and Yao consistently defended it in the incessant internecine struggles that wracked the rebel forces for the duration of the CR. This was demonstrated in a dispute that erupted over one of the many publications edited by the Writers' Group, a literary journal entitled *Zhao Xia* (Morning Glow).[52] The first monthly issue appeared in January 1974, and the journal saw only three installments before it was attacked by worker rebels contending that the three issues contained three "big poisonous weeds" that slandered the militia, attacked the worker rebels, and revived the evil spirit of the Lin Biao party line. Unions under worker-rebel leadership in Shanghai and as far away as Shanghai's "rear guard industrial base" of Anhui held mass meetings to criticize the periodical.

The controversy surrounding *Morning Glow* was part of a larger, ongoing competition between the worker and literati rebels. In January 1974, the Shanghai Federation of Trade Unions (SFTU)—a latter-day reincarnation of the Workers' General Headquarters of Wang Hongwen—convened a conference for union leaders at which Xu Jingxian of the Writers' Group delivered a keynote address. The next day, the worker rebels proclaimed Xu's remarks an insufficiently radical interpretation of the Criticize Lin Biao–Criticize Confucius campaign (CLCC) then underway (see Chapter 6). The union proceeded to develop a detailed critique of Xu that resulted in his being forced to offer an apology before the standing committee of the Shanghai Revolutionary Committee.

The humiliation of Writers' Group leader Xu Jingxian emboldened the worker rebels to stage a further offensive against their literati rivals. The decision to target *Morning Glow* was sparked by a short story in the third issue of the journal that made mention in passing to a "half-year anniversary"—a reference that the worker rebels were quick to interpret as a personal insult. Their sensitivity to this particular phrase had origins in events that had transpired years before. Only six months after the WGH was founded back in November 1966, Commander Wang Hongwen insisted on holding a gala "half-year anniversary" to commemorate the achievements of the worker-rebel alliance. At the time, Xu Jingxian had reported this unseemly event to Zhang Chunqiao, who remarked sarcastically, "Can't they even wait for one year?" The matter had led to a heated argument between Wang Hongwen and Xu Jingxian. Now, some seven years later, the worker rebels saw the allusion to a half-year anniversary as a reopening of old wounds.

In an effort to pacify the worker rebels, Writers' Group notable Zhu Yongjia offered to prepare a self-criticism concerning the publication of *Morning Glow*. But Wang Xiuzhen, top deputy of Wang Hongwen, refused to be mollified so easily. She shot back, "Don't confess. I'm not interested in hearing your confession. It's all too easy for you intellectuals to write confessions!" In the end, however, it was the workers who were required to proffer a self-criticism. Convinced that the members of the Writers' Group constituted his most reliable base of support in Shanghai, Zhang Chunqiao eventually weighed in on their behalf. The unionists duly submitted a confession, all the time insisting that their objections had been directed only against particular articles in *Morning Glow*, not against the Writers' Group as a whole.

Workers' Theory Troops

Worker and literati rebels crossed swords again over the issue of the Workers' Theory Troops (WTT) (*gongren lilun duiwu*), a network of factory-level study groups that penned essays intended to reflect a proletarian philosophy. Touted during the CR as an example of "workers occupying the superstructure," the troops largely comprised demobilized student Red Guards who had been assigned to factory labor.

Wang Hongwen's worker rebels had high hopes of taking charge of this sizable force, which in Shanghai grew to number more than 20,000 factory-level units, with over 300,000 members.[53] Ye Changming, a worker rebel who headed the trade union successor to the WGH, later recalled: "I strived to gain control of all the Workers' Theory Troops so that they would serve us."[54] To this end, the union organized a series of special training programs for WTT members. Despite the worker rebels' efforts to gain leverage over the Workers' Theory Troops, such units were generally inclined to align with the Writers' Group. The intellectually oriented former students who made up the bulk of WTT membership tended to be more impressed by the advice of trained academics than by the overtures of the relatively uneducated worker rebels.

Lin Yaohua, a leading member of Shanghai's most famous WTT, was fairly typical of these students-turned-workers in both his experiences and mentality; therefore, we will review his case in some detail.[55] Prior to the CR, Lin had been a second-year student at the prestigious high school attached to Fudan University.

Ranking at the top of his class of gifted and highly motivated students, Lin harbored but one burning ambition: to attend university. This was a goal that his father, a white-collar professional, had encouraged for him and his siblings for as long as he could remember. Permitted one elective subject in high school, Lin chose literary Chinese. He developed considerable proficiency in reading ancient texts—an erudite academic skill that, ironically enough, laid the foundation for Lin's later fame during the CR.

The Cultural Revolution completely changed Lin Yaohua's life. After a brief stint as a Red Guard, he found himself rudely transplanted from campus to factory.

The CR shattered my dream of further studies. I entered a factory as a steelworker. But I was luckier than those of my same age who were sent "up to the mountains [and] down to the villages." I went to the Number 2 Workshop of Shanghai's largest steel mill, the Number 5 Shanghai Steel Factory, to serve as a cast-iron worker. Our factory had 20,000 workers, and the workshop I was in was special because it boasted first-class equipment and products that ranked among the best in the Far East. As a steel caster, my work was physically very taxing. Even in unbearably hot weather we had to put on thick canvas uniforms to prevent skin burns from the molten steel. I didn't really mind the hardship of the work itself. . . . My suffering was because my dream of a college education had been shattered. . . . Among these poorly educated workers, my only distinction was my learning. Learning was all I really wanted to pursue. But during the Cultural Revolution learning was a primary object of revolutionary attack.

Most of my friends spent their free time playing cards and smoking, while my head was buried in the works of Mao, Marx, Lenin, and Stalin. These were the only books we were permitted to read at that time. I lived in a factory dormitory. Often, party cadres from our workshop came to my room, and several rebel workers lived in the same dorm, so I couldn't read anything but the approved books. But I liked these works. Although they weren't light reading, I felt that I got something out of them. I had a natural interest in politics.

A turning point for Lin Yaohua came in 1974, when the ongoing denunciation of former Defense Minister Lin Biao was combined with a bizarre campaign to discredit Confucianism. Newpapers and central documents were suddenly filled with classical quotations from Confucius and Mencius.

Many people, including the workshop cadres in charge of political propaganda, couldn't understand the literary language of these materials. . . . One day, the person responsible for our workshop study group—a demobilized soldier—came to my dorm room to seek my help. He explained that the party cadres had no way of transmitting recent central documents because the branch secretaries couldn't even read them. Then he said, "You're a high school student, with a good grounding in classical literature. You can help us understand these documents." So, our study group sessions became just like a language class—in which I explicated the literary texts word by word.

Lin's success at his assigned task turned his workshop's Workers' Theory Troop into a widely acclaimed model. Before long, his outfit received the personal patronage of Writers' Group leader Xu Jingxian. Although the worker rebels at his factory also endeavored to enlist his allegiance, Lin was not well disposed toward them.

> On the whole, the factory rebels were composed of individuals of shoddy character and poor work habits who didn't respect the older workers. We high school students had been instructed to humbly receive reeducation from the working class. We tended to work diligently and listen respectfully to the older workers. Since we entered the factories after the high point of [the CR] struggles was over, we hadn't participated in attacks on the factory cadres. So after some of the cadres were rehabilitated, they relied on us students and shunned the rebels—preferring to promote young students over the "new" rebel cadres.

Although the worker rebels attempted to block his nomination, Lin was handpicked by Xu Jingxian to attend an important meeting in Beijing for the study of philosophical texts. This led to further advancement.

> While attending the meeting, I went to other places, like Chengde—where I was treated as a celebrity from Party Central. And because I'd had frequent contact with the Shanghai Writers' Group, people saw me as somebody with insider information. After the meeting, I returned to Shanghai and became a member of Shanghai's leading group for the critique of Confucianism.

Despite these promotions, competition with the worker rebels continued. In 1975, Lin Yaohua was chosen as a representative to the Fourth National People's Congress (NPC). His selection came at the expense of a worker rebel.

> The rebel was just then building himself a house. His neighbors reported him for using public materials and for making other factory workers work on his house for free during regular working hours. The neighbors' incriminating letter eventually reached Wang Xiuzhen, who forced the accused rebel to step down. So I was chosen. But after the NPC I could no longer continue my work at the city level. Rebels at the factory pointed out that I had attended the NPC as a worker representative, and if I didn't return to the factory I had no right posing as a worker representative. So I went back to my workshop as deputy-secretary of the party branch. Although the SPC Writers' Group History Division wanted me to work for them, my factory wouldn't release me.

Once the Cultural Revolution was over, Lin began to appreciate the substantial gap that separated the pronouncements of his theory group from the views of the ordinary workers themselves.

> In reality, our theories couldn't possibly represent the workers' perspective. For example, when we were asked to criticize bourgeois rights, a member of our theory troop yelled out "long live 36 yuan!" This slogan was immediately picked up by Xu

Jingxian and widely publicized. Before the CR, the starting wage for Shanghai workers had been 42 yuan, but it was cut back to 36 yuan during the CR. The workers actually wanted a wage hike, but here was our theory troop acclaiming the 36 yuan standard for having destroyed bourgeois rights—and even advocating that it remain in place for another 10,000 years! Many of the ideas of the theory troops were contrary to working-class interests.

A Fragile Alliance

At least superficially, the Cultural Revolution was a notable exception to the general pattern of isolation between intellectuals and workers that characterized protest movements in the PRC. Student militants took an active lead in mobilizing rebel workers, while literati-politicos penned essays that championed working-class preeminence. Yet, crucial as this interclass interaction was, cooperation between the two groups was constrained and conflictual.

The golden age of Shanghai's Red Guards did not last long. Once the workers rose in revolt, student activism declined commensurately. A crucial element in this inverse correlation was the special relationship that developed between the worker rebels and Zhang Chunqiao during the early months of the CR. Then, the January 28 bombardment, in which Shanghai's most influential Red Guard organizations challenged Zhang's authority, resulted in a counterattack that definitively undermined their strength. The following year, the "up to the mountains, down to the villages" campaign meant the dissolution of Red Guard organizations altogether.

As we have seen in the case of the Workers' Theory Troops, however, contacts between former student militants and rebel workers continued even after the demobilization of the Red Guards. A substantial number of former Red Guards were assigned to factory work at this time. Having experienced the heady exhilaration of political activism and revolutionary responsibility, these youngsters were reluctant to withdraw from such engagement. Boasting literary skills well above those of the average worker, more than a few former Red Guards took charge of propaganda activities in their new work units. By late 1968, virtually everything published in the press in the name of workers was really written either by former Red Guards or by radical academics and journalists affiliated with the Shanghai Writers' Group.[56]

Worker rebels, as we shall see in Chapter 2, became the leading actors in Shanghai's rendition of the Cultural Revolution drama. Nonetheless, their prominence did not go unchallenged. High-placed intellectuals with close ties to Zhang Chunqiao were, as we saw in this chapter, a continuing source of competition. To be sure, the writings of these literati rebels never failed to hail the superiority of the proletariat—often with momentous repercussions. For example, Yao Wenyuan's

1968 editorial in *Red Flag*, entitled "The Working-Class Must Lead in Everything," called on workers to "seize the superstructure" and led to the formation of Workers' Propaganda Teams (WPTs), which occupied universities and scientific and cultural institutes around the country. (See Chapter 6.) Yet, for all their lip service to proletarian leadership, radical intellectuals were quick to defend their own turf when challenged by workers. And, as the *Morning Glow* incident graphically demonstrated, they were often successful.

Workers periodically expressed the opinion that, as intellectuals, literati rebels should by all rights be *targets* of the CR and could not pretend to represent the interests of the working class. The intellectuals, for their part, were inclined to look down on workers as uneducated and atheoretical.[57] Nevertheless, both sides were well aware of the intimate relationship between the Writers' Group and Zhang Chunqiao; in the end, the workers had little choice but to swallow their complaints.

2

Rebels:
The Workers' General Headquarters

If Beijing spawned the most famous social force of the CR in the form of student Red Guards, then Shanghai must be credited with producing a more enduring and politically more influential mass organization: the Workers' General Headquarters. Having dubbed his grand experiment a *"proletarian* cultural revolution," Chairman Mao was elated when a rebel movement broke out among the workers of China's industrial capital. Worker rebels were soon hailed as the main fighting force of the CR; before long, they surpassed the Red Guards in both numbers and political significance.

Previous scholarship has sometimes portrayed the rebel workers as essentially apolitical. Hong Yung Lee, in his masterful study of the CR, contrasts the motivations of rebel workers and students: "Unlike the students, who were interested in 'power,' the workers were more interested in 'money.'"[1] The rebel-workers' movement, according to Lee, was composed of those groups with the greatest economic grievances against the system: workers "from the smaller, poorer factories, the contract and temporary workers, the apprentices and unskilled workers in the larger factories, and the individual laborers."[2] Lee's is an excellent analysis of the motivations and social bases of the "wind of economism" that swept across Chinese cities in the winter of 1966–1967 (see Chapter 4), but it fails to capture the highly politicized character of the rebel-workers' movement itself. Few of the rebel leaders raised economic demands during the CR; instead, their agenda was the expressly political one of overthrowing workplace and municipal authorities.

The WGH, commanded by eventual Gang of Four associate Wang Hongwen, was an umbrella organization of rebel-worker outfits founded on November 9, 1966, whose activities were aimed at toppling party officials from the factory level right up to the Shanghai Party Committee. Buttressed by support from Zhang Chunqiao and other members of the Cultural Revolution Small Group of radical intellectuals in Beijing, the WGH became a major vehicle for seizing power from the SPC in the January Revolution of 1967 and remained a factor in both Shanghai and national politics (albeit under new names) until the close of the CR decade in 1976.

The special connection to Mao and members of the CRSG was, of course, the key to the eventual prominence of Shanghai's worker rebels. Moreover, the political benefits from the relationship flowed in both directions. The Gang of Four became a functioning clique only after WGH commander Wang Hongwen, a young security cadre and former machine operator at the Number 17 Cotton Mill, teamed up with early CR radicals Jiang Qing, Zhang Chunqiao, and Yao Wenyuan. It was Wang Hongwen's participation that gave the Gang of Four some claim to a social base, and Wang did not go unrewarded for this contribution. By August 1973, Wang Hongwen had gained a "helicopter" promotion to vice-chair of the Chinese Communist party—tapped by Chairman Mao as his putative successor in the wake of the fall of Defense Minister Lin Biao. This sort of recognition was unprecedented for a labor leader in post-1949 China and reflected Mao's high regard for Shanghai's worker-rebel movement.[3]

Buildup

Mao Zedong's initial conception of the Cultural Revolution had limited the campaign to the arenas of education and culture; he was undecided about whether the movement should eventually be expanded into the economic realm. When the CR first got underway in summer 1966, Shanghai factories were still in the midst of carrying out the Four Cleans (*siqing*)—an earlier campaign to curb the abuses of local cadres and provide experience in "class struggle" for ordinary citizens.[4] On June 30, party leaders Liu Shaoqi and Deng Xiaoping wrote Mao a joint letter, advocating that the 400,000 Shanghai workers then engaged in the Four Cleans might be used as a testing ground for the expansion of the CR. Only if the Shanghai experiment succeeded should the new campaign be extended to factories throughout the country. Two days later, Mao indicated his agreement with this proposal.[5]

The Shanghai Party Committee, following instructions from Liu and Deng, announced that at the factories where the Four Cleans had already been completed,[6] administrative work teams would not be withdrawn as previously indicated but would instead remain to develop new plans for the CR; at factories still in the throes of the Four Cleans,[7] work teams would combine that campaign with the Cultural Revolution; and at factories that had not yet begun to deal with the Four Cleans,[8] work teams would be dispatched from party and government agencies to initiate that campaign.[9] In this fashion, the CR was implemented in Shanghai factories more or less simultaneously with its development in schools. The factory version was somewhat more restrained, however: Whereas students could skip classes to participate, workers were not permitted to abandon their work posts.

Even so, criticisms poured forth from the brushes of aroused workers. On June 12, Wang Hongwen became the first factory employee to post a big-character-poster berating the leadership at his mill. By the end of that month, factories under the Metals Bureau (which had been carrying out the Four Cleans when the CR began) had singled out more than 7,000 people—over 10 percent of their employees—for poster criticism.[10]

It was not long before production was adversely affected by the escalating unrest in the factories. On July 8, the SPC notified Party Central that "industrial accidents have recently increased and equipment is not being well maintained. Products like steel and chemicals have seen a decline in output. Some research and development projects have been hampered because universities and research units are concentrating on the Cultural Revolution."[11]

Concern about the deteriorating economic situation made the SPC determined to keep work teams in place in the factories, even after Party Central leaders had announced the withdrawal of CR work teams at a meeting with Beijing student activists on July 29. Not till early December did the SPC finally order the removal of work teams from the industrial-transport sector. In the meantime, however, since Chairman Mao had declared the work teams "a mistake in line," the door was open for confrontations between restive workers and work teams still stationed at their factories. Despite the restraining efforts of work teams, factory managers were increasingly subjected to public criticism sessions at the hands of aroused workers. On the single day of August 24, from just the three sectors of shipbuilding, metallurgy, and electronics, a reported 417 factory cadres were paraded through the streets of Shanghai in dunce caps.[12]

Willing as some workers were to censure workplace authorities, however, many proved unenthusiastic about the attacks on the Shanghai Party Committee being launched by Red Guards from Beijing. When rebel students gathered in late August and early September to demand an overhaul of the SPC, thousands of workers—some spontaneously, others at the instigation of factory party organizations—converged at the SPC offices on Yan'an West Road to voice disagreement with the Beijing students. On September 2, a poster entitled "We older workers want to speak out!", signed by thirty-six individuals who identified themselves as retired and elderly workers at the Number 2 Cotton Mill, offered proletarian support to the municipal authorities.

The reluctance of many workers to criticize the city leadership was not surprising in view of the relatively favorable position that Shanghai had attained in the decade prior to the CR. Economist Christopher Howe observes, "From the eve of the Leap (1957) to the year in which the pre-Leap position is believed to have been generally regained (1965), we find that Shanghai grew more rapidly than the Chinese economy as a whole."[13] In the eyes of many Shanghai residents, "The Shanghai administration was competent, it had improved the livelihood of the citizens, and it was relatively popular."[14]

The Founding of the Workers'
General Headquarters

At the same time that most workers took exception to the radicalism of the Beijing Red Guards, a minority was inclined to emulate the student rebels. Links developed when some workers who felt stymied by the work teams posted at their factories went to the Capital Red Guards Third Headquarters Liaison Station (whose makeshift office was located in a private residence not far from the SPC) to complain about their plight and to seek advice from the students. The Red Guards, after listening to a number of tales of woe from local workers, decided it would be appropriate to help establish an all-city rebel organization of workers.

On the afternoon of November 6, 1966, a meeting to exchange experiences among Shanghai workers was organized at the Capital Red Guards Liaison Station by Central Arts Academy activist Bao Pao. To attract workers to this gathering, invitational phone calls were made to those who had recently registered complaints at the liaison station, and posters were put up in industrial centers of the city. More than thirty workers from seventeen factories showed up. The meeting began with Bao giving a summary of recent Party Central documents concerning the Cultural Revolution. Then the workers were encouraged to relate their personal experiences of repression at the hands of factory work teams, as well as their rebel activities to date.

Wang Hongwen of the Number 17 Cotton Mill responded with particular vigor to the Red Guard prodding: "Here we are holding this meeting, debating like this. What if the Public Security Bureau finds out, declares us counterrevolutionaries, and arrests us? Are you afraid or not? I'm not afraid! I'm determined to rebel!" Wang's bold opening encouraged other workers to speak out.[15] The meeting continued in this vein until ten o'clock at night. At that point, most of the workers had to return home, so it was decided that each of the seventeen work units should select a representative who would remain to discuss the name of the new organization and its leadership composition, as well as to make preparations for an inaugural meeting.[16]

As a result of these late-night deliberations, agreement was reached on a name for the new organization: Shanghai Workers' Revolutionary Rebels General Headquarters. The term "general" (*zong*) was Wang Hongwen's idea. Wang believed that worker rebels should avoid the fragmentation that had already beset the Beijing Red Guards, who were divided into several competing headquarters. He explained, "As a general headquarters, all rebel factions in the city come under our control. Later, when other people want to establish headquarters, we are 'general' and so they'll have no choice but to unite under our 'general' rubric."[17] The adjective "revolutionary" (*geming*) was added after another worker expressed reservations about the word "rebels" (*zaofan*). He pointed out that use of the term "rebels" invited people to ask: "Against whom are you rebelling?" Everyone agreed that it would be appropriate to modify the term "rebels" with "revolutionary."[18]

Among the seventeen factory representatives who remained that November night, only Wang Hongwen (a security cadre) and Cen Qilin (a technician) could claim party membership credentials. Since Cen's party affiliation had been temporarily suspended as a result of allegations raised during the Four Cleans, Wang Hongwen was chosen to chair the new organization. The fact that Wang worked at one of the largest factories in the city—and claimed to be able to mobilize 3,000 of his fellow workers to participate in the new rebel organization—also figured in his selection. Pan Guoping (a glass machinery worker) was made vice-chair, thanks to his oratorical skills. A five-person steering committee was also named.

Student inititives were critical at this formative stage of the worker-rebel movement. The Red Guards who had convened the preparatory meeting also played an active role in shaping its outcome. Noting that the Shanghai Party Committee was just then in the process of convening a high-level meeting to formulate its strategy for implementing the CR, the students suggested that the workers schedule an inauguration of their new organization prior to the conclusion of this cadre meeting so as to catch the authorities off guard. The inaugural ceremony was thereupon set for November 9, with publicity and security arrangements to be handled by the Red Guards. The founding manifesto and drafts of all keynote speeches by workers would also be penned by the student advisers.

Inasmuch as various Red Guard outfits differentiated themselves from one another by the wearing of distinctive red armbands, the organizers of the WGH agreed that the new organization should immediately issue its own armband. Like peasant rebels of imperial days, the worker rebels now faced the daunting task of procuring enough fabric to produce their identifying cloth badges.[19] Wang Hongwen, having just been named "commander" of the WGH, announced that he would assume personal responsibility for securing the requisite red cloth to make armbands for his followers. Accordingly, he gathered a dozen or so fellow workers and Red Guards for a midnight raid on a fabric store. When the store clerk demanded that the rebels pay for their bolts of cloth, Wang retorted, "Tell old man Cao [i.e., Mayor Cao Diqiu] to foot the bill!"[20] The first "rebel action" of the newly constituted WGH was thus a plundering expedition.

Only three days later, on the afternoon of November 9, the formal inaugural ceremony for the Workers' General Headquarters was staged at Cultural Plaza. Before the inauguration, the steering committee sent Vice-Chair Pan Guoping to the SPC to request the honor of Mayor Cao Diqiu's presence at the public ceremony. Uncertain about how to respond to this invitation, Cao immediately phoned Tao Zhu, secretary of the Central Party Standing Committee in Beijing, for instructions. Tao replied in no uncertain terms with what he insisted was central policy: "National or all-city organizations of workers are not permitted." Accordingly, Cao adopted the position of "no approval, no support, no participation" with respect to the founding of the WGH.[21] He later explained his reasoning at the time: "With the establishment of a WGH-type organization, contradictions that had been limited to one factory would be exported to others. Contradictions would thus be harder to resolve, the situation would be difficult to control, and production could no longer be guaranteed."[22] Cao's worries about industrial production were linked to concerns about individual personalities as well. As he confided to his secretary,

> Some of the WGH leaders are dregs of society; we must be careful. A number of impure people are mixed among the rebel ranks. Today some people are on top; tomorrow others. When an organization's composition is impure, production is adversely affected and eventually the situation breaks down. So I refused to participate in their big meeting. To have participated would have been a mistake.[23]

Perturbed by Mayor Cao's refusal to attend their inaugural ceremony, members of the newly formed WGH marched indignantly to the SPC offices. There, they staged a sit-in to demand official recognition of their organization. At the request of the SPC, the director of the Shanghai Federation of Trade Unions, Zhang Qi, met with more than 1,000 of the protesting workers at a local movie theater. Zhang called on the workers to return to their factories and expressed no opinion concerning the establishment of the WGH.

Having garnered no satisfaction either from Mayor Cao or from union director Zhang, the worker rebels decided to take their case to the citadel of the CR, Beijing, in hopes of a more sympathetic hearing from Party Central. Over 1,000 workers gathered early on the morning of November 10 at Shanghai's North Station to catch a train to the capital. One group forced its way onto a 5 A.M. train; another contingent, led by Wang Hongwen and Pan Guoping, made a 7 A.M. departure; and a third cohort, unable to board at all, proceeded along the tracks by foot. Soon after the 7 A.M. train had departed, however, the Shanghai Railway Bureau received an urgent cable from the Railroad Ministry in Beijing. The ministry was forwarding a State Council directive from Premier Zhou Enlai that the trains be grounded at stations near Shanghai so that the issue could be resolved locally. Accordingly, the earlier train was halted at Nanjing, and the train carrying Wang Hongwen and his followers was stopped at the Anting Station, on the outskirts of Shanghai, at 8:17 A.M.[24]

The Anting Incident

The Anting Incident, as it came to be known, was the first disruption of rail traffic in the Cultural Revolution. Lasting for more than thirty-one hours, it created a serious transportation snarl. According to the records of the Shanghai Railway Bureau: "Twelve trains were forced to halt to the east of Anting station. At Shanghai station, 36 trains were prevented from heading north. Between Anting and Bengbu, nearly 100 passenger and freight trains headed for Shanghai were forced to stop at various stations along the way."[25]

The symbolic import of the railway stoppage was at least as troubling as its immediate material effects, considering the key role that railroad disruptions had played in the history of China's Communist Revolution.[26] At a loss as to how to handle this volatile situation, the SPC cabled Beijing for instructions. That evening, CRSG Chair Chen Boda and Vice-Chair Zhang Chunqiao composed a joint reply, advising the SPC to send representatives to Anting to persuade the worker rebels to return to Shanghai.[27] The following day, Chen Boda fired off an urgent cable directly to the worker rebels at Anting, requesting that they "return at once to Shanghai to resolve any problems on the spot." In his telegram Chen explained,

> If you are not carrying out revolution in your spare time but are instead disrupting production, then your Cultural Revolution will come to no good end. Moreover, when production has been disrupted then no matter how righteous your cause—even if you can invoke 1,000 or 10,000 principles—it won't hold water.[28]

Chen informed the workers at Anting that Zhang Chunqiao was being dispatched to Shanghai on orders from the CRSG to handle this affair.[29] Zhang arrived at Anting in the middle of the night on November 11 and met at once with Wang Hongwen, Pan Guoping and others. After some discussion, he succeeded in talking them into returning to Shanghai for further negotiations; on November 12, the great majority of worker rebels left Anting either by train or in cars sent by their work units. A few hundred people refused to return to Shanghai, however, and insisted on continuing north by foot to lodge their complaints.

At noon on November 13, Mayor Cao convened an emergency meeting of the SPC to discuss Zhang Chunqiao's impending negotiations with the worker rebels that afternoon. Zhang attended this high-level meeting, at which it was unanimously decided neither to recognize the WGH nor to sanction its recent disruption of rail traffic. During the course of the meeting, Cao phoned Beijing and reported to CCP Standing Committee Secretary Tao Zhu, who concurred with the SPC's hard-line position.[30]

Shortly after the emergency meeting, Zhang Chunqiao hurried to Cultural Plaza for negotiations with Wang Hongwen and other worker rebels who were anxiously awaiting him there. But instead of carrying out the resolution of the SPC, Zhang took the unusual unilateral step of signing a set of "five-point demands" put forward by the rebels. The workers' demands, which directly contradicted the decision of the SPC, included the following:

1. recognition of the Shanghai Workers' Revolutionary Rebel General Headquarters as a revolutionary and legal organization;
2. recognition of the November 9 inauguration and "forced" trek to Beijing as a revolutionary action;
3. assignment of all responsibility for the outcome of the Anting Incident to the East China Bureau and the SPC;
4. public criticism of Cao Diqiu;
5. provision of various sorts of aid to the WGH to facilitate its future work.[31]

After this momentous signing, Zhang—without contacting the SPC or the East China Bureau—placed an immediate long-distance call to report to CRSG leader Chen Boda. Initially reluctant to approve Zhang's flagrant contravention of orders, Chen nonetheless agreed to consult at once with Jiang Qing. He soon called back to assure Zhang of the CRSG's full support for his audacious act. When Chairman Mao received a report on Zhang Chunqiao's handling of the Anting Incident, he responded with an imperial approval: "You can chop off their heads first and memorialize later." Mao's reaction, giving implicit sanction to Zhang's bold initiatives, rendered the Anting Incident a turning point in Cultural Revolution history.[32]

Having bequeathed to Shanghai a rebel force larger and more influential than the Red Guards, Zhang Chunqiao returned triumphantly to Beijing on November 25. In the wake of his departure, many worker militants ceased factory labor altogether to devote their full time to rebel activities. The effect on industrial production and social order proved far more disruptive than the dislocation brought about by the earlier Red Guard movement.

The Organization of the WGH

One evening, shortly after his return from Anting, Wang Hongwen joined a group of fellow worker rebels at a Shanghai pastry shop to chat about future plans. Years later, his companions recalled Wang's electrifying message to them at the time:

> The Cultural Revolution is a great upheaval; upheavals give birth to heroes. As the saying goes, "victors become kings while losers become outlaws." Right now the rebel situation is very favorable. Rebellion at the municipal-level can gain us the mayorship; at the department-level, directorships; and at lower levels, factory headships. So what if you're not party members? I can get you all into the party![33]

To institutionalize these political ambitions, Wang Hongwen announced soon thereafter that a general office of the Workers' General Headquarters would be set up, with representatives from the seventeen units that had founded the WGH serving as its core personnel.[34] Aside from a standing committee, initially there were no other regular committee members; anyone who had participated in the preparatory work of the WGH was simply included.[35] At first, the WGH established its head offices on Hangzhou Road, moving soon to Fuxing Central Road, and then to the city offices on Nanjing West Road. Finally, in February 1967 the rebels took possession of the imposing Shanghai Federation of Trade Unions building on the bund, where they remained for nearly a decade, until the conclusion of the Cultural Revolution.

The institutional changes in the WGH were especially great during the first year. By late November 1966, the general headquarters (under the command of Wang Hongwen, assisted by Pan Guoping) included seven functional divisions (*zu*): organization, secretariat, liaison, logistics, security, propaganda, and reception.[36] In early 1967, the divisions were further refined; moreover, each division director enjoyed a close personal relationship with Wang Hongwen: industry (headed by Chen Ada), transportation (Jiang Zhoufa), city government (Zhang Baolin), districts and counties (Huang Jinhai), mass movement (Wang Xiuzhen), political propaganda (Cen Qilin), administrative office (Dai Liqing), *Worker Rebel* newspaper (Wang Chenglong), secretariat of the standing committee (Ye Changming), and organization (Jin Zumin).[37] These administrative divisions persisted through the end of the CR, despite numerous changes in personnel.

Operating under the jurisdiction of the general headquarters were branches at the level of the bureau (*ju*), district (*qu*), county (*xian*), and company (*gongsi*), which came to be known as "liaison posts" (*lianluo zhan*).[38] Subsequent changes in nomenclature did not alter this basic structure. In 1972 the WGH formally adopted the name of Workers' Representative Congress, as did rebel units at subordinate levels. Later that year, when the Workers' Representative Congress reclaimed the pre-Cultural Revolution appellation of "Federation of Trade Unions," lower units were henceforth known as "union" branches.

From Minority to Majority Status

For the first several months of their existence, the rebels constituted a distinct minority in the factories of Shanghai; the overwhelming majority of workers remained reluctant to call for the removal of party authorities.[39] Not until Mao Zedong's endorsement of the January Revolution of 1967 did most workers show an interest in joining the rebel ranks. Later that year, the WGH undertook a census, which revealed that rebels had gained the upper hand in most factories. The results are shown in Table 2.1.

The change was seen in microcosm in Wang Hongwen's Number 17 Cotton Mill. In December 1966 the rival conservative organization had boasted some 5,000 workers (equal to 60% of the employees), whereas Wang Hongwen's rebels claimed only 2,000 adherents (about 25% of the workforce). But by November 1967, the rebel forces numbered an impressive 6,500 (or 73%).[40]

"Old Rebels"

The sudden influx of new rebels in 1967 (many of whom had earlier been associated with conservative factions) propelled to top leadership positions those who had stood by Wang Hongwen's side from the very start. These stalwarts liked to call themselves "old rebels" (*lao zaofan*)—an appellation that (like "old cadres") qualified those so designated for special privileges. There were, however, two competing claims regarding the cutoff date for old rebels. One interpretation restricted the label of old rebels to those who had participated in the founding of the WGH and in the Anting Incident; that is, those who had joined before mid-

TABLE 2.1   Rebel Composition in Shanghai Industry, November 1967

Sector	Number of Employees	Number of Rebels	Percentage Rebels
Textile system	362,701	216,265	59.63
Light industrial system	157,871	95,071	60.22
Instruments system	67,468	49,710	73.68
Electronics system	17,762	12,244	68.93
Ship-building system	32,881	22,765	69.23
Defense system	5,864	3,416	58.25
Metallurgy system	91,693	76,710	83.65
No. 2 Electrical Bureau	20,000	11,282	56.41
Chemical engineering system	75,802	46,514	61.36
East China Materials Bureau	3,883	2,546	65.57
Municipal Materials Bureau	11,487	8,402	73.14

SOURCE: WGH, ed., *Shanghai gongren geming zaofan zongsilingbu zaofandui zuzhi qingkuang tongji biao* [Statistical tables on the rebel organizations of the Shanghai Worker's Revolutionary Rebels General Headquarters], Shanghai, November 1967.

November 1966. By this calculation, there were only a few thousand old rebels in Shanghai. The alternative interpretation held that participation in any of the three "great incidents" of the early period of the WGH (Anting, *Liberation Daily,* and Kangping Road)—activities that occurred prior to late December 1966—qualified one as an old rebel. (Concerning the Kangping Road Incident, see Chapter 3.) By this calculation, there were tens of thousands of old rebels.

Between December 1969 and January 1970, the WGH carried out a large-scale registration of its leaders in district, county, bureau, and company liaison posts and in factory rebel brigades, which revealed that the great majority of these leaders were old rebels. According to the registration forms, of the 1,756 leaders at all levels (plus 28 for whom no entry date into the rebel forces was listed), a total of 727 (41%) had joined before November 1966 and an additional 341 (20%) had signed up by December of that year. Thus 61 percent of the rebel leaders were old rebels, in the looser sense.[41]

That old rebels were disproportionately numerous at the leadership ranks is confirmed by a detailed survey of the WGH Light Industrial Bureau Liaison Post conducted in January 1970. The investigation found 66,825 rebels among the 116,879 workers in that sector (i.e., 57% of the total), of whom only 4,438 (3.8% of the total; 6.6% of the rebels) were old rebels.[42] In other words, although the old rebels dominated the leadership echelons, they composed only a small fraction of the total rebel ranks.

The importance of the old rebels hints at a fundamental irony within the movement. Despite their claim to be making a radical break with traditional values, the rebels embraced a familiar notion of social hierarchy based upon seniority. To be labeled an "old rebel" meant that one's revolutionary contribution was considered greater than that of ordinary rebels and, having sacrificed more for the movement, that one deserved special privileges. Most of the old rebels assumed positions of power during the Cultural Revolution; even those who were temporarily forced to step down (often for disciplinary punishment), could usually parlay their identity as old rebels to stage a subsequent comeback.

Who were these "venerable" figures, and what prompted their rebellion in the first place? After the announcement formally concluding the Cultural Revolution in 1976, a barrage of criticism castigated the rebels as "social dregs" who had engaged in a variety of improper activities prior to the onset of the CR. This accusation was not without foundation. A number of the early rebel leaders had indeed been subjected to disciplinary action by their factories for transgressions ranging from embezzlement to illicit sexual affairs. Some were known as perennial troublemakers, fond of picking fights with their fellow workers. In these cases, black marks in their personnel dossiers prevented such workers from enjoying the raises and promotions to which they might otherwise have been entitled. The Cultural Revolution afforded them a chance to redress grievances. In many other cases, however, workers with clean dossiers whose ambitions outstripped the restrictions imposed by the socialist system saw the Cultural Revolution as an opportunity to get ahead.

To gain a better understanding of the composition of the rebel movement, we first introduce some summary statistics on the social backgrounds and political affiliations of the old rebels. Then we probe more intensively into the individual biographies of the top rebel leaders.

Social Background of Old Rebels

In winter 1969, the WGH undertook a thorough registration of heads of its subordinate liaison posts and rebel brigades. Surveyed units included the twenty municipal bureaus and their constituent companies and factories as well as the liaison posts of the ten city districts and ten suburban counties. Registration forms asked of each rebel leader: name, sex, age, work experience, family background, personal status, educational level, political affiliation, pre–Cultural Revolution occupation, time of joining the rebels, and current position.[43]

The investigation revealed a demographic profile of rebel leaders that was not greatly at variance with the characteristics of the workforce as a whole. For example, the overwhelming majority of rebel leaders (both old rebels and post-January 1967 recruits) came from "good" class backgrounds. Nearly 88 percent of the old rebels (and 85% of the rebel leaders as a whole) listed worker, cadre, poor peasant, or urban poor as their inherited class label.

The rebel leadership was fairly young, with more than 55 percent falling into the age bracket of 26 to 35. Since this was the largest age cohort in the Shanghai workforce, it is not surprising that it generated a substantial proportion of the

TABLE 2.2   Ages of Old Rebels as Compared to Those of the General Workforce

Age Group	Total Workforce 1966 Percentage	Old Rebels before November 1966 Number	Percentage	Old Rebels before January 1967 Number	Percentage
16–25	13.6	201	28.0	449	25.4
26–35	30.8	402	55.9	976	55.1
36–45	30.1	115	16.0	338	19.0
46–55	18.6	1	0.1	7	0.4
56+	6.9	0	0.0	1	0.1
TOTAL	100.0	719	100.0	1,771	100.0

NOTE: Due to the chaos of the CR, in 1967 the Shanghai Statistical Bureau had no way of gathering data on many aspects of the 1966 workforce, so we only have 1965 statistics on the average age of Shanghai workers. With a bit of reworking, we have estimated the 1966 figures.

SOURCES: WGH, ed., *Shanghai gongren geming zaofan zongsilingbu zaofandui zuzhi qingkuang tongji biao* [Statistical tables on the rebel organizations of the Shanghai Worker's Revolutionary Rebels General Headquarters], Shanghai, November 1967; Shanghai Statistical Bureau, ed., *1965nian Shanghai zhigong jiben qingkuang tongji—zhigong fenlei* [Statistics on the basic conditions of the Shanghai workforce in 1965], Shanghai, 1966.

rebel leaders. As the data in Table 2.2 show, however, younger workers (ages 16–25 as well as ages 26–35) were represented among the old rebel leadership at a rate almost double what we might expect from the age structure of the workforce as a whole.

The disproportionate involvement of youth is a common feature of most labor movements, or, for that matter, most social movements in general. The significant aspect of the Cultural Revolution case lies in the fact that the majority of rebel leaders were too young to have experienced the pre-Communist situation, yet were old enough to have accumulated considerable dissatisfaction with the socialist system. As the data in Table 2.3 indicate, the vast majority of old rebels had entered the workforce during the seventeen years of socialism that predated the onset of the Cultural Revolution in 1966. Having logged a number of years on the job, with scant prospects of upward or outward mobility, they were ripe for a movement that offered them a chance to challenge the status quo.

The typical rebel leader was about thirty years old at the start of the Cultural Revolution and had accrued approximately a decade of work experience. Lacking the vantage of a pre-Communist comparison, rebels had little personal stake in maintaining the new industrial order as an improvement over its "exploitative" predecessor. They were, however, sufficiently familiar with the workings of the socialist system to mount a credible challenge. Moreover, at the top echelons of the Workers' General Headquarters the average age was slightly higher than among the rebel leaders at large. Of the thirty-eight old rebels who sat on the leading

TABLE 2.3   Work Experience of Old Rebels

Work Experience (in years)	Old Rebels (before November 1966)		Old Rebels (before January 1967)	
	Number	Percent	Number	Percent
1–5	120	30.0	310	27.4
6–10	94	23.6	259	22.9
11–15	69	17.3	233	20.6
16–20	90	22.6	239	21.1
20+	26	6.5	90	8.0
TOTAL	399	100.0	1,131	100.0

SOURCE: WGH, ed., *Shanghai gongren geming zaofan zongsilingbu zaofandui zuzhi qingkuang tongji biao* [Statistical tables on the rebel organizations of the Shanghai Worker's Revolutionary Rebels General Headquarters], Shanghai, November 1967.

committees of the WGH, twenty-eight (or 74%) fell into the age 26 to 35 cohort.[44] Thanks to their considerable on-the-job tenure, these leaders could draw on substantial workplace contacts to mobilize their opposition to factory authorities.

Most old rebels had been ordinary workers before the Cultural Revolution began. According to the Shanghai Statistical Bureau, in 1965 factory workers composed 76.1 percent of the city's employees.[45] As the figures in Table 2.4 show, old rebels exceeded this percentage. The vast majority of the earliest rebels were factory employees. Workers in schools, government offices, hospitals, shops, and cultural agencies initially showed little interest in the WGH. Furthermore, within the factories themselves, party and government cadres and managerial personnel were loath to enlist on the rebel side. Only after Mao Zedong explicitly recognized the WGH as the leading rebel organization in Shanghai did cadres and managers feel compelled to change their hostile stance.

The average educational attainment of the old rebels was middle or high school, a level significantly higher than the mean for Shanghai workers at the time.[46] As the numbers in Table 2.5 indicate, nearly half of the general workforce could claim, at best, an elementary school education whereas less than one-fifth of the rebels fell into this category of the poorly educated. In part, no doubt because the Cultural Revolution began as a rather esoteric ideological debate fought out via the medium of big-character-posters, it attracted the better-educated stratum of the workforce. Moreover, younger workers, who—as we have seen—made up the bulk of the rebel leaders, tended to have a higher level of education than workers who had entered the factories before 1949. Had many rebel groups not explicitly excluded anyone with university credentials from their ranks, the proportion of this most highly educated segment of the workforce would surely have been a good deal higher.

Perhaps the most interesting finding to emerge from the registration data concerns Communist party and Communist Youth League (CYL) affiliation. Al-

TABLE 2.4 Pre–Cultural Revolution Occupations of Old Rebels

Occupation	Old Rebels (before November 1966)		Old Rebels (before January 1967)	
	Number	Percent	Number	Percent
Worker	600	84.9	1,366	80.1
Ordinary managers	94	13.3	291	17.1
Leading managers	6	0.8	18	1.1
Union cadres	2	0.3	8	0.5
Party cadres	5	0.7	20	1.2
TOTAL	707	100.0	1,703	100.0

Source: WGH, ed., *Shanghai gongren geming zaofan zongsilingbu zaofandui zuzhi qingkuang tongji biao* [Statistical tables on the rebel organizations of the Shanghai Worker's Revolutionary Rebels General Headquarters], Shanghai, November 1967.

TABLE 2.5 Education of Old Rebels Compared to the General Workforce

Level	Shanghai Workforce (1965)		Old Rebels	
	Number	Percent	Number	Percent
Illiterate	77,612	5.0	1	–
Elementary	644,294	41.5	164	19.9
Middle school	549,089	35.3	440	53.4
High school	212,154	13.6	171	20.8
University	71,096	4.6	49	5.9
TOTAL	1,554,245	100.0	825	100.0

Source: WGH, ed., *Shanghai gongren geming zaofan zongsilingbu zaofandui zuzhi qingkuang tongji biao* [Statistical tables on the rebel organizations of the Shanghai Worker's Revolutionary Rebels General Headquarters], Shanghai, November 1967.

though it is often asserted that party and league members were rare among the rebels, the information presented in Table 2.6 shows that this was not actually the case. On the eve of the Cultural Revolution, about 12 percent of the Shanghai workforce belonged to the Communist party—a figure that included such units as schools and government agencies, where party members were especially numerous. If we take factories alone, the percentage drops to under 10 percent.[47] Among old rebels, however, the proportion of party members was considerably higher. Furthermore, youth league membership was about double that of the general workforce.

These relatively high levels of party and league membership (together accounting for about one-third of the rebel leaders) indicate that old rebels tended to be more politically inclined than the general populace. Yet since few of these rebels had attained cadre or managerial status prior to the Cultural Revolution (as

TABLE 2.6   Party and League Membership

Type	Shanghai Workforce Number	Percentage	Old Rebels (before November 1966) Number	Percentage	Old Rebels (before January 1967) Number	Percentage
CCP	186,510	12.1	104	15.7	269	18.2
CYL	115,425	7.5	115	17.4	196	13.3
Masses	1,237,990	80.4	443	66.9	1,012	68.5
TOTAL	1,539,925	100.0	662	100.0	1,477	100.0

SOURCE: WGH, ed., *Shanghai gongren geming zaofan zongsilingbu zaofandui zuzhi qingkuang tongji biao* [Statistical tables on the rebel organizations of the Shanghai Worker's Revolutionary Rebels General Headquarters], Shanghai, November 1967.

shown in Table 2.4), we can presume a gap between their ambitions and their achievements. Unlike those who enlisted on the conservative side, rebel workers included a number of party and league activists who had been passed over for higher leadership posts. The Cultural Revolution, with its call to rebel against "unjust" authority, offered a golden opportunity to settle scores.

The sociopolitical profile of the rebel leaders that emerges from this investigation offers some limited support for the importance of both social groups and political networks. Although class background does not appear to have been a deciding factor, on one hand, rebel leaders did tend to be younger, better educated, and more politically active than the workforce at large. On the other hand, none of these attributes distinguishes them definitively from their conservative rivals.

To appreciate the key distinctions among different types of labor leaders during the Cultural Revolution (rebel, conservative, and economistic), we must move beyond summary statistics to probe individual biographies. The most influential old rebels in the early days of the WGH were nine individuals: Wang Hongwen, Wang Xiuzhen, Geng Jinzhang, Pan Guoping, Huang Jinhai, Chen Ada, Ye Changming, Dai Liqing, and Ma Zhenlong. Three were party members; three had been designated as "backward elements" by their work units; and three were ordinary workers prior to the CR. A review of the personal histories of these rebel leaders suggests that neither a focus on group attributes nor an emphasis on political networks can adequately capture their commonalities. The one element of similarity among these remarkably diverse individuals was their unusually forceful personalities.

Party Members Among the Old Rebels

Among the very top leaders of the rebel-worker movement were several individuals who boasted party credentials. We begin with a consideration of their backgrounds.

Wang Hongwen.   The commander of the Workers' General Headquarters, Wang Hongwen, hailed originally from Manchuria. In 1950, while still in the northeast, he joined the army and, the following year, was assigned to Korea. Although the Korean War was then raging, Wang did not face active combat. He served as a messenger in the communications department and played the horn in the army band.[48] More important, in the military Wang entered the Communist party.

In September 1956 Wang Hongwen was demobilized and sent to the Number 17 Cotton Mill in Shanghai as a machine operator.[49] The factory at which he was employed was one of Shanghai's three largest textile mills, with a workforce of over 8,000 people.[50] It was located in the city's premier industrial district of Yang-shupu and boasted a long history of political activism.[51]

Workers at the mill who knew Wang remember him as an affable and loyal friend who enjoyed a certain standing among the workers. But he was also said to be afflicted with "office addiction" (*guanyin*)—a longing for political position. Wang was known to have remarked to the master craftsman who taught him his workplace skills: "I don't want to eat skilled rice; I want to eat political rice."[52] His expressed ambition was to escape the ranks of the ordinary workers and serve as a leading cadre.

Wang Hongwen's upward trajectory was not quite as smooth as he apparently anticipated. According to an account written by the SPC Small Group to Investigate the Gang of Four,

> In 1958, Wang Hongwen was chosen as party committee member of the day shift in the number 2 spinning room, but was not made branch party secretary. He believed that he had received the most votes, but that higher levels had decided [that] the original branch secretary would continue to serve in that position, whereas Wang should remain at his work post. As a consequence, Wang Hongwen frequently refused to participate in branch committee meetings.[53]

Despite this early disappointment, Wang continued to move upward. In March 1960, he was loaned to the factory security department to handle militia work. Not long after, he was formally transferred to the security department as a security cadre in charge of militia work for the entire factory. From this point, Wang left the "blue-collar" status of productive laborer.

Wang Hongwen was known for speaking his mind. Between September 1960 and October 1962, during the terrible famine that followed the Great Leap Forward, Wang was sent to Chongming Island to participate in reclamation and flood-prevention work.[54] Despite his position as a party member and a political work cadre, he is reported to have been an outspoken critic of the policies of the day.

> In 1960, during the economic retrenchment . . . Wang Hongwen exclaimed, "Damn it! What kind of socialism forces people to go to work on an empty stomach? What kind of policy makes people starve to death?"
>
> Wang Hongwen observed, "My fellow villagers in the northeast haven't eaten, and in Anhui tens of thousands of people have starved to death. We workers should be

working in the factory. What are we doing going to Chongming to reclaim land? In my view, the natural calamities are mostly a manmade disaster."[55]

Evidently, Wang was not the obedient apparatchik—ready to champion whatever policies the party dictated—but a feisty individual willing to think and speak for himself. He read the newspapers carefully, so as to stay on top of the latest domestic developments, and even listened regularly to forbidden shortwave radio broadcasts to keep abreast of international events.[56] When the CR began, Wang Hongwen was a savvy thirty-one-year-old security cadre who had been working in a factory for nearly a decade. Undoubtedly, Wang's independent spirit contributed to his rebelliousness during the Cultural Revolution.

The beginning of Wang Hongwen's "rebellion" can be dated to June 12, 1966, when he announced his open opposition to the factory authorities by posting a big-character-poster at the Number 17 Mill. Wang (and several of his coworkers) accused authorities at his work unit, in particular, Deputy-Director Zhang Heming, of failing to grasp class struggle, practicing revisionism, and ignoring mass opinions.[57] The inflammatory poster went up at 10 A.M. Less than an hour later, the party committee secretary of the company (*gongsi*) in charge of the Number 17 Mill, Chen Zhida, arrived at the factory to convene an emergency meeting. An account written toward the end of the CR described the scene at the time.

> At the meeting, Deputy-director Zhang Heming said, "We must target big-character-posters against ox-demons and snake-spirits. Has everyone seen the big-character-poster in the security department? Everyone should go take a look and analyze it to see what its problem is. The big-character-poster in the security department is a big poisonous weed."[58]

The factory party committee then proceeded to seek out the other signatories to Wang Hongwen's poster to admonish them for their insolent act.[59]

In this heated atmosphere, the Textile Bureau dispatched a Cultural Revolution work team to the Number 17 Cotton Mill to supervise the ongoing struggle. Wang's "rebel" action received the immediate blessing of the work team. But soon, this first work team was recalled and replaced by another team sent from the SPC itself and headed by Shanghai Federation of Trade Unions vice-chair, Shi Huizhen. Shi was an older cadre who had entered the party back in 1938 and had been active in the underground Shanghai labor movement before the founding of the PRC. She did not support Wang Hongwen's precipitous attack on factory Deputy-Director Zhang Heming; instead, Shi selected the other deputy-director, Zhang Yuanqi, as the proper target of criticism.[60]

One of the signatories to Wang's poster later analyzed Wang Hongwen's conflict with Zhang Heming and the second work team.

> Why did Wang Hongwen want to oppose Zhang Heming? This was because at that time the party committee decided that eight people were to be criticized. Some of these eight had political problems [and] some were considered to be "reactionary academic authorities." The party committee decided that the criticisms could not ex-

tend beyond this limited group. Zhang Yuanqi (another deputy-directory at the factory) suggested that other factory leaders with problems could be criticized in posters, but Zhang Heming disagreed. He insisted that posters could be written only about these eight individuals. Wang Hongwen believed this was too rigid, so he put up a poster attacking Zhang Heming. At that time, we thought that the party leadership itself was riddled with problems which it didn't want exposed. As soon as you raised them, you were dubbed "anti-party" in their effort to defend themselves. So we agreed with Wang Hongwen.

The first work team was sent by the bureau, and they supported us. But the second team was sent by the city, and they disagreed with our opinions, considering our posters criticizing the party committee to be "anti-party."[61]

The disagreement concerning the two Zhangs went deeper than the question of how many struggle targets should be chosen. A conflict between the deputy-directors had developed over who would assume the vacant directorship of the Number 17 Mill. Zhang Yuanqi had relatively little formal education, but substantial work experience. Charged with overall responsibility for security matters at the mill, he had developed a close working relationship with security cadre Wang Hongwen. Like his colleague Wang Hongwen, Zhang Yuanqi was a demobilized soldier from north China. Originally from Shandong Province, he spoke with an accent unintelligible to the southern workers. By contrast, Zhang Heming had been promoted to his cadre position from among the ranks of the workers themselves, spoke with a familiar Ningbo accent, and enjoyed closer relations with the ordinary workers.

Before the Cultural Revolution, Zhang Yuanqi's portfolio at the factory included personnel as well as security matters. Wang Hongwen's support of Zhang Yuanqi apparently stemmed not only from their previous cooperation on security issues but also from Wang's calculation that Zhang's control of personnel appointments might facilitate his own promotion in the future.[62] In any event, Wang's refusal to denounce Zhang Yuanqi created substantial friction with Shi's work team.

The differences surfaced in early August, when the Number 17 Cotton Mill made plans to establish a "CR committee" to direct the struggle at the factory. Although the rebel faction among the workers nominated Wang Hongwen to serve as chair of this committee, the work team refused to consider him. At this time, the rebels were still a minority at the factory, and Wang Hongwen was not chosen.[63] Having been the favorite of the first work team posted at his factory, Wang had come to expect a position of leadership during the Cultural Revolution. Thus when the second work team of Shi Huizhen blocked his appointment, he was bitterly disappointed. Wang admitted on more than one occasion: "In the beginning if I had been permitted to serve as CR chair I would not have rebelled."[64]

In early October, Wang Hongwen put up a second big-character-poster, which attacked the work team at his factory. A few days later, he and his followers founded their own rebel group, which they dubbed "Warriors Sworn to the Death to Carry Through with the Cultural Revolution to the End." Unable to prevail at their own factory, the rebels decided to venture north to plead their case directly to Party Central. The next day, Wang Hongwen led fifteen followers off to Beijing.[65] Wang's trip to the capital was a bold move that won him the lasting admiration of other rebels among the Shanghai workforce. Prior to his foray, the "exchange of experiences" had been the exclusive prerogative of student Red Guards. Now, workers, too, were performing on a national stage. When Wang returned to Shanghai, he was lionized by rebels at nearby factories, who invited him to their workplaces to discuss the situation in the capital. Later, WGH activist Huang Jinhai admitted, "I worshipped Wang Hongwen."[66] Thus when Huang Jinhai received a telephone message on November 6 inviting him to a planning meeting with Red Guards, he immediately informed Wang Hongwen so that he, too, could participate. That afternoon, Wang Hongwen led two others from his factory to the historic meeting that would seal his fate as a worker rebel.[67]

Wang Hongwen's story does indeed highlight the significance of competing party networks in structuring the factionalism of the CR era. The long-standing conflict in which Wang's patron, Zhang Yuanqi, was embroiled became Wang Hongwen's battle as well. These networks, moreover, developed at least to some extent out of shared social backgrounds: Both Wang and Zhang Yuanqi were demobilized soldiers from north China, working on security matters at the mill. However, when we survey the biographies of the other eight top rebel leaders it becomes clear that in explaining the urge to rebel, neither political networks nor social characteristics were as important as Wang Hongwen's own restless temperament and frustrated ambition—his longing to "eat political rice," as he put it so aptly.

Wang Xiuzhen. After 1967, Wang Xiuzhen ranked second in importance to Wang Hongwen in the Shanghai rebel-workers' movement. Although she had not taken part in the preparatory activities leading to the founding of the WGH, she qualified as an old rebel by virtue of her participation in the Anting Incident. Promoted to the WGH Standing Committee only after 1967, Wang Xiuzhen moved steadily upward to assume major positions in municipal governance: vice-chair of the Shanghai Revolutionary Committee, deputy-secretary of the Shanghai Party Committee, and vice-chair of the Shanghai Federation of Trade Unions—considerably more than most other old rebels achieved.

Wang Xiuzhen's meteoric rise directly reflected Wang Hongwen's growing confidence in her. Like Wang Hongwen, she hailed originally from Manchuria. She was born to a poor peasant family in Liaoning Province and received only two years of schooling. Among the family's six daughters, the eldest girl was sold and later starved to death; the second also died young. Wang Xiuzhen was the third girl. At a very young age, carrying her younger sister on her back, she went to work as a charcoal picker.

In March 1950, at age fifteen Wang Xiuzhen entered Liaoyang Textile Mill as a weaver. Just at this time, her father died of high blood pressure. Saddled with the entire financial burden of her struggling family, she labored diligently at her factory job. After two years, Wang entered the Youth League, and at the age of eighteen she joined the Communist party. Selected as an activist in her workshop, Wang was later celebrated as an "advanced producer" and a "labor model" at city, provincial, and Northeast District levels. These were high honors; indeed, the highest to which a diligent worker might normally aspire, and Wang had achieved them when she was only twenty years old. But her accomplishments did not end there. Soon Wang Xiuzhen was named a people's representative to the city of Liaoyang and then to Liaoning Province.

In August 1956, Wang Xiuzhen was sent to the Shanghai Textile Institute to further develop her talents. Although the relocation was an opportunity for advancement, it also meant that Wang was forced to relinquish the honors and political posts she had enjoyed in the northeast. Not until the Cultural Revolution would she be able to regain the status she had possessed before her move south.

Upon graduation, Wang was assigned a job at the Shanghai Textile Design Institute. In 1961, when the Design Institute was "streamlined," she was sent to the Number 30 Cotton Mill as a technician. Later, Wang was promoted to supervisor of the weaving workshop. This promising career was threatened, however, after the birth of her two children, when she was publicly criticized by the factory director for a deterioration in her work. Humiliated by this experience, she requested a transfer. Although temporarily loaned to the Textile Bureau to handle personnel dossiers, Wang was returned to her factory shortly before the Cultural Revolution began. After her reinstatement at the Number 30 Cotton Mill, she managed dossiers in the factory director's office. Despite this promotion to the ranks of upper administration, she harbored a smoldering grudge based on her post-Liaoning tribulations.[68]

Wang Xiuzhen had always been an activist, a target of cultivation by the party. This made her unusual among the old rebels. At the start of the Cultural Revolution, thirty-two-year-old Wang Xiuzhen was even chosen as director of her factory CR committee. Most workers with this sort of background became conservatives, but Wang was an exception—not only a rebel, but an old rebel. In explaining this anomaly, Wang's fellow workers at the Number 30 Mill later pointed to her ambition and avarice, charging that she had been afflicted with the "three clamors" (*sanchao*)—for wages, housing, and position.[69]

Wang herself always insisted that her rebellion was a response to the call of Chairman Mao. However, she also emphasized that it was Wang Hongwen who had given her the personal courage to rebel. After she became CR committee chair, Wang was embroiled in a conflict with the work team at her factory. She was convinced that the team was simply criticizing the former capitalists and was even protecting the party committee at the factory, so she went to the Shanghai Party Committee to lodge a complaint. At the gate of the SPC, Wang Xiuzhen ran into an old classmate from the Textile Institute who was now working at the Number 17 Cotton Mill. Through this acquaintance she was introduced to Wang Hongwen. She later recalled,

Wang Hongwen told me how they had gone to Beijing to file a complaint against the work team at the Number 17 Cotton Mill and how the CRSG had really supported them and asked them to return to wage battle against the capitalist line of the work team and the SPC. Wang Hongwen also wanted me to use my legal status as chair of the CR committee to struggle against the work team.

I felt emboldened, and I went back and wrote a big-character-poster against the work team. A big discussion meeting was convened, and Wang Hongwen was invited to the factory to give a report about his trip to Beijing. Workers at our factory were also organized to go tour the Number 17 Mill.[70]

On November 7, Wang Xiuzhen saw a handbill announcing the inaugural meeting of the Workers' General Headquarters on November 9 at the Cultural Plaza. She quickly organized a truckload of workers from her factory to participate. After the meeting, she followed the crowd to the North Station and boarded a train for Nanjing. In this way, she acquired credentials as an old rebel participant in the Anting Incident. But, unlike other rebels who ventured to Nanjing in this incident, Wang Xiuzhen did not join the First Regiment of Dai Zuxiang. Instead, she remained loyal to Wang Hongwen.

As repayment for this allegiance, in early 1967 she was personally assigned by Wang Hongwen to the headquarters of the WGH to direct its propaganda and organization departments. From this point on, she became Wang Hongwen's most capable and most trusted lieutenant—second only to Wang Hongwen himself in the lineup of influential leaders of the Shanghai worker-rebel movement.

The lone woman among the top worker rebels, Wang Xiuzhen's rebelliousness stemmed in large measure from embitterment over her humiliation following the birth of her two children. Yet there is no evidence to suggest that Wang used her substantial influence during the CR to articulate the special concerns of women workers. Women were a distinct minority among the rebel leaders. Although they composed about one-third of Shanghai's permanent workforce at this time, women accounted for only 11 percent of the rebel-worker leadership at all levels (198 out of 1,784). Spirited as these women tended to be, their struggles seldom reflected an explicitly feminist agenda.[71]

Geng Jinzhang. Geng Jinzhang was an entirely different sort of party member than either Wang Hongwen or Wang Xiuzhen. As one of the oldest rebel workers (41 years old at the onset of the CR), Geng had been a party member for longer than any of the other old rebels, having joined the CCP in 1949. But despite his party credentials, Geng had always been an ordinary worker who never held any staff position. His educational level was also extremely low; he was functionally illiterate.

Like Wang Hongwen and Wang Xiuzhen, Geng hailed originally from north China. The child of poor peasants in Shandong, Geng was only six when he lost his father, and his mother died a year later. At age eight Geng went to live with his paternal uncle, who could not afford to keep him and put him up for sale. In desperation, young Geng fled to a nearby temple, pleading to be taken in as a novitiate. When the resident monks refused to accept him, he went off to live with his maternal aunt. At age ten Geng began a seven-year term working for a landlord. After his dismissal from that job, he was forced to resort to short-term stints as a hired hand, interspersed with periods of begging.

Like Wang Hongwen, Geng Jinzhang spent a number of years as a soldier. His military experience was considerably more diverse than Wang's, however. In January 1945, Geng enlisted in the Japanese "puppet" forces in his home county of Ningyang. When the war ended that August, for his livelihood he turned to casual labor and peddling. The following year, Geng again entered the military—this time under the command of Kuomintang (KMT) General Wu Huawen. Only when General Wu joined the Communist forces in 1948 was Geng finally incorporated into the People's Liberation Army (PLA). He advanced from ordinary soldier to squadron and battalion commander, and in May 1949, as the PLA was fighting its way south, Geng joined the CCP.[72]

Demobilized in 1957, Geng was assigned a job as a worker at the Shanghai Paper Pulp Factory. Ordinarily, an old party member like Geng at the very least would have risen to become a foreman at his factory. Yet Geng Jinzhang remained an ordinary worker; his sole position of responsibility at the pulp mill, out of consideration for his military background, was as a lower-level militia captain. The limitations on Geng's upward mobility stemmed from his reputation as a womanizer and a troublemaker. While serving in the Japanese military, Geng had been accused of rape, and as a PLA soldier he had received a stern intraparty warning for illicit sexual relations. Then, in 1963, when one of his neighbors inadvertently burned Geng's son with boiling water, Geng Jinzhang delivered a sound thrashing to the neighbor and his wife, ripped their clothing to shreds, and destroyed much of their furniture—a transgression for which he was dealt a second party warning.[73]

Later, Geng Jinzhang's workmates at the Shanghai paper mill distributed a handbill about their erstwhile comrade that colorfully described his earlier exploits.

> Geng Jinzhang was coarse by nature, violent and unprincipled. He was a ruffian who uttered a "damnation" as soon as he opened his mouth. He often got into fights at the factory. After the rectification in 1958, when he wasn't promoted to cadre he feigned mental illness and missed work without cause. Geng had lived in the Number 4 village of Tianshan, where he often fought with his neighbors. He even hit people with a cutting board. Twice he destroyed people's furniture in cases that went all the way to the Changning District Court.
>
> When the CR began, Geng Jinzhang took on airs as a party member. He mobilized the masses to put up big-character-posters, saying such and such party member was a "traitor."[74]

A roundtable discussion elicited the following evaluations of Geng from his fellow workers:

"This person is an uncouth blockhead."

"He often beat up people at the factory."

"He's simpleminded, uneducated, yet ambitious. Because he was never made a foreman at the factory, he wanted to create a stir."

"This guy was always barbarous. He was obsessed by a lust for office. He always wanted to be an official, and the CR gave him a chance to rush forth. In the past he had beaten and cursed people."[75]

Like so many of the rebel leaders, Geng's turn to rebellion followed upon the heels of retribution for having posted criticisms of his factory management. He recalled,

We prepared ten criticisms in all, and on the fifteenth we finished a big-character-poster, which we put up in the cafeteria. The poster focused on the issue of the work style of the leadership. That afternoon, the factory party branch secretary, Yang Youwei, convened a branch meeting to launch an attack against me and another worker. I felt quite uneasy, so we put up another poster. Thereupon some people in the branch organization put up posters criticizing us. I was categorized as a "four-type" (*silei*) party member, which further incensed me. I made use of my position as platoon chief of the militia to mobilize the militia to put up a poster against the party branch.

In July I organized a "warriors' group" at the factory, with more than 30 people. We used big-character-posters to expose the factory leadership, aiming the spearhead toward the factory party branch secretary.[76]

Geng's rebel initiatives made him a natural candidate for inclusion in the Workers' General Headquarters. On November 9, 1966, he was resting at home—having worked the middle shift the day before—when a fellow worker from his factory stopped by to say that he had seen a handbill on the street announcing the upcoming inauguration of the WGH later that day. The two men ate an early lunch and rushed to the founding ceremonies.[77] Later, they participated in the Anting Incident as well. It was during that incident that Geng Jinzhang was chosen as "responsible person" for the Suzhou Brigade, the forerunner of the influential Second Regiment.

Geng Jinzhang had a more independent bent than most party members. His pugnacious personality inclined him to challenge the hegemony of Wang Hongwen on more than one occasion. Indeed, as we shall see in Chapter 5, Geng and his Second Regiment presented a major source of irritation for the Workers' General Headquarters in its initial months of operation.

"Backward Elements" Among the Old Rebels

After the founding of the Workers' General Headquarters, conservative opponents charged that the new rebel organization harbored a surfeit of ruffians, gangsters, and riff-raff. Later, Zhang Chunqiao noted in a talk to the WGH that those under greatest suspicion were Pan Guoping, Chen Ada, and Huang Jinhai.

Pan Guoping.   Pan Guoping was second in the leadership lineup during the early months of the WGH. Since he had served as master of ceremonies at the inauguration, Pan became vice-commander of the WGH; Wang Hongwen, as chair of the group that had organized the convocation, assumed the role of commander. However, because Pan Guoping's talent for rhetoric far surpassed that of Wang Hongwen, he was widely mistaken for the supreme leader of the WGH during its initial days.

When the CR began in 1966, Pan Guoping was a twenty-year-old worker at the Shanghai Glass Machinery Factory. Born and raised in an ordinary Shanghai worker's family, Pan's home life was far from happy. An extramarital affair on the part of his mother had driven his father to suicide. Then his mother was fired from her factory job for "improper relations between the sexes." After graduating from middle school in 1962, Pan joined the army as an ordinary soldier. Two years later he received an early discharge because of a knee wound and was assigned to the Shanghai Glass Machinery Factory.

Pan's accomplishments were wide-ranging. In middle school he was active in athletics. While a soldier, he received second prize in an art contest. As a worker, he directed choral and theatrical troupes at the workers' Cultural Palace. Pan's artistic flair left him dissatisfied with mundane factory labor, and he asked his superiors at the factory for permission to take the entrance exam for drama school. When the authorities refused to issue the letter of introduction that would have allowed him to sit for the examination, he developed a lingering sense of resentment.[78] Pan's disaffection with his workplace was exacerbated by what he considered its unfair wage scale:

> Half a year after I had been demobilized from the military and entered the factory, I got into a row over the issue of wages. At our factory, for the same length of service and skill level we got paid at least one to two wage grades below the rate at other factories. This problem had developed shortly after liberation, when workers at the factory asked for a wage hike. Although their pay was raised to a rate even higher than at other factories, this was an "unofficial wage" (*feizhengshi gongzi*). After joint-ownership, this *unofficial* wage was abolished while at other factories where the boss had increased the *official* wage it was not reduced. In this way the wage rate at our factory became lower than at other factories.
>
> In 1957 the workers went on strike beause of this, but eventually they were suppressed. Still, the conflict over wages was intense. The factory leaders were fearful of another outburst. Later, whenever there was a wage evaluation, the workers who had entered the factory since 1958 were hardest hit, because if the recent entrants were paid according to the established standard their wages would have been higher than those of the older workers, and that would have made the older workers unhappy. I was really unlucky to have been sent to this kind of factory. After half a year I became a regular worker, but compared to demobilized soldiers at other factories my pay was many yuan lower. I was really incensed.[79]

The accumulation of grievances against his factory inclined Pan to take an active role in the Cultural Revolution. Initially, however, his embarrassing family background blocked his full participation. Rather than afford an opportunity for him to vent his dissatisfaction, the new campaign excluded Pan from its early ranks.

> They directed the spearhead at me, ferreting out my mother's problems to attack me. Naturally, I was very upset. At that time the factory established a Red Guard outfit, but they wouldn't permit me to join because of my bad family circumstances. The CR Small Group at the factory even undertook several investigations concerning my parents' background.[80]

The more skeletons that were dragged out of his family closet, the more distraught Pan became. On August 28, 1966, he took the unusual step of putting up a big-character-poster at his factory, attacking the Shanghai Party Committee. This was an act of exceptional boldness at the time. Factory posters criticizing factory party committees or work teams were commonplace, but no worker had yet dared attack the SPC itself. Pan's poster led to a debate at his factory in which he emerged as the central object of controversy.[81]

> I also participated in the debate, and I believed that the work team was carrying out a bourgeois reactionary line in criticizing me. They detained me at the factory and refused to let me go out. At that time Red Guards from Beijing also participated in the great debate at our factory. When some people at the factory wanted to lock me up, the Beijing Number 101 Middle School Red Guards pointed out that the incarceration of people was improper. So the factory released me. But they impounded my bicycle.
>
> Under these circumstances, several Beijing Red Guards took me to the capital to lodge a complaint. In Beijing I lived at the Number 101 Middle School and, thanks to the connections of some children of high-level cadres, I participated in a debate at the Chinese Academy of Sciences, where I had the opportunity to present my complaint personally to Premier Zhou Enlai. When I told Premier Zhou about my detention at the factory, the premier said he could discuss this with the SPC. So I returned to Shanghai.
>
> Now the situation was completely different from when I had left for Beijing. I joined the Mao Zedong Thought Warriors and was chosen as a committee member. At that time I had a flare-up of my knee injury and was hospitalized at the Yangpu District central clinic. Some rebels from the factory convinced me to leave the hospital and return to the factory to take a look, so—leaning on a cane for support—I exited the clinic.[82]

On his way back to the factory on November 6, Pan ran into another rebel who notified him of an exchange-experiences meeting of Shanghai worker rebels that very afternoon at the liaison station of the Capital Red Guards Third Headquarters. Knowing of Pan's extraordinary gift for oratory (enhanced by a clear Mandarin accent), the fellow rebel suggested that Pan accompany him to the meeting. Thus was Pan Guoping drawn into the founding of the Workers' General Headquarters.

Despite his glib tongue, Pan soon came to be recognized as an unreliable loafer. He was widely referred to as a "*xiao doulou*," Shanghai dialect for a hoodlum. Before long, Pan was expelled by Wang Hongwen from the policymaking center of the WGH, his vice-commander title remaining only an empty appellation.

Huang Jinhai.   Another important figure in the WGH, Huang Jinhai, was known colloquially as a "dandy" (*afei fenzi*) because of his penchant for fancy attire. Huang's attraction to fashionable clothing rendered him a conspicuous figure in the drab atmosphere of Maoist China, where simplicity of dress was the near-universal norm.

At the start of the Cultural Revolution in 1966 Huang was thirty-one years old, about the same age as Wang Hongwen and Wang Xiuzhen. Like so many of the rebel leaders, his childhood had been less than idyllic. Within a month after his birth, Huang's mother died of illness. His father was an opium addict who put his children up for adoption. When Huang was only seven or eight, his foster father also died of illness. His foster mother took in laundry and managed to pay for three years of schooling for him. But in 1947, with prices skyrocketing in the postwar environment, she could no longer afford to keep him. Accordingly, Huang was packed off to Shanghai to rejoin his natural father. While living with his still-addicted and abusive father, he completed his elementary school education.

In October 1950, at age sixteen, Huang Jinhai entered a private clothing shop as an apprentice. During the day he cooked and he looked after the children; at night he labored. In the immediate aftermath of the founding of the new socialist state, many work units were adopting new uniforms, so business at the clothing store was brisk. Huang found himself working most of the night. The slightest slipup would elicit a spanking or whipping from the owner. On occasion, he remembers his head being shoved into a bowl of glue as punishment for sloppy work.

When the Three-Antis and Five-Antis began in 1952, Huang—seeing a chance to get back at his cruel taskmaster—eagerly reported to the "tiger-beating team" (investigating capitalist abuses) that his boss had been withholding taxes. The shop was fined, and in May of that year it was closed down altogether. Huang was out of a job, but a month later he was admitted to the Yangpu District unemployed workers' training program, where free room and board was supplied, along with classes in "political culture." After eight months of this regimen, Huang attained a middle school certificate and was assigned to the Shenxin Number 5 Factory to learn to operate a lathe. Later the Number 5 was merged with two other textile mills to form the Number 31 Cotton Mill.[83]

At the Number 31 Mill, Huang Jinhai was known to be diligent at work and energetic in extra-work pursuits.

After entering the factory, I applied to join the Youth League. In my spare time, I helped write the blackboard newspaper in my workshop, led the aerobics in step to the broadcast, and later joined the company chorus, dance troupe, and basketball team. I slept at the workers' bachelor dorm. Every week on my day off I worked overtime for no pay. At that time, a master who worked overtime on his day off earned two days' wages for the day; an apprentice received no extra pay and thus could work or not as he or she pleased. Although I was an apprentice, I always worked overtime without extra pay. Additionally, I studied at night school three nights a week. My work skills also improved rapidly, giving me a 46 yuan wage in the first year, a grade-five wage of 70 yuan after 3 years, and a grade-six-and-a-half wage after 5 years.[84]

Despite Huang's success on the job, his opium-addicted father continued to present a problem. To support his drug dependence, Huang's father embezzled public funds—a crime for which he was sentenced to five years in prison. Huang Jinhai recalled, "When I heard this news I was devastated; I felt that I would never be able to cast off this terrible burden."[85] Indeed, his father's impropriety became Huang Jinhai's Achilles' heel in the years ahead, blocking the recognition he felt he deserved. In 1958, Huang and several of his fellow workers discovered a method of reusing discarded parts that resulted in a major savings in time and materials for the factory. However, when their innovation was appropriated by the workshop Youth League secretary to make a name for himself, Huang's efforts at protest proved in vain. His father's unsavory record was an insurmountable obstacle to his own advancement.

> The League secretary got a 5 yuan reward and official honors for his "rationalization proposal." Only later did we find [this] out. So at the monthly small group meeting for deciding on bonuses, I and another master exposed his deceptive act. From this point he vowed to take revenge and spread around the news about my father. I knew that my application to enter the League had been in limbo for many years, and now the prospects looked even dimmer. So I became depressed and no longer participated in extracurricular activities.

Robbed of his just due by the dishonesty of his Youth League secretary, Huang sought solace in "dissolute" pursuits.

> The more I shouldered my political burden, the more despondent I became. For a time I grew a beard and spent most of my nonworking hours playing cards in the club. On Sundays I went to the suburbs to fish instead of engaging in proper duties. I even bought a necktie and then went to a shop that sold exotica to buy a used western suit. Sometimes I ventured to the city center in coat and tie. When I saw people wearing leather jackets, I spent more than 40 yuan to buy one. I was totally preoccupied with my playboy lifestyle. My frivolous habits gave the older workers a very bad impression. I organized dances and the like, which the older workers didn't appreciate.[86]

Although we now know that Chairman Mao himself was enjoying dance parties—and more—within the protective walls of Zhongnanhai at this very time, such frivolity was not sanctioned for the populace at large.[87] As political scientist Wang Shaoguang points out, the bleak economic situation following the Great Leap Forward had generated a strong ascetic tendency: "Now one might be considered backward if any aspect of one's life-style was out of the ordinary, such as wearing brightly colored clothes, applying hair oil, going to a restaurant, cultivating flowers, raising goldfish or playing chess."[88] Personal hobbies and eccentricities became grounds for designation as a "backward element," even if one worked assiduously at one's job.

Family responsibilities eventually revived Huang Jinhai's interest in political activism:

> In 1964, I felt that to continue in this way wasn't right. I already had a child and my outlook was undergoing a major change. At that time I studied a copy of Chairman Mao's works and had a conversion. I was a small group leader of my union, and I once again actively threw myself into social activities: family visits, political study, technical assistance. In 1965, our group was named a "five-good small group" for the entire factory. I was also named a "five-good worker." I felt that this was the only meaningful kind of existence.[89]

When the CR began, Huang Jinhai plunged into the movement. At first he, like most Chinese, felt confused about the objectives and methods of the new campaign: "How were we actually supposed to carry out the Cultural Revolution? Frankly speaking, we factory workers didn't understand what the problem really was with those people named as 'revisionist elements' in the big-character-posters. Even when there was a big-character-poster about Liu Shaoqi in Beijing, no one knew what it was all about."[90]

Before long, however, Huang had figured out how to apply Mao's call for criticism to his local factory setting: "On June 25 I posted a big-character-poster written to the party general branch saying that the people 'up above' [the party general branch office was upstairs] were not diligent during political study sessions and spent their time gossiping instead. I demanded that they come down and study together with us."[91]

Huang's big-character-poster elicited a harsh reaction from the party authorities at his factory. His opprobrious family history and his own penchant for flashy apparel made him an easy target for retribution. It was this repression, he later recalled, that triggered his outright rebellion.

> They seized on the two characters meaning "come down" (*xialai*) and said I wanted the party to "fall from power" (*xiatai*) and that I was an anti-party element, a careerist. The party general branch quickly gathered a group of people to attack me and [to] post big-character-posters against me. I thought this was unfair, so I got together with some people who steadfastly supported me to write big-character-posters against the division chiefs, including the labor insurance division chief—saying they were like capitalists, right up to the party committee members. That was how the rebellion began.[92]

A deep-seated sense of injustice marked Huang Jinhai's initial turn to rebellion: "I was a five-good worker and the small group I was in was also a five-good small group. In March we'd been rewarded with bonuses, but in June thanks to a big-character-poster we'd become anti-party, anti-socialist elements. I was in the right, I had been wronged, but where could I go to make my appeal?"[93] Fueled by this resentment, Huang attached himself to the growing rebel movement. On November 6, he attended the preparatory meeting for the Workers' General Head-quarters and was chosen as a member of its leadership group. Soon he joined the first WGH Standing Committee.

Chen Ada.   Chen Ada was another worker rebel with a somewhat unsavory rep-utation. Known in Shanghai dialect as "*awu*" (a good-for-nothing), he was widely regarded as a petty gangster, prone to profanity and coarse behavior. As a com-mon saying put it during the CR, "Wherever there's an armed battle, you'll find Chen Ada."

When the CR began, Chen was a twenty-four-year-old blacksmith employed at the Shanghai Valve Factory, who had risen above difficult family circumstances. Chen was born into a poor family in rural Shaoxing (Zhejiang province); his mother worked as a servant there, and his father worked as a peddler in Shanghai. When Chen was twelve, he broke his leg, and his mother, unable to care for him at home, took him to the big city to join his father.

At first Chen lived with his father in the "poor people's district" (*pinmin qu*) in the western part of Shanghai. Every month they paid a 2 yuan fee to rent a space to sleep—father and son sharing a bed. In the same room, more than a dozen other sleeping spaces went to other vendors. During the day the peddlers ventured forth to sell their wares; at night they gathered up their stands, with nothing but time on their hands. Their chief recreation was to play cards for money and tell crude jokes. Chen Ada lived in this environment for a year. The next year, his father brought Chen Ada's younger brother to Shanghai from the countryside. Unable to survive three-to-a-bed, father and sons moved to another shantytown district and rented a small room in a hut made of bamboo and mud. Chen Ada followed the older boys to various disreputable places of recreation (dance halls, ice-skating rinks, and the like), where he learned to speak with bravado and harass girls.[94]

In 1958, as part of the Great Leap Forward, an urban commune was set up in Shanghai. To rid the city of its unproductive residents, petty gangsters and others seen as local troublemakers were rounded up and packed off for labor reform. Many of Chen Ada's friends were seized in this initiative. In view of his youth, however, Chen himself was released after a warning and assigned to the Zhonghua Shipyard as a temporary worker. At first he labored as a loader; then as a fitter. At that time, the factory's evaluation of him was quite favorable: "Chen Ada's work style is proper, his lifestyle frugal, his food and clothing economical, and his family background impoverished."[95]

Three years later, Chen joined the army. Upon his discharge, he was assigned to the valve factory. Chen's experiences in the military seem only to have exacerbated his earlier wayward tendencies, however. At the factory, he did not achieve "ac-tivist" status, and after work he spent much of his time gambling—an activity that was strictly prohibited at the time.[96]

Chen was basically uneducated. Although he studied at night school for a while after entering the factory, he admitted that he had retained precious little of the instruction. When the Cultural Revolution first got underway, his limited literacy posed an obvious problem for participation in a movement being contested via the medium of big-character-posters.[97]

Chen's early motivations for involvement did not evidence much political sophistication. Considered a backward element among the workers, he had often been subjected to criticism by the cadres. The Cultural Revolution presented an opportunity to wreak revenge. A bulletin of the WGH later reported, "Chen Ada first burst forth on the factory scene simply on the pretext that there were no portraits of the Chairman or quotations by the Chairman to be found on the premises."[98] Chen himself described his motives even more candidly: "As for the bunch of jerks in the factory, I wanted to settle accounts with all of them."[99] The "jerks" (*chilao* in Shanghai dialect) were the factory cadres.

Chen's belligerent style was demonstrated shortly after the onset of the CR, when a neighbor exposed the fact that Chen's father had been hiding a cache of gold on behalf of a former capitalist. Chen Ada's younger bother, Chen Aer, delivered a sound thrashing to the accuser, for which Aer was packed off to the police station. Chen Ada himself then gathered a large group of boisterous followers to surround the police station until the frightened authorities agreed to release his brother and post a special notice exonerating his father.[100]

It was his participation in the preparatory meeting of the Workers' General Headquarters that propelled Chen Ada to its leadership ranks. On November 6, a rebel worker who chanced to pass by the foundry of the valve factory at noontime spotted a large number of big-character-posters hanging inside. He decided to go in to make contact with the authors of the posters and inform them about the meeting to be convened by Beijing Red Guards that afternoon. Chen Ada happened to be loitering in a corner of the workshop and, hearing about the upcoming get-together, took it upon himself to attend. At the meeting, he was chosen as a member of the leading group; later Chen's fiery demeanor earned him a seat on the earliest standing committee of the Workers' General Headquarters.

Ordinary Workers Among the Old Rebels

If party members and backward elements supplied the more notorious rebel leaders, a substantial number of old rebels were drawn from the ranks of ordinary workers.

Ye Changming. Ye Changming, who rose to assume command of the Workers' General Headquarters after Wang Hongwen's transfer to Beijing, was an ordinary worker (neither activist nor backward element) prior to the Cultural Revolution. Only twenty-two years old at the start of the CR, Ye commanded considerable respect from his fellow rebels as a capable decisionmaker.

In the early 1960s, during the period of economic retrenchment following the Great Leap Forward, Ye studied at a technical institute in Jiangxi. Life in Jiangxi was difficult, so Ye asked to withdraw from school and return to Shanghai. In 1963 he entered the Shanghai Synthetic Fiber Research Institute, at first as an apprentice in the laboratory, then as a lab technician.

Only three years after Ye began to work at the Synthetic Fiber Institute, the Cultural Revolution presented an opportunity to improve his humble standing. Unlike most of the other rebel leaders, whose later testimonies emphasized injustices on the part of management as a prime stimulus for their rebellion, Ye characterized his own motives as purely instrumental. His initial expectation was that participation in the Cultural Revolution, like participation in previous political campaigns, would qualify an otherwise obscure worker for valuable party-bestowed recognition. Despite his education and intelligence, Ye demonstrated no particular understanding or interest in the deeper import of the Cultural Revolution.

> I didn't comprehend the real meaning of our great leader Chairman Mao's personally instigating and leading the CR, nor did I make any serious effort to ponder it.
>
> My so-called rebellion was just an expression of political opportunism. My initial motive was quite simply to seize the right to lead the CR at the Synthetic Fiber Institute. I hadn't been at the institute very long and had absolutely no influence there. But when the CR began, I hoped to take advantage of the opportunity to gain some prominence. So I energetically pointed the spearhead of struggle toward ordinary cadres and masses. As expected, I was rewarded by the party committee and was selected for the CR committee at the institute.[101]

Ye Changming's initial tactic for establishing his own political credentials was to attack a famous research group at the institute known as the "Red Lei Feng Youths' Study Group." Composed of eight researchers who averaged twenty-five years of age, the group was investigating a special type of synthetic fiber heretofore unavailable in China. The Lei Feng researchers had been designated by the Shanghai Party Committee as an advanced model in "studying the works of Chairman Mao." Some of the group members had entered the party, some had joined the Youth League, and some had received various awards from the factory, bureau, or municipality. Ye Changming's attack on the group was clearly strategic: "The Lei Feng Small Group was very famous, so we criticized it as a false pacesetter. By demolishing its great fame, our own fame became just as great."[102]

Although Ye's initiative won him a seat on the newly established CR committee at his institute, in the rapidly evolving political environment of that period it was not long before the CR committee was no longer functional and the party committee was unable to control the direction of the movement. When Ye realized the altered situation, he wrote a big-character-poster attacking the party committee at the institute. Later, he recalled,

> Seeing that other units had already spontaneously sprouted mass struggle groups and other organizations, I wanted to start up an organization at my institute, too. So after consulting with some other people, I founded a battle group (*zhandou zu*). The impetus was primarily my dissatisfaction in being a member of a powerless, dysfunc-

tional "CR committee." I wanted another group under my own control, so I got together with some others in the institute to kick aside the CR committee and then replace the party committee. My motives were amply revealed in my "battle manifesto."
The "battle group" I founded gathered together people whose political expression
(*zhengzhi biaoxian*) was ordinarily rather poor; those who had committed errors, including those who listened to enemy radio broadcasts; those dissatisfied with the
party and with socialism; and even cadres who had been toppled during the Four
Cleans and had exhibited serious problems. These people had low standing among
the masses, but I surmised that they were all dissatisfied with the party committee
and wanted to stir up trouble for it. This matched my own aim of creating difficulties
for the party committee. Moreover, by comparison with these people I had somewhat
better standing, and this was instrumental in my gaining control.[103]

One day when Ye was listening to a debate among Red Guards at the gate of the
Shanghai Party Committee, he spotted a notice announcing the establishment of
the Capital Third Headquarters Liaison Post. Since the address indicated that the
new liaison post was not far away, Ye went over to make contact with the Red
Guards there. As a result of these connections, on November 6 he received an invitation to attend the preparatory meeting of the Workers' General Headquarters.
In this way, Ye became one of the elders of the WGH. At the inaugural meeting of
the WGH on November 9, Ye Changming delivered a stirring speech criticizing
the Lei Feng Small Group at his institute. Soon thereafter he was appointed a
member of the first WGH Standing Committee.

Although Ye had been active in the preparations for establishing the WGH, he
did not participate in any of the landmark incidents of the early period: Anting,
Liberation Daily, or Kangping Road. Ye's absence was not accidental. Later he admitted,

I was very interested in forming a WGH. This was a way to have a broad influence in
society and to develop one's power; it matched my "appetite." But looking at the actual circumstances of the time, I wasn't confident that the WGH could really be
pulled off. So I adopted an opportunistic approach—on the one hand indicating my
active participation and rushing to give a speech at the meeting, on the other hand
refusing to handle other preparatory work or responsibility. I told the other people
who went along with me that I had no confidence at all in this project. We'd have to
see how the situation developed. This way we had some autonomy. If it could be
pulled off, we would join; but if it didn't look promising, we would withdraw our
participation. Through the entire preparatory work of the WGH, I only attended a
few meetings and didn't do any actual work. But in discussing the composition of the
leading group, I used my status as a speaker at the inaugural ceremonies to demand a
place. I knew that delivering a public address was an opportunity to expand my influence across the whole city and that to be a member of the leading group would afford
still greater power. So even though I doubted whether the WGH would really get off
the ground and didn't want to participate actively in the preparatory work, I couldn't
ignore the potential. Later on I always behaved this way, never foregoing a chance to
accumulate more power for myself. I used my so-called rebellion as capital, taking
advantage of the CR to further my personal interests.[104]

Ye's testimony—whether a genuine expression of his views at the time or a ploy to receive lenient treatment in the post-Mao era—reveals a highly calculating mentality. As he described it, the Cultural Revolution was essentially an opportunity to enhance his own standing in the intensely competitive political atmosphere of Communist China.

Dai Liqing.   Dai Liqing was also an unknown, ordinary worker before the CR. But because he was a temporary worker, his social status was even lower than that of Ye Changming. Like so many of the leaders of the worker rebels, Dai came originally from north China. Dai was born into a poor urban family in Shandong. His father had served as a policeman under the KMT. As a youngster in his teens, Dai moved with his family to Shanghai; soon thereafter he began an apprenticeship at a textile mill in the western part of the city. In 1956, Dai was sent to the Gansu Construction Bureau to help in the building of Lanzhou. A few years later, his father having been hospitalized with a terminal illness, Dai returned to Shanghai. After his father's death, Dai resigned from the electronics company in Gansu where he had been working to help out at home. Thus began a period of joblessness during which Dai operated first a cigarette stand, then a tea stand, and finally a plumbing and electronics repair stand. Thanks to the success of these entrepreneurial activities, in late 1963 Dai's household registration was officially transferred to Shanghai, and the following year he began a brief stint at the Shanghai Number 10 Steel Mill as a temporary worker. The following year Dai was introduced by his district labor office to the Jiangnan Metallurgical Factory (later renamed the Number 1 Standard Materials Factory) as an outside contract worker (*waibao gong*). Soon thereafter his classification was changed to that of a temporary worker (*linshi gong*).[105]

Dai Liqing's personal history as well as his status as a temporary worker became grounds for suspicion once the CR began. He was criticized for having returned from the interior during the period of economic difficulties following the Great Leap Forward "because he feared hardship." His efforts at petty entrepreneurship during his years of unemployment were now portrayed as "engaging in speculation and profiteering."[106] Moreover, even the other worker rebels looked down on Dai because he was not a permanent worker.[107] Dai Liqing's troubles were made worse by his own indiscretions. Forced to abandon his wife in Lanzhou when he returned to Shanghai, Dai took up with a young woman apprentice soon after he entered the metallurgical factory. Charges and countercharges surrounding Dai's peccadillos fueled the unfolding of the Cultural Revolution struggle at his factory:

> When the CR began, the factory leadership discovered that after Dai had returned to Shanghai from Lanzhou he had been a street vendor, selling homemade products, cigarettes, etc. He had even gone to other places as a peddler, engaging in profiteering and speculation. An investigator dispatched by the party branch uncovered Dai's improper liaison with apprentice Du at his factory. So the branch called Dai in for a talk, asking him to make a written statement. Dai wrote a self-criticism, but he was quite

enraged and felt a deep animosity toward Party Secretary Fu. Later, Dai learned from apprentice Du that although Fu was 37 years old he hadn't yet married and had previously pursued Du himself. This information delighted Dai; in the name of criticizing the bourgeois reactionary line of the party branch, he goaded Du into writing a big-character-poster exposing Fu.[108]

Du's big-character-poster, entitled "My accusations," galvanized the entire factory. Soon the "Red Flag Struggle Team" was established, with Dai as its head. Acting together with the deputy factory director and several worker rebels, Dai forced Secretary Fu to hand over the key to the party branch office and the archive room (which held the personnel dossiers for all factory employees). But this power seizure was soon denounced by the district work team, which criticized the deputy-director for his part in it. At the same time, another group of workers at the factory put up a poster attacking Dai. He responded by going first to the company, then to the bureau, and finally all the way to Beijing to lodge a complaint.

After staying in the capital for six months, Dai returned to Shanghai on November 9, just in time to see a flyer announcing the WGH inaugural meeting that same day. He rushed to the Cultural Plaza only to find that the meeting had already dispersed and people were debating whether to proceed to Beijing. Having just returned from the capital himself, Dai had no interest in taking off again, so he did not actually participate in the Anting Incident.[109]

Despite his lack of involvement in the earliest "revolutionary" escapade of the Workers' General Headquarters, Dai quickly became a highly placed leader within that organization. The explanation for his rapid advancement lay in his ability to offer timely advice to Wang Hongwen.

> The SPC issued a notice recognizing the WGH and its revolutionary activities. At this time I began to go over to the WGH and got to know Wang Hongwen. Later, I suggested to Wang that this chaotic clamor wouldn't work. There should be sentries posted at the gate and a clear division of labor inside. I wrote down several groupings and Wang Hongwen nodded his head in agreement. I suggested using a chop, and the next day Wang Hongwen provided a chop for the secretariat. I then became the vice-chief of the secretariat. Wang gave me the chop. In this way I gained the confidence of Wang Hongwen.[110]

Like Ye Changming, Dai Liqing saw in the Cultural Revolution a chance to shed his anonymity and gain activist status. As a temporary worker craving permanent employment, the potential benefits of his involvement in the CR were enormous. But unlike Ye Changming, Dai refused to characterize his motives as self-interested. Well after the conclusion of the movement, he continued to defend his participation:

> My constant thought was: "People must follow the king's law like the grass must move with the wind." Whenever the upper levels issue orders, the lower levels must respond. It's always this way. It's been several decades since I stepped out into society.

Beginning when I was too young to know what was going on, through my training as an apprentice worker, I grew up in the post-liberation era. I had one desire: to follow the CCP, obey Chairman Mao. . . . In ordinary times, I tried to be an activist. During the Cultural Revolution, I tried to follow the party.[111]

For Dai, uncompromising defiance to the party authorities at his own factory was justified as obedience to a higher "king's law."

Ma Zhenlong. Ma Zhenlong, an electrician at the Shanghai Enamelware Factory, was another worker rebel who refused to repudiate his Cultural Revolution militancy. Although a less colorful figure than some of the other rebel leaders, he was no less brazen. When asked by his interrogators to abbreviate his discussion of how he was unjustly suppressed at the outset of the campaign, Ma retorted heatedly,

I have to talk about this. If I don't discuss it, how can I answer you about how I came to rebel? Without that, there would have been no rebellion to discuss. Why did Chairman Mao later speak of "striking down the King of Hell, liberating the little demons"? It was in order to ferret out the capitalist roaders, right? That was how it got started. One should speak truthfully and respect history. I have to tell it like I see it.[112]

Twenty-six years before the outbreak of the Cultural Revolution, Ma had been born in the northern Jiangsu (Subei) county of Taixing, where his father worked as a grocery store clerk. When Ma Zhenlong was only four, his mother died of illness. In 1955, having graduated from elementary school and having studied briefly at a continuing education school, Ma worked for several months at a tea and food store in Taixing. The next year he moved to Shanghai as an apprentice at the Meili Machine Plant. In November 1959, this factory was amalgamated with several other plants and underwent a name change to become the Shanghai Enamelware Factory. Ma rose from machine operator to electrician at the factory.[113]

After the CR, from the materials exposing and criticizing Ma Zhenlong, the only "bad behavior" that emerged was an accusation that, during the three years of difficulty, he had used his spare time to manufacture illegally two transformers for sale. For this activity Ma was criticized as having "opened an underground factory." But he was never designated a "backward element" in his personnel dossier.

Ma Zhenlong was not involved in the preparations to set up the WGH, but he participated in the Anting, *Liberation Daily,* and Kangping Road Incidents. At that time he was just a rank-and-file member of the rebels at his factory. Ma's brother-in-law worked at his same factory and was a leader of the factory rebels. At first, Ma simply followed his kinsman into rebellion. But after a year or so, he had far surpassed his brother-in-law's status within the WGH. In December 1966, not long after his relative had assumed the leadership of the Zhabei District Liaison Post of the WGH, he recommended Ma Zhenlong for a position at the WGH. Initially, Ma worked in the secretariat, answering incoming letters and receiving visitors. But after demonstrating his personal loyalty to Wang Hongwen, Ma rose rapidly within the rebel organization.[114]

Rebel Commitment

The capsule biographies of these nine individuals offer a revealing view of the tensions brewing in the Chinese socialist system in its first seventeen years of operation. Although the official rhetoric of the Cultural Revolution would portray these contradictions as rooted in class differences, most seem to have had a more mundane basis: regional rivalries, personal ambitions, family problems, individual indiscretions, resentment against factory authorities, and the like.

Workplace grievances also played an important role in triggering rebellion. Sometimes these problems were structural (as in the unfair wage scale at the glass machinery factory where Pan Guoping worked); sometimes (as in Dai Liqing's affair with an apprentice at his factory) they were basically personal. Virtually all of the old rebels harbored resentment against their factory leadership for one or another accumulated complaint. Of the forty-one old rebels who composed the committee membership of the WGH in December 1967, at least eight had been subject to factory or party disciplinary treatment prior to the Cultural Revolution. This proportion, nearly 20 percent, was rather high, inasmuch as only about 5 percent of the workforce as a whole had received such sanctions.[115] But most workers in China, or elsewhere in the world for that matter, routinely encounter a host of workplace disappointments;. for these to translate into overt protest requires an additional stimulus.

Like previous campaigns of the PRC, the Cultural Revolution offered an opportunity for heretofore frustrated or obscure workers to rise on the basis of political activism. Both Ye Changming and Dai Liqing, who were ordinary workers before the CR, characterized their initial strategies for participation in precisely these conventional terms. In contrast to previous campaigns, however, the CR encouraged criticism of party authorities at all levels (save Chairman Mao himself, of course). Yet the boundaries of criticism were never entirely clear and the possibilities for retribution were ever present. Those willing to hazard the immense risks inherent in confronting party officials were unusually bold individuals.

Dai Zuxiang, a founder of the WGH who later became the leader of the First Regiment, recalled the reprimand that befell him when he criticized the party leaders at the Number 3 Steel Mill.[116] "In our factory I was the first to post a big-character-poster against the party committee. After I put up my poster, the party committee secretary cursed me as a bastard. Accusing me of having stirred up trouble amongst the people, he had me placed under house arrest for two weeks."[117] Jiang Zhoufa, a WGH leader who had been working at the Shanghai Railway Loading Machinery Factory, experienced similar difficulties at the hands of his party committee:

Because we had written several posters against the party organization, the authorities stirred up the masses saying that ox-demons and snake-spirits had come out of their cages and everyone must be on the alert. They also organized those people whom they had cultivated to launch a big-character-poster attack on us. Their spearhead was directed against the worker rebels; they cut our bonuses, transferred us to less desirable jobs, etc.[118]

The situation did not improve when a work team arrived at Jiang's factory.

At first we tried to seek out the work team to share our problems, but we couldn't find them. When the work team came down to the workshops they said again and again, "Our work team is experienced. At every factory whenever anyone has written posters against the work team or the factory leadership they have been ox-demons and snake-spirits." Moreover, they sent their trusted subordinates to each Small Group to say, "The factory leadership has no major problems, just a few small shortcomings. The ox-demons and snake-spirits are all in the Small Groups. You in the Small Groups must expose one another." In this way they openly incited the masses to struggle against the masses. Their backstage supporter was the work department of the city party committee.[119]

The retribution did not end there. According to Jiang Zhoufa, the party committee of the Municipal Railway Bureau dispatched a group of "conservative" Red Guards to the factory, who administered an even more severe reprimand.

Red Guards came to our factory and captured 16 of our rebels, using leather whips to torture them. They also made us kneel on little stools for as long as four hours. They shaved the heads of these 16 comrades and wrote the characters "ox-demons [and] snake-spirits" on their bodies. Fourteen workers were injured, and all 16 were tortured in a torture chamber that the Red Guards set up. More than 40 struggle sessions were convened, and some of our comrades were locked up for one to two weeks.[120]

The level of violence at Jiang's workplace was greater than the norm at Shanghai factories during the CR (although it was not uncommon at high schools and universities in the city). Nevertheless, his tale underscores the opposition that rebels might face in mounting their challenge to the system. To persist in the face of such retribution required great fortitude.

Some workers carefully weighed the odds of punishment. Rebel leader Xu Meiying, a thirty-three-year-old mother of four, who was working at a clothing cooperative at the start of the Cultural Revolution, was explicit about her calculations:

After I put up my big-character-poster, the factory leadership immediately organized a counter-attack. Some people even said they wanted to pull out my tendons and peel off my skin. Many posters were put up against me. But I wasn't scared. For one thing, I hadn't stolen anything from the factory; second, I hadn't engaged in any sexual misconduct; third, I had no historical problems; and fourth, I hadn't fought with any-body. There were no skeletons in my closet.

The factory couldn't do anything about me because at that time I wasn't a party member, so they couldn't use party discipline to repress me. The most they could do was to prevent me from joining the Red Guards.[121]

Whereas Xu figured that the odds against severe punishment were minimal be-cause of her clean record, other workers with compromised dossiers—like Pan Guoping—became more unruly as more skeletons were dragged out of their clos-ets.[122] Obviously, differences in personal considerations and temperament helped to shape individual reactions to the threat of retaliation.

When rebels bounced back undaunted from party repression, a spiraling cycle of attacks and counterattacks was put into motion. Jin Zumin, a party member at the Shanghai Electronics Factory, recounted the process of escalation:

On August 23, 1966, the director of the First Electronics Bureau led a work team to our factory. They made various reports, after which I again put up a poster saying [that] some of the points in their report were mistaken. This stirred up the whole fac-tory. The deputy-director called me in for a chat, in which he warned, "If you con-tinue to behave in this manner you will have problems. The party has cultivated you for all these years; you should really think things over carefully." The factory director also summoned me for a talk. I thereupon included everything he said in my next poster.[123]

As the cycle of tit-for-tat retribution swirled out of control, rebel workers be-came irreversibly committed to an oppositional stance.[124]

Rebel Personality

Previous scholarship on mass factionalism during the Cultural Revolution has em-phasized either group characteristics (e.g., class labels, age, skill levels, etc.) or po-litical networks (based on clientelist ties) to explain lines of association. In the case of Shanghai's old rebels, however, neither approach is entirely satisfactory. (This is in contrast to the situation among "conservative" workers—for whom, as we will see in Chapter 3, a network explanation is indeed appropriate; furthermore, a so-cial group explanation has much to say about the workers who initiated the "wind of economism"—as we will discover in Chapter 4.) For the rebel leaders, personal inclinations and ambition seem to have been key factors in inclining them to adopt the high-risk strategy of challenging party committees and work teams.

The situation was not unlike that to be found in other times and places among young radical leaders. French historian Richard Cobb's monumental study con-cerning the *armées revolutionnaires* of the Terror offers a particularly illuminating comparison. According to Cobb, "Contemporaries had no hesitation in claiming that the departmental *armées* were recruited from the dregs of urban society." He goes on to present detailed biographies of the leaders of these "people's armies," whose lives, by virtue of their tremendous diversity, undermine the credibility of previous socioeconomic or political analyses. Instead, Cobb turns to a psychological interpretation: "Most had dwelt too long in obscurity not to feel a desire to avenge past humiliations. . . . And with such men vanity always played a greater part than thought of material gain."[125] In a related vein, Kenneth Kenniston's study of young American radicals during Vietnam Summer (1968) finds that "they brought from their earlier life a sense of their own ultimate differences from others . . . and an unusually strong sense of independence."[126]

To understand such personalities seems to call for an excursion into the murky realm of popular mentalities. The Solomon-Pye approach has been roundly, and rightly, attacked for its caricature of Chinese personality formation.[127] But it would be unfortunate if such criticism were to discourage other investigations into the political culture of the CR era. Even though our study barely scratches the surface of a still largely unexplored terrain, we will venture a few preliminary thoughts on the psychology of the old rebels.

In contrast to the Pye-Solomon depiction of Chinese personality as "dependent" in the face of higher authority, our view is that the rebel leaders showed an impressive capacity for defiance. The one striking point of commonality among these very diverse individuals was their forceful personalities. A certain audacity was a prerequisite for the perilous act of challenging party authorities. The sources of this boldness were various, but they point to subcultures of opposition that were both more pervasive and more powerful than previous studies have led us to anticipate. Whereas scholarship on the political culture of Communist China has tended to portray it as an essentially static and homogeneous entity, in fact there was considerable diversity.[128] The interstices of the dominant Maoist system offered some space for creative resistance. Alien native-place origins, difficult family circumstances, dissident peer groups, and even military service seem to have provided breeding grounds for rebellious personalities.

Significantly, five of the nine top rebels (and four of the seven who remained active after the January Revolution) were northerners. As the situation at Wang Hongwen's Number 17 Mill indicates, regional allegiances could help to shape loyalties that later translated into Cultural Revolution factionalism. Cooperation along lines of native-place origin was certainly not a new feature of the Shanghai labor scene. Linguistic affinities and feelings of alienation vis-à-vis the dominant Shanghai culture had long acted to forge a sense of separateness and solidarity among recent immigrants to the city from north China.[129]

Although the "politics of place" continued to structure labor unrest in the Communist era, it operated in novel ways. With the establishment of the PRC regime, Shanghai saw a large influx of cadres from the north (the so-called *nanxia ganbu*). These cadres generally consisted of former soldiers of the New Fourth Army who, having participated in the military takeover of Shanghai, stayed on to assume top political posts in the new municipal government. As northerners whose revolutionary experiences had been centered in rural base areas, they often found themselves at odds with the more urbane southerners who had composed the heart of the underground Communist movement before 1949.[130] Seen as less likely to champion local interests than their southern counterparts, these former military men from the north (whose native dialect was a variant of Mandarin) were charged with publicizing and implementing new central policies from Beijing. As a consequence, ordinary people in Shanghai began to think of the northern Mandarin dialect as the language of revolutionary political authority. This association of Mandarin (*putong hua*) with revolution was buttressed during the CR by the several waves of Beijing Red Guards who first introduced the new campaign to Shanghai.

Immigrants from the north, rather than seeing themselves simply as second-class citizens in the southern Jiangnan culture of Shanghai (as had often been true before the Communist Revolution), have enjoyed a certain linguistic and political advantage in the PRC. As Emily Honig notes, "In the decades since 1949, the [northern] Subei community in Shanghai has consisted not only of manual laborers, but of members of the political elite as well."[131] The turn to rebellion during the CR apparently stemmed at least in part from a sense of their special revolutionary identity.

For party members who were strictly disciplined in obedience to higher authorities, outsider status as recent immigrants to the city evidently facilitated a willingness to challenge the powers-that-be. Wang Hongwen, Wang Xiuzhen, and Geng Jinzhang—the three party members among the top nine rebel leaders—all hailed from north China.

For party and nonparty members alike, arduous family circumstances seem to have helped mold venturesome temperaments. Among those from the north, combating poverty was a constant trial. Among southerners, the shame of parental indiscretions (e.g., the opium addiction of Huang Jinhai's father) may have provided a similar challenge.

Many of the rebel leaders were demobilized soldiers, individuals whose horizons had been broadened by the opportunities for travel and job mobility that came with military experience. (A number of these former soldiers served as militia captains at their factories.)

Such personal experiences encouraged some of those who felt disadvantaged by the system to thumb their noses at party leadership. Chen Ada's youthful years in the shantytowns of Shanghai exposed him to the dissolute pursuits of itinerant peddlers, as well as to the rowdy ways of local toughs. His later penchant for gambling and fighting—which earned Chen the local label of *awu* (good-for-nothing)—was, by his own admission, an outgrowth of these earlier exploits.

A number of the rebel leaders were musicians or artists of one sort or another.[132] Playboy Pan Guoping's reputation as a *xiao doulou* (hoodlum) and foppish Huang Jinhai's designation as an *afei fenzi* (dandy) were further signs of the colorful subcultures that bubbled just beneath the drab surface of Maoist China.

Although we know very little about such dissident trends, it seems clear that they helped to arm workers with cultural weapons of resistance. Yet, obviously, not all northerners, former soldiers, musicians, or shantytown dwellers turned to rebellion during the Cultural Revolution. Although certain subcultures appear to have been particularly conducive to the development of defiant personalities, it is the personalities rather than the environment in which they may have flourished that are of primary concern here. Despite differences in social background, we can detect a common feistiness in the manner in which all of these old rebels seized the initiative in denouncing party authorities. Just the opposite would be true in the case of their conservative opponents, for whom official networks of state patronage dictated a play-it-safe strategy of defending party traditions.

3

Conservatives:
The Scarlet Guards

As was true of China as a whole, in Shanghai the mass organizations spawned by the Cultural Revolution quickly divided into two opposing camps: rebel and conservative. Whereas rebels challenged the revolutionary credentials of leading cadres, conservatives supported them. China-hand William Hinton, commenting on the ubiquity of this phenomenon, notes that the basic dichotomy occurred "with such regularity and persistence that it had to be recognized as some sort of law of the political sphere as universal as Boyle's law in chemistry or Newton's law in physics."[1] Unlike the situation in many other parts of China, however, the life-span of Shanghai's conservative faction was remarkably short: from mid-November 1966 until the Kangping Road Incident of late December, a mere five or six weeks.[2]

The Formation of Shanghai's Conservative Movement

Shanghai's first citywide conservative mass organizations—like its initial rebel groups—were composed not of workers but of students. On September 12, 1966, two cross-city Red Guard outfits were formed, led for the most part by children of Shanghai Party Committee and East China Party Bureau leading cadres.[3] These students imitated the Red Guards of Beijing in criticizing their teachers and destroying the Four Olds. But when Beijing Red Guards descended on Shanghai and proceeded to attack the Shanghai Party Committee, the close connection between the local Red Guards and the top-level leadership inclined the locals to stand unabashedly on the side of the municipal party committee.[4]

Meanwhile, as we saw in Chapter 2, tensions had been escalating among the workforce. After *People's Daily* reprinted Nie Yuanzi's big-character-poster attacking the party leadership at Beijing University, workers at some Shanghai factories followed suit with their own critical posters. Other workers then rose to the defense of their factory management. These critics and defenders of workplace authorities were the earliest worker rebels and conservatives. The southern expedition of the Beijing Red Guards inspired both groups to move out of the factories and onto the streets. When Beijing Red Guards attacked the SPC, worker rebels hurried to the gates of the SPC to support the Red Guards, while conservatives rushed there to protect the municipal leadership. In the process of defending the SPC, conservative workers began to develop their own organizations. At this stage, however, such organizations remained confined to individual factories.

The Anting Incident (described in Chapter 2) generated a larger and more militant conservative movement. The first workers' organization to gain official sponsorship during the Anting Incident was a conservative outfit from the Shanghai Railway Bureau, headed by Wang Yuxi, deputy-director of the control room. Known as the "February 7 Warriors," the group was named in commemoration of the famous Communist-inspired strike on the Jinghan Railroad of February 7, 1923. All members of the organization were railroad workers, who had chosen the name to suggest a link to the revolutionary tradition of the Chinese Communist party. During the Anting Incident, the Warriors disseminated a number of highly influential handbills, which helped to sway public opinion against the rebel forces.[5]

Although the February 7 Warriors were limited to a single workplace, another conservative group born during the Anting Incident crossed both occupations and districts. This was the all-city organization known as the "Shanghai Workers' Scarlet Guard General Command," whose main membership was drawn from factories in the eastern part of the city.

After the Anting Incident, representatives from more than twenty factories in Shanghai organized a "united investigation group" to study the situation in Anting. On November 23, 1966 (two weeks after the rebels had inaugurated their Workers' General Headquarters), the united investigation group convened the first general meeting of Shanghai conservatives. Held at the offices of the Yangpu District Party Committee, the gathering attracted representatives from twenty-three factories. One representative to the provisional committee was chosen from each of the participating factories.

The chair of the meeting, Jin Ruizhang of the Lianggong Valve Factory, advocated adopting the name "Scarlet Guards" (*chiweidui*). Aside from being the appellation of the conservative workers' organization at Jin's factory, the name also had a respectable revolutionary pedigree as the term for armed militia units in the Communist base areas during the period from 1927 to 1937. Jin's proposal was greeted with unanimous approval. Since the rebels called their outfit a "headquarters" (*siling bu*), the conservatives decided to refer to their organization as a "general command" (*zong bu*).[6]

The next day another group of Shanghai conservatives—calling themselves the "Workers' Pickets to Defend Mao Zedong Thought"—held an inaugural meeting at a theater in the western part of the city. (In adopting the name Workers' Pickets [*gongren jiuchadui*], this organization implied a historical linkage to the Three Workers' Uprisings of 1926–1927, when armed unionists had formed pickets to welcome the Northern Expeditionary forces to the city.) The Workers' Pickets were organized from eighty-two factories, with leadership centered in the Shanghai Construction Materials Research Institute, and drew nearly 1,000 representatives to its founding ceremony. Among those present at the inauguration was the chief of the SPC Organization Department, Yang Shifa. When Yang noticed that the manifesto of this group was much like that of the Scarlet Guards, which had formed the day before, he took it upon himself to introduce leaders of the two conservative organizations to each other.

Following Yang Shifa's suggestion, the Workers' Pickets sent ten representatives to the Scarlet Guards to inquire about a possible merger. Satisfied with their mutual interrogation, the two groups decided to unite. Soon they were joined by the February 7 Warriors as well. These three outfits composed the mainstay of a new organization called the "Shanghai General Command Provisional Committee of Scarlet Guards to Defend Mao Zedong Thought" (known colloquially as the Scarlet Guards). The new group selected sixteen members for its provisional committee, leaving vacant a seat to be filled in future by someone from the Number 17 Cotton Mill, where Wang Hongwen worked. The expectation, which was indeed borne out, was that this key factory would soon produce an anti–Wang Hongwen force that could be incorporated into the Scarlet Guards.

The provisional committee decided to establish liaison posts (*lianluo zhan*) in every district and county of Shanghai to recruit additional personnel. Wang Yuxi of the February 7 Warriors was chosen as head of the Scarlet Guard General Command, and on December 6, 1966—just a month after the WGH had been founded at Cultural Plaza—the Scarlet Guards were formally inaugurated in ceremonies at People's Plaza in the center of the city.[7]

In contrast to the countless rebel organizations, representing competing leadership amitions, that would later spring up across the city, Shanghai's conservative movement exhibited a striking feature: Only one conservative organization emerged in each work unit. Virtually all of the leaders of these conservative organizations had been party activists in the years preceding the CR. Influenced by the norm of party unity, they were quick to link up with other organizations that shared their political outlook. Another important factor in explaining the comparative cohesiveness of the conservatives was, of course, their brief existence. After the Kangping Road Incident of early 1967, the Scarlet Guards were destroyed by the rebels and were never permitted to regroup. Thus they did not participate in the process of power seizures that led to acrimonious splits within the rebel ranks over the distribution of resources and authority (see Chapter 5).

Despite the brevity of their existence, the conservative forces presented a serious challenge to the newly founded Workers' General Headquarters. Within days of their inauguration, the Scarlet Guards were already mounting impressive counteroffensives against Wang Hongwen and his rebel followers. One of the first such confrontations occurred at the Number 24 Yarn-Dyeing Factory, where rebels who had detained an SPC work team were ransacking personnel dossiers and attacking the factory party leadership. To aid in the rebel assault, Wang Hongwen dispatched some 60,000 to 70,000 of his followers to surround the factory. Almost immediately, the Scarlet Guards mobilized an even larger number of supporters. (Their forceful response was fueled by a rumor, which turned out to be unfounded, that the WGH was using the Number 24 Factory as a launching pad for a "day of red terror" in which all cadres of rank seventeen and above would be subject to house searches.) After consulting with union chief Zhang Qi, the Scarlet Guards briefly detained Wang Hongwen, Pan Guoping, and other WGH leaders and seized a substantial cache of sensitive WGH records. Involving at its height approximately 200,000 Scarlet Guard participants, the confrontation—which lasted for nearly one week—graphically demonstrated the muscle of the new conservative organization.[8]

The Composition of Shanghai's Conservative Organizations

Unlike the conservative Red Guards, which were led for the most part by children of high-ranking cadres who rejected the student leadership of the pre-Cultural Revolution period, leaders of the worker conservatives were drawn overwhelmingly from among pre-Cultural Revolution activists, Communist party and Youth League members, and from labor models and advanced producers. Such workers had been the mainstay and prime beneficiaries of seventeen years of communism. In the past their work had been rewarded and praised; some had been selected as political or production exemplars at municipal or national levels. According to Andrew Walder's analysis of the relationship between this subset of the Chinese workforce and the Communist party,

> A group of "activists" or "backbones" is closely associated with the party organization. The party carefully cultivates relationships with these activists and through them extends control over the shop floor. Activists are people who are positively oriented to the party and who do its bidding. Many are members of the Communist Youth League, which has an organization that replicates, and is directly subordinate to, that of its parent organization. These activists are a minority of the workforce, roughly as numerous as party members themselves, that the party is grooming for eventual membership and often for later promotion to posts of leadership. The party is able to build and maintain this network of loyalties through its influence over promotions, raises, and other rewards—in addition to its ability to apply punishments to those who challenge it.[9]

A look at the biographies of the principal Scarlet Guard leaders reveals the extent to which they were enmeshed in these party networks.

The vacant seat on the Scarlet Guard General Command was soon filled by Ma Ji, a cadre in the Number 17 Cotton Mill who rose to the challenge of countering Workers' General Headquarters commander Wang Hongwen. A respected party member, Ma was thirty-three years old at the outset of the Cultural Revolution. He had been born into a Shanghai family of modest means; his father worked at a bean curd shop. His mother gave birth to ten children, but only Ma Ji and a younger brother survived. Ma began factory work at age seventeen as an apprentice. He studied at night school, where he joined the Communist Youth League and chaired the student association. Following the February 6, 1950, shelling of Shanghai by American-supplied KMT forces, Ma Ji participated in rescue teams, gaining a reputation as an activist. Soon he was assigned to the Yufeng Spinning Mill, the precursor of the Number 17 Cotton Mill. Initially, Ma worked as an oiler and then as an accountant. At the same time, he continued to build his political credentials, advancing from secretary of the Youth League branch in his workshop to the factory Youth League committee. After joining the Communist party, Ma Ji was made party secretary of his workshop. In 1955 Ma's factory sent him to a cadre school for training. Upon his return, he requested a transfer to the factory security department. There, he took an active part in the Anti-Rightist campaign and remained centrally involved in the supervision of cadres until the start of the Cultural Revolution.[10]

Li Jianyu, another top Scarlet Guard leader, had entered the Shenxin Number 6 Mill in 1956 at the age of seventeen, in the last group of managerial trainees (*lianxisheng*) at that mill. Although Li's parents had been ordinary workers, Li himself joined the factory as a staff member, thanks to his relatively high level of education. After completing the initial training period, he became an accountant in the dye room. Like Ma Ji, Li was sent away for special education at the expense of his factory. In March 1957 he was dispatched to a cadre school of the East China Textile Bureau (later renamed the Shanghai Textile Bureau) for further training in statistics.

When Chairman Mao called on urban cadres to go to the rural villages in 1958, Li went with other members of his factory party committee to an agricultural cooperative in Nanxiang, in the suburbs of Shanghai. After half a year in the countryside, he enlisted in the military and was sent to the Number 2 Aviation Institute in Qingdao (Shandong) to study mechanics. Six months later, Li was retained at the institute as a district captain (*qu duizhang*). In December 1962, he joined the Communist party. The following year, Li Jianyu was demobilized and sent back to his original factory in Shanghai, which had already changed its name to the Number 31 Cotton Mill. There, he was assigned to the Organization Department of the factory's Party committee. In the latter half of 1964, as the Socialist Education movement turned into the Four Cleans campaign, Li was assigned to a Four Cleans work team at the Textile Bureau. Then, just as the Four Cleans movement was winding down, along came the Cultural Revolution.[11]

To a person, the top Scarlet Guard leaders were trusted party members, serving as political cadres at their work units, who had been specially nurtured by the party. Their promotions from the ranks of ordinary workers had come as a reward for active participation in previous party-sponsored campaigns.

Wang Yuxi, commander of the Scarlet Guards, was deputy-director of the Shanghai Railway Bureau's control room and a party member. Chen Achun, adviser to the Scarlet Guards, was a Party member who served as personal secretary (*mishu*) to the director of the Railway Bureau. Yi Ping, member of the Scarlet Guard Command, was a staff secretary in the security department of the Shanghai Compressor Factory and a party member. Xu Yunsheng, also on the Scarlet Guard Command committee, was a cadre in the Shanghai Number 2 Machine and Electronics Industrial Bureau and a party member.[12]

These leaders were lower staff (*ganshi*), paid according to the wage scale for regular workers, but they enjoyed close relations with leading cadres, and they wielded considerable discretionary power. For example, as secretary in charge of security, Ma Ji had the authority to detain for interrogation any suspicious worker. Li Jianyu, as secretary of the organization department, was in a position to investigate the personal, family, and political conditions of cadres as well as workers. Although none of these people had attained the status of "leading cadres" (*lingdao ganbu*) in their work units, they were all basic-level cadres (*ji-ceng ganbu*) charged with serving as links between the party and the ordinary masses.

Because so many highly placed cadres became targets of struggle during the Cultural Revolution, factory-level Scarlet Guard organizations generally excluded from recruitment cadres above the level of department chief (*kezhang*)—and even clerical personnel who were not on the ordinary workers' pay scale. For example, the Scarlet Guards at the Number 31 Cotton Mill adopted a regulation that read:

> We hereby stipulate that those on cadre wage scale may not participate; only those on worker wage scale may join. Any party cadre in the branch committees who is paid on the workers' wage scale may join. The great majority of cadres sympathize with us and many of them want to join up, but we should beseech them not to participate.[13]

The Scarlet Guards took such precautions to avoid being upstaged by rebels who had accused them of "royalist" tendencies. They wanted to demonstrate that theirs was an independent organization that was not subject to manipulation by powerholders. Had such regulations not been adopted, the proportion of cadres among the Scarlet Guard ranks would have been even higher.

If the rebels represented countercultural undercurrents in Maoist China, then the conservatives embodied the mainstream reaction. Among both leaders and followers of the Scarlet Guards were a large number of pre–Cultural Revolution activists: especially Communist party and Youth League members, labor models, and advanced producers.[14] But the rank and file also included a substantial representation of individuals with questionable dossiers, for whom enlisting on the conservative side was a deliberate attempt to minimize risk. Before Chairman Mao intervened to make clear his preference for the rebel faction, the conservatives grew rapidly to outnumber their rivals in virtually every factory in Shanghai.[15] For instance, in the Number 31 Cotton Mill, the rebels at first claimed 108 followers, known as the "108 generals," but the conservatives soon boasted more than 700 followers. By late December, official Scarlet Guard armbands had been issued to 756 employees.[16] Similarly, at the Number 17 Cotton Mill, according to the recollection of Scarlet Guard leader Ma Ji, "As soon as our group was established, it gained great support from the workers. In a flash, some 4,000 to 5,000 people joined. By contrast, Wang Hongwen's organization in August-September of 1966 could count at most 100 to 200 followers."[17]

The industrial sectors where the deleterious effects of the Cultural Revolution were particularly visible generated an especially large number of conservatives. The railway system was severely disrupted by the Anting Incident, as well as by the Red Guard movement to "exchange experiences" (*da chuanlian*). Accordingly, many conductors, train service personnel, and workers in the control room enlisted in the Scarlet Guards. Similarly, the Shanghai postal system was interrupted by the *Liberation Daily* Incident (described in Chapter 2), in which the rebels insisted on having their tabloid delivered to newspaper subscribers. Numerous postal carriers thereupon joined the ranks of the Scarlet Guards.

The participation of labor models and advanced workers lent legitimacy and luster to the Scarlet Guard cause. For example, famous labor model and worker-engineer Wang Linque; advanced producer and pedicab driver Cheng Dewang; advanced producer and worker-electrician Cai Zuquan; advanced worker and 1958 national "heroes of the masses" representative Meng Dehe; and even veteran of the 1927 Shanghai workers' three armed uprisings, Sun Changsheng, all served as advisers to the Scarlet Guard General Command.[18] At the factory level as well, labor models and advanced producers enlisted on the conservative side in droves.[19] Labor models had been carefully selected by the party cadres as figures for national emulation; they enjoyed public acclaim as well as material benefits and wages well beyond the reach of ordinary workers. Naturally, such workers felt considerable attachment and loyalty toward the leading cadres who had selected them for these privileges.

Thanks to the influence of these advanced workers, a large number of their colleagues also enlisted on the conservative side. For example, virtually the entire Small Group of famous labor model Yang Fuzhen joined the Scarlet Guards. Similarly, of the more than twenty pedicab drivers in Cheng Dewang's work unit, all but one became Scarlet Guards.[20] Only two weeks after the formal inauguration of the Scarlet Guards, they already claimed 400,000 members. At their height, they enrolled twice that following.[21]

The Relationship of the
Scarlet Guards to the SPC

The conservative organizations of the Cultural Revolution era appear relatively autonomous if judged against worker associations during the preceding seventeen years of Communist rule, when labor activism was largely monopolized by the official trade unions.[22] Yet, if compared to their rebel rivals, the conservatives are most notable for the close relations they enjoyed with local party authorities.

The recollection of Scarlet Guard leader Li Jianyu concerning the establishment of a conservative organization at his Number 31 Cotton Mill confirms the mix of spontaneity and consultation involved in its inauguration. Recounting a meeting between Mayor Cao Diqiu and conservative workers on November 20, 1966, Li notes,

> Since the rebels had established an all-city organization, I asked whether we might not also establish an all-city organization to counter them. Cao Diqiu replied that the issue of whether or not all-city organizations were permissible rested with Party Central and that at present such a move was inappropriate. He advocated that we establish a provisional-style organization as a more flexible alternative. Then if, in future, the center did not approve, we would have an escape hatch. I was the one who proposed establishing an all-city organization at that time.
>
> A few days later, center issued a bulletin calling on representatives from all factions to participate in the destruction of "black materials." At our factory, the work team composed one faction, the rebel "Warriors to Defend Mao Zedong Thought" were another faction, and the factory CR committee was yet a third faction. I said to work team captain Wang Ming, "We also want to participate." Wang retorted, "We represent organizations; what do you represent?" I said, "Then I'll establish an organization, too!" Wang Ming said, "If you want to establish one, that's your business. It doesn't concern me!" We had this conversation at 3 P.M., after which I immediately distributed an invitational handbill. At 5 P.M. we held our inauguration. I had notified representatives from all factions and had even invited the rebels. Now that I think back on it, that meeting really was convened on short notice. Only afterwards did I learn that the SPC was committed to permitting the majority faction to form organizations if they were so inclined.[23]

Li Jianyu insisted that the conservative organization at his factory was a spontaneously established entity rather than an artifact of cadre manipulation, as charged by the rebels.

> It can be said that the establishment of the Scarlet Guards at our factory was our own idea. The rebels had their organization. Without our own organization, we had no power to constrain or challenge them. The party committee and the municipal committee were in favor of our establishing an organization. They didn't directly instruct us, although they did give us covert encouragement. But it really was our organization.[24]

Although party authorities at both factory and municipal levels were eager to see the development of organizations to counter the rebel forces, they were not free to express such views openly. The result was an intriguing combination of creativity and caution by conservative forces.

The formation of the February 7 Warriors further illustrates the general pattern. The February 7 Warriors, it may be recalled, were founded during the Anting Incident as a reaction against the disruption in rail traffic. The first to appreciate the seriousness of the situation were employees in the Shanghai Railway Bureau control room, the nerve center of rail transport for the East China region. Workers in the control room prided themselves on their serious work habits, which called for precise timing and a high degree of organized discipline. They were thus appalled by the unruly behavior of the rebels. When the deputy-director of the control room, Wang Yuxi (who was on duty at the time of the Anting Incident), decided to make a public appeal to the people of Shanghai to put a stop to the rebels' actions and restore rail traffic immediately, the vast majority of workers in the control room applauded his approach. One of the workers penned a supportive handbill on the spot.

This initial burst of spontaneity was immediately tempered by caution, however. Wang Yuxi was a Communist party member who was accustomed to reporting to the party organization before taking any action. He thus sought out the director of the Shanghai Railway Bureau Party Committee Political Department, Tian Zhou, who indicated his firm support. Additionally, Wang notified Shanghai Railway Bureau Party Secretary Wang Huasheng and Li Gancheng, vice-mayor of Shanghai in charge of traffic and transportation. Both officials also offered their encouragement. That night, Tian called together Wang Yuxi and others from the control room to discuss the situation and revise a draft document written by Chen Achun, secretary to the director of the Shanghai Railway Bureau, on the basis of the earlier handbill. The two leaflets composed by this group were the first concrete reactions of the Shanghai conservatives to the Anting Incident. To alert the public to the fact that the handbills had been written by railway workers, they were signed "February 7 Warriors." Only after the distribution of these handbills were the Warriors formally established as an organizational entity based primarily on workers in the control room. The members of the new group voted Wang Yuxi as their leader and Chen Achun as adviser to the group.[25]

The process by which the February 7 Warriors formed, which was typical of the conservative faction as a whole, demonstrated a spontaneity quite unlike the pre-Cultural Revolution situation. The same sort of autonomy was seen in the formation of the Scarlet Guards General Command as well: The leadership was entirely chosen by the members themselves, in contrast to the pre-Cultural Revolution situation, when it was necessary to secure party approval of "mass association" leaders; the membership was also recruited according to criteria established by the participants themselves, unlike the pre-Cultural Revolution situation when the party made such decisions. (During the 1950s, for example, the party had stipu-lated that temporary workers could not become union members, so unions sim-ply did not recruit among such workers. By the same token, when the party de-creed in the early 1960s that research and educational units did not need unions, the unions at such places were dissolved.)

After the Kangping Road Incident of late 1966, the rebels charged that the Scar-let Guards had been a creation of the SPC. From the above account, we can see that this charge was not entirely accurate. Yet the rebels' claim was not groundless; conservative organizations did in fact receive major support from the SPC, as well as from various levels of party branches. This was in stark contrast to the estab-lishment of the Workers' General Headquarters, toward which the party initially took the "three nos" (*sanbu*) stance of "no support, no recognition, and no partic-ipation." From Li Jianyu's memoir it is clear that both the work team and Mayor Cao Diqiu offered tacit support to the formation of a conservative group at the Number 31 Cotton Mill. And from other sources we know that the SPC urgently desired a conservative force to further its own political ends. Shanghai trade union chair, Zhang Qi, explained:

> As soon as the revolutionary rebels arose among the workers, Chen Pixian and Cao Diqiu thought up a way to organize the "majority faction" to counter them. More than once I heard with my own ears Cao Diqiu say words to the effect that "the rebel numbers are small but their capacity for action is great. It would be good if a major-ity faction also arose." More than once I heard him complain, "The majority faction is useless; why hasn't it risen up yet?"[26]

When the Beijing Red Guards attacked the SPC, party authorities called upon the Federation of Trade Unions to respond in a variety of ways. On August 29, Cao Diqiu convened a meeting of responsible cadres from bureaus and depart-ments, at which he requested the mobilization of labor models and advanced and older workers: "They are a banner (*qizhi*), a force with prestige among the massses. Let them come forth and speak."[27] The practice of asking older workers to take a stand (*biaotai*) was a party tradition. Since 1949, the proletariat had been hailed as the leading class of the nation. Moreover, older workers, having experi-enced the pre-Communist situation, were regarded as the most politically con-scious and most influential segment of the working class. During the Three-Antis and Five-Antis campaigns of the early 1950s, it was these workers who had first been mobilized. At the start of the Anti-Rightist campaign in 1957, the newspa-pers had published an article entitled "The Workers Have Spoken." (After the Tiananmen Incidents of 1976 and 1989, the papers also carried such articles.) Similarly, at the outset of the Cultural Revolution, the Shanghai Federation of Trade Unions (SFTU)—under prompting by the SPC—organized meetings of such workers to "respond to Chairman Mao's call to join the Cultural Revolu-tion." This was a means of notifying the reliable sector of the workforce of its re-sponsibility to stand up for the party authorities.

With this as prelude, big-character-posters entitled "We older workers want to speak out" and "Yang Fuzhen and other comrades send Chairman Mao an urgent telegram" were posted on the gates of the SPC offices to oppose the Beijing Red Guards' offensive. This was the first public action of the conservative workers under the influence of the SPC. Trade union chair Zhang Qi later recalled that as soon as the Scarlet Guards were established, the SPC directed the SFTU to contact them and provide an office in the union building for their use. As Zhang put it, "The SPC handed over the Scarlet Guards to the SFTU."[28] Trade union Vice-Chair Zhou Bingkun elaborated:

> The point was to use the orthodox status of the SFTU among the workers to dupe the masses and facilitate a rapid expansion of the Scarlet Guard organization. That evening, [union chair] Zhang Qi told me that the decision to take charge of the Scarlet Guards was made by Comrade Cao Diqiu himself. He wanted the Scarlet Guards placed inside the SFTU and wanted us to clear out one or two rooms for their use. He asked me to send a cadre the next day to SPC offices on 33 Yan'an West Road, to consult about this.[29]

After the Scarlet Guards were established, the SPC provided substantial material assistance. Unlike Wang Hongwen's WGH, the Scarlet Guards faced no difficulty in procuring identifying armbands, for example. A deputy sent from the SFTU to the Scarlet Guards reported that

> Beginning on November 26, the SPC wanted the SFTU to contact the Scarlet Guards, so the higher levels sent me as a liaison officer. When I asked how to handle the Scarlet Guards' finances, Zhang Qi [member of the SPC Standing Committee and chair of the SFTU] said meaningfully, "The union has so much money, now is the time to use a little." And within ten days we had issued 125,000 armbands to the Scarlet Guards.
>
> After the Scarlet Guards emerged, they were greatly praised by cadres at all levels, who provided covert and overt support, helping them with tactical planning and offering all sorts of material assistance. Some factory-level unions, following the lead of the SFTU, also allocated office space for the Scarlet Guards. Within 3 to 5 days, the Scarlet Guards had grown to number in the tens of thousands. By December 6 they numbered more than 200,000, and by mid-December 400,000.[30]

Scarlet Guard Jin Ruizhang admitted that the SPC was a source of substantial aid:

> The day after Cao Diqiu approved the formation of the Scarlet Guards, he arranged for us to have an office in the SFTU. Immediately we were given pens and paper, typewriters, printing presses, bicycles, and many other supplies. Later we also used the union's jeeps to procure 50 bolts of red cloth and commissioned 6 workers to sew Scarlet Guard armbands.[31]

The SPC's material generosity stemmed, of course, from an interest in controlling the conservative movement. As the SFTU liaison officer to the Scarlet Guards recalled,

The SPC went through the Industrial Political Bureau deputy-chair, Yang Huijie, to send a phone message to the union: "You must strengthen political leadership of the Scarlet Guards; don't just serve as a supply station!" They wanted the SFTU to dispatch a section-chief-level cadre to strengthen the liaison work and they instructed SFTU Vice-Chair Zhou Bingkun to engage personally in work with Scarlet Guard commanders whenever necessary so as to implement "political leadership" (*zhengzhi lingdao*).[32]

Scarlet Guard leader Wang Yuxi had a similar recollection concerning the SPC's interest in his organization's activities: "Over the space of five months they sent five liaison officers to us, to assist with strategy and tactics, to help us with 'manifestos,' [and] to revise our proclamations and some criticism materials."[33] In their first week of existence, the Scarlet Guards convened three meetings to accuse Zhang Chunqiao and to oppose the Double-Five Points raised by the Worker's General Headquarters during the Anting Incident. Through the mediation of the SPC, three telegrams attacking Zhang Chunqiao were sent to Party Central.[34] Li Jianyu of the number 31 Cotton Mill recalled of those telegrams,

> When we requested that the SPC contact Party Central, Cao Diqiu immediately responded, "I will certainly assume responsibility for notifying the Center." On November 26, when Cao met with [conservative] representatives from 38 work units at the West Shanghai Workers' Cultural Palace, he reported "I have already informed the Center."[35]

The SPC's investment was repaid by repeated shows of loyalty on the part of its client organization. This was particularly evident during the *Liberation Daily* Incident when the Scarlet Guards—with the encouragement of the SPC—dispatched a huge contingent to the gates of the newspaper offices to protest the rebel initiative.

Conservative Motivations

The Scarlet Guards formed as an indignant reaction against what its members perceived as rebel excesses. Those who organized conservative groups were appalled by the lawless initiatives of those on the rebel side. The worker rebels engaged in a series of sensational manueuvers—lying on the railroad tracks, stealing dossiers, assaulting leading cadres and work team representatives—that provoked the ire of many of the party activists among the workforce. As we have seen, the impetus for the establishment of the February 7 Warriors was opposition among elite workers in the control room to the rebels' obstruction of the rail lines at Anting.

A number of the rebel leaders had been targets of criticism by party activists before the Cultural Revolution began. Now, these former victims had managed to turn the tables and had become CR activists themselves. Needless to say, this dramatic role reversal did not sit well with those who had previously enjoyed a privileged status because of their sterling party credentials. Li Jianyu of the Number 31 Cotton Mill recalled of the earliest rebels at his factory:

> Those who put up big-character-posters all belonged to a group of people whose performance (*biaoxian*) was usually pretty poor. Some of them were not diligent workers, who even after the CR didn't change their ways. They were careless and irresponsible. Some of them had engaged in corrupt behavior, like Cheng Lin, who later became top dog at the Yangpu District branch of the WGH. Before the CR, Cheng had been an accountant in the factory nursery, but he had embezzled money, as well as milk powder for the infants, and was forced to pay a fine of 100 yuan. Some of these people were guilty of adultery or extortion; one, after being exposed, scaled the wall of the British Consulate in a futile attempt to escape. There were also some people who suffered from problems that today we wouldn't consider problematic. For example, if one's father had been a KMT officer, it was said that one's family background was bad (*chushen buhao*). But even if we adopt today's standards, many of these people were of shoddy character: adulterers, extortionists, embezzlers—people who would be shunned in any era.
>
> So at that time I was really dismayed. I felt that these people's basic character was bad and yet here they were, issuing commands and criticisms of the SPC. Their own ass wasn't clean but they were collecting "black materials" on others. Today they would attack this factory cadre; tomorrow they would attack that party committee member. Whenever they got off work they just went wild.
>
> In early August 1966, I wrote my first big-character-poster, "The rising wind augurs the coming storm," in which I disagreed with the attacks on the SPC. Although I didn't name names, everyone could tell who was being referred to. As soon as it was posted, it was attacked by the minority faction, who said my poster was a life raft for the SPC.[36]

In addition to distaste for the rebels' unruly personalities and disorderly behavior, conservatives disapproved of the rebels' negation of the basic system of party control. In some cases, these sentiments took a while to sink in. Ma Ji, from the Number 17 Cotton Mill, where Wang Hongwen also worked, happened to be away on business when Wang put up the first big-character-poster at the factory. But Ma confessed that had he been at the factory at the time, he would surely have added his own signature to Wang Hongwen's poster. In fact, after he returned from his business trip, Ma penned a big-character-poster supporting Wang Hongwen. It was only when Wang Hongwen opposed the second work team dispatched to the factory that Ma Ji withdrew his support for the rebels. He recalled,

> I didn't oppose the idea of criticizing the leadership, since the CR was calling on everybody to rise up and criticize. But I did oppose the idea of doubting everything and destroying everything. At that time Wang Hongwen was seldom at the factory (often he was off exchanging experiences), and I began to sense that he was overly ambitious. My public fallout with him came later, when he established his "Warriors Forever Loyal to Mao Zedong Thought." By the time of the Anting Incident, our differences had exploded. I was upset that Wang Hongwen's rebel ranks had admitted an awful lot of people who had previously been reprimanded for various infractions.

Wang Hongwen and his followers took quotations from Chairman Mao that had been meant for criticism of landlords and used them against cadres and party members. I couldn't stand that. I believed that Wang was no longer rebelling against the capitalist class, but rather against the proletariat. Thus at almost the same time that Wang established "Forever Loyal," we established "Warriors to Defend Mao Zedong Thought" to counter Wang and his followers. When Wang Hongwen seized the materials of the work team, we protected them. We believed that since the work team had been sent by the party, it wasn't right to wantonly criticize them. We should believe in the party.[37]

The conservatives supported the Cultural Revolution, just as they would have supported any political campaign. Many of them, like Ma Ji, wrote numerous big-character-posters at the start of the movement. But they certainly did not want to topple the authorities in the process; still less did they want to negate the entire order of the past seventeen years. They anticipated that, as in previous movements, a small number of "bad" people would be exposed, the majority of "good" people would be educated, and the party ranks would be rendered purer as a consequence.

This mentality produced a striking phenomenon: The more militant the rebels were at a particular factory, the more active the conservatives became as well. Those factories that generated leaders of the WGH were the same factories that produced Scarlet Guard leaders. For example:

- Wang Hongwen's Number 17 Cotton Mill also had Ma Ji;
- Huang Jinhai's Number 31 Cotton Mill also had Li Jianyu;
- Pan Guoping's glass machinery factory also had Pan Yuefa;
- Chen Ada's Lianggong Valve Factory also had Jin Ruizhang;
- Jiang Zhoufa's Shanghai Railway Bureau also had Wang Yuxi.

These rebels were founders of the WGH and members of its standing committee, just as their conservative opponents were founders of the Scarlet Guards and members of its general command. The conservative leaders were all longtime activists whose interests were intimately linked to the fortunes of their party patrons.

When leading cadres came under attack from rebel challengers, their clients felt compelled to defend them. Pedicab driver Cheng Dewang recalled that after the Beijing Red Guards stormed the SPC on September 4, 1966, the Shanghai Federation of Trade Unions called together labor models and advanced personnel like himself to garner support. At the meeting, the workers were assured that the Beijing Red Guards did not understand local conditions in Shanghai and were reminded that as labor models they shared responsibility for making the real situation known to Party Central. Then the union officials pulled out a draft that they had prepared in advance of the meeting to which four "five-good" workers eagerly signed their own names. It was sent off as a telegram from the workers of Shanghai to Party Central. Cheng Dewang had always seen the SFTU as "top-level leadership," and since the top-level leadership was asking for his support, he readily complied. Later, "when the Scarlet Guards General Command was formed, I saw that the stage was filled with five-good workers with whom I was familiar and I felt that the personnel in this organization were upstanding, so I also joined and agreed to serve as adviser."[38]

Scarlet Guard leaders and advisers evidenced a strong loyalty to party authorities, but for rank-and-file members of the Scarlet Guards the principal motivation was the more prosaic one of "following the mainstream" (*sui daliu*). Because the Scarlet Guards boasted so many party and Youth League members who had been esteemed as activists by the party leadership, people naturally assumed that it was a safer political bet to enlist on the conservative side. Workers had learned during seventeen years of political movements that in any campaign the decision of what was correct and incorrect lay ultimately in the hands of the top party cadres; it was simplest and safest just to follow their lead.

In the face of political uncertainty, the great majority of Scarlet Guards were trying to "follow the mainstream" so as to avoid later retribution. This included a number of people with "bad" class labels and compromised political dossiers, whose initial participation on the conservative side was a defensive strategy designed to divert attention from their suspicious pasts. When it turned out that the rebels, rather than the conservatives, were the recipients of Mao Zedong's support, the rebel side became the "mainstream" to which workers—"good," "bad," and indifferent—immediately gravitated.

The Demise of the Scarlet Guards

The heyday of the Scarlet Guards was brief indeed. As Party Central's backing of the rebel challengers became increasingly obvious, even the Shanghai Party Committee was forced to withdraw its support for the Scarlet Guards in favor of their arch rivals, the Workers' General Headquarters.

When the WGH was first established, the Shanghai party secretary had remarked, "The ranks of the WGH are impure"; "they are not really working class"; and "many of them have this or that problem."[39] But by the end of December 1966, the vice-chair of the SPC secretariat was pinning the "impure" (*bu chuncui*) label on the Scarlet Guards: "The Scarlet Guards are seriously impure, suffering from five too-manys: too many labor models, too many party members, too many League members, too many advanced producers, too many older workers."[40] These five types in the past had served as the stalwart ranks on whom the party depended; now they had become "impure elements." With the cadres who had held power for the past seventeen years in serious jeopardy as a result of the Cultural Revolution, workers who had attached themselves to these officials were also endangered. Allegations of impurity signaled the reversal in fortunes that accompanied the deterioration of their patronage networks.

The change in attitude by the Shanghai Party Committee began with Ma Tian-shui, SPC secretary in charge of industry, who was an experienced and articulate cadre with considerable prestige. In November-December 1966 Ma attended a national conference on industry in Beijing at which he expressed indignation toward the Cultural Revolution because of the havoc it was wreaking on the Shanghai economy. Ma's hostility drew criticisms from Lin Biao, Jiang Qing, and Zhang Chunqiao alike. Then, just before Ma was to return to Shanghai, Zhang Chunqiao took him aside to convey a pointed message:

1. the Cultural Revolution is a "dynastic change" (*gaichao huandai*);
2. the members of the proletarian headquarters, down to Yao Wenyuan at the bottom, include only eight people; and
3. revisionism rests with the major responsible people at Party Central, provinces, and municipalities—who must be expelled from office.[41]

Zhang's pithy communication had a determining impact on Ma's attitude toward the Cultural Revolution. After his return to Shanghai, Ma indicated to a meeting of leading cadres from all of the districts and counties in the municipality that he had decided to support the aims of the rebels. This change of heart on the part of so prominent a figure as Ma Tianshui exerted a major impact on leading cadres of the SPC as well as on rank-and-file workers. A transcript of Ma's remarks was printed and distributed to every factory, and tape recordings were made available to ordinary workers.

Aware that the end was drawing nigh, Scarlet Guard leaders made a desperate bid to maintain support. Taking a page out of the rebels' book, they switched from defending the Shanghai Party Committee to rebelling against it. On December 23, 1966, the Scarlet Guard General Command convened at People's Plaza a meeting of some 300,000 people to "criticize the reactionary line of the SPC." After the convocation, the erstwhile conservatives demanded SPC recognition of their status as a "revolutionary mass organization" and insisted that in future the SPC must refrain from engaging in unilateral agreements with any mass organization. The first point was an attempt to gain legitimacy for the Scarlet Guards and the second was to restrict the development of the Workers' General Headquarters. Mayor Cao Diqiu signed the demands, and the Scarlet Guards printed 80,000 copies of the agreement. However, before the copies were even circulated, the SPC Secretariat met to denounce Cao's action. First Party Secretary Chen Pixian pointed out that the SPC had already agreed to support the rebels and therefore Cao's signing of this agreement was a mistaken political stand.[42]

The next afternoon, rebel organizations throughout the city, led by the WGH, met at Cultural Plaza and forced Cao publicly to rescind his agreement with the Scarlet Guards. Cao was compelled to make a public confession:

On December 23, the Scarlet Guards held a mass meeting which I attended. At the meeting, the leadership committee raised demands that they asked me to sign. Pressured by a small group of people, I didn't stick to principle and signed. This was not even discussed with the secretariat. I committed a major error, and now I announce the rescinding of this agreement. I resolutely stand on the side of the revolutionary left, support the revolutionary left, thoroughly criticize the bourgeois reactionary line of the SPC headed by myself, and thoroughly criticize a small handful of capitalist roader authorities in the party.[43]

When Cao's confession was broadcast, it infuriated the rank-and-file Scarlet Guards, who streamed to the SPC offices on Kangping Road to lodge a protest. Dismayed by Cao's betrayal, the Scarlet Guards demanded that the mayor meet with them to clarify his attitude regarding the previous agreement.

By the morning of December 28, 20,000 to 30,000 angry Scarlet Guards had amassed at the courtyard on Kangping Road. That day, from a stammering phone conversation with Ma Tianshui, Zhang Chunqiao surmised that an incident had erupted on Kangping Road. Realizing that Scarlet Guard forces must be standing at Ma's side, making it impossible for him to speak freely, Zhang immediately phoned his wife to learn more about the situation. When he heard that the Scarlet Guards were seeking recognition from the SPC as a legitimate organization, Zhang instructed his wife to tell Writer's Group leader, Xu Jingxian, "The rebels cannot tolerate these Scarlet Guard activities." Zhang also had his secretary phone Geng Jinzhang, leader of the rebel Second Regiment, who was then in Beijing, to request that Geng return at once to Shanghai to handle the Scarlet Guards. Finally, Zhang placed a call to Wang Hongwen in Shanghai, asking him to mobilize his forces to "engage in blow-for-blow combat with the Scarlet Guards."[44]

Following Zhang's instructions, the next day the WGH and SPC Agency Liaison Post gathered more than twenty heads of rebel organizations in the vicinity of Kangping Road to establish a "united command post" to surround the SPC courtyard. By that evening, over 100,000 rebels had assembled to face the 20,000 or so remaining Scarlet Guards. Early the next morning, Geng Jinzhang notified the Scarlet Guards that he was commencing the attack. The "Kangping Road Incident," as it came to be known, was the first armed battle of the Cultural Revolution in China. Many Scarlet Guards sustained injuries in the confrontation; ninety-one were wounded so seriously that they required hospitalization.[45]

At the same time that Scarlet Guard forces were surrounded at Kangping Road, their offices at factories around the city were ransacked, armbands were confiscated, and many of their leaders were seized. According to a later report by a special investigatory team of the Shanghai Revolutionary Committee, the roundup targeted 247 "backbone elements" of the Scarlet Guards at city and district levels: eight were legally arrested, eighty were sent to the public security organs for reeducation and were then released, ninety-six were subjected to mass criticism, and sixty-three went unpunished.[46] These figures underrepresent the extent of the purge, however. At the Number 17 Cotton Mill alone, twenty-five Scarlet Guards were sent to public security; among them, Ma Ji was detained for more than a month.

On the early morning of December 30, the Scarlet Guards who had evaded the WGH dragnet decided to head north to lodge a complaint about their maltreatment at the hands of the Workers' General Headquarters. The next afternoon, some 20,000 Scarlet Guards took off en masse from the North Station, marching toward Beijing. Before long, the marchers reached Kunshan County in Jiangsu, on the outskirts of Shanghai. Just as they were hesitating about whether to continue northward, more than 10,000 troops of Geng Jinzhang's Second Regiment arrived on the scene. At 5 P.M. another battle between rebels and Scarlet Guards erupted—later dubbed the "Kunshan Incident."

The Kunshan Incident, like the Anting Incident of the previous month, disrupted the railway lines; traffic on the Shanghai-Nanjing line came to a standstill for twenty-six hours. When news of the railway stoppage reached Beijing, Premier Zhou Enlai phoned Shanghai's first party secretary, Chen Pixian, with instructions to get the trains moving again at once. Chen immediately dispatched emissaries to Kunshan to negotiate with the Scarlet Guards.[47] At the same time, he called upon the rebel organizations of Shanghai to draft a handbill criticizing the disruption in transportation and industry. Entitled "Grasp revolution, promote production, thoroughly smash the new counterattack of the capitalist reactionary line—an urgent letter to all city dwellers," the handbill positioned the rebels decidedly on the side of economic order.[48]

Although the Kunshan and Kangping Incidents resulted in a serious depletion of the Scarlet Guard ranks, the conservative organization did not collapse until the newspapers exposed an alleged "triple stoppage" (*santing*) plot by the Scarlet Guards that would have shut down water, electricity, and transportation services across the city. Actually, Shanghai's industrial production was already in a state of semiparalysis. The "wind of economism" (see Chapter 4) had exacted a severe toll on the city's economy. Moreover, during the Kangping Road Incident, some 50,000 to 60,000 Scarlet Guards and more than 100,000 rebels had left their work stations. Soon thereafter, the rebel assault on conservative organizations in the factories and the attendant arrest of Scarlet Guard leaders and harrassment of rank-and-file members convinced many on the conservative side, including a large number of cadres, to leave the factories and go into hiding. The sudden departure of so many basic-level cadres was followed by a precipitous decline in industrial production. The *Annals of Shanghai's January Revolution*, a tract written to celebrate the achievements of the Cultural Revolution, reported the situation in the textile industry:

> Because a large number of benighted Scarlet Guards abandoned their work stations, the textile mills in Yangpu District experienced a partial work stoppage; then some factories in Putuo and Changning Districts followed suit. Both revolution and production were severely harmed; during the ten days from December 29, 1966, to January 9, 1967, losses totaled more than 1.5 million yuan in value.[49]

The triple stoppage is mentioned in only one public document of the Cultural Revolution era. The *Workers' Rebel*, the official newspaper of the Workers' General

Headquarters, printed a confession by Scarlet Guard leader Li Shiyin in which he admitted that the Scarlet Guard Command had made plans for an industrial shutdown. But fifteen years later, Scarlet Guard Command member Li Jianyu adamantly denied the accusation that his organization had really planned for a triple stoppage. He insisted,

> There was definitely no "triple stoppage." Li Shiyin was a spineless type. His exposé in *Workers' Rebel* of an alleged "triple stoppage" had an extremely deleterious influence. At that time, it's certainly possible that some people spoke in anger, saying, "The SPC is like a candle; if you don't ignite it, it won't give off light. The rebels' obstruction of transportation and [their] factory walkout was 'revolutionary'; shouldn't we also shut down production?" But such statements were, at most, spoken in anger, and in the end no such decision was made. Our policy at the time was to engage in a protest demonstration. If we were not permitted to demonstrate, we would send a delegation to Beijing. But Li Shiyin's confession made it seem as though the Scarlet Guards had actually passed a resolution to engage in a "triple stoppage" and had even started implementing it. This is completely at odds with the facts.[50]

Former Scarlet Guard leaders later denied this event; and even leaders of the WGH, such as Huang Jinhai (at Li Jianyu's factory), later said on many occasions, "I never could see that the triple stoppage really amounted to anything."

From the primary sources at hand, it seems clear that a triple stoppage was proposed in anger by some Scarlet Guard leaders who did actually debate the merits of such an action. However, in the end, there was no resolution; still less was there any implementation. Had a shutdown been launched, with 800,000 Scarlet Guards mobilized to participate, industrial production in Shanghai would certainly have been brought to a standstill. But even without any attempt at implementation, mere discussion of the matter was grounds for culpability. Although the Kangping Road Incident had seriously depleted the Scarlet Guard ranks, the crime of a triple stoppage had given the rebels an excuse to thoroughly crush their opponents.

In the end, however, the fatal blow to the conservatives was dealt by Chairman Mao himself. Mao's insistence on a joint congratulatory telegram to the WGH, recognizing it as the legitimate representative of the working class, shattered any remaining hopes on the part of the conservatives and forced them to repudiate their previous stance. On January 12, the day after the congratulatory telegram was sent, Scarlet Guards posted a big-character-poster at the Shanghai offices of *People's Daily*. Entitled "Begging Forgiveness from Chairman Mao," the poster acknowledged that opposing the rebels had been a mistake.

Later Li Jianyu of the Number 31 Cotton Mill recalled the impact of the congratulatory telegram on his position toward the Cultural Revolution,

> What caused me to change my mind was the telegram sent by [Party] Central to the rebels. When the cable arrived, I was incarcerated. At that time I believed our inherent shortcomings had alienated the support of Chairman Mao. I thought: With even Chairman Mao on the side of the rebels, how can I remain obstinate? I'd better reverse my position.[51]

The famous "advanced producer," Cheng Dewang, remembered the shock he experienced from learning of the congratulatory telegram:

> At that time I was in great mental conflict. Party Central, the State Council, the Military Affairs Committee and the CR Small Group had sent a telegram of congratulations to the WGH conveying the views of Chairman Mao. Old Chairman Mao supported the revolutionary rebels! It was like a clap of thunder, jolting me awake. The general direction of the Scarlet Guards had been in error. I was standing on the wrong side, taking the wrong road.[52]

After the Fall

Many labor models and advanced producers who had previously joined the Scarlet Guards now wrote open letters to the newspapers confessing to how they had been "duped by capitalists." Just as they had once convinced their fellow workers to enlist on the side of the conservatives, so now they brought many of their colleagues over to the rebel side. Textile worker Yang Fuzhen, a well-known advanced producer, was typical of this trend: "Before long, [Scarlet Guard adviser] Yang Fuzhen joined the rebels; she talked about her decision with her Small Group and mobilized others to turn the tables on their former friends. Three days after Yang joined the rebels, thanks to her influence half of her Small Group had also switched sides."[53]

Like Yang Fuzhen, pedicab driver Cheng Dewang actively mobilized workers in his Small Group to join the rebels. He recalled,

> I thought that to add another person was to add another force to the revolution. Our Small Group had more than 20 people; at first only one was a rebel. So I joined with him to organize comrades from the Small Group into a study session to raise their consciousness. Before long, most of the comrades joined the rebels. There remained one comrade who just wouldn't change his thinking. He couldn't stand the rebels, and he would get angry if a rebel tried to offer him help. So I went to his home to have a heart-to-heart chat with him, and in the end this comrade also joined the rebels.[54]

Labor models and advanced producers were not the only Scarlet Guards to reverse their stand. A number of cadres at various levels, for whom the seeds of doubt had already been planted by Ma Tianshui's personal testimony, lost their nerve after learning of Mao's congratulatory telegram. The exposés and testimonials of these repentant cadres—in criticism meetings and in the pages of newspapers—proved far more damaging to the conservative cause than any criticism from the rebel side. With experienced cadres folding under the pressure, how could ordinary workers not succumb as well?

To make the decision as painless as possible, the WGH issued a proclamation welcoming former Scarlet Guards to the rebel ranks. This open invitation was Wang Hongwen's idea. Although many in the WGH opposed the notion of "recruiting rebels from among the old conserves," Wang was insistent that the former Scarlet Guards not be excluded from the rebel ranks. He repeatedly advocated at WGH Standing Committee meetings that ordinary Scarlet Guards be absorbed into the rebel organization. Three years later, Wang recalled a decisive meeting of the standing committee held at the Number 31 Cotton Mill on January 21, 1967:

> We argued from 6 at night till 6 the next morning, pounding on the table and throwing stools. The heart of the debate was whether or not to admit Scarlet Guards to the rebel ranks. Many people disapproved, and some of these comrades didn't change their minds even after the January Revolution. But practice proved that this course was correct. We were able to unite people of different viewpoints to work together, convincing these comrades to go forward with us to improve the situation. If it can be said that the situation in Shanghai was "extremely good," I believe that the correct resolution of this sort of issue was a factor. Of course, the primary factor was the personal concern of Chairman Mao and the direct leadership of the CRSG. But had this issue been incorrectly handled, after the January Revolution the whole city would have split into two huge factions.[55]

Wang Hongwen's policy of reconciliation, which applied to all but the top echelon of Scarlet Guard commanders, spelled the organizational destruction of the conservatives and spared Shanghai the sort of bloody factional conflict that wracked much of China. Unlike so many other places, where rebel and conservative organizations fought against one another for months to come, in Shanghai, after the Kangping Road Incident, the conservatives never regrouped to oppose the rebels. Elsewhere in China, the unwillingness of rebel organizations to accept "old conserves" turned conservative organizations into implacable enemies. The conservatives changed their names and slogans, altered their programs, proclaimed themselves to be "rebels," and then proceeded to undertake sustained opposition to the rebel organizations.

Later events proved that Wang Hongwen's strategy was a remarkably astute one, which resulted in the effective elimination of the conservative threat. According to an April 1, 1968, report commissioned by the Shanghai Revolutionary Committee, the previous year a total of fifteen "concentrated study sessions" had been organized for some five hundred former "backbone elements" of the Scarlet Guards at city and district levels. Of the 264 people surveyed, 144 (54.5%) now supported the rebels wholeheartedly, and 104 (39.5%) acknowledged their own errors but still harbored reservations about the rebels; only 6 percent remained adamantly opposed to the rebel forces.[56]

Although most former Scarlet Guards were quick to jump ship as soon as the direction of the political tide was clear, some remained unaffiliated. In a few cases, former conservatives simply returned quietly to their pre-Cultural Revolution role as ordinary workers. But in most factories, Scarlet Guards who refused to join the rebel side faced economic sanctions.

The Kangping Road Incident had occurred just before the annual year-end bonus was to be issued. At that time, workers' bonuses were of three types:

monthly, seasonal (every three months), and annual. Generally speaking, factories gave either monthly or seasonal bonuses, but not both. However, every unit granted annual bonuses, which were the primary source of funding for the lunar new year celebrations. In the aftermath of the Kangping Road Incident, factories withheld monthly, seasonal, and even annual bonuses from former Scarlet Guards who failed to reenlist under the rebel banner. The losses were no meager sum, amounting to one-third to one-half of a worker's monthly wage. In many cases, the suspension of bonuses continued for months.

Those who had served as top Scarlet Guard leaders suffered the greatest reversals. Such individuals had long been trusted party allies, vested with considerable authority; now they suddenly found themselves "set aside." Prior to the Cultural Revolution, Ma Ji, Li Jianyu, Chen Achun, and Wang Yuxi had worked in important divisions of their factories. After the Kangping Road Incident, however, they were all incarcerated. Upon their release, these former leaders—and sometimes their family members as well—were subjected to public humiliation and denunciation. Later, they were demoted to demeaning work assignments. As Ma Ji recalled,

> When they attacked me, they took my Scarlet Guard armbands and made them into a vest that they forced me to wear as I was paraded around for [the] struggle [session] in every workshop. I didn't mind their attacking me, but they attacked my wife too. My wife was also at the Number 17 Cotton Mill. She worked the early shift and got off at 2 P.M. They struggled against her at the factory gate until 9 at night. When the middle and late shifts got off work, they also struggled against her. My son was at the Shanghai Number 5 Steel Mill, my daughter had been sent down to the countryside, [and] my younger brother was at the maritime academy; they were after all of them. I thought about changing my environment, switching jobs, but they wouldn't agree. They said they wanted to choke me to death.[57]

Ma Ji was given janitorial duties, and, even after the 1972 policy adjustment (*luoshi zhengce*), he was assigned to the cafeteria rather than to his former post in the security department. Similarly, when Li Jianyu was released from prison, he was first made a street sweeper and then later was sent back to his factory as an auxiliary worker (*fuzhu gong*). Only in 1973 was he assigned to the planning department of the factory supply division. Even then, Li was not permitted to resume his original job in the organization department, where he had once wielded such authority over personnel decisions. After Wang Yuxi completed his sentence and was released, he worked as an ordinary laborer on the railroads. Chen Achun lost his position as secretary to the bureau chief and was also assigned as an ordinary railroad worker. Later, these former Scarlet Guard leaders faced a variety of roadblocks in terms of promotions, wages, party membership, and so forth.

People such as Wang, Ma, and Li were "old conserves" who before the Cultural Revolution had served as political cadres in positions that had involved substantial responsiblity and that had afforded considerable latitude of action. Their past status made them reluctant to submit to rebel instructions, even after the defeat of the Scarlet Guards. When Wang Yuxi fulfilled his jail term and was released as an ordinary worker in the cargo division of the railroads, the rebels pressed him for a show of allegiance. But Wang kept his silence, declining to express any opinion about the political movements that ensued in the later stages of the CR: movements such as Criticize Lin Biao–Criticize Confucius, Criticize Deng, and Criticize the Tiananmen Incident.[58] Ma Ji was even less cooperative. After his release from a month in the Public Security Bureau, Ma wrote a letter to Zhang Chunqiao complaining about Wang Hongwen. In 1969, when a party committee was reestablished at the Number 17 Cotton Mill, Ma was one of only three party members at the factory who did not vote for Wang Hongwen; for this, he was put into solitary confinement at the factory for more than a month. Later Ma recalled his sentiments at the time:

> The higher Wang Hongwen rose, the more confused I became. It seemed to me that in educational level, working ability, consciousness, and oral skills he and I were about equal. To be a factory head or a party secretary was already good enough; how could he be promoted to the city and then [to] the [Party] Central? I knew his shortcomings. How could such a vast China be entrusted to this sort of person? I just couldn't figure it out. I also believed that one day his downfall would come.[59]

Like Ma Ji, Li Jianyu could never bring himself fully to accept rebel leadership. He reminisced,

> I always had lingering doubts, but I tried my best not to think about them. Yet sometimes I just couldn't stop myself from engaging in private conversations, for which I was then made an example. I was a (negative) example in the campaigns to criticize the reversal of verdicts concerning rightists, to criticize Deng, etc. In 1972 our factory had to criticize the Seventy Articles for Industry [which outlined a system of centralized factory management, deemed "revisionist" during the CR]. I felt there was nothing wrong with the 70 points and refused to criticize them, whereupon I was again subjected to criticism. In 1974, at the time of the anti-reversal of verdicts on rightists, a big-character-poster was hung on my desk.[60]

Other unrepentant Scarlet Guard activists suffered similar treatment over the course of the Cultural Revolution. Even though some of them were later "cleared" in the policy adjustment of 1972, they were still only assigned jobs that were considered especially degrading or physically taxing.

Not all Scarlet Guard leaders and "backbones" were henceforth excluded from positions of authority during the Cultural Revolution, however. The rebels welcomed those who readily confessed their own errors and exposed the offenses of others. Such turncoats were drawn heavily from the ranks of labor models and advanced producers. Yang Fuzhen, after submitting to a very brief period of criticism, quickly continued her upward trajectory, rising well above her pre–Cultural Revolution standing. During the CR, she occupied the posts of SRC standing committee member, vice-secretary of the Putuo District party branch, member of the WGH Standing Committee, and standing committee member of the Fifth Shanghai Workers' Representative Conference. Cheng Dewang gained membership on the revolutionary committee of the Shanghai Public Utilities Management Bureau, as well as the Fifth Shanghai Workers' Representative Conference. Although both Yang and Cheng were renowned advanced producers before the CR, they had not previously enjoyed political assignments.

In contrast to such former political cadres as Li Jianyu or Ma Ji, who had in the past held positions of some authority, these labor models had attained their fame simply by following the party line. In the past, the party had wanted them to take the lead in production; now the party wanted them to take the lead in supporting the Cultural Revolution. Whatever reservations they may have harbored about the rebels, they were not inclined to express them openly. On the contrary, many were quick to demonstrate public endorsement of the rebels. In virtually every subsequent phase of the CR, Yang Fuzhen offered her support in newspapers and public meetings. Before the CR she had been typecast as "Chairman Mao's good worker," a role that she continued to play during the CR itself.

A series of investigations undertaken by the Workers' General Headquarters in the years following the Kangping Road Incident revealed the rapid accommodation that labor models had made to the Cultural Revolution. According to a report in spring 1968, of 110 pre–Cultural Revolution five-good workers and labor models surveyed at 89 industrial and service enterprises in the city, some 50 people (45.5%) now exhibited "good" political orientations (*biaoxian*), 44 people (40%) were "average," and 16 people (14.5%) were still "relatively poor." More tellingly, 43 of those investigated (39%) had recently been chosen as workers' representatives, and 50 of them (45.5%) currently served in rebel committees at factory, bureau and district levels.[61]

The proportion of pre–Cultural Revolution labor models joining the rebel side increased over the course of the CR.[62] A survey conducted in January 1972 among 735 of the more famous labor models in Shanghai found that 561 (76%) demonstrated "good" political orientations, whereas only 29 (4%) were still rated as "poor."[63] The category "poor" was further explained as "cannot properly deal with mass movements" (i.e., resists the CR). Although this figure of 4 percent does not necessarily capture the genuine feelings of these people toward the Cultural Revolution, it is clear that by 1972 most former labor models were at least *acting* in accord with Cultural Revolution standards. Such compliance propelled many of them into important leadership positions.

Party Networks

Rebels and conservatives were both embroiled in a high-stakes political contest, but conservatives drew upon the resources of established party-state networks in mounting their offensive. As Walder has noted, "The party reaches out to the citizenry through constantly cultivated patronage relationships, in which active support and loyalty are exchanged for mobility opportunities, material advantages, and social status."[64] Although rebel condemnation forced the conservative Scarlet Guards to disavow any intimate connection to higher-level patrons, party backers did in fact play a crucial role in promoting their activities.

Such political networks are sometimes seen as having been created de novo by the Communist state during the 1950s, but they had important roots in the pre-1949 Communist labor movement—as the conservatives' preference for historical nomenclature borrowed from the revolutionary struggles of the past suggested. At the start of the Cultural Revolution, the Shanghai Party Committee and the Shanghai Federation of Trade Unions were replete with old cadres from the Jiangnan Region who had been active in the pre-1949 labor movement. Both SFTU Vice-Chair Shi Huizhen (who led the work team that condemned the rebellion of Wang Hongwen at the No. 17 Mill) and SFTU Chair Zhang Qi (who authorized the provision of material aid to the Scarlet Guards) were former activists in the underground Shanghai labor movement, whose initiatives during the CR offered clear encouragement to the conservative forces. Long accustomed to a modus operandi that favored reliance upon fellow party loyalists from Jiangnan, they continued this familiar tactic during the early months of the CR.[65]

Had Chairman Mao not intervened to indicate his personal support for the rebels' assault on established party networks in Shanghai, the Scarlet Guards would undoubtedly have emerged victorious. Their rapid development into the majority faction demonstrated the magnetic pull of the party's patronage system among the urban workforce.

Once the tables turned in favor of the rebels, however, thousands of former members of the party underground (who hailed for the most part from the Jiangnan Region) were viciously attacked by the worker-rebel leadership (which, as we have seen, was disproportionately composed of northerners). Of the ninety-nine former underground activists who held top party and government posts in Shanghai at the outset of the CR, sixty-five were subsequently arrested on rebel orders.[66]

The swift demise of the Scarlet Guard movement revealed the limits of the loyalty of the rank-and-file to their party patrons. Although the top Scarlet Guard commanders—accustomed to positions of some political authority and committed to their defense of party superiors—remained steadfastly opposed to the rebels, the great majority of conservatives proved much more fickle. Once they detected a clear shift in political winds, ordinary workers and advanced producers alike were quite willing to transfer their allegiance to the favored side. Wang Hongwen's policy of openly welcoming (all but the very top) former Scarlet Guards to his WGH did much to facilitate this trend. The ease with which erstwhile conservatives reenlisted under the rebel banner was indicative of a general fluidity among the workforce that found its fullest expression during the "wind of economism"—when both rebel and conservative followers joined with less-privileged members of the workforce to voice insistent demands for material improvements.

4

A Cry for Justice:
The Wind of Economism

The Cultural Revolution saw the unfolding of what political scientist Sidney Tarrow has termed a "cycle of protest." Tarrow observes of these cycles that "in the presence of such general periods of turbulence, even the poor and disorganized can draw upon opportunities created by the 'early risers' who trigger the cycle."[1] After the actions of rebels provoked the reactions of conservatives, battles between these relatively fortunate workers (most of whom were permanently employed at state enterprises) afforded space for the have-nots of Chinese socialism to demand socioeconomic justice.

In the winter of 1966–1967, a new type of labor association, neither rebel nor conservative in orientation, appeared on the Cultural Revolution scene. These orgainzations were dubbed "economistic" because of their relative disinterest in the political debates of the day; they were not centrally concerned with the issue of attacking or defending party leaders. Their focus was directed instead on redressing socioeconomic grievances. We have records of 354 such organizations in Shanghai alone.[2] In most cases, their names indicated their objectives: "Rebel Revolutionary Headquarters for Housing Difficulties," which demanded a resolution of housing complaints; "Rebel Headquarters for Revolutionary Bachelor Workers," which demanded transfer to Shanghai of workers' families; "Revolutionary Rebel Headquarters for Permanent Residents with Temporary Household Registration," which demanded resolution of residency problems; and so forth. Although their activities were short-lived (just a little over a month), they exerted a significant impact on the course of the Cultural Revolution—creating a "wind of economism" (*jingjizhuyi feng*) that brought industrial production to a virtual standstill in some parts of the country and that elicited a harsh reaction from top party leaders in Beijing.

The demands of workers in these organizations were various, but in Shanghai they boiled down to three kinds of requests: (1) increased compensation in the form of higher wages, subsidies, and the like; (2) a change in household registration (*hukou*), from rural to urban or from small town or distant province to Shanghai; and (3) new work assignments or job classifications: Workers who had been sent to the countryside asked to return to their previous jobs in Shanghai, and temporary and contract laborers demanded promotion to permanent worker status. Although denigrated by party authorities as "economistic," these concerns were life-and-death issues to workers who had been shut out of the benefits of the command economy.

In contrast to rebel and conservative organizations, whose principal animus lay in criticizing or protecting party leaders, economistic associations represented a relatively apolitical and autonomous expression of worker concerns. Taking advantage of the uncertainty afforded by the Cultural Revolution, disprivileged workers raised demands for material improvements. Since the socialist economy was controlled by party cadres, struggles for economic gain inevitably brought the protesters into conflict with local officials. Nevertheless, the protesters' chief concern was to ameliorate their own downtrodden status rather than to seize power from alleged "capitalist roaders" within the party. This was not the first time that economic grievances had been voiced by the have-nots of Chinese socialism.[3] And, just as in the past, such complaints would not elicit a sympathetic response from the authorities this time either.

According to Chairman Mao and the other radical promoters of the CR, the movement was fundamentally a struggle over political, not economic, matters. As Zhang Chunqiao had put it in his November 1966 message to Ma Tianshui (see Chapter 3): "The Cultural Revolution is a change in dynasties"; that is, a political transformation rather than an economic reform. By characterizing demands for job transfers, pay hikes, and changes in household registration as "economistic" (Lenin's scornful term for the benighted mentality of workers bereft of Communist party leadership), Party Central was able to dismiss these concerns as unbefitting so noble a quest as the Cultural Revolution. Beyond this ideological consideration was the simple fact that any serious effort to redress such grievances would have proven extremely expensive for the Chinese government to underwrite.

Although ostensibly committed to the creation of an equitable socioeconomic order, Chinese socialism had given rise in practice to a variety of systemic inequalities.[4] People experienced enormous differences in status and material benefits depending upon what kind of city they lived in (directly administered, provincially administered, district, county, or town), what type of unit they worked at (state-owned or collective), their work status (permanent, contract, or temporary), their wage scale (cadre or worker), and so on.

Household registration was typically determined by one's parents' place of residence; moreover, unless one were fortunate enough to join the military or pass the university entrance examination—both of which were highly competitive opportunities—one was permanently condemned to an inherited residential status. To be saddled with a rural registration meant a life of exhausting labor and economic deprivation as a peasant, with next to no welfare provisions. In Maoist China, the worst punishment that might befall an urbanite—aside from imprisonment—was to lose one's household registration. Without urban status, one had no access to grain rations, no opportunity of permanent employment at an urban work unit, and no chance to educate one's children in city schools. Even among the cities there was a ten-grade pecking order. Shanghai was classified as a grade-eight region, with a high basic wage; the Shanghai suburbs were a grade-five district, with a much lower wage scale. The level of city affected not only one's wage but also the quality of medical care, education, and welfare benefits.[5]

To the accident of birth, which determined one's household registration, the government added other sources of differentiation. For example, whether one's work unit was state-owned or collectively owned, and—within collectives— whether it was a "large" or "small" collective (i.e., managed by a district or county industrial bureau or by a neighborhood) was a product of government decree. The benefits offered by these different types of enterprises were markedly different. A union member at a state-owned factory could enjoy "big labor insurance," by which one's dependents were also covered for half of their medical expenses, whereas workers in collectives were resigned to "small labor insurance," which provided no coverage at all for dependents. Similar discrepancies pertained to pensions. Wage grades were also ordained by the government, with workers differentiated by skill level into eight grades, and cadres classified according to occupational status as engineer, teacher, doctor, technician, manager, and the like.

In any country, regional and occupational differences are reflected in varying levels of income, benefits, and social status. But in China's command economy, personal choice or individual effort appeared to play next to no role in creating this differentiation; hence, virtually all socioeconomic divisions were viewed as a consequence of government fiat. The fact that the official ideology of the Cultural Revolution put such stress on egalitarianism only exacerbated the feelings of injustice on the part of those condemned to low socioeconomic status. Moreover, the Cultural Revolution's guiding credo—"to rebel is justified"—presented an opportunity for people who felt deprived by the system to articulate their accumulated resentment.

The planned economy was one source of dissatisfaction. The legacy of the Great Leap Forward was another. Although the city of Shanghai had not suffered as severely as other places during the Great Leap, many temporary and contract workers (who came from the surrounding countryside) had never recovered fully from its disastrous impact. A further contributing factor was the tendency of some ambitious cadres arbitrarily to alter the State Council's set policy on wages so as to curry favor with higher authorities. For more than a decade prior to the Cultural Revolution (from October 1954 right up to his death in April 1965), the radically inclined first party secretary of Shanghai, Ke Qingshi, had insisted on an exceptionally harsh implementation of wage policy in the city.

Although these were long-standing concerns, insofar as we can determine all of the economistic demands that erupted in Shanghai during the Cultural Revolution were raised only after the Anting Incident. The insistence of Wang Hongwen's Workers' General Headquarters that the Shanghai Party Committee sign off on the rebels' five-point demands was apparently the trigger for the wind of economism. An obvious lesson of the events at Anting was that, in the name of rebellion, cadres could be forced to succumb to worker pressure. A March 1967 report of the Shanghai Revolutionary Committee traced the upsurge to that period.

> In mid-November of 1966, temporary workers who had been sent down to the countryside gathered at the cultural hall in Jing'an District to criticize the "simplify and settle" policy and [to] demand a change in the allocation system.
>
> At the same time, temporary and contract workers arose in rebellion, criticizing the government for being inequitable and exposing irrationalities in the labor system and the economy.[6]

Early "Economistic" Organizations

The cry for socioeconomic justice originated not within the factories, but in the streets and on the farms: among long-term irregular workers and workers who had been mobilized to go to the countryside to support the peasants. Later, the demands of these groups spread to workers in the interior and to intellectual youths who had been part of the "up to the mountains, down to the countryside" resettlement campaign. Eventually, the economistic fever infected even permanent state employees with secure urban *hukou*.

The earliest type of economistic organization was composed of temporary workers (*linshi gong*), contract workers (*hetong gong*), and outside contract laborers (*waibao gong*). The largest and most influential such organization in Shanghai—with branches in other cities as well—was the "Revolutionary Rebel General Headquarters of Red Workers," known colloquially simply as the "Red Workers."

Use of temporary and contract labor had functioned as a standard means of supplementing the workforce since 1949. During the economic recovery of the early 1960s, State Chair Liu Shaoqi advocated expanding the temporary and contract system so that labor might be allocated more flexibly. The system had obvious advantages for the Chinese state, in terms of both efficiency and cost. However, the workers relegated to this lowly status experienced discrimination on several levels. Unlike permanent workers, temporary and contract laborers received no lifetime securities, no pensions, no subsidies, no disability coverage, no health insurance for their dependents, and so forth. Often they were paid not by the month, but by the day or by piecework rates. Whereas the lowest monthly wage for a permanent worker at the time was about 40 yuan, many temporary and contract workers earned less than 30 yuan a month. They tended, moreover, to be assigned the most backbreaking types of labor and were subject to dismissal on short notice. Temporary and contract workers were also barred from membership in trade unions, the Youth League, or the Communist party. In short, these laborers were excluded both economically and politically from the benefits of the socialist system.

As soon as Liu Shaoqi was fingered as China's "Number One Revisionist" during the Cultural Revolution, the injustices of the temporary and contract labor system were held up as evidence of his foiled "capitalist restoration." For a brief time, it appeared as though the campaign against Liu might perforce present the have-nots of the Chinese workforce—many of whom were women—with a powerful backstage supporter for their economistic demands. On the evening of December 26, 1966, core members of the Cultural Revolution Small Group—Jiang Qing, Chen Boda, Kang Sheng, Zhang Chunqiao, Yao Wenyuan, and Qi Benyu—met in the Great Hall of the People in Beijing with representatives of the "National Revolutionary Rebel Delegation of Red Workers."[7] In discussions that lasted for nearly five hours, the worker representatives castigated the exploitation and oppression suffered by temporary and contract laborers at the hands of "capitalist roaders."

Moved by this emotional outburst, Jiang Qing reportedly shed tears in sympathy with the workers' plight and issued an order summoning leaders from the State Council Labor Ministry and the All-China Federation of Trade Unions. To their face, she rebuked them: "What kind of labor minister is it that doesn't labor? Let him be a section chief!" Yao Wenyuan interrupted, "Better yet, let him be a contract worker. On with the rebellion! This system treats its workers just like capitalism does!" Jiang Qing continued, "This is completely capitalistic, reserving a certain number of hired laborers to reduce the burden on capital. Feudalism couldn't be more cruel than this system! Make them [i.e., the minister of labor, the chair of the All-China Federation of Trade Unions, etc.] serve as contract workers. . . . The contract labor system is a system of the reactionary bourgoisie. The contract workers must revolt!"

The worker representatives chimed in, "Yesterday we sealed up the Labor Bureau and tomorrow we're going to seal up the All-China Federation of Trade Unions!" Jiang Qing responded, "Terrific! It's best to seal them up! I salute you!" Then she proposed that a notice be issued immediately in the name of the CRSG, permitting contract and temporary workers to participate in the Cultural Revolution without prejudice and protecting them from job dismissal or the withholding of wages. Workers who had lost their jobs during the previous six months would be allowed to return at once to their original work units and would receive back wages.[8]

Jiang Qing's instructions were immediately printed up as a handbill and distributed nationwide. The handbill made a major impact on industrial hiring policy. When authorities in Shanghai cracked down on economism in February 1967, they pointed to the effects of Jiang's intervention.

> Originally the contract and temporary workers would come and go from factories according to production schedules and seasonal needs. After last December 26, when Comrade Jiang Qing spoke with Red Workers' representatives, all temporary and contract workers who had been dismissed since June 1 of that year returned to their original factories. Now some factories face a surfeit of temporary and contract workers. For factories which engage in seasonal production, the glut of idled workers is especially acute. Conversely, other factories that desperately need temporary and contract workers are afraid to hire them, and the Labor Bureau has no way to allocate them efficiently among enterprises.[9]

The deleterious economic impact of Jiang Qing's attempt to redress the griev-ances of disprivileged workers quickly eroded top-level support for her experi-ment.[10]

Before the leadership rang down the final curtain on the wind of economism, however, temporary and contract laborers did manage to introduce a socioeco-nomic tone to the otherwise relentlessly political discourse of the Cultural Revo-lution. As an eyewitness to the inaugural ceremonies of the Workers' General Headquarters remembered the distinctive contribution of the temporary workers to the convocation:

> Those up on the platform were criticizing the capitalist reactionary line of the SPC, but down below the platform were a group of women workers between 30 and 40 years of age wearing tattered work clothes and hats. These women didn't look like factory workers, but like temporary workers who pulled carts. They weren't paying any attention to the speeches on the platform, but periodically shouted out, "We want to become permanent workers!" "We want a pay raise!"

Wang Hongwen's wife, Cui Gendi, was actually a temporary worker from Subei who during the "economist wind" went several times to the offices of the Shang-hai Federation of Trade Unions to protest the discriminatory labor system. Ac-cording to the recollection of the staff person at the SFTU who received her,

> Cui Gendi first came to the SFTU in late November 1966, not long after the Anting Incident. Her hair was done in a small pigtail and she wore a purplish-red coat. Lead-ing more than ten other women workers, she arrived at the SFTU reception room. She explained that she was a child care worker at a workers' residential district nurs-ery operated jointly by the Number 17 Cotton Mill and a nearby printing factory. However, she was not part of the factory wage system, an injustice which she asked to be changed. At this time, Cui's attitude was still quite good. She appeared inexperi-enced and shy with strangers. The staff person from the women's bureau who re-ceived her at the SFTU had been part of the work team sent to the Number 17 Cotton Mill during the Four Cleans, so she knew that Cui was Wang Hongwen's wife. Be-cause the delegation was so large, they were taken to the garage next to the main building, where they were seated on mats. After [the SFTU staff had] listen[ed] to their story, it was agreed that their concerns would be reported to the relevant agen-cies. Cui even pointed out that she herself had come after finishing her work shift, so her work was not being adversely affected.
>
> Later, Cui Gendi came several more times, each time with a worse attitude. More-over, now she was accompanied by male rebels, who insisted that the union leader-ship meet with them. Later, they simply occupied the conference room on the fifth floor and refused to go back to work, insisting that the union supply them with three meals a day. Finally, they found an opportunity to seize SFTU Vice-Chair Zhou Bingkun and keep him locked up in the conference room. They departed only after the SFTU agencies rebelled in late December.[11]

The exact nature of the relationship between organizations of temporary work-ers and the WGH remains obscure. It was widely rumored that Wang Hongwen's wife had joined the Red Workers and that Wang's initial lack of enthusiasm for opposing economism was related to his wife's protest activities. As we saw in Chapter 2, Dai Liqing—later a central figure in the WGH and a member of the WGH Standing Committee—was also a temporary worker. Many people, including fellow WGH leader Huang Jinhai, alleged that Dai had joined the Red Workers. However, Dai himself never admitted to participation in any organization other than the WGH itself.[12]

Groups of contract and temporary laborers like the Red Workers were structurally quite loose. They lacked regular procedures for registration and admission; when they wished to pressure some cadre into signing an agreement, they simply gathered a group of people who dispersed as soon as they had accomplished their mission. This organizational laxity made it possible, when the wind of economism came under attack, for many temporary and contract workers who had participated in these mass activities to deny that they had formally joined any organization.

A second type of economistic organization was composed of employees who had been mobilized to return to their native places as a result of the retrenchment campaign of the early 1960s. The largest of this type of organization was the "Revolutionary Rebel General Headquarters of Shanghai Workers Supporting Agriculture Returned to Shanghai," known colloquially as Support Agriculture Headquarters. On January 18, 1967, this group mobilized some 100,000 followers for a sit-down demonstration at People's Plaza. Calling repeatedly (but fruitlessly) for Zhang Chunqiao to come forth and meet with them, the protesters roared: "We want to return to work!" "We want to eat!"[13]

In the years 1960–1962, during the severe economic crisis after the Great Leap Forward, many factories had been forced to halt or severely curtail production. In view of the surplus labor problem, the government had asked overstaffed urban factories to relocate those workers who had relatives in the countryside or some other means of resettling outside the city. This was in essence a mass layoff, with the explicit promise that as soon as the national economy improved the repatriated workers would have first option on returning to their old jobs. Of the hundreds of thousands of Shanghai laborers laid off in this relocation effort, the majority (unlike the situation in other cities) were experienced workers who had entered the labor force before 1957. Workers hired since 1958 were usually dismissed outright.[14]

By 1963, the Chinese economy had begun to improve. However, the intervening demographic explosion put such pressure on urban employment that factories were loath to make good on their previous promise to reinstate repatriated workers. In an effort to defuse mounting tensions, the city of Shanghai decreed that workers who had been resettled in the suburbs of Shanghai could be reabsorbed into the industrial workforce as temporary laborers. More than 30,000 repatriated workers were returned to factory work as "part-worker-part-peasant" in this initiative. Such workers retained rural household registrations, however, and their income was split 40–60 with the production team of the village where they were located. Moreover, the vast majority of relocated workers—who had been sent to places distant from Shanghai—received no benefit whatsoever from this remedial effort.

The resentment of repatriated workers was heightened when it was discovered that the Shanghai authorities had taken liberties with Party Central guidelines in implementing the layoffs in the first place. In an apparent attempt to save money, Shanghai had violated Party Central policy by targeting more experienced workers (who of course garnered higher paychecks) for the relocation effort. A February 1967 report on the origins of economism highlighted this discrepancy.

> When Party Central previously decreed that the urban population be reduced, their principal target was the "new workers who had come from the countryside since 1958." However, Shanghai tampered with the Central instructions and forced older workers who had been employed before 1958 to return to the countryside (some 70% of the dismissed workers had worked for more than 10 years, and more than 12,000 were skilled workers of the fourth grade). At present, approximately 500,000–600,000 of these workers have returned to Shanghai to ask for reinstitution in their former jobs.
>
> Among those who lost their jobs, more than 100,000 were employed at neighborhood factories. After dismissal, about half of them went to work in street factories. At present, they are also demanding reinstatement at their old factory jobs.
>
> The main justification that the above two types of workers offer in demanding to return to the factories is: (1) Shanghai's method of reducing population was not in accord with the spirit of the Central directive; and (2) at the time of retrenchment, the leadership promised that once the national economy improved [these workers] would be the first to resume work.[15]

In contrast to other cities, where repatriated workers were mostly recent additions to the industrial labor force, those expelled from Shanghai tended to be longtime city dwellers with considerable work tenure. Eager to reclaim their rightful privileges as urbanites, these repatriated workers converged on Shanghai from every direction, involving cadres at all levels in their demand for resettlement. According to a report of the Shanghai Labor and Wage Committee on December 15, 1966,

> The repatriated workers have established two rebel commands and have raised demands for permanent worker status, changes in the method of income allocation, and improved work benefits. We have learned that a "revolutionary committee of repatriated employees" with more than 10,000 registered members has been established in Wuxi (Jiangsu) and has disseminated numerous handbills. They are requesting either a return to work or an official retirement settlement. At present, a number of other places have also seen groups of repatriated employees demanding an immediate return to Shanghai.[16]

A third type of economistic organization was composed of workers helping out with construction in the interior. As the premier industrial city in China, Shanghai for many years had sent a large number of people to support construction projects in other parts of the country. In some cases, whole factories had been re-located to the interior. Some of these transfers were carried out according to Party Central directives, but others were direct transfers from Shanghai to the interior. The CR provided an opportunity for these transferred workers to stream back to Shanghai. According to *Annals of the January Revolution in Shanghai,*

> The phenomenon of returned workers is quite severe. In just the three bureaus of in-struments, chemical engineering, and number one electronics, of 26,000 transferred workers, nearly 20,000 have now returned to Shanghai.
>
> For example, the 1,500 workers at the Xi'an Transformer Factory were all trans-ferred from Shanghai factories and have now all returned to the city. The Yongyang Electric Meter Factory was also entirely staffed with Shanghai workers, all of whom have decamped—leaving only the factory director and the party secretary in place.
>
> This large number of returned workers puts great pressure on city services. Some have brought back their entire families, demanding to live in hotels, buy monthly bus passes, receive cost of living subsidies, etc. They have struggled against the per-sonnel who originally sent them to the interior, even going to their homes to harass them.[17]

Many of the relocated workers were apprentices in the middle of their training periods. After the Cultural Revolution began, these apprentices protested the un-welcome disruption in their training schedule.

> In the past, when the city of Shanghai relocated its factories, there were problems in the way in which personnel were transferred. Hence we request reassignment to jobs in Shanghai, regular wages, and urban household registration. . . . During the ap-prenticeship training period no one should be transferred to the interior to help out with construction, and anyone having been so assigned should be reinstated in his/her old job in Shanghai at once.[18]

Workers who returned from construction projects in the interior, such as de-mobilized soldiers, had gained valuable comparative experience as a result of their travels. As we have seen, more than a few rebel leaders in Shanghai emerged from such backgrounds. Both Ye Changming and Dai Liqing, for example, had served as transferred workers. Among those transfers who returned to the city, some (such as Ye Changming) found new work in Shanghai; others (such as Dai Liqing) were unable to find regular employment and could only serve as temporary work-ers; and still others—many of whom publicized their plight during the wind of economism—remained unemployed.

A fourth type of economistic organization was composed of young people who had been mobilized in the "up to the mountains, down to the countryside" and "support agriculture, support the frontiers" campaigns of the 1960s. To reduce the unemployment problem, Shanghai had mobilized a large number of "social youths," who were unemployed or who had just graduated from middle school or high school, to go to the suburbs of Shanghai or to more distant locales to labor on state farms. In the single year of 1963, some 20,000 Shanghai youth were sent to Xinjiang, for example.[19] During the Cultural Revolution these workers also took advantage of the general disruption to hurry home. As a report of February 1967 indicated,

> At present, the great majority of intellectual youths sent to neighboring state farms, as well as some of those sent to the military farms in Xinjiang, have already returned to Shanghai. They claim that "mobilizing city youths to go up to the mountains and down to the countryside to support agriculture and support the frontiers is a giant plot." They demand to return to Shanghai and to reclaim their household registrations so as to participate in the Cultural Revolution.
>
> Moreover, according to a report from the Xinjiang Industrial Office, more than 4,000 part-work-part-study students were participating in the industrial construction of Xinjiang last August and September. Many of these students have already returned to Shanghai, requesting readmission to their former schools to continue their studies.[20]

Another report noted that on Changxing Island in the suburbs of Shanghai "more than 10,000 intellectual youths sent down to the state farms have run away, resulting in the deaths of a large number of abandoned sheep and cattle."[21]

Yet a fifth type of organization—one that quickly succumbed to repression by the Public Security Bureau—was formed by private entrepreneurs. The city's largest such association, the "Shanghai Private Entrepreneur Laborers' Revolutionary Rebel Headquarters," was deemed "capitalist and anti-revolutionary" and its leaders were apprehended by the authorities. A rebel handbill reported unsympathetically on its operations.

> This organization was founded in December 1966. In addition to a general headquarters, it established branches in 10 districts and 4 counties. To entice recruits, it promised that "those who join our organization in future can enter state enterprises with labor insurance, permanent jobs, and old age welfare and disability."
>
> Its members charged [that] "policies of utility, restriction, and reform are big poisonous weeds, left in form but right in reality." They claimed that in seventeen years of liberation the working people have "turned over" and become masters, but the private entrepreneurs are still oppressed by the powerholders. More than 30 criticism sessions were held in every district to attack the policies of "utility, restriction, and reform," and the taxation policy. They charged that three big mountains rest on the heads of the peddlers: the Taxation Bureau, the industrial-commercial department, and the market management office.
>
> In the name of striving for a state enterprise, they engaged in economism. They demanded that "private merchants and peddlers must be state employees," and they rejected the current system of cooperatives.
>
> They even hoped to seize power from the Shanghai Industrial and Commercial Administrative Management Bureau and the industrial-commercial bureaus in each district. As a result, they were chased out by the rebel faction at these units.[22]

Although the private entrepreneurs appear to have been better organized than some other economistic groups, their commercial activities rendered them an easy target for repression in a campaign directed against capitalist roaders. The entrepreneurs' attempt to use the Cultural Revolution as an opportunity to attain the status of state employees with full entitlement to the benefits of socialism resulted in further discrimination and exclusion.

Out of the Streets and into the Work Units

The so-called wind of economism first gained momentum among those who lacked secure jobs or household registrations in Shanghai. Denied the privileges that came with permanent employment at state enterprises or fixed residency in a major city, the have-nots demanded access. But even those more favored by the system were certainly not free from dissatisfactions. With wages having been basically frozen since 1957, permanent workers also had cause to grumble; eventually they, too, raised demands for redress.

Indeed, the wind of economism can be read as a kind of weather vane, measuring the level of deprivation among the Shanghai workforce, shifting direction over time from the most disadvantaged elements toward more privileged sectors: from contract and temporary workers to repatriated workers to apprentices and, finally, to permanent state employees with Shanghai *hukou*. Apprentices, who occupied a kind of intermediate position on the employment roster (promised permanent employment and secure benefits in the future, yet still laboring long hours for low wages on a trial basis) were instrumental in redirecting the wind of economism from the streets into the factories. As the Shanghai Revolutionary Committee noted in its chronology published in March 1967,

> On December 27, 1966, some apprentices in the ninth district of the Port Authority, while searching for black materials, discovered documents concerning the official wage scale for apprentices. Realizing that their wages did not match what was stipulated in the documents, they went to the district bureau to demand a supplement. Li Guang, party secretary of the Maritime Transport Bureau of the northern district, agreed to issue a year's wages as recompense.[23]

Buoyed by this wage victory, apprentices began to press for other demands as well.

> The State Council had ruled that apprenticeship periods could vary in length, depending upon the difficulty of the skill to be acquired. But in Shanghai the period was set universally at three years. Now the apprentices are demanding that Shanghai comply with the national regulation and that supplemental wages be paid to those whose training time exceeded the required length.[24]

According to State Council regulations, certain relatively simple jobs (e.g., transporting goods within the loading district of the port) required no apprenticeship at all—merely a six-month probationary period. Yet in Shanghai, even these jobs were designated as demanding a three-year apprenticeship. During the economistic wind, a group calling itself the "Shanghai Apprentice Rebel Committee" formed for the purpose of reclassifying the requisite training periods.[25] The potential gains for the workers were considerable: Apprentices at the port were paid a mere 18 yuan per month, whereas the monthly wage for someone who had fulfilled the training period began at 42 yuan. The wage settlements for these discrepancies turned out to be substantial. According to a telegram from a Shanghai bank to Party Central on January 6, 1967, "The Shanghai Port Authority's fourth loading district disbursed nearly 40,000 yuan in one installment, with each worker receiving on average 300–400 yuan. Some garnered nearly 1,000 yuan."[26]

News of the apprentices' success spread like wildfire, and soon, not a single enterprise in the city was unaffected by monetary demands from its workers. Insisting that previous wage hikes had not kept pace with official directives, employees requested subsidies to compensate for years of substandard treatment. Even newly hired workers rushed forward to press wage claims; a group known as the "58 Regiment"—the membership of which was primarily young workers who had entered the factories in 1958—charged that new hires had been subject to wage discrimination for which compensation was due.[27]

Pressured by worker demands, cadres at all levels felt compelled to turn over huge sums of money as restitution. At the East China Electrical Bureau, "Originally, every month the wage bill had totaled 330,000 yuan, but on January 5, a sum of 1.28 million was disbursed—equivalent to about four months' wages for the Bureau."[28] At the Zhoujiadu Shipyard, the per capita payments were even larger: "The capitalist roaders gave 22,600 yuan to make up for wage discrepancies for 18 workers. One woman worker and her husband together collected 4,128 yuan."[29] In some cases, several years' worth of back pay was issued.

> Workers at the Shanghai Pen Factory claimed that, in the past, evaluations of wage grades had been irrational. Now that they've rebelled against the unit leadership, the leaders have agreed to raise the wages of all those workers whose pay currently falls below the average 1963 wage in the factory. Moreover, back pay to 1963 is to be issued. The factory owes 70,000 yuan in the first installment. (It is estimated that the 700 workers at this factory will receive 130,000 yuan in all.)[30]

Another strategy for raising wages was to change the ownership form of an enterprise, thereby altering the employees' status. In a number of instances insistent workers convinced SPC Secretary Chen Pixian and Vice-Secretary Cao Diqiu to sign agreements that converted formerly private and collective enterprises into new state-owned units. A group known as the "Elementary Teachers' Headquarters," claiming at its height more than 10,000 members, was established to demand that private schools be redesignated as publicly owned institutions.[31] In the case of one privately run elementary school, the conversion to state ownership resulted in a 70 percent wage hike for teachers.[32]

Wages constituted only a fraction of an urban employee's total income—much of which was in the form of subsidies. Workers at state enterprises received cash allowances for transportation, baths, meals, nutritional supplements, uniforms,

TABLE 4.1   Economistic Allocations in the Number 2 Commercial Bureau

"Economistic" Item	Money Allocated (yuan)	Percentage of Total
Wage hike for regular workers	637,576	54.00
Subsidies for travel to exchange revolutionary experiences	181,990	15.40
Wage hike for temporary workers	79,803	6.76
Subsidy for uniforms for apprentices	40,600	3.44
Expenses of personnel aiding agriculture	52,014	4.40
Increase in workers' insurance and welfare	66,767	5.65
Increased subsidy for breakfasts, dinners	28,249	2.40
Other	94,315	7.95
TOTALS	1,181,314	100.00

SOURCE: *Guanyu gua jingjizhuyi yaofeng de qingkuang huibao* [Situation report on the blowing of the evil wind of economism], from Shanghai Number 2 Commercial Bureau to State Council's Ministry of Commerce (June 6, 1967).

towels, soap, shoes, gloves, and so on. The wind of economism stirred up a concern over subsidies that was almost as feverish as that over wages. In some cases, workers at collective enterprises demanded treatment equivalent to that enjoyed by workers at state enterprises; in other cases, workers at state enterprises asked for the restoration of benefits that had been lost during the economic troubles of the years 1959–1962. Along with wage and subsidy increases, workers cleverly raised a demand for various Cultural Revolution "living expenses." Fees to exchange revolutionary experiences, spread propaganda, produce armbands, purchase broadcasting equipment, procure vehicles for transportation, and so forth were requested.[33]

Taken as a whole, these various allocations could amount to a sizable sum. The data in Table 4.1 show the amounts allocated to the 160,000 workers in Shanghai's Number 2 Commercial Bureau, as reported to the State Council's Ministry of Commerce.

A particularly costly manifestation of the economistic wind was a call to divide up various pots of money—such as operating expenses, year-end production accumulation funds, shares of co-ops, and so on. In Yimiao District, one cooperative disbursed the entire 50,000 yuan it had accumulated since 1963; similarly, the Huaihai Weaving Factory completely divided up its union's 16,000-yuan cash surplus account.[34]

Disbursements to individual workers, which ranged from several tens of yuan to several thousand yuan, amounted to a significant sum of money. (At this time, an average state worker's wage ranged from 40 to 60 yuan per month.) Many of the recipients rushed to market with their allotments in hand, able at last to fulfill long-standing dreams: "An apprentice at a service company in Xuhui District took his payment of 888 yuan and immediately purchased furniture and got married."[35] Long-suppressed demands from consumers frustrated by the years of frozen wages burst forth. According to *Annals of the January Revolution in Shanghai,*

> From January 1 to January 8, Shanghai's largest department store saw a rise in sales of 25.1% over the previous month, an increase of 36.3% over the same period of the previous year. Many products were sold out. As soon as the doors opened, hundreds of people rushed to the basement of the department store to buy sewing machines, while others raced to the bicycle counter. Watches were in even greater demand. Imported watches costing 400–500 yuan, which in the past had seldom drawn customers, were now being cleaned out. Sales of high-class nylon material increased many fold.[36]

In addition to claims for monetary compensation—whether in the form of higher wages, subsidies, Cultural Revolution expenses, or shares of accumulated funds—workers demanded the right to unionize. Behind the quest for unionization lay a desire for medical benefits, welfare provisions, and retirement provisions (a package known as labor insurance) accessible only to union members. According to China's trade union regulations, workers at private or collective enterprises were ineligible to join unions. This meant that such people were denied the benefits obtainable only through union membership. According to a report by the SFTU at the time,

> In Shanghai there are approximately 420,000 employees in collective and privately owned enterprises, widely distributed: more than 250,000 are in industry (street factories, cooperative factories); 110,000 are in trade (cooperative stores, vegetable markets); 30,000 are in education and health (privately run schools, local hospitals); and 20,000 are in other lines of work (e.g., real estate, public health, etc.) Except for a few cooperative factories belonging to the Handicraft Bureau, none of these units has a union organization. But the workers' demand to organize unions is quite insistent.[37]

In late August 1966, hundreds of workers from street factories; private schools; local hospitals; and trade, government, and construction industries marched with cymbals and drums to the SFTU to demand unions.[38] But soon, the Federation of Trade Unions itself came under attack as part of the Cultural Revolution assault on bureaucratism, rendering unionization an unfeasible option.

One of the more violent manifestations of the economistic wind was the seizure and occupation of housing. Population pressure had created a severe housing shortage in the city. The Cultural Revolution offered a convenient opportunity to appropriate residences in the name of "rebellion." Acts of confiscation were carried out by individuals or groups of individuals, usually in the name of the rebel faction at their work unit. Under the pretext of expelling "capitalist roaders," "four pests," and "reactionary authorities," workers took possession of housing that they had coveted for themselves and their families. In the space of five days—from December 30, 1966, to January 3, 1967—"all the housing in the city that had been awaiting allocation was forcibly occupied."[39]

The Role of Rebels

After the wind of economism spread from the streets into the factories, the basic ranks of rebel and conservative workers alike became vociferous in raising material demands. Some of the rebels were affiliated with Wang Hongwen's Workers' General Headquarters, others with splinter groups like the Second Regiment or the Workers' Third Headquarters. As far as we can determine, however, the rebel organizations themselves did not raise such demands—aside from asking for subventions of expenses associated with Cultural Revolution activities. Their handbills indicate that their actions as well as their slogans were fundamentally "political" attacks on powerholders, rather than "economistic" requests for increased income.[40] Thus, although rank-and-file rebels were deeply involved in the cry for socioeconomic justice (which Wang Hongwen initially refused to condemn), organizationally the rebel forces were relatively free of such entanglements. As a consequence, when Party Central issued a directive opposing the economistic wind, rebel organizations were quick to place the blame entirely on the shoulders of those cadres whom their ordinary followers had forced into signing disbursement agreements—charging that these cadres had used money to corrupt the rebel ranks.

The Workers' General Headquarters took the lead in denouncing economism. On the evening of January 6, 1967, its leaders drafted a proclamation, announcing that "beginning at 5 P.M. on January 7, the banks are prohibited from issuing wage hikes or other welfare benefits; union funds, factory accounts, collective accumulation funds, etc. are all frozen."[41] A handbill issued by the WGH on January 7 underscored its explicitly political agenda.

> We are rebelling against a small handful of authorities [who are] taking the capitalist road, rebelling against the reactionary bourgeois line, and not primarily over "money."
>
> The worker comrades must emphasize the long-term revolutionary interest and must not rebel for the sake of a wage hike. That would be a mistake! We raise the banner of politics, not the banner of economics!
>
> Our major target is a small handful of authorities [who are] taking the capitalist road inside the Shanghai Party Committee and the East China Bureau in order to consolidate the political power of the proletariat. Political power must be controlled by the revolutionary rebels of the proletariat; this is the core issue! Otherwise, all temporary short-sighted economic interest is empty![42]

Clearly, the rebel command viewed power seizure as more important than monetary gain. Some of the individual rebel leaders showed a similar commitment in their personal actions. An investigation of Xu Meiying, one of the founders of the WGH, reported: "During the economist wind, Xu Meiying was working at the WGH general office when her factory notified her to come and collect 100 yuan in extra wages. When Xu heard this, she rushed back to the factory to refuse the offer of money."[43]

This is not to say that individual rebel leaders evidenced no interest in material gains from their participation in the Cultural Revolution. Only months after the wind of economism had subsided, in the summer of 1967 the very WGH leaders (i.e., Wang Hongwen, Chen Ada, Dai Liqing, and Wang Xiuzhen) who had so confidently criticized the "bourgeois tendencies" of others all moved into new, and much larger, housing. Later, they all relocated again, in every case into more spacious accommodations. Moreover, despite the fact that workers around the country had been laboring under a several-decade wage freeze, the leaders of the WGH treated themselves to a "special subsidy" of about 100 yuan two or three times each year.[44]

On January 11, Party Central issued a directive sternly opposing economism and implying that the fault for this unseemly phenomenon lay with the cadres who had yielded to worker pressure. Three days later, the WGH organized a huge demonstration in which hundreds of cadres—from members of the SPC down to factory party secretaries—were paraded through all the main thoroughfares of the city and cursed for their economistic "crimes."[45] The alleged criminality of the cadres in fanning the winds of economism became the pretext for the rebel seizure of power from the Shanghai Party Committee.

The Attitude of the Shanghai Authorities

In view of the fact that so many ordinary rebels were involved in pressing monetary demands, party authorities in Shanghai found themselves in an impossible position. If they acceded to rebel claims, they violated a long-standing commitment to holding the line on expenditures; but if they refused to go along with the demands, they were guilty of the crime of opposing "revolutionary rebels."

As early as mid-November 1966, the Shanghai Labor Bureau launched a reform of the workers' allocation system in an attempt to steer a moderate course between these contradictory pressures. The *Annals of Anti-Economism*, an account critical of SPC initiatives, described the situation as follows:

> Sent-down workers who had returned to the city's enterprises as temporary workers gathered at the Jing'an Cultural Palace to criticize the problems connected with the streamlining program and to demand changes in the allocation system. At that time, Wang Shaoyong, representing the old Shanghai Party Committee, forged a four-point black proclamation intended to resolve the economic difficulties and cover up the problems which remained from the streamlining program. At the same time, according to the spirit of Wang Shaoyong's four-point proclamation a work group led by Wang Ke was established to handle the allocation issue. It approved two agree-

ments to the effect that, beginning in 1967, sent-down workers should receive 100% of their wages, with grain and oil rations supplied by the production team, and 5% of the collective accumulation fund and collective welfare fund to be paid by the state. This committed the state to 2 million yuan a year in payments. This resolution was a plot by Shanghai's black party committee heads, Chen Pixian and Cao Diqiu, to change the direction of struggle and marked the start of the evil wind of economism.[46]

On November 22, East China Bureau representative Huang Yuji and Shanghai Labor Bureau Vice-Director Yu Yongshi co-signed an agreement "not to dismiss temporary and contract workers without just cause" and "to find jobs within two weeks for all temporary and contract workers dismissed during the Cultural Revolution."[47] The next day, Shanghai Labor Bureau Chief Wang Ke signed off on the demands of workers sent back to the countryside to help out with agriculture; the main import of this agreement was to recognize their actions as revolutionary and their organization as legal, as well as to promise a modest degree of material assistance.[48] These two agreements were made formal documents of the Labor Bureau on December 2. As local officials, Shanghai Labor Bureau cadres sympathized with the plight of workers who lacked regular employment. The deputy director of the Labor Bureau spoke of "owing a debt to the repatriated workers."[49] However, the household registration system and the wage policies were all dictated by Party Central; the local government was powerless to effect major changes.

From the moderate tone of these two agreements, it is apparent that the Labor Bureau was in fact trying to hold the line on spending. In negotiating with disgruntled workers, Shanghai authorities endeavored to honor current policy without angering the rebels. This was a no-win situation, however. According to a November 24, 1966, report by the Shanghai Labor Wage Committee,

> The wind of economism came very fiercely and rapidly gained momentum. Thousands of people gathered for eight days and nights, surrounding the responsible comrades and refusing to disband unless their demands were met. Now the masses have already established three "rebel headquarters." They are raising numerous economic demands whose resolution has widespread implications; many are national issues which are not at all easy to settle.[50]

On November 29, the city's Labor Wage Committee wrote an urgent letter to Party Central, requesting guidance on how to deal with the economistic upsurge.[51] Nearly a month later, having received no clear response from Party Central, the SPC agreed on a seven-point "opinions on temporary measures for handling several concrete problems in negotiating with the masses." The focus had expanded from questions of temporary and repatriated workers to include state and collective workers' labor insurance, sick leave, maternity leave, apprenticeship periods, transportation subsidies, and so forth.[52]

Subjected to increasing mass pressure, cadres involved in direct negotiations with the protesting workers faced a difficult dilemma. If they did not accept the demands, they were forced to submit to round-the-clock criticism at the work site, with no food or sleep and often no access to the lavatory. Not until they signed off on an agreement were they permitted to return home.

Unable to endure the intense pressure, many cadres simply caved in to the workers' demands. On December 27, Wang Litian, deputy director of the Shanghai Labor Bureau, signed an accord on behalf of the postal service to raise the wages of workers with families from 30 to 41 yuan. That same day, the city Labor Wage Committee accepted the sixteen demands of a group calling itself the "Rebel Heads of Households of Revolutionary Youth Sent to Settle the Frontiers." Two days later, according to a critical account,

> Capitalist roaders at the city Civil Affairs Bureau signed an agreement raising the wages of workers at the factory for the blind and deaf from 30 to 50 yuan, a 70% increase. Capitalist roaders at the municipal Labor Bureau signed an agreement giving the 250 workers at the Geology Bureau wage hikes amounting to 60,000 yuan. The Party Committee agreed to a change in the wage rate for temporary workers from daily to monthly wages, resulting in a monthly increase of some 80,000 yuan.[53]

On January 1, 1967, Cao Diqiu chaired a meeting at the SPC guest house on Xiangshan Road during which he transmitted Chen Pixian's admonition: "Relax a bit on the economic issue, don't be obstructionist; fight independently, think independently." Remarked Cao, "For these current issues, it's useless to ask for instructions from Party Central or the State Council, we'd better just go ahead and take action!"[54] At the meeting, five points were approved:

1. All workers sent down as part of the streamlining campaign after 1958 must be given work in their original factories.
2. Unemployed youths must be assigned jobs.
3. Street industries can wear the "hat" of state enterprises and augment their insurance and welfare systems appropriately.
4. Grade-five suburban wages may be raised to the level of grade-eight.
5. Long-term temporary and contract workers can become regular workers.[55]

The next day, the deputy-director of the city Labor Bureau, Yu Yongshi, convened a cadre meeting at the bureau to transmit the SPC's five points.[56]

Both the *Annals of Shanghai's Anti-Economism* and Song Yongjia's *Annals of the January Revolution in Shanghai*, written in celebration of the rebels' power seizure, present the January 1 meeting at Xiangshan as proof that the SPC was the chief culprit in the economistic wind.[57] The effort to appease the rebels through economic means had clearly backfired.

Economic Impact

The wind of economism exacted a noticeable toll on the Shanghai economy. According to a report of the Shanghai Revolutionary Committee, during the one month of January 1967 some 35 to 40 million yuan was paid out in higher wages, subsidies, welfare, divisions of accumulation funds, stocks, and the like as part of the economist wind. As workers left their posts to participate in protests for higher wages and, after receiving cash handouts, rushed off to enjoy their new-found wealth, productivity declined commensurately. The problems were especially acute in the transportation sector. A contemporary report on the Shanghai Railway Bureau noted:

> Some drivers, conductors, signalmen, and stevedores were deceived into stopping work to engage in economic rebellion. At that time, the four gates of the North Station were opened wide, but there was no one to collect tickets.
>
> From the first to the eighth, the passenger trains from Shanghai to Nanjing and Hangzhou—which according to schedule should have numbered 21 per day—totaled only 17, and were, moreover, all late. The freight trains were supposed to number 23 a day, but in actuality numbered only 3. Measured in tonnage, only about 11% of the planned freight was actually hauled.[58]

The situation at the Port Authority was equally chaotic.

> Between the first and the ninth, the various districts under the Port Authority disbursed more than 14 million yuan. At the port, 5,904 people had left their jobs and, of a scheduled 90,000 tons of cargo, only 35,000 tons were loaded. In the nine days, more than 70 ships on average per day were idled by the lack of stevedores. One day, as many as 114 ships were held up.
>
> Of the 198 ships of the Shanghai Fishermen's Company, only 5 or 6 a day went out to sea. Less than 10% of a normal day's catch went to market.[59]

Industrial production was similarly affected. According to the transcript of a February 27, 1967, meeting of all Shanghai bureaus convened to "grasp revolution, promote production,"

> Textile Bureau: of the 11 companies under the bureau, 5 have been unable to complete their production plans for the season. The absentee rate in the bureau is now at 10%.
>
> Light Industry Bureau: of the 562 factories in the bureau, 308 have not fulfilled their January production responsibilities. In January, of 3,800 workers at a bicycle factory, 600 have gone elsewhere to exchange revolutionary experiences. As a result, in the electroplate workshop three shifts have been reduced to two, and even those two are not filled.[60]

Beginning in February, as units started to account for moneys disbursed during the wind of economism of the previous month, they demanded that workers return whatever handouts they had received. Some workers quickly complied, but many refused.

> One approach was to leave the money in the bank and take a wait-and-see attitude. A foodstuff company in Huangpu District (which supervised cooperative stores) disbursed 9,000 yuan; to date (June 6, 1967) only 82 yuan (0.1%) has been returned. A

worker at the foodstuffs company received 5,700 yuan in traveling expenses for a trip north, but because the trip never materialized he deposited the money in the bank and did not return it.

Another approach was to point out that "the Party Central document just talks about investigation and study, so it's possible that in [the] future supplemental payments will still be permitted." Rather than return the money immediately, they stressed that "this could be dealt with in the later stages of the movement." Others refused to repay the cash, with the simple argument that "the money I received was not economism."[61]

Some workers spent all their newfound wealth at once and had no immediate means of returning it. For example, the apprentice who used his money to get married could not repay the sum when it was demanded of him. So every month, 15 yuan, nearly one-third of his wage, was deducted from his paycheck to make up for the allocation. Even so, it took him more than four years to pay off the debt.[62]

After the crackdown against economism, most of the temporary and contract workers and repatriated workers were sent back to the countryside, where it was extremely difficult to recover any money that had been issued to them. By April 1967, the two commercial bureaus had recouped only 488,000 yuan, a sum that represented less than half of what they had disbursed.[63]

Redressing Grievances

Although most of the organizations that had formed spontaneously during the wind of economism were soon suppressed,[64] a number of the demands raised in that period later came to be accepted as official policy. For example, in late 1968, apprenticeships were set at variable periods, ranging from half a year to three years, depending upon the skills to be acquired. Differences between union and nonunion members in medical and other welfare provisions were abolished in 1971 by the Shanghai Labor Bureau. At the same time, temporary workers who had entered Shanghai factories before 1966 were converted to permanent status.[65]

These changes were certainly a reaction to the economistic pressures of early 1967. Sobered by the widespread labor discontent that manifested itself on this occasion, authorities took steps to placate the restive workforce. There were, however, obvious limits to the redress of grievances. The emphasis was clearly on mollifying the workers residing in Shanghai, among whom the potential for creating urban unrest was greatest. Repatriated workers enjoyed no such consideration. The promises that had been made to them in 1960 concerning their future return to the city were not acted on for twenty years. And even in the 1980s, they were only permitted to have one of their children return to Shanghai to work.

As an outburst by the downtrodden elements of Chinese socialism, the cry for worker justice is well explained by a conventional focus on socioeconomic divisions. This approach has stressed the influence of favored versus disfavored backgrounds in generating a kind of "interest group" behavior among ordinary Chinese. Hong Yung Lee's characterization of rebel mass organizations as comprising disprivileged social groups—"from the smaller, poorer factories, the contract and temporary workers, the apprentices and unskilled workers"[66]—is an accurate portrait of those who spearheaded the wind of economism.

Previous scholarship has erred in conflating economism with the rebel movement. Followers of both rebel and conservative organizations quickly joined the clamor for improved compensation, but the rebel leadership was careful to distinguish its basically political objectives from the materialistic upsurge. Unlike either rebellion or conservatism, economism was in essence a protest against the socioeconomic inequities of the command economy. Groups of workers criticized the administrative methods that arbitrarily divided them into different categories with differential access to benefits. Those least favored by the system—contract and temporary workers, relocated workers, apprentices, collective and private sector employees—raised the most strident complaints. In pointing the finger of blame at the flagrant injustices inherent in the operations of China's socialist system, economism represented in some respects a more fundamental criticism than did the rebel movement.

5

Renegade Rebels:
Regiments and Lian Si

Battles between rebels and conservatives were mercifully brief and bloodless in Shanghai as compared to many other Chinese cities in which the January power seizure unleashed a torrent of hostility between attackers and defenders of the powers-that-be. In Shanghai the swift demise of the Scarlet Guards effectively eliminated the conservative alternative. This did not mean, however, that the city was thenceforth free from disruptive strife. Instead, battles erupted within the rebel camp itself.

Led by hot-headed individuals for whom the Cultural Revolution presented a chance to transcend their previous marginality, the rebel groups composing the Workers' General Headquarters had always formed an uneasy partnership at best. With the establishment of revolutionary committees from the municipal level down to basic work units—a process that began in February 1967 and continued for several months thereafter, internecine warfare exploded within the rebel ranks.

According to incomplete official statistics, Shanghai witnessed 156 armed battles during the latter half of April 1967. In just the first eight days of May, more than 140 such incidents occurred—an average of eighteen a day. The weapons ranged from bricks, stones, wooden staves, bamboo spears and iron poles to nitric acid, ammonia, guns, and even fire engines. The confrontations were often sizable in scale and costly in casualties. For example, a battle at the Number 9 Cotton Mill drew participants from nearly two hundred work units across the city; some forty combatants were wounded in the conflict, sixteen of them seriously. The level of violence escalated over time: the more than 150 battles that erupted in the first half of August resulted in 4,500 injuries and twelve fatalities.[1] Despite a thin veneer of ideological debate (with rival leaders accusing one another of "rightist opportunism"), these struggles had more to do with power and personalities than with political principles.

Internal Challengers: Regiments

For some time after its establishment, the Workers' General Headquarters was little more than a loose amalgam of rebel outfits from various factories throughout the city. The independent personalities of the "old rebels" militated against submissive obedience to the dictates of any single leading organization. Shortly after its inauguration, the WGH faced an internal threat from the five "regiments" (*bingtuan*) ostensibly under its command. These regiments included:

1. The Shanghai Workers' Revolutionary Rebel General Headquarters First Regiment Returned to Shanghai from Beijing (known colloquially as the "First Regiment").
2. The Shanghai Workers' Revolutionary Rebel General Headquarters Second Regiment Returned to Shanghai from Beijing (known colloquially as the "Second Regiment").
3. The Shanghai Workers' Revolutionary Rebel General Headquarters Third Regiment Returned to Shanghai from Beijing (known colloquially as the "Third Regiment").
4. The Shanghai Workers' Revolutionary Rebel Headquarters Steel Regiment (known colloquially as the "Steel Regiment").
5. The Shanghai Workers' Revolutionary Rebel Field Regiment (known colloquially as the "Field Regiment").

The First, Second, and Third Regiments were all outgrowths of the Anting Incident. Attempting to take their case to Beijing, one group of worker rebels had boarded a north-bound train, which was later stopped at Nanjing. Another party was halted at Anting Station, on the outskirts of Shanghai. Yet a third contingent never managed to get on a train, but walked to Anting to link up with the rebels being detained there. After Zhang Chunqiao went to Anting to negotiate with Wang Hongwen and Pan Guoping, most of their followers returned to Shanghai and formed the bulk of the old rebels loyal to the WGH. However, some of those assembled at Anting refused to go home and instead marched on to Suzhou. Only after Zhang Chunqiao went in person to Suzhou for direct negotiations with this group did its members finally return to Shanghai.

The outfit that was detained in Nanjing later formed the First Regiment, under the leadership of Dai Zuxiang. The band that returned from Suzhou, led by Geng Jinzhang, established the Second Regiment. The Third Regiment was a much smaller organization, comprising those who had set off for Anting by foot. Refusing simply to hand over their followers to the Workers' General Headquarters, leaders of these three regiments chided the WGH for "opportunism" in having rushed back to Shanghai from Anting. In February 1967, members of the Second Regiment issued a handbill, entitled "The Second Regiment was Born in the Midst of Revolutionary Storm," which justified their defiance as a natural reaction to the WGH's callous disregard for their "revolutionary struggles."

Several days after returning to Shanghai from Suzhou, the Workers' General Head-quarters still had sent no one to inquire about us. We repeatedly sought contact with the WGH on our own initiative, but we were never given admission to the main gate of their offices and could never make contact with anyone in a position of authority.[2]

This was the official rationalization for the split, as presented in a public handbill. A more complete explanation was provided by Sun Yuxi, a leader of the Second Regiment imprisoned in the Yangpu District Public Security Office in February 1967 by the WGH. When pressed about why he had helped to mobilize a competing rebel force, Sun offered the following answer:

First, at that time the WGH top leadership was in a state of disarray and we feared it could not withstand attack. We were apprehensive about entering its ranks and were therefore reluctant to disband our own organization.

Second, when we returned to Shanghai, the Shanghai Party Committee assigned more than 30 people to our case. They encouraged us to disperse and return to our original work units to "grasp revolution and promote production." We assumed this was a plot of the SPC and thus believed it necessary to preserve the regiment.

Third, we felt that the WGH didn't value us highly. When we went to collect provisions we weren't given any. So we believed that if the regiment were disbanded our subsequent status would be even more precarious.

Fourth, we worried that if the regiment were dissolved our former achievements would amount to naught and the CR would be adversely affected.

Fifth, we feared that as soon as the regiment was disbanded and we had "turned our swords into plowshares" by returning to work we would become identified with counterrevolution.[3]

When First Regiment leader Dai Zuxiang testified in 1979 about why he had previously mobilized an alternative force, his explanation was consistent with that of Sun Yuxi. Dai recalled that in late November 1966, after he had led his forces back from Nanjing,

We opened an office on Wuyuan Road to serve as a temporary reception post for re-turned workers. The evening after we moved into the new offices, [Second Regiment leader] Geng Jinzhang came over to say that we must guarantee that those comrades who had returned from Nanjing and Suzhou would be protected from attack in their factories and that we must help them in resolving any difficulties they might en-counter back in the factories. He advocated working together to establish a united regiment. Out of selfish considerations, I agreed to help found such an organization.[4]

From these firsthand accounts it seems clear that the splinter activities of the regiments were not the reflection of any basic ideological disagreement within the WGH. The situation at the time was chaotic and the rebels feared that they would be attacked after reentering their factories. Leery of becoming embroiled in the conflicts in which the WGH was already implicated, they decided to seek refuge under their own banner.

A key impetus for the renegade movement lay in the desire of the regiment leaders to safeguard their own freedom of action. In Suzhou and Nanjing these old rebels had acted independently for some period of time and had even engaged in separate negotiations with Zhang Chunqiao. Were they simply to be absorbed into the WGH, their own records of rebellion would amount to nothing.

The largest of the rebel contenders, the Second Regiment, grew rapidly from an initial membership of 100,000 at the time of the Anting Incident in November 1966 to more than 500,000 just three months later.[5] The period of greatest expansion occurred after the Kangping Road Incident of late December 1966, with the incorporation of a large contingent of defeated rank-and-file Scarlet Guards.

When the WGH later criticized Geng Jinzhang for setting up an independent kingdom upon his return from Suzhou, Geng defended himself by saying that, at that time, it had been very hard to make contact with Wang Hongwen or Pan Guoping. Afraid of being attacked by Scarlet Guards, the top commanders of the WGH moved about from one place to another and spent little time at the WGH offices. The offices themselves were also frequently relocated to evade enemy assault. By contrast, the Second Regiment publicized the location of its office and the intrepid Geng himself showed up there every day. Many workers thus found it easier to attach themselves to Geng's Second Regiment than to enlist under the banner of the WGH. The reach of the Second Regiment expanded commensurately. As Geng Jinzhang described his empire at its height,[6]

> In the ten districts of the city, as well as Minhang and Wusong [two large industrial districts in the suburbs of Shanghai], there were district-level branches. Anting had a regiment, and a Kunshan headquarters had been founded with help from three of our comrades. Wujing and Bengbu [also large industrial districts of greater Shanghai] had branches as well. Within the city proper, there was a paper manufacturing headquarters, an instruments regiment, a materials regiment, a foreign trade branch, a coal company, and a construction company branch. These were quite large. In all, the Second Regiment had somewhere between 500,000 and 600,000 members.
>
> Several hotels were also ours. The Nanjing Hotel, Jinjiang Hotel, Shanghai Mansion, Hengshan Guest House, Park Hotel, Peace Hotel, and Xinya Hotel [the city's largest hotels at the time], the Sino-Soviet Friendship Building, etc., all belonged to us. The Number 2 and Number 3 Stations of the public transport company were in our hands as well.[7]

Connections in the public transport sector afforded the Second Regiment easy access to vehicles with which to move personnel rapidly. For his main fighting force, Geng recruited a large contingent of disgruntled youths who had been working at state farms on Changxing Island. Given free lodging at the Shanghai Mansion in the heart of the city, the grateful youngsters were an effective source of committed combatants.[8]

The Second Regiment had become a formidable rebel organization in its own right. Although still claiming to be operating under the aegis of the Workers' General Headquarters, it was in fact challenging the hegemony of Wang Hongwen and the other top commanders of the WGH. That some of the leaders of the Second Regiment had explicit ambitions of setting up an independent rebel force was demonstrated as early as December 1966, when they advocated leaving the WGH altogether and changing their name to "Shanghai Workers' Revolutionary Rebel Committee." Several hundred armbands were actually printed up with the new appellation before it was learned that this particular name had already been assumed by another organization.[9]

A startling demonstration of his regiment's prowess occurred when the flamboyant Geng Jinzhang ordered his followers to seize SPC leaders Chen Pixian and Cao Diqiu. These symbols of discredited party authority were first imprisoned at the Second Regiment's offices and then (for fear that conservatives would come to rescue them) relocated at an egg factory on Xumin Highway, remote from the city center. Later, they were again transferred—this time to the Huangdu Feedlot in the suburbs. Any rebel organization wanting to criticize Chen and Cao first had to "borrow" them from the Second Regiment.[10]

Although less powerful than Geng's Second Regiment, the other regiments also created headaches for the fledgling WGH. First Regiment leader Dai Zuxiang made energetic efforts to mobilize new followers, claiming that in the Anting Incident it was his troops who had "suffered the most, accomplished the most." Although professing that his regiment was a subsidiary organization of the WGH, Dai refused to meet with Wang Hongwen or to participate in WGH initiatives.[11]

The Steel Regiment grew out of a branch of the WGH directed by a worker at the Shanghai Number 15 Radio Factory, Chen Hongkang. Originally, this outfit had served as a kind of palace guard for Wang Hongwen. In late 1966, when Scarlet Guard pressure on the WGH was severe, WGH offices were relocated to an elementary school on Hangzhou Road in Yangpu District; the Steel Regiment remained at the original office to guard the gate. At this time, Chen Hongkang still claimed, "I listen to the commands of Wang Hongwen alone." But on January 7, 1967, Chen declared his independence, changing the name of his organization to the Shanghai Workers' Revolutionary Rebel Number 3 Headquarters, or Workers' Third Headquarters. (This was in imitation of the Capital Red Third Headquarters of the Red Guards; Shanghai had no Second Workers' Headquarters.) The Workers' Third Headquarters commanded some 100,000 followers at this time.

The Steel Regiment's break with the WGH was prompted at least in part by a desire to procure independent financing for its activities.

WGH Steel Regiment leader Chen Hongkang had for some time harbored desires of setting up an independent kingdom and planned to hold an inaugural meeting for the Workers' Third Headquarters. Notices had already been printed up, but later he feared criticism from various mass organizations, so he temporarily called a halt to the plan. Chen Pixian saw an opportunity which he hoped to seize by saying, "It's all right for you to want money, but you have to have an independent organization and name with which to sign for it." Thereupon the Steel Regiment split off from the WGH and established the Workers' Third Headquarters.[12]

The situation of the Field Regiment was quite similar to that of the Workers' Third Headquarters. At the time of its inauguration, the Field Regiment issued only cards, not armbands, to its followers, and claimed to be aiding the WGH. However, in early 1967, the Field Regiment announced its independence and characterized itself as enjoying "fraternal relations" (i.e., egalitarian status) with the WGH.

Relations Between the Regiments and the WGH

The top command of the Workers' General Headquarters was of two minds about these fledgling regiments. Although many WGH leaders adamantly insisted on the need to disband the challengers, Wang Hongwen himself took a more tolerant attitude. Huang Jinhai remembered, "On the matter of the regiments we were in constant disagreement with Wang Hongwen. But Wang Hongwen was obeying Zhang Chunqiao, so we had no recourse. When Wang was head of the WGH, he seldom went to its offices, yet he frequently visited Geng Jinzhang's place. A lot of people in the WGH were unhappy about this."[13]

According to the notebook of Chen Bin, personal secretary to Wang Hongwen, a meeting specifically to discuss the regiment matter was held on the evening of December 27, 1966, in the conference room of the Shanghai Glass Machinery Factory. On that occasion, Wang Hongwen declared, "It's easy to issue an order to dissolve the regiments, but we have to take responsibility toward the revolutionary enterprise. To simply disband them would create major contradictions and conflicts."[14] Wang Hongwen's conciliatory attitude toward the Second Regiment in particular was in fact heavily influenced by Zhang Chunqiao. From the start, Zhang had thought highly of Geng Jinzhang. According to Geng's recollection, shortly after the Anting Incident Zhang summoned both Wang Hongwen and himself to the place where he was staying on Xingguo Road and told them,

> I must return to Beijing to make a progress report, but the work here in Shanghai is very pressing. In the WGH, you two are party members and thus bear a heavy burden. At present, the most important task in Shanghai is to mobilize the masses. The key points that must be seized are the railroads, the port, the municipal committee agencies, and especially Chen Pixian and Cao Diqiu.
>
> You two divide up the work, with Wang Hongwen in charge of the key points and Geng Jinzhang in charge of the overall picture.[15]

Later, during the Kangping Road Incident, Zhang Chunqiao had his secretary solicit Geng Jinzhang's help in subduing the Scarlet Guards. Geng's successful handling of this assignment contributed greatly to the fame of the Second Regiment. In early January 1967, after Zhang Chunqiao had returned to Shanghai, members of the Lian Si faction at the Shanghai Diesel Engine Factory (see the discussion later in this chapter) tried one night to scale the walls of the party compound to gain access to him. Thinking he was under attack, Zhang again called Geng to the rescue. In view of Zhang's debt of gratitude toward Geng, Wang Hongwen was reluctant to disband the Second Regiment.

Before the conservatives had been decisively routed in the January Revolution of 1967, rebel factions were united by their common enemy. Cooperation among these groups was essential in countering the numerically superior Scarlet Guards. As Zhang Chunqiao reportedly noted, "After the Anting Incident, the WGH relied on the Second Regiment to gain control of the situation. Without the Second Regiment, the very survival of the WGH would have been in jeopardy."[16]

Only after the conservatives had been thoroughly quashed could the WGH finally afford to turn its attention to the problem of internal dissension. On January 14, 1967, at a meeting to prepare for the Shanghai power seizure, Wang Hongwen announced that the regiments could not participate as independent organizations because they were all under the direction of the WGH. This precipitated a noisy row. According to the recollection of one participant in the meeting,

> Both sides pounded on the tables, upended benches, and jumped up on stools to give speeches. The main line of conflict was between the WGH of Wang Hongwen on one side and the WGH's Second Regiment of Geng Jinzhang on the other. Wang considered himself the representative of orthodoxy, while Geng believed that because he had so many followers and enjoyed the personal trust of Zhang Chunqiao he deserved to share in the spoils.[17]

With his forces having played a leading role in the Kangping Road Incident, Geng argued that the Second Regiment had earned the right to participate in the power seizure on an equal footing with the WGH. He later complained, "I thought: The Second Regiment has a substantial following, so why shouldn't it join the People's Commune?"[18]

Similarly, Dai Zuxiang recalled of his numerically smaller forces,

> Our First Regiment participated in the Anting Incident, and in the *Liberation Daily* Incident we were the first to rush into the newspaper office. During the Kangping Road Incident our regiment stood at the front lines and we also dispatched troops in the Kunshan Incident.[19]
>
> We always protected the WGH, but the WGH never recognized us, saying, "There is no such organization as the First Regiment under our jurisdiction."[20]

Unfortunately for the regiments' ambition of improving their status during the January Revolution, Zhang Chunqiao decided at this critical juncture to throw his full support behind Wang Hongwen. Eager to put an end to the wind of economism and to reestablish some semblance of government authority in the city, Zhang was willing to restrict the degree of worker participation in favor of a more orderly process. As Andrew Walder has argued, "The January Revolution was not a power seizure by workers' organizations . . . but an effort organized by Chang Ch'un-ch'iao [Zhang Chunqiao] to bring mass political action under control and to restore the normal operations of Shanghai's economy."[21]

Excluded from the January Revolution, the regiments became convinced of the need to unite in opposition to the WGH. On the same day that Wang Hongwen announced their exclusion from the power seizure, the regimental leaders proclaimed the formation of a "Shanghai Workers' Revolutionary Rebel Liaison Post," with fourteen constituent organizations.[22] Although the WGH was listed first on the roster of member organizations (followed by the First, Second, and Third Regiments and the Workers' Third Headquarters), this was only for the sake of appearances. Actually, the WGH was not notified about meetings of this amalgamated group of rebel challengers. In fact, at one such meeting a person was seized for interrogation on suspicion of being a spy for the WGH. Among the constituent organizations, only the First and Second Regiments and the Workers' Third Headquarters were well known. The other small and uninfluential groups were hoping to capitalize on the power of the Second Regiment by linking up with it.

When Wang Hongwen (advised by Zhang Chunqiao) decided in early February to set up a new power structure—dubbed the "Shanghai People's Commune"—to replace the toppled Shanghai Party Committee, he again refused to permit participation by the regiments on grounds that they were nothing more than appendages of the WGH. In response, Geng Jinzhang and his confederates expanded their liaison post to include thirty-six organizations in the "Grand Alliance Committee" (*da lianwei*) opposed to Wang Hongwen's Shanghai People's Commune.[23] The alliance announced plans to form its own power structure known as the "New Shanghai Commune."[24]

Hearing the news of this direct challenge, Zhang Chunqiao sought out Geng Jinzhang to indicate that he and Yao Wenyuan could not possibly endorse Geng's "new commune." However, Zhang also promised that, in the future, more rebel organizations would be permitted to join the Shanghai People's Commune. In deference to Zhang's wishes, Geng agreed to disband his Grand Alliance.[25]

On February 5, 1967, the inaugural ceremony for the Shanghai People's Commune was held at People's Plaza. Some thirty-eight rebel organizations participated in the founding. In referring to these participating organizations, Zhang Chunqiao proposed that the term "constituent units" (*zucheng danwei*) be changed to "founding units" (*faqi danwei*) so as to minimize arguments with organizations that had not participated.

The question of military involvement in the new power structure was a particularly sensitive issue. Writers' Group leader Xu Jingxian, in a 1970 interview with American journalist Edgar Snow, recalled,

Comrades [Zhang] Chunqiao and [Yao] Wenyuan reported our plans to the Chairman, who pointed out that, in addition to representatives of revolutionary masses, there should be revolutionary cadres and military representatives to compose "revolutionary triple combinations." After we received the Chairman's instructions, we postponed the meeting for two days to discuss our commune's organizational format according to the triple combination principle. We especially discussed the role of the military. Chen Pixian was first political commissar of the Shanghai military. If the military supported Chen, this would have created a big headache for us. . . . We insisted on criticism of Chen, supplying a large amount of material so that military comrades could see that Chen was a die-hard capitalist roader.[26]

As a consequence, the military—in the form of the Shanghai Garrison—participated only partially in the power seizure. Parris Chang explains, "Although the PLA adopted a hands-off policy before 1967 and had co-operated with the municipal authorities on some occasions, the central leadership, in a change of policy, had ordered PLA units to intervene on the side of the leftists on 23 January, and the Shanghai Garrison under commander Liao Cheng-kuo complied with the order and switched support to Chang [Zhang], thereby greatly strengthening his hand."[27]

As it turned out, however, Mao was not satisfied with the name "Shanghai People's Commune" for the new power structure. On February 12, he summoned Zhang and Yao to Beijing to insist that the new entity be called the "Shanghai Revolutionary Committee" (SRC). Twelve days later, another 10,000-person meeting was held to celebrate the name change.

Mao's initial silence on the Shanghai People's Commune—because of his reservations about both the organizational format and the nomenclature—fueled the hopes of the regiments. In early February, Geng Jinzhang often remarked, "Chairman Mao has not approved the People's Commune, the CRSG doesn't know about it, and *People's Daily* has not publicized it. With Party Central expressing no opinion, there's definitely a problem."[28] As late as February 14, Geng's Second Regiment issued a handbill proclaiming "We have always believed that if the views of the WGH were correct we would resolutely uphold them, but if the WGH could not raise high the banner of the Shanghai worker rebels, then we would have to do so."[29]

The conflict between the WGH and the regiments grew increasingly intense. Geng Jinzhang later remembered,

In mid-February, I called a meeting at a pharmaceutical factory of all the leaders of district branches of the Second Regiment—more than 300 people. I pushed the "down with Wang Hongwen" idea, and we even decided to seize Wang and fight a bloody battle to the end against his forces. We would not recognize the Shanghai People's Commune. Later, a similar meeting was convened at the Friendship Movie Theatre, and the spirit of the meeting was conveyed to the basic levels of the Second Regiment. At this time [WGH leaders] Chen Ada and Huang Jinhai were leading their followers to attack our basic-level organizations, generating armed struggles at the

Shanghai Cement Plant, the Number 8 Plastics Factory, the Number 5 Steel Mill, etc. I even went to Zhongshan Hospital to visit wounded members of the Second Regiment. We issued notices warning that responsiblity for the dire consequences would have to be borne by the WGH. I phoned Zhang Chunqiao, but couldn't get him on the line. When members of the basic-level branches sought me out, I wanted them to stand their ground and prepare to retaliate.[30]

At first, Wang Hongwen had treated the various regiments rather differently. The Second Regiment, although the most powerful, had, after all, accomplished some important tasks for the WGH, and it enjoyed a close relationship with Zhang Chunqiao. Thus, initially, Wang called on only the other regiments to disband, admonishing the rank and file to join the WGH as individual followers. WGH leader Ye Changming testified,

In handling relations between the WGH and other mass organizations as the "sole revolutionaries," we tried to swallow up the lesser outfits. For example, there was a small organization known as the "Workers' Oppose Thoroughly," which had repeatedly requested to join the WGH and even indicated that it would be completely subservient to us, retaining only its name. But we refused. All other organizations had to disband before they could be permitted to join the basic ranks of the WGH.[31]

Only the Second Regiment of Geng Jinzhang was allowed to retain its own identity. Wang Hongwen indicated that even if the Second Regiment refused to disband it should be absorbed. He encouraged the Second Regiment to move into the offices of the WGH and cooperate in directing the rebel movement, giving Second Regiment leader Sun Yuxi the title of "picket brigade captain" in the WGH and providing him with his own office space in the building on the bund, which had formerly housed the SFTU and was now occupied by the WGH. However, several rounds of conciliatory talks in this vein failed to achieve results. Ye Changming remembered,

The influence of Geng Jinzhang in the WGH was immense. He was Wang Hongwen's most significant rival. Huang Jinhai and I always feared that the expansion of the power of the Second Regiment would undermine the status of the WGH. At first we advocated abolishing the regiment organizations. But Wang Hongwen wouldn't hear of it. Not until February–March 1967, when Wang Hongwen believed he was in a more secure position and began to see the regiments as a threat to himself, did he decide to demolish them. Our strategy was to present the WGH as a united organization that could not accommodate independent organizations within it so as to force the regiments to disband of their own accord. But several chats with Geng Jinzhang failed to win his concurrence.[32]

Geng later insisted, "I myself agreed to move into the WGH, and conduct business alongside them, but the members of the standing committee disagreed. I argued with them for quite a while, but they still refused so there was no choice but to forget it."[33]

The public reason for the Second Regiment's not amalgamating was that several of its standing committee members disliked Pan Guoping, Chen Ada, and Huang Jinhai of the WGH, considering them ruffians (*liumang afei*). But in view of Geng Jinzhang's own unsavory reputation, this rationale was hardly convincing. The primary consideration was reluctance on the part of the Second Regiment to relinquish its hard-won power. Later Sun Yuxi acknowledged, "At that time we feared a plot of the WGH, thinking amalgamation was just a word under which we would actually be disbanded. Thus we refused to merge with them."[34]

The unwillingness of these standing committee members to amalgamate also involved another concern that they were loath to disclose publicly: the unwelcome prospect of returning to their factories as ordinary workers. In heading a semiautonomous regiment, the Second Regiment leaders continued to draw wages from their original work units without actually showing up for work. Having tasted the excitement of political participation, they were unenthusiastic about returning to monotonous factory routines. If the regiments amalgamated with the WGH, the great majority of standing committee members would lose their administrative status and thus be forced back to work.

The recalcitrance of the rival regiments prompted Wang Hongwen to seize the initiative. On February 11, 1966, the WGH issued a notice.

> Originally the First, Second and Third Regiments were a subsidiary of our headquarters, but some of their leaders instigated conflicts and factionalism and for a long time opposed the general headquarters. Now the above three regiments and our headquarters have no organizational links whatsoever. The Workers' Third Headquarters is an independent organization born of conflict and has no connection at all with our headquarters.[35]

This announcement by the WGH indicated that the conflict with the regiments had already reached a showdown. A few days later, Geng Jinzhang mobilized several hundred truckloads of his followers for a boisterous demonstration, punctuated by shouts of "Down with Wang Hongwen!" In a move that foreshadowed the demands of student protesters during the Tiananmen Uprising of 1989, Geng's followers posted notices around the city calling for a televised debate between their leader and Wang Hongwen. The demonstrators concluded their show of strength by surrounding the Number 17 Cotton Mill, where they attempted—unsuccessfully—to drag forth Wang Hongwen for a public reckoning.[36]

On February 24, Zhang Chunqiao returned to Shanghai to convene the first committee meeting of the Shanghai People's Commune. He conveyed Mao's wishes that the commune be transformed into the Shanghai Revolutionary Committee and in his speech touched on the question of dissolution of the regiments. Senior cadre Ma Tianshui later remembered that it was at this juncture that Zhang Chunqiao decided to make explicit his preference for Wang Hongwen over rival Geng Jinzhang: "Zhang Chunqiao said to me that he had met individually many times with both Wang Hongwen and Geng Jinzhang. He said he felt that Wang was superior to Geng and thus he supported the WGH."[37]

That evening, Wang Hongwen sought out the most adamant opponent of the regiments, Huang Jinhai, to convey the long-awaited message: "Zhang Chunqiao agrees; now is the time."[38] The next day, Geng Jinzhang was seized and imprisoned in the Yangpu District Public Security Bureau. Soon Dai Zuxiang of the First Regiment and Chen Hongkang of the Workers' Third Headquarters were also apprehended. Reading the handwriting on the wall, the Field Regiment hastily announced its amalgamation with the WGH; its leaders thereby avoided incarceration. A founder of the WGH, Fan Zuodong, recalled,

> At first Wang Hongwen was unwilling to dissolve the regiments. I always advocated dissolution, as did the great majority of WGH leaders. We all felt that the existence of the regiments sowed dissension at the basic ranks, leading to factionalism in the factories. Moreover, we disapproved of Geng Jinzhang's crude style. He believed [that] the WGH was an empty shell and that real power lay in his own hands.
>
> In the end, Wang Hongwen's decision to seize Geng Jinzhang was made possible because Zhang Chunqiao said at a Small [Group] meeting, "In future I will not protect Geng Jinzhang."
>
> Actually the power and political influence of the Second Regiment did not match that of the WGH. I felt that the rank-and-file workers in Shanghai joined the regiments because of the prestige of the WGH. People didn't know that the regiments and the WGH were vying for autonomy; they were under the mistaken impression that we were one family. All we had to do was to issue a notification explaining that these regiments had no connection to the WGH and that the WGH didn't recognize the regiments as their subordinates and no one would follow them.[39]

After Geng Jinzhang's detention, his Second Regiment was accused of having developed so rapidly only because "it absorbed all the organizations with different viewpoints from the WGH and all the organizations that the WGH had refused to authorize."[40] The same strong arm tactics that had been used against the Scarlet Guards were now being applied with equal effect against the rebel challengers.

Although Zhang Chunqiao's decision to withdraw his support was the critical factor in Geng's demise, Zhang was not immediately informed of the depths to which his erstwhile client had plunged. Only after Geng had been incarcerated for more than two months did Zhang actually learn of the matter. He ordered an immediate release, enabling Geng to return home on May 3. Zhang continued to press for Geng's collaboration with the WGH. Later, Wang Xiuzhen recalled Zhang's Chunqiao's words at the time.

> Geng Jinzhang is meritorious. . . . Wang Hongwen had him imprisoned, but if I had known of it I would not have agreed to it.
>
> You should not think poorly of "Commander Geng" because his Second Regiment remains powerful. After the Anting Incident, I talked with him individually on a number of occasions. I understand him; he is a person with great rebel spirit who can lead the ranks and command in battle.[41]

Perturbed as he may have been about Geng's arrest, Zhang Chunqiao could not condone the Second Regiment's challenge to the WGH. Soon after his release, Geng participated in a meeting of some forty or fifty WGH leaders with Zhang Chunqiao. Zhang greeted him with a rebuke.

You've been released. You've been put to great inconvenience. How many times did I tell you not to form an independent kingdom? But your kingdom grew larger and larger and in the end you created dissension. You didn't listen to what I said. It was necessary to offer you protection, otherwise Shanghai would have experienced great chaos. Had you not been detained, the newly born agencies in Shanghai would have been in danger of annihilation. You people just looked out for yourselves, becoming a sheet of loose sand. How could that situation have been controlled?

Had you not agitated for an independent kingdom, Shanghai would have been more peaceful. In future, it'll be up to you. Look, Wang Hongwen is more solid than you. I hope you will unite.[42]

Initially, Geng had been assigned to the industrial division of the WGH, under Chen Ada. When the industrial division was transferred to the city revolutionary committee, Geng was reassigned to the political propaganda division of the WGH. Later he became deputy-director of the basic construction division of the Bureau of Light Industry.

Although Geng Jinzhang was gradually demoted from a top commander of the WGH to an obscure figure on the Shanghai scene, his connections to the WGH still afforded considerable advantages. In 1969 and again in 1973, when charges of economic crimes were brought against Geng, Wang Hongwen insisted, "Unless Zhang Chunqiao gives the nod, no one can move against Geng Jinzhang."[43] When Geng requested a larger residence, Ma Tianshui relocated him at once. When Geng complained that he was in financial straits, Wang Xiuzhen on several occasions approved a cash subsidy for him. When Geng's wife, a worker at a neighborhood cooperative, wrote a letter to Wang Hongwen requesting a better job, Wang Xiuzhen immediately arranged for her to enter the Shanghai Number 1 Tire Factory as a permanent worker.[44] Geng was particularly appreciative of the arrangements made for his wife. In 1974, during the Criticize Lin Biao–Criticize Confucius campaign, he commissioned someone to write a summary of his thoughts in which, after deprecating his own contribution to the revolution, he praised that of Wang Hongwen. Geng presented the summary to Wang Xiuzhen, who thought it was excellent and immediately had copies made for Wang Hongwen and other WGH commanders.[45]

Some of the other regiment leaders suffered a good deal more than Geng. Dai Zuxiang was imprisoned until March 1968, after which he became an ordinary factory worker. Chen Hongkang was once again arrested after his release in 1968 and was only freed in 1973 to return to his factory as a common laborer. Many subordinate regiment leaders were subjected to repeated imprisonment and interrogation.

Lian Si: A New Constellation of Anti-WGH Forces

Having weathered the threat posed by the unruly regiments, the Workers' General Headquarters soon found itself faced with another challenge to its leadership. The new rivalry came from "Lian Si" (Allied Command), a rebel organization based in the Shanghai Diesel Engine Factory.

The Diesel Engine Factory had been founded by the famous minister of finance under the KMT, T. V. Soong, but after the Communist victory it was taken over by the Shanghai city government. By the time of the CR, the factory operated under the direct supervision of the Number 8 Machine Bureau of the State Council. With a workforce of nearly 10,000, it ranked as China's largest diesel engine factory. Throughout the first seventeen years of the PRC, the factory was considered an "advanced enterprise" and occupied a pivotal position in the industrial economy of Shanghai.

As a major producer of diesel engines for military use, the plant enjoyed a close relationship with the navy. One of the workshops in the factory had for some time been supervised directly by military representatives sent from the navy to assist with production. Moreover, many demobilized naval cadres were assigned to the diesel plant. The number of these demobilized naval officers increased substantially after 1958, with most of them serving at the *workshop* level. By contrast, the majority of *factory*-level cadres at the plant were locals.

As a Red Guard, who was a member of the Shanghai Diesel Engine Factory investigation team, later noted, the cadre situation had a major influence on the development of factionalism at the plant.

> Their many years of military life had imbued these demobilized sailors with a particular work style and mind set. During successive political campaigns, the demobilized sailors were more leftist than the local cadres and more apt to subject people to criticism. This was principally due to the fact that political work received particular emphasis in the military, especially from the 1960s on, when the PLA stressed "class struggle" more than society at large. Furthermore, the military cadres lacked technical competence. [Because they had] been assigned as cadres, their management style consisted of "grasping politics" and "grasping class struggle." Local cadres, by contrast, were relatively familiar with the production process and more comfortable in using techniques of persuasion and education rather than coercion. The locals had little patience for demobilized sailors who talked in empty political slogans.
>
> Over the long haul, these interpersonal relations generated latent contradictions between the former military cadres and the local cadres. The contradictions erupted over issues like cadre promotions [and] wage increases . . . and especially during political campaigns like the CR.[46]

Conflicts among cadres were a common phenomenon in Shanghai factories. At the Shanghai Diesel Engine Plant, the main division was between demobilized military cadres and local cadres; at other factories, however, it was between intellectual cadres and worker-peasant cadres, or between cadres who had served in the "white areas" (Japanese and KMT-occupied territory) and cadres who had worked in the Communist-base areas during the revolutionary era. Whatever the initial dividing lines, tensions were exacerbated by previous political campaigns in which grudges had developed over who criticized whom. Some of these animosities grew out of differences in political principles or policies, but the more common complaints concerned personalities and work styles.

Because the diesel plant had a pre-1949 history as a KMT-operated factory, many of the senior workers had been KMT members. After 1949, these "elder workers"—who should, under normal circumstances, have been the backbone of Communist party strength at the factory—were considered politically unreliable. Their former KMT ties meant a black mark in their dossiers that rendered them targets of struggle in successive political campaigns.

Misgivings escalated when on several occasions in the 1950s someone was seen launching signal flares from a vegetable garden located near the diesel plant. The perpetrator was never caught, but the behavior was generally thought to have been the work of a KMT secret agent, leading to further suspicion of the former KMT members at the factory. When the Four Cleans movement was introduced to the plant in 1964, the elder workers became primary targets of struggle. The campaign was carried out by cadres dispatched from the navy, who called upon the factory's armed militia (comprising activists and party and Youth League members) to rough up the struggle targets. Long-standing animosities among ordinary workers at the factory were intensified by the brutal manner in which the Four Cleans was executed.

In this charged atmosphere, an alleged "KO counterrevolutionary clique" was uncovered at the factory, when some workshop cadres noticed that many of the younger workers had scratched the English initials "KO" onto their leather belts. Some of these same youngsters had posted inflammatory slogans on the factory walls, designed to incense their elders: "We can't but feel ashamed that half a month's wage is barely enough to buy a pair of leather shoes!" "Our spring has already lost its radiance!" "Let's hold dance parties at once!" "Long live women!"[47]

Most of the young workers lived in the factory dormitory or in the workers' residential district adjoining the factory. Far removed from the city center, recreational activities were virtually nonexistent, and leisure time often spelled boredom. Moreover, the economy had barely recovered from the disastrous period of 1959–1962, and material pleasures were still in short supply. It was hardly surprising that disgruntled youths with time on their hands would turn to countercultural means of entertainment. Like many of the top leaders of the Workers' General Headquarters, the "KO" adherents were searching for some means of self-expression in the highly constrained environment of Maoist China. Nevertheless, in openly airing their frustrations, these young people were branded as dangerous elements. Although the selection of the "KO" insignia had been intended playfully (perhaps as a pun on the English word "okay," perhaps as an abbreviation for "knockout"), it was misconstrued as the secret password of some clandestine organization. Thus a "KO counterrevolutionary clique" was conjured up.[48] Altogether some thirty to forty youths were accused of participation in the organization.[49]

During the Four Cleans and its aftermath, cadres mobilized party members and activists to attack, first, the former KMT members and, then, the alleged "KO conspirators" among the workforce. This recent history of internal strife structured lines of factional conflict within the workforce that erupted during the Cultural Revolution.

When the CR began, workers divided over the issue of how to evaluate the factory director. Director Zhu was a local cadre; and some characterized him as "a traitor, a capitalist roader, and a time bomb waiting to explode," whereas others regarded him quite favorably. On September 15, 1966, the anti-Zhu faction established an "East is Red Headquarters" with some 2,300 followers.[50] Exactly one week later the pro-Zhu forces founded the "Shanghai Diesel Revolutionary Rebel Allied Command"—known as "Lian Si"—with 3,000 members.[51]

The great majority of demobilized sailors among the cadres—who were concentrated at the workshop level—supported East is Red's attack on the factory director. Workers who enjoyed good relations with their shop floor cadres also tended to join the anti-Zhu East is Red faction. Thus this faction was composed heavily of party members, Youth League members, and older workers and cadres with "clean" political records. Militia members who had carried out the Four Cleans assault against former KMT members at the factory just two years earlier were especially well represented among its ranks.

A number of ordinary workers, especially those who had been criticized during previous campaigns, resented the workshop cadres. These disgruntled workers insisted that the real capitalist roaders were the shop floor cadres themselves. Charging that East is Red's "rebellion" against Factory Director Zhu was nothing more than an effort by the basic-level cadres to save their own skins, workers with an axe to grind against their immediate supervisors joined Lian Si.

As was generally the case with factory factionalism during the CR, a decision to join Lian Si or East is Red grew out of previous personal relationships. Within factories, friendships had solidified into "circles" (*quanzi*) comprising workers with roughly comparable social status and educational backgrounds, who felt an emotional bond with each another. Successive political campaigns had imbued workers with an acute sense of insecurity, inclining them to rely heavily on their circle of friends.[52] Individual calculations and preferences were readily subordinated to the lead of opinion-makers in one's particular circle.

Political ideology took a definite backseat to personal connections in shaping the lines of conflict at the diesel plant. As the constituency on whom the workshop cadres had relied during the Four Cleans, members of East is Red protected these cadres and followed their example in pointing the finger of blame at the factory directors. By contrast, Lian Si members' resentment of the workshop cadres resulted in a more positive attitude toward their superiors at the factory level.

In one sense, the Shanghai Diesel Engine Plant was typical of factories throughout the country during the CR: Two hostile factions split over whether to attack or protect particular party leaders along lines in which long-standing disputes among cadres dovetailed with personal rivalries and relationships among workers. But in the leadership and composition of its WGH-affiliated "rebel" forces, the diesel engine case was unusual: The East is Red rebels were drawn overwhelmingly from party and Youth League members and included others with "good" records of conduct. This peculiarity, it would soon become clear, rendered the situation at the diesel plant highly volatile.

The two factions at the diesel engine plant characterized each other (both groups with some justification) as dyed-in-the-wool "old conserves." Wang Hongwen once remarked, "Any organization with a large number of party and League members is without question an old conserve organization." By this criterion, East is Red certainly qualified for the designation. However, in fingering Factory Director Zhu as its object of struggle, the East is Red group was assuredly acting as a rebel organization.

Factory Director Zhu had long enjoyed close relations with the Shanghai Party Committee. East is Red insisted that the SPC's patronage of Zhu was an issue of line that required, first, criticizing Zhu and, then, getting to the root of the trouble—the SPC itself. The anti-Zhu forces were therefore also anti-SPC. Thus the East is Red faction participated as part of the combined forces of the WGH in the Anting Incident, the *Liberation Daily* Incident, and the Kangping Road Incident—the three "revolutionary" initiatives of worker rebels in Shanghai.[53]

Later, when the fierce struggle at the diesel engine plant attracted the attention of the entire city, many student Red Guard organizations sent special Small Groups to the factory for on-the-spot investigations. A common finding was that

East is Red is not only an authentic rebel organization of the Shanghai Diesel Engine Plant; it also stands as an authentic rebel organization of the entire Shanghai region. The criterion for an "authentic" rebel organization lies not only in its opposition to the capitalist roaders in the SPC but, more important, in that the mainstay of its membership is drawn from party and League members and activists. During the CR these people must rise up in rebellion. However, this type of authentic rebel faction is actually very rare. In all of China, only at the Shanghai Diesel Engine Plant are class relations clear.[54]

These student observers hoped that proletarian "rebellion" during the CR would be spearheaded by workers who had been regarded as reliable party backers during the pre–Cultural Revolution era. Clearly, the rival Lian Si faction did not accord with this view. Lian Si attracted a large number of young and obscure workers, most of those designated as the "KO clique" during the Four Cleans, and others (including former KMT members) who had been targets of struggle in successive campaigns. Like many rebel outfits at other factories, Lian Si's motley composition contributed to an explosive demeanor. Indeed, according to the recollection of one Red Guard who participated in an investigation of the Shanghai Diesel Engine Plant, Lian Si was actually the more radical faction.

> For seventeen years they had been oppressed; the oppressed are the most revolutionary. Moreover, their rebellion was directed against the workshop cadres. These workshop cadres were all their immediate superiors and held their fate in their hands. To engage in this type of rebellion entailed great personal risk. Thus they were the authentic rebels. How could the actions of the East is Red be considered rebellion? They were rebelling against the SPC, but the SPC was far removed from them and incapable of retaliating against factory workers. This type of risk-free rebellion didn't count as rebellion. Furthermore, members of the East is Red protected their immediate superiors, so they were old conserves rather than rebels. Only those rebels who dared to rebel against their immediate superiors were authentic rebels.[55]

No matter how "authentic" Lian Si's rebellion may have been, the organization committed a number of strategic errors in its pursuit of its rebel objectives. Appreciating the need to link up with an all-city umbrella organization to buttress its immediate strength and ensure its long-term security, Lian Si decided to apply to Wang Hongwen's WGH for admission. As it turned out, however, the more politically astute workshop cadres had beaten Lian Si to the punch. A few days before the Lian Si representatives reached the WGH offices to plead their case, East is Red leaders had already secured WGH recognition. Unable to affiliate with the premier rebel organization, and more concerned with their parochial factory struggle than with the larger political implications of their actions, Lian Si turned to the Scarlet Guards as a means of bolstering their challenge to East is Red. Welcomed into the ranks of the conservatives, Lian Si subsequently participated as a vital force in all of the Scarlet Guards' major initiatives.

After the dissolution of the Scarlet Guards, Lian Si's leaders appreciated the seriousness of their strategic error and endeavored to redeem their reputation. A small organization with which Lian Si enjoyed friendly relations was connected to the Yangpu District Branch of the WGH, so Lian Si announced itself as a brigade of that branch in an attempt to establish an eleventh-hour affiliation with the WGH. However, as it turned out, the Yangpu Branch was not directly under Wang Hongwen. As a result, when Wang moved to eliminate opposition to his leadership within the WGH in early 1967, the Yangpu District Branch was crushed.[56]

Faced with this setback, Lian Si made a daring attempt to outmaneuver its rivals by going directly to Zhang Chunqiao. Upon learning one night that Zhang was back in Shanghai, Lian Si leaders went to his residence to request a personal meeting. To their surprise, they were stopped outside the gate by security guards. A few intrepid Lian Si members thereupon scaled the walls of the compound. Thinking that he was under attack, Zhang immediately telephoned Geng

Jinzhang of the Second Regiment to request help. The next day, this incident was portrayed in the press as "Lian Si terrorists attack Comrade Zhang Chunqiao's home."

The alleged assault on Zhang Chunqiao, misunderstood though it was, escalated tensions between the two factions at the diesel engine plant. East is Red requested assistance from the WGH, whereupon Wang Hongwen dispatched more than two hundred people, including Public Security police, to advance on the diesel engine plant and seize Lian Si leaders.[57] Lian Si members quickly surrounded this group, prompting Wang Hongwen to send more than 10,000 additional adherents to the factory in a counterencirclement. In this encounter some two hundred Lian Si followers were apprehended and taken to the Yangpu District Public Security Bureau.[58]

The incident resulted in an open declaration of war by Lian Si on Wang Hongwen's rebel headquarters. As Lian Si leaders saw it,

> Considering themselves to be the elder brother among Shanghai's rebel factions, WGH was always going around interfering with CR activities in other units, attacking and crushing those who disagreed with them. This was revolutionary solipsism (weiwo duge). We of Lian Si refused to buy this. The CR meant liberating oneself. No one could serve as nursemaid and no one could always be correct.[59]

Annoying though it was, Lian Si's opposition to the WGH was not terribly threatening, so long as its reach remained limited to the diesel plant. However, after February 1967 the situation changed dramatically, thanks to the intervention of a person known during the CR as Quan Xiangdong (an alias meaning "completely partial to [Mao Ze]dong"), a teaching assistant at Jiaotong University, whose real name was Tang Fukun. On February 19, Quan held a very cordial meeting with leaders of Lian Si. He especially hit it off with a technician in the foundry shop of the diesel plant who had recently completed a degree in mechanics at Qinghua University. As fellow university graduates, the two men had much in common.

Quan Xiangdong concurred with the viewpoint of Lian Si that since most of the East is Red members had been beneficiaries of the previous seventeen years they could not be considered true rebels, whereas the Lian Si partisans, having been oppressed in the past, qualified as authentic rebels. He charged, "Shanghai's leadership authority is not in the hands of the proletariat," and "Shanghai needs another period of great chaos!" Quan's ideas were not antirebel or anti–Cultural Revolution, but were concerned with the questions of who qualified as genuine rebels and who should assume control in the aftermath of the power seizure. His opposition was aimed above all at the hegemony of the WGH and its backstage supporter, Zhang Chunqiao.

Quan proposed that Lian Si seek support from society at large and, under the name of a worker-student movement, mobilize public sympathy against the WGH. Together with the chair of the revolutionary committee at the Shanghai

Automobile Parts Factory, Chen Puchang, he advocated establishing a series of liaison posts (*lianluo zhan*) across the city to support the activities of the Lian Si. This bold recommendation was immediately adopted. With a clear organizational alternative now available, groups holding a grudge against the WGH were quick to enlist under the Lian Si banner. Lian Si liaison posts sprang up across the city; a "little support–Lian Si post" was even established for children.

On the surface, the support–Lian Si liaison posts looked like a new organizational development, but to a large extent they were simply a realliance of groups that had previously suffered run-ins with the WGH. Units disbanded by the WGH (e.g., First Regiment, Second Regiment, Third Regiment, and Workers' Third Headquarters), organizations attacked by the WGH (e.g., the Red Revolutionary Committee, Bombard Command), and rebel outfits excluded by the WGH from the January Revolution and the Shanghai People's Commune, as well as individuals who were dissatisfied for one reason or another with Wang Hongwen and Zhang Chunqiao, joined forces to challenge the hegemony of the WGH. In August 1967, the newspaper of the WGH, *Worker Rebel*, published an article entitled "Why I Supported the Lian Si and Opposed the WGH," written by Dai Zuda, the younger brother of former First Regiment leader Dai Zuxiang and the head of an organization allied with Lian Si. The article was written under coercion after his capture by Wang Hongwen, but it reflected the attitude of those who had participated in the support–Lian Si posts. Dai Zuda noted that after his elder brother had been captured in March of 1967,

> He remained in custody. Because of this, I hated Wang Hongwen's guts, blaming him for my elder brother's detainment. I was always looking for some way to get even, so I linked up with Lian Si of the Shanghai Diesel Engine Plant. This was an action against the WGH and the leadership of the city revolutionary committee. Then in late July, I formally organized the *Yawusha* [Shanghai dialect for "irrepressible"] Warriors.[60]

The Lian Si problem had escalated from an intrafactory factional struggle to a much broader contest between the WGH and other disgruntled rebel groups. The liaison posts constituted the most powerful organizational opposition to the WGH since the Scarlet Guards.

Lian Si's growing antagonism toward the WGH was fueled in large part by the attitude and actions of Zhang Chunqiao. On the evening of January 24, 1967, when Wang Hongwen reported to his superior on events at the Shanghai Diesel Engine Plant, Zhang responded adamantly, albeit inaccurately: "Most of the Lian Si members are cadres and technicians instigated by the old Party committee; it is an old conserve organization."[61]

Two months later, Zhang sent a Mao Zedong Thought–Propaganda Team from the army, navy, and air force to occupy the diesel engine plant. After a month at the factory, the team announced its conclusion that Lian Si's general orientation was mistaken. Angered by this pronouncement, Lian Si members that night trashed the office of the propaganda team. In response, the propaganda team seized two Lian Si leaders and trundled them off to the municipal Public Security Bureau. Lian Si thereupon mobilized several thousand workers and family dependents for a protest at the gates of the city Public Security Bureau on Fuzhou Road. A week later, on May 27, more than 2,000 Lian Si members staged a sit-down demonstration outside the bureau. At the same time, Quan Xiangdong and Chen Puchang mobilized all the support–Lian Si posts across the city (which now numbered 627) to converge at People's Plaza in an expression of public sympathy.

The challenge of Lian Si (and its supporters) was becoming increasingly bold—directed not simply against the WGH, but against the whole structure of power ushered in by Zhang Chunqiao's January Revolution. As Chen Puchang put it in several meetings,

> People say we're bombarding the city revolutionary committee. So what?
> With the city revolutionary committee madly oppressing the revolutionary masses and attacking the revolutionary masses, we have to bombard!
> I believe the city revolutionary committee is following a capitalist reactionary line. It's like a spokesman for the capitalists. I want to overturn it![62]

Lian Si support posts now characterized themselves as "an alliance of all revolutionary rebels in the city who were suppressed after February 5, 1967."[63] February 5 was the date on which the Shanghai People's Commune, the precursor of the Shanghai Revolutionary Committee, had been founded. Thus the spearhead of Lian Si was aimed squarely toward the new Shanghai Revolutionary Committee.

At the same time, the Lian Si leadership prepared to establish an all-city "support–Lian Si general post." Wang Hongwen understood the threat to his control that this development implied.

> The Shanghai Diesel Engine Factory Lian Si and the support–Lian Si posts emerged in opposition to the newly born revolutionary committee and our WGH. They wanted to destroy the revolutionary committee and the WGH and establish a second workers' organization to replace the WGH and seize power from the municipal revolutionary committee. The support posts were the product of the reactionary theory of multiple centers (*duo zhongxin lun*) and they advocated redistribution of power. This was ultraleftism. The leaders of the support posts wanted to create major chaos in Shanghai, during which they would seize power from the revolutionary committee. Had we permitted the liaison posts and Lian Si to develop, it would have been very hard to deal with. Shanghai really would have experienced great chaos and the labor movement would have split into two big factions.[64]

At this time, Wang Hongwen served as vice-chair of the Shanghai Revolutionary Committee as well as commander of the WGH. In other words, he was both an official government representative and a "mass" leader—a dual status that he put to good effect in dealing with the threat from Lian Si. In mid-June, Wang established a secret base in the Shanghai Garrison Command (with the code name of "888," taken from the last three digits of its office phone number) for the express purpose of gathering intelligence on Lian Si and its support posts and developing a counterstrategy.

As the external environment grew more polarized, the situation inside the diesel engine factory became increasingly tense. On June 29, the Lian Si and East is Red factions engaged in an armed battle that led to more than two hundred injuries. A month later, another large-scale struggle erupted in which several East is Red members were nearly killed.

To buttress its defenses both inside and outside the factory, Lian Si called a preparatory meeting of leaders of its general headquarters and district posts on July 31. The next morning, leaders of the local liaison posts assembled for a strategy session. When Wang Hongwen learned of these gatherings, he decided to take immediate action. On August 1, Wang dispatched his forces to the liaison post meeting to seize at one fell swoop all of the principal Lian Si leaders. Only Quan Xiangdong eluded immediate capture by arriving late to the meeting, but before long he, too, was apprehended. The effort to oppose the WGH by organizational means had been stymied.

Although his operation against Lian Si was based in the Garrison Command, Wang Hongwen staged the assault in the name of the WGH rather than the Shanghai Revolutionary Committee. This was because SRC members Wang Shaoyong and Wang Chenglong had resolutely opposed Wang Hongwen's intended plan of action. At a meeting of the SRC on June 29, Wang Shaoyong complained that such an important issue should have been formally brought before the revolutionary committee, but Wang Hongwen insisted that the WGH—as a mass organization—could resolve this matter on its own. Only if something unexpected occurred would it become necessary to involve the SRC.[65]

Disregarding the dissenting opinion of fellow SRC official Wang Shaoyong, Wang Hongwen set the date for a full-scale attack on Lian Si forces at the diesel plant as August 4. On the night of the August 3, by the time that Wang Shaoyong learned of the WGH's preparations for a military assault, the troops had already been dispatched. Wang Shaoyong immediately phoned Zhang Chunqiao for advice. Zhang responded, "When the masses have arisen they must act; let them act!"[66]

On August 4, hundreds of thousands of combatants converged to encircle the Shanghai Diesel Engine Factory. Shanghai's second large-scale armed battle of the CR (following the Kangping Road Incident of December 1966) began at 10 A.M. and lasted until 6 P.M. More than 1,000 Lian Si members were taken prisoner in the offensive.

The August 4 attack on Lian Si occurred at a time when armed struggles around the country were reaching a high point.[67] In comparison to what was happening elsewhere in China, the battles in Shanghai were actually remarkably tame. Shanghai's continued economic growth during this troubled period was a by-product of the relatively low level of strife among the workers.[68] In the struggles that did erupt, casualties were modest by national standards. Much of the credit for this must go to the Shanghai Garrison commander who, just after the Kangping Road Incident, confiscated the arms and ammunition of the militias at all Shanghai factories.[69] Combatants were thenceforth limited to spears, iron bars, catapults, high-pressure hoses, and homemade bottle bombs. Even so, hundreds of workers were injured in the August 4 assault, and many of them became permanently crippled as a result.

In the Shanghai Diesel Engine [Factory] Lian Si incident, 983 people at the factory were injured, 663 were detained, of whom 11 were locked up for 8 years and one was sentenced to 36 years. Some 121 people became handicapped from their injuries, and 18 later died of them. The economic losses were also shocking. Because of the August 4 armed battle, production was halted for two months, with a loss in production value of 5 million yuan and a loss of 1.75 million yuan in profits, as well as a loss of 3.55 million yuan in materials and 148,000 yuan in repairs to factory equipment and buildings. In the period from 1967 to 1969, 118,600 yuan was spent on medical costs for the factory's employees.[70]

After the August 4 assault, the WGH set about destroying Lian Si support posts around the city. The major leaders of these posts had already been rounded up on July 31 and, leaderless, the rank and file offered little resistance. At the same time, subordinate organizations under the WGH used the pretext of smashing the support posts to eliminate other rival outfits. Organizations that had shown any inclination to oppose the WGH in the past were virtually all eliminated in the offensive.[71] From this point on, with the notable exception of the Writers' Group (see Chapter 1), no rival organization was able to mount a credible challenge to the hegemony of the Workers' General Headquarters.

Intra-Rebel Dissension

The saga of resistance and repression within the rebel ranks is testimony both to the independent spirit of the rebel leaders and to the eventual taming of the rebel movement by the reimposition of party norms and networks. Considering the unruly personal history of Geng Jinzhang—marred by sexual transgressions and rows with neighbors and coworkers—it was not surprising that he resisted ready submission to the authority of Wang Hongwen. Moreover, as a demobilized soldier from Shandong whose membership in the Communist party predated that of Wang Hongwen, Geng fully expected to enjoy a commanding role in the Workers' General Headquarters. The Second Regiment was largely an extension of his own recalcitrant temperament. Geng's special relationship to Zhang Chunqiao greatly facilitated his bid for autonomy, but, ultimately, Zhang's insistence on unity ended the Second Regiment's defiance toward the WGH.

Lian Si presented a somewhat more complex challenge, directed ultimately against the new order imposed by the January Revolution. The situation at the Shanghai Diesel Engine Factory, though unusual, revealed the complicated possi-

bilities inherent in factory "rebellion." Whereas shop floor supervisors were at
odds with higher-level management, competing worker "rebels" faced a choice of
targets. The involvement of such radical intellectuals as Quan Xiangdong on the
side of Lian Si helped further to fan the flames of resistance. Yet in the end, Lian
Si, like the regiments before it, suffered crushing defeat at the hands of the WGH.

Why was Wang Hongwen's WGH able so quickly and decisively to emerge victorious in its conficts with recalcitrant rebels? The most important reason was
quite obviously the role of Zhang Chunqiao, who enjoyed a secure position in
Party Central throughout the duration of the Cultural Revolution. This distin-
guished the Shanghai scene from other places where local organizations were supported by CRSG members who themselves soon fell from power. The groups they
had promoted were then easily divided or defeated.

Because Zhang Chunqiao's national political status was assured, in Shanghai he
was widely seen as the embodiment of the "correct line" and thus was able to exert
enormous influence over the local situation. Moreover, the January power seizure
had resulted in Zhang being named chair of the Shanghai Revolutionary Committee and party secretary of Shanghai. In other places, splits occurred when mass
organizations jockeyed for position in the post–power seizure triple combinations by allying with the cadres with whom they had connections and hurling the
invective of "old conserve" at their rivals. In Shanghai, with Zhang Chunqiao in
charge of cadre selection, rebels could not as easily accuse those chosen of conservatism.

Once Zhang's special relationship with the Workers' General Headquarters became widely known, factory-level groups were generally eager to enlist under the
WGH banner. In linking up with an umbrella association, leaders of mass organizations sought a reliable means of protection, such that future political changes
would not suddenly find them accused of counterrevolutionary tendencies. Thus,
in recruiting followers, the regiments had always used the name of the WGH. This
was precisely why the rank-and-file regiment forces offered next to no resistance
when their leaders were arrested on orders from Wang Hongwen. Elsewhere in
China, seizures of factional leaders erupted into violent conflict and even full-
scale war.[72]

Zhang Chunqiao was not the only factor in moderating the factional struggle
in Shanghai. A second important reason for the relatively stable situation lay with
Wang Hongwen—a party member with an unorthodox style. In ordering the
Kangping Road attack on the Scarlet Guards, the arrest of Second Regiment
Commander Geng Jinzhang, and the August 4 smashing of Lian Si, Wang acted
over the strong objections of almost all the other party members in the rebel
movement. The Writers' Group, for example, argued adamantly for using propaganda and education, rather than force, to reform rival organizations. However,
judging by the violence that erupted elsewhere in China, the call for moderation
appears, in retrospect, a risky recommendation. Had Wang Hongwen's policy of
repression not prevailed and had the Scarlet Guards, the regiments, or Lian Si

been permitted to expand further, Shanghai might well have proven as susceptible to large-scale armed factional battles as the rest of the country.

On other issues, however, Wang did side with his fellow party members. Thus after the Kangping Road Incident, over the howls of many of his nonparty colleagues among the rebel leadership, Wang insisted upon absorbing rank-and-file members of opposing groups into his own organization. Subsequent developments showed that Wang had again made a prudent decision.

Yet a third factor in Shanghai's comparative tranquility was the lack of direct military interference. As we saw in this chapter, the PLA and the Shanghai Garrison Command threw their full support behind Zhang Chunqiao at the time of the January Revolution. Thenceforth, civilian leadership—in the persons of Zhang and Wang Hongwen—was decisive. The confiscation of factory militia weaponry further limited the scale of conflict.

After an initial period of uncertainty, Wang Hongwen—thanks to his relationship with Zhang Chunqiao, as well as to his own political acumen—emerged as the supreme authority within the Shanghai labor movement. Like party leaders of the pre–Cultural Revolution era, he moved quickly to consolidate his personal patronage network. Fellow WGH leader Ye Changming recalled,

> Wang Hongwen relied on the fact that he was strongest among the commanders of the WGH to seize opponents and detain them illegally. Moreover, he adopted a string of policies to expel those leaders within the WGH who disagreed with him. The great majority of those who remained with the WGH were intensely loyal to Wang Hongwen. In order to expand his personal power, Wang transferred trusted people directly from the factories to work at WGH and dispatched Wang Xiuzhen to a number of large and important factories to select some additional leaders.[73]

"Patriarchs" within the ranks of the old rebels who used the occasion of the January Revolution to challenge the supremacy of Wang Hongwen—most notably Geng Jinzhang and Pan Guoping—were forced out of their positions within the WGH at this juncture. Conversely, individuals close to Wang Hongwen who had not participated in the early preparatory activities leading up to the establishment of the WGH—that is, Wang Xiuzhen, Ma Zhenlong, and Dai Liqing—ascended rapidly to the top ranks of the WGH after January 1967. Leadership positions were basically allocated according to one's relationship with Commander Wang Hongwen. Ye Changming, Chen Ada, Huang Jinhai, Dai Liqing, and Ma Zhenlong were known thenceforth as Wang Hongwen's "five tiger generals" and, along with Wang Xiuzhen, their importance within the WGH persisted until the close of the CR.

The case of Ye Changming illustrates the changing fortunes of WGH leaders at this time. Because Ye had not actively participated in the early initiatives of the WGH, he exercised relatively little influence within the organization at first. Feeling excluded, Ye found an excuse to leave the WGH. According to Pan Guoping's recollection, "In December 1966, Ye Changming wrote Wang Hongwen and me a letter, the main point of which was that he had resigned because he had been pre-vented from working by Chen Ada and others."[74] Ye Changming used the excuse of carrying on the movement in his original work unit to return to the Synthetic Fiber Institute. After the January Revolution, however, he realized that his depar-ture from the WGH had been a major mistake. The status of the Workers' General Headquarters had risen considerably during the course of the power seizure; and after the Shanghai Revolutionary Committee was established, the WGH occupied a central spot in the new power structure. Later Ye recalled,

> After the municipal revolutionary committee was established in February 1967, I felt very regretful. I shouldn't have left the WGH at the outset. I had forfeited a big op-portunity. I realized that the WGH exerted a huge influence over the whole city and couldn't be ignored. I then wanted to return to the WGH.[75]

As it happened, Wang Hongwen was at the time embroiled in a feud with Fan Zuodong, a powerful member of the WGH Standing Committee. Learning of this dispute, Ye sought out Wang to tell him that his earlier departure from the WGH had occurred only because Fan had squeezed him out. Ye was soon reinstated as Fan Zuodong's replacement. Wang's juggling of personnel in this manner shaped the WGH into a loyal organization, responsive to his wishes. As Ye Changming summarized the result, "Workers' General Headquarters became Wang's General Headquarters."

Over the ensuing years of the Cultural Revolution decade, the Workers' General Headquarters—operating under a succession of names—became a key vehicle for institutionalizing the political gains of rebel workers. To be sure, many of the pro-grams and procedures of Wang Hongwen's WGH came in time to replicate pre–Cultural Revolution practices. But in a number of significant respects, the victory of the WGH did signal a new chapter in the saga of the Chinese labor movement under communism. It is to that story that we now turn.

6

Institutionalizing
Rebel Gains

One of Mao's stated objectives in launching the Cultural Revolution was to enhance the status of the proletariat in national political life. Workers, he proposed, should replace "capitalist roaders" who had been occupying positions of authority. The title of an article by Yao Wenyuan became a stock slogan of the day: "The working class must exercise leadership in everything" (*Gongrenjieji bixu lingdao yiqie*)![1] Despite such pronouncements at the time, it is usually assumed in retrospect that the CR brought a general decline in the political influence of workers. According to Mark Selden, the outcome of the CR "was not new heights of power in Shanghai or elsewhere. . . . Far from strengthening the position of workers, heightened controls in an arbitrary and military-dominated political system reduced worker autonomy and increased dependence on local and regional leaders."[2]

We will argue in this chapter that Yao Wenyuan's slogan calling for proletarian leadership was more than empty verbiage, however. For nearly a decade after the January power seizure of 1967, the core leadership at all levels of Shanghai's municipal government included a substantial number of worker rebels. During the previous seventeen years of Communist rule, worker representatives had been selected for their diligence at work or their obedience to party directives and had served as little more than tokens at people's congresses. By contrast, the "new cadre" corps of worker rebels evidenced a keener understanding of political operations and a greater willingness to speak their minds. Having successfully challenged party authorities in the early months of the CR, they were seldom content thereafter simply to mouth the party line.

During the January Revolution, Wang Hongwen hoped at first simply to substitute his rebel organization for the preexisting power structure, but Zhang Chunqiao refused to approve so naked a power grab. Instead, the rebels were forced to bide their time for a few months. Nevertheless, during the process of restoring social order later that year, the WGH sent "worker representatives" and "workers' propaganda teams" to staff government agencies with their own personnel. As preparations for the Ninth Party Congress got underway in late 1967, rebel groups in other parts of the country were systematically dismantled. By contrast, the Shanghai worker rebels not only maintained their own organizational system but used it as a base to gain a secure foothold in higher echelons of administration.

After the January Revolution, leaders of the WGH immediately set their sights on positions with real authority: party and government posts from the factories, right up to the municipal and national levels. At the same time, worker rebels developed a military presence in the form of factory militia. Even more important, they rejuvenated the union apparatus so that this "mass association" would be poised to exercise a genuine influence on official policies. The effort to challenge the party's monopoly over policymaking by beefing up mass associations persisted until the Tenth Party Congress, when there was a call to restore party hegemony. But the party never fully recovered its previous control.

Impressive as the worker-rebels' political inroads were in this period, compared to the pre–Cultural Revolution era, they also faced serious barriers. Perhaps the biggest deterrent to the institutionalization of worker-rebel gains was the independent spirit of the "old rebels," many of whom were soon removed from office for one or another infraction or indiscretion. The feisty proclivities of the worker rebels led not only to intrarebel dissension but also to clashes with intellectuals and senior cadres—most of which were ultimately resolved by Zhang Chunqiao in favor of the latter groups.

Worker Participation in Municipal Administration

The first instance of formal participation in political administration by the Shanghai worker rebels came with their January 1967 establishment of a "Frontline Command Post to Grasp Revolution and Promote Production."[3] The combination of the recent Kangping Road Incident and the wind of economism had severely disrupted Shanghai transportation; railways were blocked, the wharves and loading stations lacked stevedores, and nearly 400,000 tons of cargo had piled up.

Frontline Command Post to Grasp Revolution and Promote Production

On the night of January 7, Wang Hongwen convened a meeting of representatives from WGH liaison posts at all district and bureau levels, together with some Red Guard leaders in the city, for a conference to discuss how best to resolve the transport mess. According to the recollection of Wang Minglong, a WGH leader at the time,

> In his address to the meeting, Wang Hongwen noted that some Red Guard organizations and rebel liaison posts of several bureaus connected to the transport system had

reported that the railway system was blocked and the North Station and surrounding streets were filled with people waiting for trains—even sleeping in the streets at night. The port had basically closed down. A few ships had sailed into harbor, but there was no one to unload them. Other cargo had been piled high on the wharf for a long time. No one in the SPC or the railway or port bureaus was handling this problem. This was a plot by capitalist roaders to destroy production and suppress revolution, to alter the direction of the struggle. We Shanghai Revolutionary Rebels had to get involved. The railway had to immediately be opened, the goods at the harbor speedily moved. Production must not cease. After this, Wang Hongwen suggested establishing a "Shanghai Grasp Revolution, Promote Production Frontline Command Post" [Frontline] to take charge of both passenger and freight trains and of cleaning up the chaos at the harbor. For personnel, it was decided to rely primarily on the six transport bureaus liaison posts of the WGH. Red Guard organizations in the city also sent people to participate in the formation of "Frontline."[4]

Wang Hongwen's immediate concern in founding Frontline was to alleviate the congestion in the Shanghai transportation and communication system. But the action had important political consequences. In effect, the establishment of Frontline meant a takeover of the administration of this sector by the worker rebels and their student allies.

According to Xie Pengfei, a leader of Frontline, the new organization undertook the following activities: (1) restoring transportation and communications in all transport bureaus; (2) issuing proclamations about seizing revolution, promoting production, and opposing economism (most proclamations were written by Zhu Yongjia of the Writers' Group; some were sent to Zhang Chunqiao for approval); (3) contacting all industrial bureaus for information about production conditions, which were then reported to Zhang Chunqiao; (4) convening congresses to seize revolution and promote production in the industrial and transport systems; (5) handling the Shanghai Mansion "Support Agriculture Returned to Shanghai Rebel Command Post" Incident (in which workers who had returned to Shanghai during the wind of economism were sent back to the countryside); and (6) organizing the movement of some 400,000 tons of accumulated goods (by mobilizing student Red Guards to go to the wharves and train stations to relieve the bottleneck).[5]

Initially, Wang Hongwen asked Pan Guoping to serve as general commander of Frontline, but Pan did not wish to be saddled with the difficult job of solving transport snarls, and he went only once to the Frontline offices. Wang thereupon designated Ye Changming to take charge. Ye also quit after only one day on the job, bequeathing this challenging task to Wang Minglong.

The main leadership of Frontline's four departments—core, office, propaganda, and liaison—comprised some forty-odd people. The seven people in charge of the core department were all WGH members. Besides Wang Minglong, others included WGH Railway United Command Post leader Xie Pengfei, and representatives from the Long-Range Navigation Liaison Post, Transportation Liaison Post, and Seaport Command Post. But according to Wang Minglong, except for himself (with overall coordination responsibilities) and Xie (who handled railway affairs), the other five members of the core command were mere figure-heads who seldom attended meetings and, at best, sent representatives in their place.[6]

The operations of Frontline reflected the uneasy cooperation between workers and intellectuals that characterized much of the political activity of the Shanghai rebel movement. Most of the concrete work of Frontline was shouldered by Red Guards. At that time, the only social force that could be effectively mobilized for the task of relieving transportation snarls were university and high school students. Harboring illusions of uniting with the proletariat, they rushed to the docks and train station to undertake volunteer labor.

The office, liaison, and propaganda departments of Frontline were handled by thirty-five university students and two cadres. Zhu Yongjia, originally a member of the SPC Writers' Group, who later participated in the SPC Revolutionary Rebels Liaison Post, was one of the cadres assigned to Frontline. After a few days there, he reported to Zhang Chunqiao, whose response was very encouraging: "The SPC and Shanghai People's Committee is already moribund. This new agency of yours is tantamount to seizing leadership of economic work and indus-trial and transport work from the SPC. I support your efforts." Later, Zhang Chunqiao and Yao Wenyuan met with Frontline leaders, saying, "This is a newly born thing, a new form of political power. We must really sum up this experi-ence." Zhang added, "Frontline can be called an 'economic soviet' replacing the Shanghai people's government."[7]

Zhang Chunqiao was known for being very particular about matters of politi-cal organization and nomenclature. His statements thus signaled the momentous possibilities implied by Frontline, inviting the worker rebels to tackle even more ambitious operations. Wang Minglong and Xie Pengfei quickly consolidated the organizational structure, establishing departments of industry, transportation, re-search, finance, health, reception, and so forth. In short, offices that had belonged to the Shanghai municipal government before the January Revolution were being recreated in Frontline. The number of leading personnel soon increased to more than one hundred.[8]

With the expansion of Frontline, tensions among workers, cadres, and intellec-tuals became more pronounced. At this time, some employees in the municipal government had formed rebel groups that were planning to take over the opera-tions of the agencies in which they had been working. However, Xie Pengfei ar-gued that these government cadres were merely feigning rebellion and that only worker rebels were genuine rebels. He insisted that factories and bureaus report directly to Frontline, instead of to cadres who had served in government posts. Xie was also hostile toward such writers as Zhu Yongjia, who had been sent to Frontline from the Shanghai SPC Revolutionary Rebel Liaison Post. Suspecting that these intellectuals were inclined to listen to former cadres rather than to the workers themselves, Xie refused to issue work permits or write recommendation letters for such liaison personnel and barred them from attending policy-planning meetings.[9]

Rebel cadres fought back. Wang Chenglong, a leader of the SPC Revolutionary Rebel Liaison Post, gathered intelligence on Wang Minglong and Xie Pengfei and then submitted a damaging situation report about Frontline to Zhang Chunqiao.[10] The report had the intended effect: When the Shanghai People's Commune was established on February 5, Zhang Chunqiao demoted Frontline to a temporary department of the commune, stipulating that its sole duties were some emergency responsibilities in the production sector. No longer was Frontline presented as a substitute for the municipal government; a month later, it was dissolved. When the People's commune gave way to the Shanghai Revolutionary Committee (which set up its own departments of industry, transportation, and economic planning), Xie Pengfei was sent back to his original job in the Railway Bureau.[11]

Xie Pengfei's effort to rely exclusively on the working class and to shun former cadres—even members of the Writers' Group—ended up alienating Zhang Chunqiao and undermining the WGH's first foray into government administration. Publicly, Zhang Chunqiao (like Mao Zedong) expressed great esteem for the working class and characterized the worker rebels of Shanghai as a progressive social force capable of struggling against the revisionist capitalist roaders. But having had direct contact with these worker rebels, Zhang harbored genuine reservations about their leadership potential. In April 1967, when Zhang met in Beijing with Wang Xiuzhen, Wang Hongwen's trusted colleague in the Workers' General Headquarters, he asked her pointedly,

> Wang Xiuzhen, tell me, who can represent the workers in your WGH? Wang Hongwen is a cadre from the security department and has never touched a machine; Pan Guoping is an apprentice and hasn't yet completed his training period; Chen Ada has also only done a few days' work; you, Wang Xiuzhen, were sent from the Northeast to Shanghai to study at the textile institute and have yet to work at a machine! Can you represent the Shanghai working class? I think none of you can! If we're going to talk about someone who can really represent the working class, it would be Geng Jinzhang, a party member with 12 years of work experience, calluses on his hands, and a bit of standing among the workers. But the Second Regiment wouldn't listen to us and was divisive. We supported you instead of them, so the Second Regiment fell and your WGH developed. Without our support, I believe you wouldn't have defeated the Second Regiment![12]

Although some of the particulars were mistaken (e.g., Wang Hongwen had actually worked as a machine-operator at the Number 17 Mill before entering its security department, and Pan Guoping had already become a regular worker), Zhang's negative assessment of the worker rebels was clear. He reiterated these sentiments in a speech to Party Central some months later. By that time, Wang Hongwen was nationally famous, but in Zhang's address on the CR in Shanghai he did not mention the name of a single WGH leader. At the end of his remarks,

Zhang noted, "For a mass association the WGH is good, progressive. But it has not given rise to any influential worker-leaders."[13]

The Shanghai People's Commune

Despite his doubts about the leadership of the Workers' General Headquarters, Zhang Chunqiao appreciated the critical importance of a working-class constituency in institutionalizing Mao's ostensibly "proletarian" cultural revolution. After the January power seizure, any new system of governance established to replace the discredited party committees would require worker participation in one form or another. Among the thirty-eight groups that formed the Shanghai People's Commune were three worker-rebel outfits: the WGH, the Frontline to Grasp Revolution and Promote Production, and an organization of temporary workers known as the "Shanghai Mao Zedong Thought–Workers Revolutionary Rebel Headquarters."[14] Frontline, we have seen, was an agency of the WGH. The temporary workers' group was a tiny organization (unlike the enormous Red Workers organization, which was banned during the January Revolution) that was included in the People's Commune only as public window dressing for the campaign to combat economism that was underway at the time. In effect, then, the WGH was the sole labor organization represented in the People's Commune. The nineteen-person provisional committee established to guide the activities of the new commune included five leaders of the WGH—more than from any other mass organization—and three members of the Writers' Group.[15]

The WGH, thanks to its cachet as a revolutionary working-class organization, was poised for a key role in the development of the new power structure. According to the recollection of Wang Minglong, who served as the WGH representative in charge of preparations for the commune, the guidelines for the configuration of the new entity were proposed by Wang Hongwen.

> In mid-January of 1967, I convened a meeting of heads of various organizations at the old SPC party school to discuss the question of units' participation in the commune. At the meeting Wang Hongwen insisted that the commune not become too much of a hodgepodge. Organizations which had attacked Zhang Chunqiao, conservative organizations, and guild organizations were all prohibited from participating in the preparatory work for the commune.[16]

Wang Hongwen saw the People's Commune as ushering in a new era of working-class political participation. On February 5, 1967, the day the commune was founded, the WGH distributed a handbill with the title "Hail the Birth of the Shanghai People's Commune." According to the handbill, "November 6, 1966 [i.e., the founding of the WGH], was the start of our Shanghai workers' participation in the CR. . . . The birth of the Shanghai People's Commune is a joyous event in the political life of the Shanghai revolutionary people. It opens a new chapter in the Shanghai laboring people's control of our own fate."[17]

When, because of Mao Zedong's intervention, the Shanghai Commune was hastily transformed into the Shanghai Revolutionary Committee, the composition of the new body was initially quite confused. Some members, like Wang Minglong, were no sooner appointed than they were dropped from the list. Nevertheless, in summer 1967 the WGH sent eight people—including Wang Hongwen—to the SRC to assume regular administrative positions. Whereas the People's Commune had been staffed by representatives of rebel organizations who did not serve as individuals, this staffing of the SRC was a more formal arrangement. At this time, for example, Chen Ada became the director of the municipal industrial department—a position he retained until the end of the CR.[18]

Only in January 1970 was the namelist of the SRC membership officially reported to Party Central.[19] Although the 1970 roster listed Zhang Chunqiao and Yao Wenyuan as chair and first vice-chair, respectively, they were already preoccupied with national affairs. Day-to-day responsibilities resided with the other vice-chairs: Wang Hongwen, Xu Jingxian, Wang Xiuzhen, Ma Tianshui, and Wang Shaoyong. Ma Tianshui and Wang Shaoyong were experienced government cadres, Wang Hongwen and Wang Xiuzhen were worker rebels, and Xu Jingxian represented the Writers' Group. Among the thirty members of the SRC Standing Committee, seven were worker rebels.[20] In November 1972, an additional thirteen names were added to the standing committee, of whom four were workers.[21]

Revolutionary Committees

After the formation of the SRC, subordinate revolutionary committees were established at all levels as the approved post-power seizure organizational form. Members of these committees were selected according to Mao's "triple combination" formula, with representation from mass organizations, old cadres, and military cadres. The mass representatives were, for the most part, drawn from activists in rebel organizations, but they also included pre–Cultural Revolution labor models and some "old conserves" who had turned over a new leaf, like the tractable Yang Fuzhen (see Chapter 3).

The general establishment of revolutionary committees afforded the rebels an opportunity to enter political leadership ranks at all levels of administration. In sectors where workers were heavily concentrated, such as industry, transportation, basic construction, and the like, worker rebels gained substantial influence. For example, the revolutionary committee of the Shanghai Machine and Electronics Bureau, established in July 1967, included forty-six committee members, of whom twenty-one were worker rebels. When a new revolutionary committee was formed in November 1968, worker rebels contributed thirty-five of the forty-five members.[22]

Numerical superiority on revolutionary committees was an important, but insufficient, achievement in the rebels' quest for political influence. Real policymaking authority rested with the working agencies (*gongzuo jigou*) of the committees, where worker rebels initially were not well represented. For example, in 1968, the revolutionary committee of the Bureau of Light Industry had 109 working personnel (*gongzuo renyuan*), of whom only twenty were former workers; the rest had held cadre positions in various agencies of the Bureau prior to the CR.[23] Moreover, the twenty from worker backgrounds complained, "We were just put in charge of secondary matters and administrative details. The majority of us handled production work; few handled political work."[24] The situation was comparable—or worse—at other bureaus responsible for industrial production.[25]

The rebels criticized the comeback of the former cadres as a counterattack by conservative forces. Under the pretext of opposing restoration (*fan fubi*), numerous attacks on revolutionary committees and their working personnel were launched in 1967 and 1968. Many committees were forced to reorganize to increase the proportion of rebels. When the revolutionary committee of the Handicraft Bureau was established in 1967, the 120 working personnel at the three department offices were all cadres from the bureau; in August 1968 they were reduced to eighty-five, of whom fourteen were newly added worker rebels.[26] The situation at the Yangzi River Navigation Bureau was similar: At first, all working personnel of the revolutionary committee were cadres from the bureau; later, ten workers were added to "fill vacancies."[27]

To allow worker rebels a meaningful role in revolutionary committees, in a situation report Wang Hongwen put forth the notion of "one leading group, two signboards" (*yitao banzi liangkuai paizi*).[28] On December 31, 1968, Wang explained the system in a report from the WGH to the Shanghai Revolutionary Committee:

> Currently in the great majority of basic units, some responsible persons and some working personnel for the rebels have joined the revolutionary committee and have been assigned work in their departmental offices. Normally the pattern of "two committees" (*liang weihui*) is adopted, in which the rebel committee and the revolutionary committee participate in joint discussions to decide major issues in the factory. After the revolutionary committee makes a decision, if it is appropriate for the mass organization to implement it, then the mass organization does so, and if it's appropriate for united implementation then that's what's done. This pattern is generally called "*yitao banzi, liangkuai paizi*."
>
> After the implementation of "one leading group, two signboards," overlapping layers of bureaucracy were eliminated, streamlining was carried out, unified leadership was strengthened, the revolutionary committees were infused with new blood and replete with youthful vigor, [and] the problem of policy emanating from too many bureaus was avoided, as was the duplication of effort. The rebels held regularly scheduled committee meetings to exchange experiences and to study the work of mass political thought and the direction of class struggle, as well as some issues pertaining to the rebels themselves. Everyone agrees that with implementation of "one leadership group, two signboards" the rebels' fighting function has been enhanced and expanded under the strengthened leadership of the revolutionary committee. . . . Thus

it is recommended that bureau and company liaison posts and bureau and company revolutionary committees, as well as district and county liaison posts and revolutionary committees, amalgamate into a single working group to overcome these contradictions.[29]

As soon as this report was submitted, without even waiting for the approval of the SRC, the WGH ordered lower levels to execute its recommendations. On March 20, 1969, the WGH composed a follow-up report. It noted that thirteen bureaus had already implemented the "one leading group, two signboards" method and further advocated that heads of WGH liaison posts who had already joined bureau revolutionary committees be gradually promoted to leading positions on their standing committees.[30] This was an all-too-transparent ploy by the WGH to take over the revolutionary committees, and in the end Zhang Chunqiao did not endorse it.

After the Ninth Party Congress was convened in 1969, many more pre–Cultural Revolution cadres were admitted to the revolutionary committees. The result was a decline in the leadership role of worker rebels. A 1970 survey of revolutionary committee leaders (i.e., chairs and vice-chairs) of bureaus, districts, and companies in the city showed that the percentage of worker rebels ranged from a high of 9.6 percent (in the ten companies of the Bureau of Light Industry) to a low of 4.1 percent (in the ten municipal districts).[31] Similarly, an investigation of worker-rebel leaders in December 1969 revealed that only 9.9 percent served as chairs or vice-chairs of revolutionary committees.[32] Declining participation in revolutionary committee leadership posts helps to explain the worker rebels' continuing demand for a greater political role.

Worker Representatives

Reluctant though Zhang Chunqiao was to vest too much authority in Wang Hongwen's worker rebels, he was even more troubled by the routinization that beset the revolutionary committees soon after their establishment. As more and more cadres returned to their former administrative posts, the revolutionary committees began to look like replicas of their predecessor party committees in everything but name. To combat this retrogression, Zhang settled on a program of "worker representatives" (*gong daibiao*) to be sent to municipal-level offices. The representatives were expected to take charge of key government agencies so as to prevent pre–Cultural Revolution cadres from regaining the upper hand.

During a return to Shanghai in July 1968, Zhang called together SRC Industrial-Transport Department leaders Huang Tao and Chen Ada, along with Wang Hongwen and SRC Vice-Chair Wang Shaoyong, to request that they undertake the urgent task of selecting some 140 to 150 "worker representatives" for assignment to city-level agencies. Zhang characterized his program as a process of "mixing sand"—a metaphor Mao had coined about adding sand to cement in order to prevent its becoming too rigid. Zhang asked that a list of names be drawn up within a few days.

The next day, Huang Tao notified each bureau of a strict four-day deadline by which to complete this task, since it was of such urgency to Zhang Chunqiao. Each bureau was required to have its companies report back within two days, leaving just one day for the basic-level agencies to submit nominations to the companies. Because of the narrow time frame, in the end only 128 names were selected.

The assembled personnel were put through a two-week training session run by Jin Zumin, head of the organization department of the WGH. Zhang Chunqiao, Yao Wenyuan, Wang Hongwen, and Xu Jingxian all met with the entire group of worker representatives to stress the gravity of their mission. Zhang Chunqiao admonished the selectees: "Now that you've been chosen, you must have the courage to weed out the tired work style of the old fogies. You are the authentic worker representatives. The credit for cleaning house will go to you, but I will take responsibility for any mistakes."[33] The SRC put a good deal of emphasis on the job assignments of these workers and insisted that the work units to which the representatives had been assigned welcome them with drums and cymbals as "authentic worker representatives."[34]

Zhang Chunqiao's motives in promoting this program of "authentic" worker representatives were not entirely clear. As it was, each unit already had a group of worker rebels who had been added to the leadership ranks. Evidently, Zhang was hoping to buttress the proletarian presence in municipal administration without further augmenting the control of Wang Hongwen and company. WGH leader Huang Jinhai raised the obvious question, "What does it mean that they're 'authentic worker representatives?' Does that then mean that those WGH people who joined revolutionary committees as mass representatives are false worker representatives?"

All the work of selecting worker representatives had been carried out by revolutionary committees rather than by the rebel apparatus under the command of the WGH. As a result, the group of 128 delegates included not one member of the WGH Standing Committee, nor a single head of a rebel liaison post at district, county, or bureau levels. A total of eighty-seven, or 68 percent, were party members. A slight majority (52%) had been workers before the CR, but a substantial minority (48%) had been basic-level cadres—that is, party or Youth League branch secretary or committee member, union chair, production team leader, and so on.[35] There were 108 men and twenty women among the selectees. Four had received a college education through spare-time schooling, seventeen claimed a high school education, sixty-seven were middle school graduates, and forty had only an elementary school background.[36]

Of these 128 worker representatives, thirty-three were sent to nine departments of the SRC, and thirty-one were dispatched to district revolutionary committees.[37] The largest contingent was assigned the unpopular duty of serving on the investigation teams, or "special case groups," established to ferret out conspiracies of "class enemies."[38] According to the recollection of then SRC office director Wang Chenglong:

> The city special case groups (*zhuan'an zu*) were allocated the most [workers representatives]—some 40 to 50 people. These worker representatives resisted the assignment, wanting instead to be sent to various work departments. In accord with Zhang Chunqiao's instructions that "triple combinations must be implemented in special case groups, and worker representatives certainly must participate," I convened a special discussion meeting to execute this order.[39]

By the conclusion of the CR in 1976, fifty-one worker representatives had returned to their original factories; among them a sizable number had been dismissed for uncooperative behavior. Of the remaining seventy-seven, the great majority became leaders of Small Groups under the various departments of the SRC or leaders of offices of revolutionary committees at district, county, or bureau levels. Despite what appears to have been a strategy by Zhang Chunqiao to use the worker representatives to dilute the authority of the WGH, in fact a number of the representatives were subsequently co-opted as important figures in the rebel organization as well.[40]

Workers' Mao Zedong Thought–Propaganda Teams

A more favorable opportunity for enlarging the political participation of worker rebels came with the establishment of Workers' Mao Zedong Thought–Propaganda Teams in summer 1968. Dispatched to schools, factories, and even party offices across the country, the Workers' Propaganda Teams (WPT) were charged with restoring order in work units beset by factional strife.[41]

On July 28, 1968, the SRC established a six-person "leading Small Group" for WPTs—whose membership included three soldiers sent by the Shanghai Garrison, and Wang Hongwen, Chen Ada, and Zhang Baolin of the Workers' General Headquarters. Soon, a WPT office was set up under the Small Group to handle units with especially serious and long-standing problems (*laodanan*). Under the *Laodanan* Office, as it came to be known, were two subordinate offices: the Cultural and Educational Battlefront Office, led by Wang Xiuzhen, and the Industry and Transport Battlefront Office, headed by Dai Liqing. These two offices were responsible for sending WPTs to resolve conflicts at work units where factionalism was most acute.

Immediately following the publication of Yao Wenyuan's essay, "The Working Class Must Exercise Leadership in Everything,"[42] the SRC convened a series of meetings to discuss the implementation of Yao's recommendations. At one such assembly, WGH leaders Jin Zumin and Wang Hongwen suggested that WPTs be sent to all municipal, bureau, and district agencies. Moreover, they insisted that these workers be dispatched in large numbers to prevent them from being assimilated by intellectuals. In the end it was decided that

> the WGH would take responsibility for picking a group of good workers from the factories to be added to each "mouth" (*kou*)—i.e., system, and each district. This was the first step. The "mouths" of the SRC included industry-transport, trade-finance, technology, suburban counties, education-sanitation, and propaganda. No one was sent to the public security-procuracy-courts [which had been amalgamated under military control at the start of CR] or to the special case department. In all, some 100,000 workers were chosen.[43]

Termed the "army of 100,000," Shanghai's WPTs were assigned to every university, high school, and middle school, as well as to all SRC offices and to each district, county, and bureau agency.[44] In systems or units that did not employ industrial laborers, WPTs were dispatched as "occupiers" to "take charge of everything." As a consequence of this massive deployment, workers gained unprecedented clout in city administration.[45] Under Yao's slogan of the working class leading in everything, the WPTs dismissed the SRC working groups, which had been established the year before, and assumed power for themselves. It was at this time that Wang Xiuzhen and Huang Jinhai assumed major administrative duties in the municipal government, with Wang eventually taking over effective control of the SRC.

Initially, the jurisdiction of the WGH had been confined to industrial workers, but with the sending of WPTs, its authority expanded to encompass all occupations in the city. SRC departments already had their own rebel organizations, many of which had been founding units of the Shanghai People's Commune during the January Revolution. However, after the arrival of WPTs, the indigenous rebel leaders lost their previous status.

> When WPTs occupied various units, they first carried out "great uniting" (*da lianhe*), then "cleansing ranks" (*qingdui*), then "party rectification and reconstruction" (*zhengdang jiandang*). People called this process the "triple hatchet" (*san futou*) of the WPTs. In the process of "struggle, criticize, reform" (*doupigai*), they used the methods of "mixing sand," "layering amalgamation" (*cengceng jiehe*), etc. Leaders of WPTs forced their way onto the leadership groups of these units and assumed party and government authority.[46]

The tactics of the WPTs varied according to the severity of the factional conflicts in the units they occupied. At work units considered to have serious and long-standing problems, employees were not permitted to return home and were required to participate in intensive on-site criticism meetings. Dubbed "Resistance College-Style Training Sessions" (*Kangdashi xuexiban*), in commemoration of the Yan'an cadre training school, this technique was actually a kind of detention and investigation. After the training sessions were completed, a "big changing of the guard" (*da huanban*) occurred, in which WPT members replaced the previous leaders at all levels. Toward units considered to be "unhealthy" or "less than ideal," the WPTs adopted the method of "adding to the stage without destroying it" (*butai bu chaitai*)—WPT members simply took over major leading posts as "number one boss" (*diyi bashou*) or "number two boss" (*dier bashou*). In the few units considered to be in good shape, WPTs and the "two committees" (revolutionary committees and rebel committees) held joint meetings to decide major issues.[47]

Although the WPTs were a key vehicle for expanding the political influence of worker rebels, they also generated dissension within the rebel ranks. As we have seen, the Cultural Revolution produced three waves of worker involvement in political administration. These "three workmen" (*san gong*) included (1) WGH liaison post heads at district, county, bureau and company levels; (2) worker representatives; and (3) WPTs—all of whom were rebel forces that ostensibly were under the auspices of the WGH. Actually, however, members of the three groups seldom got along well, and in some units conflicts among them became heated. In August 1968, the WGH carried out an investigation of these tensions from the perspective of its liaison post heads.

> With respect to the worker representatives, the liaison posts think [that] "we liaison posts are an organization of the WGH. We're also worker representatives, why can't we lead everything? We ferreted out the capitalist roaders in the districts and established district revolutionary committees. Though we struggled for such a long time, we still can't serve on the standing committees, but as soon as these so-called 'worker representatives' appear on the scene they're made standing committee members."
>
> The liaison posts believe that since the WPTs carried out their struggle, criticism and reform under the jurisdiction of the districts, they should only take charge of work at units which they had infiltrated and should not participate in the leadership of the district revolutionary committees.
>
> [Because they] gained their status by attacking cadres in the various district, county, bureau and company agencies where they were stationed, liaison post rebels are not regarded fondly by the cadres. So when worker representatives and WPTs were sent to these units, some cadres exclaimed, "We welcome the authentic workers coming to lead in everything," implying that the liaison post rebels could not really represent the working class. This further incensed the liaison post rebels.[48]

As the first to rebel, liaison post leaders maintained that they should enjoy the right to rule now that the realm had been taken. However, the worker representatives prided themselves on being a leadership core sent by the SRC, and the WPTs assumed that they were Mao's chosen instrument for "leading in everything." Hence relations among the "three workmen" were strained, with "each group doing its own thing and failing to communicate with one other."[49] The friction abated only when a number of liaison post heads were named chairs of revolutionary committees. After the Ninth Party Congress in 1969, which stressed the strengthening of party leadership, WPTs were required to submit to the direction of the party committee at the same level. Wang Hongwen was reluctant to relin-

quish his control over the WPTs, however. As he put it to Wang Xiuzhen, "In cultivating cadres, I am relying on two channels: One is the factories, the other is the
WPTs."[50]

On August 6, 1972, Wang Xiuzhen—as SPC party secretary—convened a meeting at the Shanghai Federation of Trade Unions to request that the SFTU pay special attention to the concerns of the WPTs. After the meeting, SFTU director Ye
Changming held a discussion with WPT leaders of thirty-one units in the cultural
and educational sector.[51] The face-to-face encounter had a sobering effect. Soon
after his get-together with WPT leaders, Ye submitted a report to Wang Xiuzhen
in which he stated, "The WPTs have become unmanageable in three respects: the
units from which they came and the units to which they have been assigned cannot control them and neither can the higher levels. The higher levels use the
WPTs, but don't cultivate them."[52] At the conclusion of his report, Ye requested
permission for the SFTU to assume full responsibility for WPT work. Wang Xiuzhen agreed. Accordingly, in September 1972 the SFTU established the
WPT–Work Small Group, charged with: (1) establishing dossiers and name lists
for WPT cadres; (2) increasing the number of WPT members at occupied units;
(3) investigating and reporting to the SFTU on the conditions of WPT members;
and (4) transmitting the plans and documents of the SFTU to WPT members.[53]

Ye Changming's effort to tame the WPTs was apparently successful. A 1974 report revealed that approximately 60 percent of Shanghai's WPT members now
belonged to the party;[54] the great majority of these emissaries had assumed
prominent positions as secretaries or deputy-secretaries of party committees in
the work units they occupied.[55] Zhang Chunqiao summed up the situation with
evident satisfaction: "The Shanghai working class really controls the Shanghai
scene. This is a result of the Cultural Revolution, especially after the WPTs were
dispatched."[56]

Party Reconsolidation

The relationship between "new" rebel influence and "old" party hegemony was a
complicated one, however. As early as October 27, 1967, Party Central and the
CRSG had called for restoration of the party's unitary leadership. But in Shanghai, as elsewhere, party reconsolidation did not actually get underway for another
year. In November 1968, the Shanghai Revolutionary Committee selected three
enterprises that had been bases of "old rebel" power as test points for party
restoration: Shanghai Lianggong Valve Factory, Shanghai Port Number 7 Loading
Zone, and Shanghai Number 17 Cotton Mill. Party reconstruction was formally
endorsed by the Ninth Party Congress of April 1969. By February 1970, more
than 80 percent of the work units in Shanghai had resumed party activities.[57]

In this process of reconsolidation, party members were required to undergo
"mass evaluation" (which actually meant evaluation by the rebels) before they
were permitted to resume activities; those who failed to pass muster were made to

wait or even to relinquish party membership. According to an October 1972 SRC report, "Through this September, 18,941 people were processed, of whom 4,137 were expelled from the party, 2,227 were persuaded to relinquish their memberships, 4,166 were denied the right to resume membership immediately, and 8,411 received other forms of party discipline or punishment."[58]

As soon as party members resumed their party activities, however, their political advantage over the rebels became readily apparent. In reestablishing party committees and party branches, elections were held in which only party members could vote. The situation at the Shanghai Electric Machinery Factory, where old rebel Jin Zumin was employed, was typical.

> In recruiting candidates, the factory revolutionary committee repeatedly insisted that the leading group must be "new" [i.e., CR rebels], but the great majority of the 50-odd candidates nominated by the party were actually "old" [i.e., pre–Cultural Revolution cadres]. After numerous discussions, it was finally decided to settle on six old and five new [candidates].
>
> In the election, the old cadres garnered the most votes. The new candidates (including Comrade Jin Zumin) received very few votes. In the pre-election poll, Comrade Jin Zumin received only three votes fewer than the most popular old cadre and was ranked third, but in the official election he trailed by more than 30 votes and was ranked fifth. The other four new candidates trailed by more than 100 votes.[59]

The rebels pointed out that Jin was an alternate delegate to the Ninth Party Congress who should therefore have received unanimous support in an election for factory party committee. Moreover, some party members at the factory obviously were not following higher-level instructions: "When it came time for the formal elections, on dozens of ballots there were no marks by the names of new cadres." During the workshop party branch elections, as well, party members were not inclined to elect those valued by the rebels. In some cases, party members expressed their spiteful sentiments quite openly: "In restoring organizational life, you rebels restrained us. Now it's our turn and electoral power is in our hands."[60]

Only party members could gain decision-making authority within leading organizations, but the great majority of worker rebels were not party members at the onset of the CR. Admission to the party thus became their most pressing demand. As one worker rebel explained, "Party power was the power of all powers. Without party power, rebellion was in vain."[61]

According to CCP regulations, however, entrance to the party required discussion and approval by party members—many of whom were former conservatives who realized that rejecting the rebels' applications for party membership was the last line of defense in thwarting their political influence. A party branch secretary in the Shanghai Electronics Factory later recalled of his effort to block the rebels from entering the party,

> I knew that as soon as I admitted any rebels to the party, the higher levels would immediately appoint them as workshop party leaders and then they would become fac-

tory leaders. But if this sort of person became a leader, workshop production would be adversely affected. So I bucked the tide and refused to admit them.[62]

To get around the roadblocks to party admission being erected by long-standing party members, the WGH submitted a request to Zhang Chunqiao, Yao Wenyuan, and the SRC for permission to recruit party members directly. This demand was rejected, however, on grounds that it violated a long-standing party regulation stipulating that new members must be enrolled by the units that paid their wages. At that time, rebels working at the WGH still received their wages from their original factories; thus, they could only be admitted to the party through their factory branches.

Stymied in the effort to recruit party members directly, worker rebels hatched various alternative schemes to enlarge their party membership. At the enamelware factory where Ma Zhenlong worked, the rebels insisted that all major decisions required an agreement between the party branch, Ma, and another rebel leader. In self-defense, the party branch immediately targeted Ma and the other rebel as top candidates for recruitment.[63] At the East Shanghai Ship-building Factory, rebel leaders demanded that half of the seats on the reconstituted party committee be reserved for rebels who would be admitted to the party in the future, claiming, "If you don't attract new blood and don't reserve some spaces, there's no manifestation of the achievements of three years of cultural revolution." Ten out of twenty seats were duly set aside to be filled in the future by new party recruits.[64]

As noted previously, Wang Hongwen's Number 17 Cotton Mill was one of three "test points" for the restoration of basic-level party organizations in Shanghai. In late 1968, the first group of party members cultivated during the CR—sixteen workers in all—were enlisted at the mill. As soon as they joined the party, most of these rebel workers were sent to city, bureau, and company agencies as influential leaders.[65] Wang Hongwen also prevailed upon party committees at other factories to admit rebel activists. He took a special interest in Huang Jinhai at the Number 31 Cotton Mill. Wang's argument was simple: "Huang Jinhai is already the director of the finance and trade department of the SRC. If he's not admitted to the party, how can he do his job?" Later, Huang recalled that as soon as he had achieved party membership, he immediately recruited other rebels into the party:

> The original heads of rebel forces, except for those with huge problems that could not be covered up, were practically all admitted to the party and became cadres. Some of them I personally recruited.
>
> In the foreign trade bureau which I administered, more than 200 new cadres were chosen by imposing deadlines, applying coercion, and in some cases "flying over the ocean" (feiguo hai)—i.e., if the party branch at their original unit wouldn't accept them, they would be transferred to another unit that would.[66]

Similarly, after Ye Changming was admitted to the party, he recruited eighteen party members from among the rebels in the Synthetic Fiber Institute where he

TABLE 6.1   Party Status of Worker-Rebel Leaders in July 1970

WGH Liaison Posts	Party Members Admitted Pre–Cultural Revolution (%)	Party Members Admitted Since Ninth Party Congress (%)
Textile Bureau	28.6	10.2
Light Industry Bureau	37.6	12.0
Industrial, Transport, and Construction Bureaus	23.3	6.1
Districts	10.8	3.3

SOURCE: WGH, *Xin ganbu qingkuang huizong tongjibiao* [Statistical tables summarizing the condition of new cadres], Shanghai, December 1969 and July 1970.

had previously worked. Sixteen of these new recruits became cadres at middle ranks and above, altering the balance of power in the party branch.

Across most of China, the restoration of the party organization meant that conservatives regained power at the expense of rebels. The situation in Shanghai was somewhat different because of the unusual resilience of the rebel forces. Nevertheless, it was not easy for worker rebels to win admission to the party. As the data in Table 6.1 show, even in the companies of the Bureau of Light Industry (where the proportion of worker rebels was highest), new party members among WGH liaison post leaders stood at a mere 12 percent in July 1970.

If the earlier development of triple combinations, worker representatives, and WPTs had served as opportunities for rebels to expand their political reach, then admission to party membership was a chance to consolidate newly won gains. Difficult though that goal was to accomplish, party recruitment initiatives did permit a subset of worker rebels to become formal, long-term leaders at all administrative levels, right up to Party Central.

The Military Face of the Worker Rebels

Alongside the effort to acquire party credentials, the worker rebels sought to gain military prowess as well. In contrast to much of the rest of China, the establishment of revolutionary committees in Shanghai had not involved a major role for the military. The prominence of Zhang Chunqiao reduced the need for the armed forces to serve as arbiter in determining which cadres and which mass organizations could participate in the new power structure. After May 1967, Zhang became political commissar of the Shanghai Garrison, a post that augmented his prestige and further diminished the influence of the armed forces in Shanghai.

Unlike other places where military representatives wielded the upper hand in the new "triple combination" revolutionary committees, in most Shanghai work units the military was represented by a single individual, whose authority was subordinate to that of the worker rebels. The relative lack of military involvement worked both to enhance the position of the WGH and to lessen the chance of factional conflicts escalating into bloody battles.

As we have seen, two major armed battles occurred in Shanghai during the Cultural Revolution: the December 1966 Kangping Road Incident and the August 4, 1967, assault on Lian Si. In neither confrontation was anyone killed.[67] Nevertheless, the attack on Lian Si at the Shanghai Diesel Engine Factory prompted the WGH to establish its own armed forces. Picking up on a slogan of Jiang Qing's, the WGH dubbed its new paramilitary units the "Attack with Words, Defend with Force Troops."[68] These were the units that successfully spearheaded the August 4 battle at the diesel plant. The following month, a "Defend with Force Troops" Shanghai Command Post was formally established (by authorization of the Shanghai Revolutionary Committee), under the leadership of the WGH.

At first the command post was confined to the industrial sector, but soon the WGH began to develop armed forces in commercial and educational units, and in the suburban counties as well. By March 1970, the Shanghai Command Post exercised jurisdiction over seven divisions (*shi*), 72 regiments (*tuan*), 151 battalions (*ying*), and 623 companies (*lian*)—and the WGH had enlisted some 210,000 soldiers. Once the Defend with Force Troops had subdued the factional enemies of the WGH, rather than disband they proceeded to carry out widespread dragnets. Under the pretext of "strengthening social order [and] attacking gangsters and ruffians," the Shanghai Command Post caused some 104,000 people over the years to be detained.[69]

In 1969, Mao Zedong approved a document that abolished the "defend with force" paramilitary organizations and restored the preexisting militia system. Even so, the Shanghai Command Post remained intact until May 1970; at that point, pressured into following the national pattern, the WGH changed its name to the "Shanghai Militia Command Post." In contrast to other cities, however, Shanghai's militia was only nominally under the jurisdiction of the military. Actual leadership remained with the Workers' General Headquarters. From city to district levels, the directors of the so-called militia were all WGH leaders.

The Shanghai militia was thus, in reality, the armed force of the Shanghai worker rebels. By the conclusion of the CR decade in 1976, the WGH-sponsored militia had established branches in virtually every factory in Shanghai. Even the rural militia units in outlying villages were led by the WGH Command Post. The number of its divisions had increased to nine, the regiments stood at 602, battalions numbered 1,287, and there were more than 18,700 companies with three million soldiers. In addition to infantry, there were communications, engineering, naval, and motorized units. The militia possessed more than 226,000 guns, 1,900 cannons, 2,600 rocket launchers, 500 tanks, and a warship. This was now a force capable of challenging the regular military.[70]

The Reestablishment of Unions

Institutionally even more important to the worker-rebel cause than the formation of militia was the buttressing of their own organizational base. To avoid the fate of annihilation that befell virtually all rebel factions when Mao called for "grand alliances" under party supervision, the Shanghai WGH underwent a number of metamorphoses—changing its name first to "Shanghai Municipal Workers' Representative Congress" and then to "Shanghai Federation of Trade Unions." Under these two appellations, the WGH was able to maintain its original organizational system and personnel more or less untouched.

Although 1968 marked the end of the mass movement phase of the Cultural Revolution—with former Red Guards packed off to the countryside and Mao Zedong Thought–Propaganda Teams dispatched to pacify the factories—Shanghai differed from the rest of China in the continuing institutional presence of the worker rebels. Despite a name change to "workers' representative congresses," the WGH maintained organizations at district, county, and bureau levels. Even when the old name of the Shanghai Federation of Trade Unions was restored, the structure and personnel remained basically that of the original Workers' General Headquarters. On January 19, 1967, the WGH—acting with the explicit encouragement of Zhang Chunqiao—seized power from the old SFTU and moved into the union's tower on the bund; but organizationally the WGH did not formally revive the union until April 1973, with the convening of the Fifth Shanghai Workers' Representative Congress. Later, Ye Changming, who was put in charge of the reconstituted SFTU, recalled,

> I decided that the leadership positions at all levels of the union hierarchy could only be occupied by "new cadres" from the rebel ranks. A few "old cadres" could help out with concrete work at the basic union levels, but could not enter the leadership ranks.
>
> Among the leaders at district, county and bureau levels of the union, only one "old cadre" could serve [but] . . . could not be in charge. All the directors had to be "new cadres."
>
> When I approved union leaders, I paid primary attention to whether or not they had been rebels. This was the main criterion for deciding if leaders were good or bad.[71]

Although Mao had called for representation from former cadres, military personnel, and mass representatives in rebuilding pre–Cultural Revolution institutions, in Shanghai the reestablished trade union was essentially a metamorphosis of the WGH. Wang Hongwen viewed the SFTU as his personal organization and brooked no interference into its affairs from those who were not part of his rebel clique. By the same token, worker rebels who remained loyal to Wang were rewarded, first, with union positions and, then, with party and government offices. Ye Changming recalled of Wang's faithful followers, "The 'little brothers' (*xiao xiongdi*) formed a 'gang' (*bang*) in both the municipal party committee and the municipal revolutionary committee."[72] Yet, as Ye readily acknowledged, Wang Hongwen's new cadres had both strengths and weaknesses when compared to cadres chosen according to more conventional criteria.

> The new rebel cadres had sprung out of the CR. At that time the struggles were difficult, and if you didn't have fighting spirit you couldn't spring forth. In the course of these struggles, they gained considerable experience. On the other hand, a few cadres had been selected by the party committee—usually because they were honest and obedient. After they appeared on the scene they were like a sailboat following the wind, without any struggle experience. I believe that those new rebel cadres who had sprung forth on their own couldn't avoid making some mistakes in the movement and would surely offend some people. Some of them really did have a number of shortcomings and were looked down upon by others. But these people were very sharp in understanding problems during the midst of big struggles and were invariably correct in fundamental matters of line. By contrast, the cadres who had been handpicked for their honesty and obedience did not easily get into trouble and generally gave people a good impression; but in times of struggle they were incapable of seeing through issues, lacked fighting spirit, and very easily made mistakes of line.[73]

In choosing his union cadres, Ye Changming emphasized both independence and loyalty.

> I considered whether or not they had been rebels, [or] old rebels [or] whether or not they had rebel spirit and fighting spirit as well as "guts" (dadan pola) [and] a willingness to speak out and make suggestions. I then considered whether or not these people had feelings for the "gang of four"; whether they would stick by us was a most important question. Evidence to consider was whether or not they had participated in the attack on Zhang Chunqiao, whether or not they had supported Lian Si, [and] whether or not they had opposed the WGH during the CR. After using these cliquish (bang) criteria to make the initial cut, direct meetings and discussions were held to choose the people we needed. Then there was plenty of cultivation (peiyang) and investigation (kaocha).[74]

Union cadres who did not prove sufficiently congenial to the rebel perspective were replaced. As Ye Changming recalled, "We often used the cover of investigation and rectification groups to get rid of those cadres with whom we were dissatisfied." For example, in the case of Yang Fuzhen, the chameleon-like model worker who had been an "old conserve" in the early CR and who later became a leader in the Putuo Union,

> We always believed she wasn't one of us, so we schemed to replace her, but at first without success. Then on the eve of the Criticize Lin Biao–Criticize Confucius cam-

paign, with the express approval of Wang Hongwen and Wang Xiuzhen and taking advantage of the fact that the district workers' representative congress was being convened, Ni Shuying and Liu Cha were sent down to her union. Under the pretext that Yang Fuzhen was overworked, they did not permit her to continue as district union director (she was at the time Putuo District party committee secretary), and instead Ni became union director and Liu Cha took over the administrative work.[75]

Even if someone had been selected for union leadership by the rebels, any subsequent hint of disloyalty could be grounds for dismissal. The directors of the Jing'an District Union were rebels who had been handpicked by Ye himself. However, before long, Ye decided that these unionists had been "co-opted" by the district party committee. At the time of the district workers' representative congress, Ye sent more trustworthy replacements to take charge of the Jing'an union.[76]

The SFTU of the Cultural Revolution, though identical in name to the official union organization during the pre–Cultural Revolution era, was actually quite unlike its namesake. The reconstituted SFTU had no "industrial unions" (*chanye gonghui*), only "system unions" (*xitong gonghui*), which paralleled the administrative departments of the municipal government. In terms of activities and personnel appointments, the new SFTU was considerably more autonomous than its predecessor, which had been totally subservient to party dictates. In the past, for example, union cadres all had to be approved by the party authorities at that same level. Now the tables had turned. Ye Changming remembered,

> We publicly usurped the power of appointment of union leaders by the party committee. The Number 2 Machine and Electric Bureau and the Urban Construction Bureau party committees decided they wanted to increase their bureau[s'] union standing committees by several people, but because they hadn't first discussed this with the SFTU, we openly announced that we would not approve it. Moreover we made the district party committees confess their errors and undertake some remedial procedures vis-à-vis the SFTU.[77]

Although Ye's SFTU enjoyed substantial independence, as reflected in its powers of hiring and firing, in some respects the new union was even less a champion of worker interests than its pre–Cultural Revolution forerunner. Wang Hongwen explicitly cautioned the new unions against becoming bogged down in mundane labor issues. Eschewing any interest in "economistic" questions of wages and benefits, he focused squarely on political objectives.

> The unions should grasp major issues, grasp class struggle, grasp ideological education—and not get involved in other matters. They shouldn't grasp production, mass livelihood, labor emulation drives, industrial safety, etc. If they grasp these things they fall into the old path. . . . Since our WGH was established, it has grasped the big picture and has never let go of [the] struggle with the capitalist roaders. So our WGH has fighting power. The SFTU must grasp the big picture, must resolutely struggle against the capitalist roaders.[78]

Concretely, "grasping the big picture" meant above all the transfer of cadres via unions to various levels of party and government office. Since 1949, no organization had so closely monitored the administrative gains of its personnel. In its ten-year existence, the WGH and its successor organizations, the Shanghai Workers' Representative Congress and the restored SFTU, carried out surveys nearly every year to tally up the party and government positions of worker rebels. Wang Hong-wen considered this statistic the most important indicator of workers' political participation, the tangible "fruits of the Cultural Revolution."

During the CR, the SFTU employed several methods in sending worker cadres to party and government agencies (in addition to the program of WPTs, discussed previously). The first step was to take advantage of the reestablishment of district, county, and bureau unions. The SFTU would directly appoint worker rebels to occupy leadership positions in these unions. Then it would send "new cadres" from the unions to reorganized party and government agencies. Through this process, many worker rebels became party committee secretaries or revolutionary committee leaders. With the SFTU setting the fashion, subordinate unions soon followed suit.

A second strategy was to dispatch worker rebels directly to party and government agencies in which workers were scarce. Ye Changming remembered,

> Especially in the ten districts, I used the fact that there were few industrial workers in the districts to argue that we were supporting the districts by sending worker cadres. [Major factories belonged to bureaus and were not administered by districts.] In selecting personnel we even decided exactly which positions these people would assume after being dispatched.[79]

The bureaus were handled in a similar manner. If the SFTU concluded that a particular bureau party committee or revolutionary committee had a deficit of worker rebels, it simply dispatched its own personnel. Wang Xiuzhen remembered,

> The SFTU could send cadres to all the districts, counties and bureaus. It sent not only union cadres but also party committee cadres. According to incomplete statistics, after 1970 the SFTU sent more than 100 people to occupy leading positions at district, county, and bureau levels and higher (including various department offices of the SRC). Moreover, if the district, county, and bureau party committees wanted to appoint or transfer union cadres, they needed to procure the approval of the union.[80]

Cadre assignments had always been monopolized by the party. The SFTU's arrogation of this function was thus a frontal challenge to party authority. In 1974, during the Criticize Lin Biao–Criticize Confucius (CLCC) campaign, Jin Zumin (a WGH "old rebel" who headed the municipal party committee organization department) proposed that, within two to three years, fully one-half of the top party leadership posts should be held by new cadres. Emboldened by such calls, some union cadres tested the waters and bypassed the party committee organization department altogether, investigating (*kaocha*) new cadres themselves. If the relevant party committee organization department refused to write them letters of introduction, the unions themselves prepared such documents.

A third strategy was to rely on the personal authority of top municipal party committee leaders—most notably Jin Zumin, Wang Xiuzhen, Ma Tianshui, and Xu Jingxian—to send personnel to units where worker rebels were not in control. The heads of the district party committees in Jing'an and Putuo, for example, were replaced by worker-rebel cadres dispatched directly by the municipal party committee.

In addition to promoting their own people to important administrative positions, the rebels worked on enhancing the prestige of the union itself. Later, Ye Changming recalled that this involved a three-pronged strategy: (1) having worker rebels who already occupied party and government posts also assume union positions; (2) having worker rebels who were in line for party and government cadre posts go first to the unions for a transitional period; and (3) establishing regular union standing committee meetings. Ye noted,

> I really encouraged district, county, and bureau unions to develop their own organizational style. In the leadership groups of these reorganized unions, I always insisted on including some new cadres who were in responsible positions in party committees and revolutionary committees. This created an abnormal situation in which union cadres held major posts in key party and government agencies. Because the great majority of district and bureau union leaders were concurrently district or bureau party committee secretaries or vice-secretaries or standing committee members, and most other union personnel had party or government leadership positions, their approval of some union issue was tantamount to party and government approval. To report to them was equivalent to reporting to party or government. In this way, the union avoided party supervision. This group of people could enforce union wishes on the party committee, allowing the unions to override the party organization.[81]

With respect to the method of sending targets of recruitment and promotion to the unions for a "transition," Ye Changming recalled,

> I frequently said: "After the new cadres depart from having worked in the SFTU, their feelings and attitudes are unlike those new cadres who were directly appointed to higher levels." So I regarded a working transition at the SFTU as an important means of training new cadres. The great majority of the personnel we selected came to the SFTU for a period of time. After training and investigation, they were placed in other work. . . . We used every possible means to cultivate these people's feelings toward us.[82]

So that the worker rebels who had been dispatched to party and government posts would not forget their old home in the union, Ye Changming (as head of the SFTU) ordered that each level of the union must convene regular meetings involving these personnel: "Party and government leading cadres who held union positions were asked to return to the unions to participate in organizational activities such as standing committee meetings. District committee worker representatives and WPT members were also asked to participate in district union activities."[83]

Through these various means, the SFTU effectively eroded the pre–Cultural Revolution pattern of union subservience to party committee leadership. Among the seven chairs and vice-chairs of the new SFTU, the only ones who held exclusively union positions were Ye Changming, pre–Cultural Revolution SFTU Vice-Chair Shen Han, and Yang Fuzhen, who was a vice-chair only because she had been a labor model. The other four (Wang Hongwen, Wang Xiuzhen, Jin Zumin, and Chen Ada) retained their union positions well after they had left day-to-day work at the WGH for higher political office. To establish firmly the national prestige of the SFTU, Wang Xiuzhen made the unusual proposal that new cadres among the Central Committee and delegates to the national Tenth Party Congress all be absorbed into the SFTU Standing Committee[84]—a recommendation that Wang Hongwen approved.[85]

Although the SFTU Standing Committee was nominally expanded by these measures, only the worker rebels on the standing committee were generally permitted to join in its most important activity—its brainstorming sessions (*pengtou hui*). Thus labor model Yang Fuzhen, for example, was excluded from such meetings. The main participants in the sessions were Chen Ada, Huang Jinhai, Ma Zhenlong, Ye Changming, Dai Liqing, Jin Zuhai, and Wang Xiuzhen. Ye Changming referred to these individuals as "the standing committee of the standing committee, the core of the core."[86]

The brainstorming sessions were, in effect, planning meetings for the worker rebels to increase their leverage over party and government affairs. Wang Xiuzhen's notes of a typical brainstorming agenda read as follows:

1. "Be concerned with the big picture," "discuss current events," analyze the "current direction of class struggle," [and] discuss which activities worker rebels must engage in.
2. Transmit the speeches of Wang Hongwen, Zhang Chunqiao, Jiang Qing, and Yao Wenyuan and have the unions implement their instructions, thereby putting the unions at the forefront of the campaign.
3. Analyze SPC, SRC, and district, county, and bureau party and government agencies' relationships with union cadres and discuss how to plant our own people in these agencies to counter our opponents. Later we can utilize Wang Xiuzhen and Jin Zumin's control of organization and personnel in the SPC and SRC to realize this.
4. Discuss Wang Xiuzhen's planned speech to SPC and SRC and revise it according to ideas proposed.
5. Mutually encourage struggle on behalf of Wang Hongwen and Zhang Chunqiao.[87]

Wang Xiuzhen recalled that "after a brainstorming session of the standing committee, 'little brothers' [i.e., worker rebels] took the contents of the session to all departments of the SRC and concerned bureaus."[88] Thanks to such strategies, the influence of the unions over party and government decisions loomed larger than at any time since the socialist transformation of 1957. This was especially true at municipal and submunicipal levels in Shanghai. Wang Hongwen on more than one occasion remarked, "In Shanghai the union holds the upper hand."[89]

Because the union had assembled a loyal network of supporters in the party and government, it was able to position itself at the forefront of campaigns during the CR era. The 1974 Criticize Lin Biao–Criticize Confucius movement and the 1976 Criticize Deng initiative were both directed in Shanghai by the SFTU. During these campaigns, the union convened mass meetings and assumed the supervisory role that had been played by the party apparatus in earlier years.

Exerting National Influence

In addition to municipal-level initiatives intended to augment the presence of worker-rebel cadres in Shanghai's party and government agencies, there were two major drives to send worker cadres to the center in Beijing: (1) the "cultivate worker ambassadors and worker diplomatic personnel" program of November 1971 to May 1976, and (2) a special initiative to send "new cadres" to Central Party and government agencies in the years 1974–1975. Although neither effort proved particularly successful in the end, they symbolized the political ambitions of Shanghai's worker-rebel movement.

The idea of worker ambassadors was first raised by Zhang Chunqiao during two trips to Shanghai in 1971 and 1972. Senior cadre Ma Tianshui remembers Zhang complaining at the time: "Today's ambassadors all wear glasses; there are no young ones. They are all men; there are no women. They are all intellectuals; there are no workers. We should cultivate a group of worker ambassadors and women ambassadors. Only then can we improve the situation."[90]

To honor Zhang's wishes, 113 workers were chosen from the industrial and transport systems. Of these, thirty-three were trained at several units under the SRC Foreign Affairs Department and the other eighty at a special "workers' diplomatic cadre training session," operated at Fudan University. As it turned out, however, the trainees were never actually assigned to diplomatic posts. After the training was completed, the SRC contacted the Foreign Ministry of the State Council, but "the Foreign Ministry did not respond, indicating it did not need these people. The Foreign Ministry only valued old diplomats and didn't want this newborn force of ready-made worker diplomats."[91] Instead of the international assignments they had anticipated, the worker ambassadors were placed with the foreign affairs department of the SRC. At the end of the CR, they returned to their original work units.

Both Wang Hongwen and Zhang Chunqiao emphasized the importance of sending new cadres to the center. On March 23, 1974, SPC secretary Wang Xiuzhen recorded in her work notebook the following statement by Wang Hongwen, "Shanghai is an important place, with considerable national influence. All aspects of work must be done well and two points must be grasped: first is class struggle, second is cultivation of cadres. Lin Biao's gang managed to cultivate Zhou Yuchi and Yu Xinye. Why can't we cultivate some young cadres?"[92] At another meeting that year Wang Hongwen is reported to have said, "We should prepare 20 ministers. Can it be that among the 1.8 million workers in Shanghai we can't find 20 exemplars?!"[93]

Similarly, Zhang Chunqiao was eager to replace toppled cadres with abrasive young rebels. At the Fourth National People's Congress in September 1973, Zhang, alluding to the devilish imagery embraced by the rebels, advocated that "Those cadres with long horns on their heads and long thorns on their bodies should be sent to the center to raise a ruckus."[94] At the Tenth Party Congress the following year, Zhang confided to Xu Jingxian, Ma Tianshui, and Wang Xiuzhen (the three Shanghai Party Committee secretaries), "I originally didn't particularly want to select cadres from Shanghai; if too many were chosen, people would say it was a Shanghai gang. But now it has become necessary to select them and we can no longer afford to be above suspicion."[95]

Zhang Chunqiao was not unaware of the fact that most worker-rebel cadres lacked a good education and were inexperienced in leadership work. His stated reasons for sending such people to the center were twofold: to rebel; that is, to "kick up a ruckus"; and to gather intelligence. As he informed the Shanghai party secretaries, "I'm planning to send a worker to *People's Daily* as an office manager. He won't be concerned with editorial matters and thus the intellectuals won't be able to best him on that score. At the very least he can report to us directly on the situation there."[96]

In August 1974, after discussions among Ma Tianshui, Xu Jingxian, and Wang Xiuzhen, as well as SPC Organization Department Chief Jin Zumin, eighteen names were chosen as candidates for State Council ministers and vice-ministers. In early 1975, another sixteen names were proposed for ministers, vice-ministers, and Central Party and government offices. The great majority of these nominees were old rebels. However, when the list of names was sent to Beijing, opposition by old cadres prevented all but ten of the nominees from actually serving as ministers or vice-ministers.[97]

After the Cultural Revolution, the new SPC criticized both the worker-ambassador initiative and the sending of worker-rebel cadres to the center as "conspiracies to seize party and government leadership authority." In a report issued on December 26, 1980, by the SPC office, these two programs were characterized as "important criminal acts of Gang of Four remnants in Shanghai." However, Shanghai's combined security-procuracy-court reached a different conclusion, reasoning that

1. Mao Zedong and Zhou Enlai had both indicated that Shanghai should
   recruit worker cadres to be sent to the center; and

2. those who had been assigned to leadership positions in the center had all been duly approved by the appropriate central agencies, in accordance with legal procedures.[98]

Wang Hongwen, under interrogation in Beijing after the conclusion of the CR, also emphasized the importance of higher-level support for these initiatives: "Premier Zhou discussed with me the matter of sending cadres from Shanghai to the center. He even criticized Shanghai's thinking as conservative in not sending enough cadres to the center."[99]

Wang's testimony is corroborated by the remarks of Wang Xiuzhen at a July 1974 SFTU organizational work conference, during the height of the workers-to-the-center effort.

> Several days ago, all the central ministries requested people from Shanghai. More than ten ministries, including the Ministry of Culture, asked for Shanghai to send people. To dispatch the most outstanding Shanghai workers is a big task and we can't manage it at present. The All-China Federation of Trade Unions, Communist Youth League and Women's Federation are all looking for young successors. To handle this job properly is to consolidate the dictatorship of the proletariat.[100]

Selecting and training ordinary workers for cadre roles was not a new practice. Before the CR, the unions had routinely identified promising workers for party and government leadership positions. As we have seen, those who led the conservative workers in the early CR period were drawn from the ranks of precisely such individuals. But whereas the pre–Cultural Revolution standard for selection primarily was obedience to party authority, during the CR the chief criterion was "rebelliousness." Only those who had demonstrated a willingness to challenge party leadership at the outset of the CR were eligible for selection. This very consideration proved to be a double-edged sword for the durability of the rebel victory, however.

The Erosion of Worker-Rebel Ascendancy

Despite their domination of the 1967 January power seizure, the worker rebels ran into difficulties during the period of consolidation that followed. The same personality traits that had facilitated their rebellion became liabilities in conforming to the subsequent demands of a more routinized style of political behavior. A certain recklessness had permitted rebels to play a critical role in attacking cadres at the beginning of the CR, but as the movement developed, their continued penchant for unruly behavior rendered many of these individuals targets for censure and expulsion.

In late 1967, the WGH Standing Committee ordered an investigation into the behavior of 449 top rebel leaders.[101] The inquiry revealed that well over half of the leaders (260, or 58%) were beset with one or more "serious problems."[102] Among those with problems, thirty were arrested. Their crimes were listed as: (1) carrying out counterrevolution in viciously attacking the proletarian headquarters; (2) evidencing serious problems in his/her political history and continuing to do bad things during the movement; (3) involvement in murder, arson, and assassination; (4) graft and embezzlement, rape, moral depravity; and (5) participation in beating, smashing, and looting, with grave results.[103]

Some of the crimes of which these rebels were accused were political, but most were straightforward criminal acts. This was an early investigation carried out by the rebels themselves to ferret out the most problematic among their leaders. Later, as conservatives regained positions in party organizations, more rebel offenses were uncovered.

The 1968 Cleansing of Class Ranks campaign and the 1970 One Strike, Three-Antis campaign (to strike down those who practiced counterrevolution and to oppose graft and embezzlement, speculation and profiteering, and extravagance and waste) were two important tests for the rebel leaders. These national campaigns targeted people with so-called problems of political history as well as those who had evidenced shortcomings in their work or lifestyle. The sweep of the two campaigns and the ease with which victims were named and forced into making confessions was unprecedented in the history of the PRC.

Cleansing Class Ranks

The first public call for a campaign to cleanse class ranks came in a November 27, 1967, speech by Jiang Qing to a workers' symposium in Beijing. Later, *People's Daily*, *Red Flag*, and *Liberation Daily* printed editorials about the impending crusade. The movement involved the persecution of both cadres and masses on an amazing scale. In Shanghai, more than 169,000 people were investigated in Cleansing Ranks cases, and more than 5,000 lost their lives in the campaign.[104] Of the twenty leading cadres who had served before the Cultural Revolution as SPC secretary, standing committee member, mayor, or vice-mayor, only Zhang Chunqiao, Ma Tianshui, and Wang Shaoyong escaped detention as traitors, spies, and capitalist roaders. Of the 1,019 cadres who had served at bureau-level and above in Shanghai, 853 people (83.7%) were interrogated; of 6,161 at department (*chu*)-level or higher, 5,868 (95.2%) were apprehended. When Wang Hongwen made the inflammatory statement, "Not a single person in the party underground was good," the entire pre-1949 Communist underground in Shanghai was subjected to investigation; thirty-nine "major cases" (*da an*) and 845 "minor cases" (*xiao an*) were examined, involving 3,675 people.[105]

The Cleansing Ranks campaign took a heavy toll on industrial workers, as well. As Wang Hongwen noted in August 1968, "The number [of workers] ferreted out in two months was greater than in the entire previous two years."[106] Figures contained in bulletins issued by the WGH suggest the scope of the campaign at the factory level.

- Of 1,000 employees at Shanghai's Number 26 Radio Factory, sixty-four were targets of cleansing.[107]
- Of 1,100 employees at the Shanghai Electronic Information Instruments Factory, 120 were targets.[108]
- Of more than one-hundred employees at the Number 16 Dyed-Silk Factory, ten were ferreted out.[109]
- Of 160 employees at Shanghai's Oxidized Steel Factory, twenty were discovered to be "secret agents, traitors, hegemons or counterrevolutionaries," and nine were found to be "class enemies."[110]
- Of 300,000 employees at the Textile Bureau and nearly 40,000 in the Handicraft Bureau, by November 1968 14,000 class enemies and 4,500 others had been uncovered.[111]

Severe punishment consisted of incarceration and beatings; light punishment meant deduction of wages or public criticism. Of the two-hundred employees at the Huangpu District Finance Bureau, sixty were "dug out"—of whom forty-seven suffered wage cuts or freezing of savings.[112] At the Shanghai Number 2 Steel Mill, 209 (4.9% of the employees) were ferreted out; of these, fifty-nine suffered wage cuts, 185 were subjected to public criticism, and 170 were assigned to long-term labor.[113]

In contrast to the way in which the campaign was carried out in most of the country, in Shanghai the targets included a large number of rebels and rebel leaders. Many of the worker rebels had been sanctioned prior to the CR—whether for deficiencies in their work or lifestyle or for certain problems in their family background or personal political history. Those who fell into the latter category were easy marks during the Cleansing of Ranks campaign.

As Wang Hongwen readily recognized, the movement provided a golden opportunity for those who had lost out during the power seizure to wreak revenge on their victorious opponents.

In the January Revolution those who had been ox-demons and snake-spirits now use the pretext of cleansing class ranks to seize on some shortcomings among rebels and revolutionary committee members or some small problems persisting among some cadres to make judgments about the whole. They attack and slander and everywhere ferret out "bad people" and "black hands."

A bureau in the transport system, without higher-level authorization, tied up the rebel leader and convened a mass meeting to publicly declaim him as a "bad leader." Then they sent some sort of "leading Small Group to investigate the masses" down to the basic levels and summarily sealed up the doors of the rebels' "attack with words, defend with force" and revolutionary committee, forcing them to hand over their chops and documents. Calling this a "power seizure," they forced most of the rebel leaders in [the] factory and workshops to step aside and undergo labor under surveillance.

Conservative forces in every unit have taken advantage of the opportunity to raise a ruckus. In some factories, former Scarlet Guard leaders are secretly plotting and have posted big slogans . . . [such as] "sweep away all ox-demons and snake-spirits" at the entrances to rebel offices. They also have organized big-character-poster brigades to attack the rebels.

Some people are really keen on ferreting out rebel "bad heads," but show little interest in struggling against capitalist roaders, traitors, and secret agents.[114]

Wang Hongwen concluded, "This is an evil rightist wind whose obvious characteristic is a repudiation of the revolutionary rebels, a repudiation of the January Revolution, an attempt to reverse verdicts on the bourgeois reactionary line, [on the] capitalist roaders, traitors, and secret agents, and [is] a plot to destroy the revolutionary rebels organizationally."[115]

One Strike, Three-Antis

Despite Wang Hongwen's objections, an even more severe attack on the worker rebels was yet to come. The One Strike, Three-Antis campaign, which rolled across Shanghai from February 1970 to December 1972, was an initiative that laid bare the contradictions between worker and student rebels. The high school classes of 1966 and 1967 had not graduated because of the CR, and in late 1968, they were put directly to work instead. Unlike in most of China, where students were often sent off to distant communes to labor as peasants, in Shanghai the students were mainly assigned to factories and nearby state farms. Hundreds of thousands of politically active youngsters were thereby added to the ranks of the working class.

When Red Guards had first gone to the factories to link up with the workers, they supported the factory rebels without reservation. But after these students actually became workers themselves, they quickly discovered the wide gulf that separated their own perspective from that of the worker rebels. (See Chapter 1.) Idealistic and relatively well educated, the students realized that, in terms of personal style, they shared much more in common with the conservatives than with the rebel workers. Having just left the politicized atmosphere of the schoolyard, their activist inclinations were still strong. The One Strike, Three-Antis campaign was the students' first chance for political participation since entering the factories. So, with the tacit support of the conservatives, they put up big-character-posters against the rebel leaders.

The One Strike, Three-Antis campaign was extensive in scope;[116] by the time of its conclusion, the movement had fingered 131,645 people in Shanghai said to be guilty of various economic crimes adding up to more than 56 million yuan in losses.[117] A total of 29,242 people were dubbed "counter-revolutionaries," and more than 1,600 died abnormal deaths during the campaign.[118] Although some of the demoted rebel leaders lost their positions because of long-standing political problems, the great majority (approximately 80%) were dismissed because of disreputable activities or poor job performance after seizing power in the January Revolution.[119]

Typical of the industrial sector as a whole was the Clock and Watch Company of the Shanghai Light Industry Bureau, where 243 rebel leaders (out of 348 rebel leaders at 31 factories) were removed from office because of recent political, economic, and personal mistakes or poor job performance. This amounted to the dismissal of nearly 70 percent of the rebel leaders in the entire company.[120] The situation was similar in the bureaus. Of the 121 rebel leaders at the General Liaison Station of the ten companies belonging to the Bureau of Light Industry, sixty-four (i.e., more than half) were dismissed from their posts for transgressions of various sorts.[121]

The combined impact of the two campaigns on rebel workers was substantial. An investigation by the WGH in 1972 concluded,

> After the Cleansing of Ranks and the One Strike, Three-Antis, a group of new cadres was dismissed for various reasons. The nine industrial bureaus of Number 1 machinery, textiles, light industry, chemical engineering, instruments, watches, Number 2 machinery, metallurgy, [and] electronics suffered 137 dismissals, equal to 44.5% of the total of new cadres. In the finance and trade bureaus, 49 [cadres] were dismissed (equal to 36.3%); among the districts, 135 were dismissed (equal to 43.5% of the new cadres). Add to these the fact that a number of cadres were demoted without actually being dismissed and the proportion grows considerably higher.[122]

These campaigns struck a severe blow to the highest levels of worker-rebel leadership. Of the seventeen workers who had remained late on the evening of November 6, 1966, to finalize plans for the founding of the WGH—all of whom became top leaders in that organization (see Chapter 2)—seven were sent to the Public Security Bureau or were detained at their work units, and another two were returned to their original factories for supervised "labor" as a consequence of these two campaigns.

The Dilemma of the WPTs

Old rebels were not alone in facing difficulties during the years following the January power seizure. Despite the personal endorsement of Chairman Mao, Workers' Propaganda Teams also ran into problems in trying to occupy the commanding heights of party and government leadership. Although WPTs were sent, for the most part, to academic and cultural institutions, the educational level of the team members was quite low. From available statistics, we estimate that about 65 percent of the WPT members sent to universities or research units had a middle school education, and the remaining 35 percent claimed only an elementary education; among those sent to middle and elementary schools or districts or neighborhoods, the educational level was even lower—with more than half having only an elementary school education. The few members who boasted some college training were permitted only a supporting role in WPT operations; leadership was invariably vested in the hands of the less educated.[123]

It was impossible for these poorly educated workers to assume a guiding role at higher-level academic institutions or scientific research institutes. So, as a WGH report noted, they "nodded their heads without confidence or shook their heads without reason. . . . When it was time to remember the bitter and the sweet [i.e., to discuss class exploitation], the bitter waters came pouring out, but when it was time to discuss professional matters they had nothing of import to say."[124]

When WPTs were first constituted, they composed about 10 percent of the Shanghai workforce. But this loss of labor power exerted an adverse effect on production, and by July 1974 the number of WPT members in the city was down to 10,713—about one-tenth of the initial figure.[125] Although the upper leadership of the WPTs were stalwarts of the WGH, the main membership was not composed of prominent worker rebels. Rebels who saw some prospects of gaining power in their units were uninterested in abandoning this possibility to join WPTs. Thus the early rank-and-file WPT members were largely rebels who were being shunned at their own units.

After 1969, a substantial number of cadres from factories were added to WPTs. These cadres had been "set aside" by the rebels when their factories established revolutionary committees, and they were barred from resuming their former positions. Having no obvious shortcomings that qualified them for attack, however, they were sent to be "educated" in WPTs. By January 1974, nearly 30 percent of all WPT members stationed in the city's cultural and educational system were former cadres; in some individual units the proportion of cadres was considerably higher.[126]

Additionally, the factories sent a number of elderly and sickly individuals to join WPTs. This was generally done out of concern for the ailing workers—rather than for the institutions to which they had been assigned.

> Some sent the WPT backbones back to the factories and replaced the strong with the weak. People with various illnesses who couldn't engage in normal work were sent off. Workers on the verge of retirement were also sent. For example, the Shanghai Glass Factory dispatched 7 workers, suffering from 8 illnesses, to the North Station Clinic. The Shanghai Number 22 Cotton Mill sent a 49-year-old woman worker with asthma and a 53-year-old worker with gallstones to the Xinhua Hospital as WPT members.[127]

According to another investigation, "Among WPT members dispatched to middle and elementary schools, the elderly were numerous, the poorly educated were numerous, those unable to engage in public speaking were numerous, and the sick were numerous. The factories simply sent them to the schools to recuperate."[128]

Under these circumstances, leadership by WPTs was a farce. Unable to take charge, team members busied themselves with observing the scene, repairing the grounds, or sweeping the floors. At some schools, "When the students got into fights, the WPT members became policemen; when teachers argued, the WPT members became mediators; when the schools opened, the WPT members became liaison officers; when the schools built new buildings, the WPT members acquired the materials."[129] But in many other cases, WPTs were less benign, stirring up "class struggle" to compensate for their lack of professional expertise, raising political objections to the content of the curriculum or the way that films were being made, and the like.

Temporary Respite: The Second Seize-Power Movement

Among the many unsolved puzzles of the Cultural Revolution, the Criticize Lin Biao–Criticize Confucius campaign of the years 1973–1974 remains one of the most perplexing. Many clues point to the CLCC as an attack on Premier Zhou Enlai, yet a search of Mao's speeches and essays about the campaign reveals no references to Zhou. Whatever the motivation of the top CCP leadership, for Shanghai's worker rebels the CLCC campaign became in essence an "antirestoration" movement aimed at stemming the erosion in their now-precarious authority. In trying to consolidate their position, the rebels' slogan was "protect the fruits of the Cultural Revolution." Wang Xiuzhen more than once announced at various meetings that

> There is a group of old cadres who were criticized at the outset of the CR who harbor revenge which they want to vent. They want to reverse verdicts on the CR and settle accounts with the CR. They want to restore things to the pre–Cultural Revolution situation. They engage in "two denials," whereas we want to criticize the two denials and criticize this restoration.
>
> Now other places think ill of Shanghai and attack us. This sort of attack is an indication of line struggle. Actually this sort of attack is not only directed against Shanghai, but even more is directed at the three leading comrades in the center [i.e., Jiang Qing, Zhang Chunqiao, and Wang Hongwen]. So we must strive to do our work well.[130]

Wang's allusion to "two denials" referred to "denying the Cultural Revolution" and "denying the newborn things of the Cultural Revolution." The latter included revolutionary committees, workers' propaganda teams, and, especially, new cadres promoted from among the worker rebels. Wang was particularly alarmed about the roadblocks being raised to prevent rebel cadres from joining the party or from assuming administrative responsibilities.

Although harbingers of the new campaign had appeared as early as 1972 (in a seemingly arcane academic debate on the periodization of ancient history),[131] Wang Xiuzhen did not grasp its full import until January 1974, at the time of the Chinese New Year, when a group of leaders from the Shanghai trade union gathered at her home to celebrate the holiday.[132] After dinner, the assembled unionists placed a long-distance call to Wang Hongwen in Beijing (who was then vice-chair of the CCP), to seek his advice for the coming year. (At the Tenth Party Congress of August 1973, at which the ongoing crusade against Confucius was explicitly linked with the criticism of Lin Biao, Wang Hongwen had been catapulted into the third spot in the leadership hierarchy—preceded only by Mao Zedong and Zhou Enlai; Wang's long-time patron, Zhang Chunqiao, now ranked beneath him.) Over the phone, Wang Hongwen alerted the Shanghai union leaders to the significance of the unfolding campaign: "Today the agencies under direct control of Party Central are convening a 10,000-person meeting to promote the CLCC; tomorrow, the army is also going to convene a 10,000-person meeting, mobilized by Jiang Qing herself." Wang Hongwen admonished his friends in Shanghai to seize the initiative in the campaign, explaining that "the CLCC must be linked to practice, linked to the practice of the ninth and tenth line struggles.[133] The union must grasp the big picture; the CLCC is the big picture. The union must stand at the forefront."[134]

In response to Wang Hongwen's counsel, the SFTU took immediate action. A week later, on February 2, the "Shanghai Workers' Penetratingly Criticize Lin and Confucius Meeting" was convened at Cultural Plaza, with more than 10,000 people representing municipal, district, county, and bureau-level unions and WPTs. Heads of party organizations at all levels also attended the convocation to "receive education." Wang Xiuzhen spoke at the meeting, enjoining unions at all levels to expose the "two denials" and "restorationist retreat" and calling on the rebels to develop the spirit of the January Revolution and protect the fruits of the CR.

Systems, bureaus, districts, and factories rushed to respond, with the unions leading the mobilization drive.[135] Ye Changming, directing the SFTU work, advocated using this movement to "establish the martial authority of the unions." He saw the CLCC campaign as an occasion to reverse the routinization that had beset his organization in recent years: "The prestige of the WGH exploded out of the Cultural Revolution. But, more recently, union work had become insipid, colorless, and its prestige had declined. We wanted to take advantage of the opportunity of this campaign to energize the unions and raise the prestige of the unions in the course of [the] struggle."[136]

With unions at all levels pushing the offensive, the posterboards again overflowed. The rebels saw the CLCC as tantamount to a second power seizure. In February 1974, Zhang Chunqiao wrote a letter to Ma Tianshui, which read in part,[137]

> Frankly speaking, in some units power could not be seized during the January storm, and in other units seized power was lost. The persistence and complexity of the struggle lie in this. Otherwise, why the fuss over criticizing Lin . . . [and] Confucius. . . [and over] restoration and retreat? Why must cultural revolutions be undertaken repeatedly?[137]

A new power seizure was indeed launched in many Shanghai industrial agencies and factories.[138] At the Jiangnan Shipyard, for example, the military propaganda team that had assumed control during the January Revolution was accused of "two denials" and "restorationism," after which the entire leadership body—some 348 cadres from factory level down to department, workshop, and production team—was summarily replaced.[139]

TABLE 6.2   Shanghai Party Recruitment During the Cultural Revolution

Year	Number of Party Members Recruited	Percentage Increase in Party Membership over Previous Year
1968–1971	28,807	7.35 (over 1966)
1972	27,416	6.26
1973	45,028	9.69
1974	38,275	7.34
1975	29,581	5.23
1976	22,074	3.65

SOURCE: Shanghai Party committee, ed., *Zhongguo gongchandang Shanghaishi dangyuan he dang zuzhi tongji ziliao huibian* [Compilation of statistical materials on party members and party organizations of the Chinese Communist party in Shanghai], Shanghai, May 1986.

To better understand the aims of this campaign, the Shanghai Party Committee sent Wang Xiuzhen to Beijing in late March for three days of consultation with Wang Hongwen, Zhang Chunqiao, and Yao Wenyuan. The central leaders expressed the hope that their old bailiwick of Shanghai would spearhead this movement, using the campaign as an occasion for recruiting rebel cadres who might be transferred to the center. Upon her return to Shanghai, Wang Xiuzhen encouraged the unions to mobilize new cadres at all levels.

A big-character-poster at the Number 2 Bureau of Commerce (where Huang Jinhai was now in control) noted, with a hyperbolic flourish, that the real issue behind the criticism of the two denials and restorationism was the declining fortunes of the rebel faction: "During the great alliance period, the rebels lost 50 percent of their positions; during the triple combinations, they lost two-thirds of their positions; when the party organizations were restored, they lost out 100 percent."[140]

Having achieved only limited success in their earlier bids to gain admission to the Communist Party, rebel workers in Shanghai took advantage of the 1973–1974 CLCC campaign to launch another, more effective, effort. The newly reconstituted SFTU convened an organizational work conference aimed specifically at the goal of increasing party membership among its activists. Thanks to the clear Party Central endorsement of this initiative, the results were immediate. Within three days, the Number 1 Machine-Electric Bureau ordered its personnel department to appoint a group of old rebels to important posts at bureau and factory levels. Similarly, the Foreign Trade Bureau quickly admitted more than two-hundred rebels to the party and promoted a number of rebel leaders to company and bureau leadership positions.[141]

The CLCC campaign resulted in the recruitment of a large group of new party members in Shanghai. As the data in Table 6.2 show, the city drafted about 83,000

TABLE 6.3   Occupations of New Party Recruits in Shanghai

Year	Workers[a]		Peasants		Cadres, etc.	
	Number	Percentage	Number	Percentage	Number	Percentage
1962	11,561	20.3	33,696	59.1	11,758	20.6
1967–1971	15,514	53.9	5,717	19.8	7,576	26.3
1972	13,580	49.5	5,884	21.5	7,952	29.0
1973	22,283	49.5	9,363	20.8	13,382	29.7
1974	17,528	45.8	9,108	23.8	11,639	30.4
1975	14,720	49.8	5,001	16.9	9,860	33.3
1976	9,985	45.2	4,785	21.7	7,304	33.1

[a] "Workers" do not include cadre or white-collar employees at factories

SOURCE: Shanghai Party committee, ed., *Zhongguo gongchandang Shanghaishi dangyuan he dang zuzhi tongji ziliao huibian* [Compilation of statistical materials on party members and party organizations of the Chinese communist party in Shanghai], Shanghai, May 1986.

new party recruits in the years 1973–1974, nearly double the number that had been inducted during the preceding five years. Of these new recruits, workers composed a substantial proportion.

As the figures in Table 6.3 indicate, workers contributed the lion's share of party inductees throughout the CR decade. Whereas, previously, only about one-fifth of party recruits had been drawn from workers, during the CR the proportion rose to about one-half. The number of party members among the city's workforce nearly doubled over the course of the CR decade, as seen in Table 6.4.

Along with this impressive growth in party membership went a commensurate increase in rebel promotions to top cadre posts. According to a summary report of the SFTU, in 1974 some sixty-six worker new cadres were advanced to leading posts at the municipal level.[142] Ye Changming credited the CLCC campaign with raising the prestige of his union: "In the past the party committee did not respect the unions, but as soon as this movement came along we gained respect. Some party committee secretaries never used to go to union offices, but now they rush there for news updates. Now just as soon as the SFTU convenes a cadre meeting those party secretaries get agitated."[143]

The "second power seizure" was not without its detractors, however. Cadres, party members, and ordinary workers were generally unhappy to see their units plunged into conflict once again. Moreover, intrarebel dissension erupted as well. Rebels who had been disciplined for bad behavior in earlier campaigns tried to make a comeback, often without success. Victorious rebels resisted the demands of their erstwhile comrades, likening their efforts at reinstatement to "burning incense to attract demons."[144]

TABLE 6.4   Party Members Among the Shanghai Workforce Before and During the
Cultural Revolution

Year	Number of Worker Party Members	Total Number of Workers	Percentage
1962	3.21	232.46	13.80
1965	3.45	271.19	12.74
1970	4.23	306.53	13.81
1976	6.44	397.82	16.19

unit=10,000 people

SOURCE: Shanghai Party committee, ed., *Zhongguo gongchandang Shanghaishi dangyuan he dang zuzhi tongji ziliao huibian* [Compilation of statistical materials on party members and party organizations of the Chinese communist party in Shanghai], Shanghai, May 1986.

Meanwhile old cadres who had returned to power were subjected to harsh criticism. The situation was especially complex in Shanghai, however, inasmuch as a number of the returned cadres were actually promoting rebel-worker interests. The contradictions came to a head in spring 1974, when the party committee of Yangpu District, under worker-rebel instigation, launched a virulent attack against its party secretary, old cadre Zhang Jingbiao. Subsequently, Zhang was dragged from factory to factory for public criticism.[145]

The assault on Zhang Jingbiao proved to be a turning point in Shanghai's rendition of the CLCC campaign. Zhang was serving concurrently as director of the SPC office, a right-hand man of senior cadre Ma Tianshui. Outraged by this treatment of his trusted lieutenant, Ma called Zhang Chunqiao to file a complaint. Concerned about the level of disruption that had been stirred up by Shanghai's worker rebels during the course of the campaign, Zhang Chunqiao responded sympathetically to Ma's objection: "If things continue in this fashion, today they can drag forth Zhang Jingbiao, tomorrow they can drag forth Wang Xiuzhen and Xu Jingxian, and the next day perhaps they'll drag forth you, Ma Tianshui. If things continue like this, won't it mean disaster for the likes of us?" He asked Ma to instruct the SFTU to curb the campaign.[146] Ma immediately notified Wang Xiuzhen, who passed along the word to Ye Changming of the SFTU. The CLCC was thus brought to an abrupt halt in Shanghai during the summer of 1974.

Having been encouraged to regard the CLCC as a second power seizure, the worker rebels were naturally disappointed by Zhang Chunqiao's unceremonious termination of it. Huang Jinhai complained, "It's not at all easy to get a fire going. Then to suddenly snuff it out leaves the campaign with only half-cooked rice."[147] When such criticisms reached Zhang Chunqiao's ears, he insisted that the union leaders engage in self-criticism. In late 1974, the SFTU drafted a summary report of its annual activities that expressed abject regret for its aggressive role in the CLCC movement.

> Because we had not studied enough or investigated enough, before and during the CLCC campaign we could not clearly analyze the political situation. We either over-estimated or underestimated the severity of the struggle. For example, in the early part of the campaign because we heard and saw many things relating to the Cleansing of Ranks and the One Strike Three–Antis, we became hotheads and proposed some intemperate slogans, generating the error of "opposing restoration" (i.e., opposing the return to power of old cadres). Our emotions influenced some districts, counties, bureaus, and basic-rank union cadres. Had the SPC leadership not offered timely criticism, it would have been very dangerous.
>
> We carry out the instructions of the SPC, but are not respectful of district, county, and bureau party committees. There is a tendency for us to issue commands to them. It's as though, if they don't obey us unionists, they aren't relying on the working class and have a problem of line. Under our influence, individual district, county, and bu-reau as well as some basic-level cadres don't fully obey the party committees of their same rank. There is even a tendency to evade party leadership altogether. . . . Some comrades during this campaign dredged up old "rebel" and "conservative" dividing lines of 8 years ago.[148]

The SFTU statement indicated the difficult position in which the worker rebels found themselves by this point. Practices considered "revolutionary" at the outset of the CR were now deemed "intemperate." Although the CLCC campaign breathed new life into the rebel movement, it was a temporary resuscitation. By the end of the campaign, Shanghai's worker rebels had been humbled for their "hotheaded" excesses.

The List of 181 Old Chiefs

As the status of the worker rebels declined, the question of how to deal with their former victims assumed increased salience. In spring 1973, just before undergo-ing surgery for cancer, Premier Zhou Enlai requested that the Organization Min-istry compile a list of names of cadres to be "liberated." Among the names in-cluded on the roster was Shanghai's former first party secretary, Chen Pixian. Chairman Mao concurred with the reversal of verdicts on Chen, even stating that Chen was not a "black demon," as his rebel detractors had alleged, but a "red demon" instead.[149]

As early as the February adverse current of 1967, a point of debate between Vice-Premier Tan Zhenlin and Zhang Chunqiao had been the question of Chen Pixian. Several vice-premiers and PLA marshals criticized Shanghai for not hav-ing liberated Chen, but Zhang disagreed. Later, Wang Hongwen announced on several occasions: "If Chen Pixian returns to the stage, I'm stepping off it!" Zhang Chunqiao and the old rebels took Chen Pixian and Cao Diqiu as symbols of the rectitude of the CR. In each political movement after 1949, there had been such symbolic personages.[150] Were Chen to be liberated, this would have been tantamount to declaring that Shanghai's January Revolution had been a colossal mistake.

To argue against Cao Diqiu's return to office, Zhang Chunqiao and Wang Hongwen insisted that most underground party members before 1949 had been enemy agents and that those who had been arrested and imprisoned were, to a person, traitors. As a former activist in the underground who had been imprisoned, Cao Diqiu was deemed a "turncoat" (*pantu*). However, Chen Pixian by contrast, had been active in the Communist army in base-area work rather than in the Shanghai underground. Because Chen had never been arrested, there was no "historical evidence" to hold against him; he was therefore assigned the label of "black demon" (*hei xiaogui*).

When Party Central forwarded to Shanghai the list of cadres to be liberated, including Chen Pixian, the local authorities at first simply let the matter rest. But pressure from the center continued. In fall 1974, Mao asked repeatedly about Chen Pixian, advising that his case should be handled as a contradiction among the people.[151] On October 9, Wang Hongwen phoned Wang Xiuzhen to inform her that, in view of Mao's stated position, it seemed that Chen Pixian would have to be exonerated after all. To soften the blow, Wang Hongwen suggested that a substantial number of ousted rebels be rehabilitated at the same time; as he put it, "Chen Pixian is to be liberated, so you should quickly put together a list of rebel chiefs from the January Revolution who should also be dealt with properly. This will show Chen Pixian that his opponents are still around."[152]

Soon thereafter, Ma Tianshui received a phone call from Zhang Chunqiao asking that he make arrangements for the rehabilitation of a group of Chen's erstwhile opponents before the former party secretary himself was liberated.[153] When Ma Tianshui communicated the ideas of Zhang Chunqiao and Wang Hongwen to SFTU's Ye Changming, Ye rushed back to the union and worked through the night to compile a list of 147 old rebel chiefs. After its inspection by Ma Tianshui and Wang Xiuzhen, a few former Red Guard leaders were added to the roster. Based on these recommendations, the SPC Organization Department produced a list of 181 ousted rebel leaders.[154]

The erstwhile rebel chiefs included three types of people: First were leaders who had challenged the hegemony of Wang Hongwen; for example, WGH cofounder and vice-commander Pan Guoping, Second Regiment leader Geng Jinzhang, First Regiment leader Dai Zuxiang, Workers Third Headquarters leader Chen Hongkang, and so on.[155] Second were those who had been expelled for extramarital affairs, rape, extortion, murder, violence, and other crimes.[156] Third were leaders of non-worker-rebel organizations such as the Finance Revolutionary Committee, the Elementary Teachers' Headquarters, the Public Security Bureau Revolutionary Committee, and the like. There were also some Red Guard leaders included. More than 70 percent of those listed for rehabilitation had been affiliated with the WGH and its militia and liaison posts; 8 percent with the Finance

Revolutionary Committee and its subsidiary organizations; 11 percent in mass organizations of culture and education, public health, and science and research systems, as well as municipal party committee and government agencies; and 10 percent in Red Guard student organizations.[157]

On the morning of October 11, the list was printed and sent by plane to Beijing. A few days later, Zhang Chunqiao and Wang Hongwen circled the names of more than thirty people on the roster, with instructions that these people be immediately reinstated in appropriate positions. Zhang put Pan Guoping at the top of his list for rehabilitation. As Wang Xiuzhen recalled,

> In 1974 when Chen Pixian was about to be liberated, Zhang Chunqiao—in order to firm up the opposition—stipulated that he [i.e., Pan] must be properly placed. Ye Changming and Jin Zumin suggested [that] Pan be made a member of the SFTU Standing Committee, but I feared [that] that position was too low and would not serve to buttress the opposition, so I phoned Wang Hongwen to propose that Pan be made vice-chair of the SFTU. But Wang didn't agree, and in the end Pan was designated a standing committee member."[158]

In this way, Pan Guoping returned to the SFTU from his stint at hard labor. Similarly, Geng Jinzhang became a member of the standing committee of the Bureau of Light Industry. Ye Changming approved the reassignment of a total of twenty-seven old rebels, but because the CR ended sooner than expected, the process of reinstatement was never completed.[159]

The End of the Cultural Revolution in Shanghai

The year 1976 was a momentous one in Beijing. Zhou Enlai's death gave rise to the April Fifth Tiananmen Incident, in which hundreds of thousands of mourners gathered to express grief at Zhou's passing and dissatisfaction with the radical policies of Jiang Qing and company. Sympathetic demonstrations erupted in dozens of other cities across China.[160] But Shanghai remained placid. In contrast to the droves of protesters who converged on Beijing's Tiananmen Square, in Shanghai's People's Plaza a lone, young worker raised a white flag in memory of Zhou Enlai. The hapless fellow was immediately apprehended and jailed.[161]

As the curtain was rung down on the CR in Beijing, however, Shanghai came alive. When Party Central announced the gravity of Mao Zedong's medical condition on June 27, Wang Hongwen immediately ordered his rebel supporters in Shanghai to strengthen the militia. An additional 75,000 guns, 200 mortars, and over ten million rounds of ammunition were disbursed to the Shanghai militia over the next two months. On September 10, the day after Mao died, Wang Xiuzhen made the rounds of major factories in the city to warn the militias of impending military action. That same day, the Shanghai militia detonated 600 cartridges and 15,000 artillery shells in a fiery display of unswerving support for Mao's widow and her colleagues.[162]

Less than a month later, however, the stunning arrest of the Gang of Four (Jiang Qing, Zhang Chunqiao, Yao Wenyuan, and Wang Hongwen) shattered Shanghai's ties with the CR clique in Beijing. The arrests were not immediately announced, but on October 7, the day after the roundup, with no explanation senior cadre Ma Tianshui and Shanghai Garrison Commander Zhou Chunlin were called to Beijing for an urgent meeting. When Ma's trusted secretary phoned back to Xu Jingxian in Shanghai with the cryptic message that his old stomach ailment was acting up again, Xu, who knew of no previous intestinal afflictions, suspected the worst.

As still-unconfirmed rumors of the arrest of their radical patrons reached Shanghai, Zhang Chunqiao's literati allies and Wang Hongwen's worker rebels were equally distraught. Leaders of these groups met on several occasions to plan armed resistance. The militia was put on full alert and special forces were dispatched to guard the newspaper offices, broadcast stations, and party archives.[163]

The worker rebels retained their feisty demeanor to the end. Wang Xiuzhen, Wang Hongwen's top deputy, took personal responsibility for mobilizing the militia. At a meeting of SFTU old rebels and militia commanders to discuss military action, she exploded: "Look here. Chairman Mao has only just passed away and they couldn't wait to stage a palace coup. This is more Khrushchevian than Khrushchev!" Chen Ada jumped to his feet to second her sentiments, "If Party Central goes revisionist, never fear. We'll counter it. I didn't die during the Cultural Revolution. Now I'm ready to die, but I'm not afraid." Then Huang Jinhai chimed in, "We can instigate a strike, organize workers' demonstrations, post slogans and manifestoes." Ye Changming concurred, "We can't surrender; we can't become traitors." Wang Xiuzhen concluded the meeting with a call for the worker rebels to draw on their earlier history of struggles: "You all have the experience of having fought Lian Si. At that time our forces were divided into a first line and a second line. When the fighting begins, you must all go to the various command posts and take charge."[164]

Two Shanghai Militia command headquarters were established; one at the Jiangnan Shipyard in the west of the city and the other at the Chinese Textile Machinery Factory, in the east. A flurry of consultations ensued in which the Public Security Bureau agreed to provide additional weapons and vehicles, the Writers' Group took responsibility for radio broadcasts and newspaper editorials, and so forth. In the midst of this commotion, Wang Xiuzhen and Xu Jingxian were summoned to Beijing; again, without explanation.[165]

Bereft of these key leaders, the remnant rebels persisted in their determination to fight on. After news of the Gang of Four's arrest circulated via Taiwan radio broadcasts, the worker rebels convened another meeting to discuss their response. The mood was still uncompromising. Declared Chen Ada, "Give me revolution or give me death! Everyone should swear an oath. Who wants to be a traitor, damn

it?! Even in death I'd take three bites out of such a person!" Huang Jinhai continued, "Right! Whether or not we swear an oath, I'm organizing a 'dog-beating
brigade'!"[166] Not to be outdone, Ma Zhenlong sobbed, "From my childhood I had
to work to make ends meet. It was the Cultural Revolution that liberated me. I'm
going to carry through no matter what the consequences." The rebels thereupon
decided to recall fellow WGH founder Dai Liqing (who was then away at a May
Seventh cadre school) to serve as front-line commander for their military initiatives.[167]

Meanwhile, Zhu Yongjia of the Writers' Group called in worker rebel Ma Zhenlong to stress the need for cooperation between the two groups. As Zhu put it, "In
the past we had a bit of conflict, but now we must unite and work together. With
the unions taking the lead, the militia will act. We literati rebels will offer full support." Old suspicions were not easily erased, however. When Dai Liqing arrived
back on the scene to take charge of the militia, he remarked of the Writers' Group:
"Those old fogies don't mean it when they say they want action. If they won't act,
let's go ahead on our own." Ye Changming was more cautious: "Without party authorization, people won't listen to the union or the militia. Before the militia can
move, the army will crush it."[168]

While the debate continued, time was running out for the worker rebels. On
October 13, Ma Tianshui, Xu Jingxian, and Wang Xiuzhen returned to Shanghai,
their release having been made contingent upon an agreement to persuade their
fellow rebels of the need to accommodate to the new post–Gang of Four order. At
first, it looked as if persuasion would be extremely difficult to achieve. On the ride
back from the Shanghai Airport, Ma, Xu, and Wang sat mute while Zhang Jingbiao, the SPC cadre who had been meeting continuously with the worker rebels
during the absence of his superiors, harangued his fellow passengers. Although
Jiang's rough kidnapping by worker rebels had brought the CLCC campaign to a
screeching halt two years earlier, he had come to develop a genuine respect for his
former detractors.

> These young people [i.e., the worker rebels] are really precious (*kegui*). What they say
> makes sense. They have deep emotions about the CR. Only for your sake have they
> not yet taken action. They are unafraid of death. . . . You weren't here on the night of
> the twelfth when these young comrades all congregated. They were all so lovable
> (*keai*) and all of them were prepared to die. We old folks have so many years on them,
> it's no big deal for us to die. But can you really talk them out of it?[169]

That night the returned emissaries convened a meeting of district, county, and
bureau leaders to explain the momentous changes at Party Central. If the words
of their turncoat superiors left any room for doubt in the minds of the old rebels,
the actions of the Shanghai citizenry soon settled the issue definitively. Before the
militia could be called into service, the streets of Shanghai were flooded with
huge, spontaneous demonstrations of workers and other residents proclaiming

their joy at the downfall of the Gang of Four. Old rebels were quickly rounded up and forced to suffer precisely the same sort of public humiliation that they themselves had once so eagerly meted out. The Cultural Revolution, which had begun in Shanghai with Yao Wenyuan's criticism of *Hai Rui Dismissed from Office*, ended there with the workers' militia powerless to follow through on its plans for military resistance.

Limited Gains

In light of the widespread suffering wrought by the Cultural Revolution, it is tempting to see the mass organizations that sprang to life at that time as little more than elite-sponsored instruments for perpetrating terror.[170] Moreover, the masses themselves are often pictured as having gained nothing but further repression from their involvement in this whole sorry enterprise.

Most mass organizations were dissolved only two and a half years after the start of the CR, just as they were beginning to demand a real voice in the new power structure, but Shanghai's Workers' General Headquarters was a notable exception.[171] Despite several name changes, Wang Hongwen's WGH remained fundamentally intact throughout the duration of the CR decade. Moreover, it succeeded in gaining an unprecedented degree of authority for its worker activists. Despite opposition from old cadres, intellectuals, and conservative rivals, the WGH emerged as a critical political force. Wang Hongwen's own "helicopter ascent" to the commanding heights of party power was the most dramatic indication of this phenomenon, but the takeover of Shanghai administration by his followers was hardly less impressive.

The tendency for workers to assume new political roles during the CR, though most pronounced in Shanghai, was not limited to that city. Stephen Andors concludes on the basis of his national study that "the CR saw a marked influx of workers and new cadres from factories into organs of local government."[172] Despite these striking developments, there is little evidence that either Wang Hongwen in Beijing or his "little brothers" in Shanghai or elsewhere around the country used their newfound authority to advance the socioeconomic interests of their fellow workers.[173]

Although inequalities inherent in the operations of China's socialist system had certainly helped to fuel the mass strife of the CR, most notably during the wind of economism, the victorious rebels undertook few concerted efforts to redress these underlying grievances. Even though the replacement of factory party committees by new revolutionary committees may have muted some of the resentment against workplace managers that had initially triggered the rebel leaders' own activism, the subsequent elimination of bonuses and other material incentives was hardly a popular measure with the workforce at large. With unions focusing more attention on augmenting their political clout than on improving the welfare of ordinary workers, the factory cafeterias, clinics, bath houses, child care centers, and so on suffered a noticeable deterioration in services.[174]

The series of factory strikes that erupted in Hangzhou toward the end of the CR decade was symptomatic of the general worker dissatisfaction. As Lowell Dittmer notes, these strikes were launched by workers "whose worldview may have more closely approximated that of Deng Xiaoping than that of the Gang of Four—they wanted bonuses and higher wages, which were taboo from the Maoist perspective."[175] Indeed, when Wang Hongwen went in person to Hangzhou to settle the disturbance, his modus operandi was to toss the "economistic" strikers behind bars.[176] To the end, the worker rebels were engaged in a personal quest for political recognition rather than a class crusade to improve the lot of their fellow laborers.

7

Conclusion

The Cultural Revolution marked a major watershed in the study of contemporary China. The remarkable political activism displayed by ordinary citizens during the course of that movement served to discredit the prevailing totalitarian model and to engender new approaches that assigned greater influence to social forces. These post–Cultural Revolution interpretations differed in identifying the bases of popular activism; some stressed socioeconomic interest groups, others clientelist networks, and yet others psychocultural orientations. In this book, we have argued for the relevance of all of these considerations.

Three Faces of Activism

Important as social forces were in the unfolding of the Cultural Revolution, they tugged in contrary directions. Within the working class of Shanghai, we have identified three different tendencies. *Rebels* challenged party authorities, *conservatives* defended them, and *economistic* organizations demanded socioeconomic justice. Labor was working at cross-purposes: Rebellion, conservatism, and economism were promoted by different sorts of leaders acting on the basis of dissimilar motivations. These distinctions, we have suggested, are best comprehended by different analytical traditions.

The "wind of economism" that blew across the urban Chinese landscape in the winter of 1966–1967 graphically demonstrated the significance of socioeconomic cleavages among the populace. Many of these divisions had been created or exacerbated by state policies; the segmentation of the citizenry—in terms of "good" versus "bad" class labels, urban versus rural household registration, permanent versus temporary or contract labor, state versus collective ownership of enterprises, and the like—was clearly a product of socialist initiatives. Yet, even if they were state imposed, such categories generated competing social interests that laid the groundwork for a form of group politics not entirely unlike what can be found in more "pluralist" systems.[1] Demands raised during the high tide of economism call attention to the socioeconomic cleavages that lurk, like fault lines, just beneath the surface of the Chinese political system. Although temporarily stilled in the winter of 1967, and then redrawn in the post-Mao reforms of the 1980s and 1990s, their rumblings continue to pose a threat to the stability of the Communist order.

To be sure, the Communist system has not lacked defenders. Beneficiaries of the state's divisive tactics gravitated toward conservative organizations during the CR. As Andrew Walder notes, the conservative reaction was mounted by workers "closely aligned with informal networks of party-sponsored patronage before the Cultural Revolution. They were prototypical 'activists,' group leaders and assistant group leaders, rank-and-file party members, model workers, youth league members, and other recognized 'backbone elements.'"[2] Although distinctively shaped by the imperatives of the socialist state, clientelist networks—like interest groups—find analogues in other political systems as well.[3]

It is in addressing the rebels, the most complex and ultimately the most influential strain of worker activism during the Cultural Revolution, that our explanation departs furthest from conventional analyses—turning Pye and Solomon's "dependent" representation of Chinese personality on its head, so to speak.[4] Whereas Pye and Solomon portray Chinese political culture as marked by an essentially unchanging and uniform craving for authority, we point to subcultures of opposition from which bold individuals sprang forth to challenge authority figures. Although such rebellion was carried out in the name of Chairman Mao, the ultimate political authority, it nonetheless reflected a surprising degree of individual ambition and ingenuity. These were hardly "dependent" personalities yearning to submit to their superiors. Rather, they endeavored first to unseat party leaders and then systematically to replace them with their own personnel.

Rebel leaders, like their conservative opponents, were playing a political game whose operating rules had been laid down by higher levels. As was true in previous campaigns, the *rewards* of the game remained the promise of political office—yet the *rules* of the game changed dramatically during the CR. Uncertainties over proper targets of struggle permitted those outside or on the edges of established party networks to seize the initiative in a manner unthinkable in earlier political movements.

In contrast to conservatives, the allegiances of the old rebels cannot be understood simply as a product of preexisting party networks. And, unlike those who participated most vocally in the wind of economism, neither is their behavior well predicted in terms of group analysis. Some rebel leaders were party members, others ordinary workers, and yet others were considered "backward elements." We have thus sought an alternative explanation by tracing the biographies of the most influential of these old rebels. Harold Lasswell once wrote that "political science without biography is a form of taxidermy."[5] In detailing the personal histories of these colorful individuals, we have tried to revive them as flesh and blood personalities. Additionally, we hope to have identified some points of commonality worthy of further exploration.[6]

Those who rose to the challenge of criticizing party committees and work teams were, to a person, unusually audacious and ambitious individuals. Often, their feisty personalities had been born out of difficult family circumstances and had been nurtured in rowdy subcultures that operated on the margins of orthodox party life. Northern origins, shantytown childhoods, and youth gang participation all played a role in fostering rebel leadership.

Regional identities seem particularly salient in promoting rebel factionalism. Although Chairman Mao sometimes referred to the Gang of Four radicals (Jiang Qing, Zhang Chunqiao, Yao Wenyuan, and Wang Hongwen) as a "Shanghai clique" because of their close association with that city, two of the members actually hailed from the northern province of Shandong. Moreover, their backstage patron was none other than Secret Police Chief Kang Sheng, also of Shandong origin. Northern rebels were able to tap into long standing political divisions in Shanghai. Among officials sent from the north to help take charge of the city after the Communist takeover of 1949, demobilized soldiers from Shandong were especially numerous. These individuals, who became leading cadres in many Shanghai factories, represented a rural, northern military culture that clashed with the more restrained operational style of the southern cadres who had controlled the urban Communist underground. For the first decade and a half of the PRC, southerners held the upper hand—dominating the top ranks of the Shanghai trade union, for example. The Cultural Revolution offered the northerners a chance to get even.[7]

Unfortunately, we know very little about such dissonant currents in Communist China.[8] But it is quite clear that not all Chinese exhibited a submissive orientation toward authority.[9] Even one of Wang Hongwen's most faithful rebel colleagues, a party member himself, criticized many of the other rebel leaders for their unrestrained temperaments.

> Wang Hongwen never forgot those who rose in rebellion with him and was always looking out for them. . . . However, I couldn't stand those other WGH leaders like Huang Jinhai, Chen Ada, or Dai Liqing. They were rascals. We were, after all, party members and were used to strict demands on ourselves. During the CR I never could get along with those other people.[10]

If a rebel could express such distaste for his fellow rebel leaders, we can appreciate the feelings of revulsion that gripped those on the conservative side. The disgust with which conservative leaders regarded their radical adversaries reflected the cultural gulf that distanced the persons and actions of the rebels from accepted party practice.

Mao's preference for the rebel challengers unleashed many of the disruptive consequences of the Cultural Revolution decade. Eventually, party networks in work units were reestablished, but not without a marked deterioration in discipline. The irreverent style of the rebels was fertile soil for the growth of a general disrespect for party authority, with serious implications for the future of Chinese politics.[11]

Shanghai in National Perspective

The power of the worker rebels in Shanghai was of considerable national significance, thanks to the prominent position that Zhang Chunqiao, Yao Wenyuan, and Wang Hongwen came to occupy in central-level politics. As the only real social base that the CR radicals could claim in their quixotic crusade to remake the face of China, the worker rebels gained extraordinary influence.

Unlike the situation in other cities, in Shanghai the rebels retained—and improved—their political standing well after the army had wrested control from mass organizations across most of the country. With Zhang Chunqiao serving concurrently as vice-chair of the Cultural Revolution Small Group, chair of the Shanghai Revolutionary Committee, and political commissar of both the Nanjing Military Region and the Shanghai Garrison Command, Shanghai was spared the military takeovers that occurred in other places where civilian authorities proved incapable of imposing order. Aside from enterprises engaged in the production of military equipment, Shanghai factories were not assigned military representatives during the Cultural Revolution.[12] Although military representatives were dispatched to universities and middle schools to quell factional struggles among students, in the industrial sector the worker rebels remained firmly in charge. The local "political opportunity structure" in Shanghai was thus much more conducive to rebel hegemony than was the case elsewhere in China.[13] Rebel domination, in turn, dampened the flames of factional strife that led to scenes of mass violence in so much of the country. In Shanghai, after the January Revolution, power was largely shared by worker and literati rebels. Buttressed by their control of the urban militia, the worker rebels spoke with a decisive voice in municipal politics. Workers were no longer mere figureheads in showcase people's congresses, as had been the case for the previous seventeen years. At all levels, unions challenged party committees.

With workers in key positions of authority from municipality to factory floor, how did labor fare during the CR? As we have seen, the economic welfare of the working class was not a priority for the rebel leadership. Thus, although state workers in Shanghai were spared the cuts in overtime and wage subsidies that affected workers elsewhere in the country,[14] there is little evidence, on one hand, that the CR brought improvement in the living standards of the average worker. On the other hand, the "iron rice bowl" privileges enjoyed by state workers appear to have been strengthened during the CR, with fewer punishments meted out for infractions of rules or poor on-the-job performance and greater latitude for workplace freedom. Moreover, workers and their children were now favored in university admissions, government employment, and as marriage partners. Perhaps most important, the visible career advancement of the old rebels served to instill a sense of political efficacy among the working class. More than a few workers in Shanghai and elsewhere were undoubtedly cheered to see a young worker catapulted to the commanding heights of power. Much touted programs of Workers' Propaganda Teams, Workers' Theory Troops, worker ambassadors, "new cadres," and the like encouraged the belief that, at last, the People's Republic was trying to live up to its pretensions as a proletarian state.

Although the worker rebels of Shanghai were by no means engaged in a class struggle to improve the plight of the proletariat, their political success may well have contributed to a general growth in class consciousness among the Chinese workforce. A notable feature of labor unrest in the post-Mao era has been the centrality of class imagery in protest slogans and strike manifestoes.[15] Chinese workers remain divided, to be sure, but the CR experience seems to have bequeathed a newfound pride in their proletarian status as well as a powerful language of class with which to challenge unwelcome policies.

Labor's Political Influence

Working-class activism during the Cultural Revolution suggests a need to reconsider the political impact of labor in Communist China. Most analyses of the Maoist work unit (*danwei*) have emphasized the subservience to higher authority engendered by party control. For some, workplace relations under communism are seen as reminiscent of an allegedly "traditional" feature of Chinese political culture: dependency in the face of authority. In Richard Solomon's infamous yet influential formulation, this dependency was linked to the essential "orality" of Chinese personality.[16] In Andrew Walder's very different model of neotraditionalism, it is the new Communist system that renders workers economically and socially dependent on their enterprise, politically dependent on factory management, and personally dependent on their workplace supervisors.[17] Gail Henderson and Myron S. Cohen summarize the prevailing wisdom in their book, *The Chinese Hospital: A Socialist Work Unit*: "Overall, it appears that the structural characteristics of the unit system reinforce the traditional dependent modes of interaction."[18]

Leaving aside the dubious representation of "traditional China" that such characterizations imply, there is a serious question to be raised about their portrayal of the situation under communism. As this study has shown, some workers (i.e., those who became Scarlet Guard leaders) were indeed deeply enmeshed in party-sponsored networks of patronage that inclined them toward a strategy of compliance. However, other workers (the old rebels) drew strength from dissonant subcultures to challenge the hegemony of party authorities. And yet others (those most infected by the wind of economism) exhibited a far greater interest in material restitution—higher pay, improved labor conditions, greater job control, and so on—than in playing the political game of either defending or defeating party leaders.

The variety of ways in which workers responded to the Cultural Revolution cautions against too facile a portrait of working-class politics in Maoist China. The institution of the *danwei* induced not only dependency, but also defiance[19]— both toward individual workplace authorities (on the part of the rebels) and toward structural features of the system itself (when those most disprivileged by the *danwei* system demanded a redress of grievances during the wind of economism.)

In part because of source limitations and in part because of the prevailing image of Chinese workers as basically quiescent, studies of protest in the PRC until quite recently have focused almost exclusively upon students and intellectuals. This is the case not only for the Cultural Revolution but for the Hundred Flowers campaign, Democracy Wall movement, and the Tiananmen Incidents of 1976 and 1989 as well. Increasingly, however, we are discovering that workers played a key role in all of these movements.[20] Indeed, one might well propose that the draconian fashion in which each of these upsurges was eventually suppressed was due above all to the Beijing regime's deep-seated anxieties about a restive workforce. Moreover, as Poland's Solidarity movement dramatically demonstrated and as new theories of democratization underscore, the Chinese leadership was hardly being irrational in harboring such fears. In the industrial age, regime transitions are closely associated with labor movements.[21]

Upcoming transformations of the Chinese polity will surely bear more than a casual relationship to this history of worker unrest. And yet, as in the past, labor organizers are likely to continue to work at cross-purposes. Only by uncovering the divergent political, psychocultural, and socioeconomic strains within the Chinese labor movement can we hope for a reliable guide to its future bearings.

Theoretical Implications

In emphasizing diversity within the labor movement, our account runs against the grain of the latest trend in analyses of collective action in contemporary China. Although the dramatic Tiananmen Uprising of 1989 heightened scholarly interest in mass politics, recent theorizing has tended to portray Chinese social forces under communism as singularly homogeneous. Thus sociologist Xueguang Zhou argues that the uniformity of contemporary Chinese society—induced by the strength and penetration of the socialist state—has given rise to a surprising degree of "unorganized collective action." As Zhou states his thesis, "The very institutional structure of state socialism that prevents organized interests facilitates collective action based on unorganized interests. . . . State socialism reduces the barriers to collective action by producing 'large numbers' of individuals with similar behavioral patterns and demands that cut across the boundaries of organizations and social groups."[22] For Zhou, the homogeneous living and working conditions of contemporary Chinese generate a consistency of behavior analogous to the phenomenon of swarming bees: "Social groups in China not only live in a similar political and economic environment but also tend to share similar life experiences. . . . Like bees that always swarm, individual behaviors in China are also present in large numbers."[23]

Similarly Daniel Kelliher, in his book on the post-Mao rural reforms, notes that, contrary to what we might have anticipated on the basis of Western theories of state-society relations, Chinese peasants played a key role in initiating the reform process. The reason for this surprising outcome, he suggests, is that "by placing great numbers of people in very similar, prescribed circumstances, state socialism unwittingly creates the possibility of mass action by disorganized, atomized individuals."[24] Like Zhou, Kelliher proposes that the very structure of state socialism gave rise to a potentially influential brand of collective action whose power derives not from its organization but from its homogeneity vis-à-vis the state: "Peasants . . . confronted a nearly identical face of state power. Dealing with a state that appeared everywhere the same made peasants behave with a more singular identity than they actually possessed."[25]

We have no quarrel with Zhou and Kelliher's emphasis on the overbearing nature of the Chinese Communist state. Any explanation of collective action in Communist China must take full account of the conditions of extreme politicization under which it has developed. Models based on market economies with liberal politics are of only limited applicability in this effort. As Zhou argues, "To understand mass mobilization in China, the logic of collective action cannot be uncritically accepted from a literature that has been largely built on non-Communist (mainly Western) experience."[26]

Our disagreement stems instead from the image of amorphous social homogeneity that accompanies this state-centric approach. Worker activism during the Cultural Revolution disputes the contention that "although individuals are unorganized, their actions in pursuit of their own self-interests tend to convey similar claims, share similar patterns."[27] Popular activism during the CR was neither unorganized nor uniform. The motivations and methods of labor leaders exhibited an impressive degree of variation and organization. Both characteristics, moreover, were a direct outcome of state initiatives. In dividing its citizens according to class background, residential location, party membership, job status, and so forth, the socialist state reinforced and reconfigured deep cleavages among the populace. Such inequities have fueled mass protests from the initial decade of Communist rule right up to the present. Participants in this collective drama have acted not as an undifferentiated mass of "swarming bees" but in distinctive patterns of association that reflect dissimilar—even conflicting—constraints and concerns.

These findings also caution against too ready an acceptance of any single general model of popular protest. The Cultural Revolution was, we can all agree, an exceptionally politicized movement in which the ultimate authority of Chairman Mao imposed severe constraints on the degree of popular autonomy.[28] If even during such an orchestrated movement as this we can identify three distinctive forms of popular participation—one prompted by grievances, another by political resources, and yet another by personal identities—should we not expect to find at least as much variety in less tightly controlled protest movements? If so, then perhaps social scientists should abandon the search for one master key to unlock all collective action doors in favor of a recognition that different types of activism may call for different explanations.

Notes

Notes to Introduction

1. Although certainly more dramatic than earlier precedents, the CR was not the first time that citizens of the People's Republic of China (PRC) had responded to Mao's call. The Hundred Flowers Movement of 1956–1957 also saw an impressive display of mass participation. See Roderick MacFarquhar, *The Origins of the Cultural Revolution, vol. 1, Contradictions Among the People, 1956–1957* (New York: Columbia University Press, 1974), esp. chap. 16.

2. Franz Schurmann, *Ideology and Organization in Communist China* (Berkeley: University of California Press, 1968), vii, 504.

3. Michel Oksenberg, *The Cultural Revolution: 1967 in Review* (Ann Arbor: University of Michigan Center for Chinese Studies, 1968); Lowell Dittmer, *Liu Shao-ch'i and the Chinese Cultural Revolution: The Politics of Mass Criticism* (Berkeley: University of California Press, 1974); Hong Yung Lee, *The Politics of the Chinese Cultural Revolution: A Case Study* (Berkeley: University of California Press, 1978); Anita Chan, Stanley Rosen, and Jonathan Unger, "Students and Class Warfare: The Social Roots of the Red Guard Conflict in Guangzhou (Canton)," *China Quarterly*, no. 83 (September 1980): 397–446; Stanley Rosen, *Red Guard Factionalism and the Cultural Revolution in Guangzhou (Canton)* (Boulder: Westview Press, 1982).

4. Gordon A. Bennett and Ronald N. Montaperto, *Red Guard: The Political Biography of Dai Hsiao-ai* (Garden City, N.J.: Doubleday, 1972); Ken Ling, *The Revenge of Heaven: Journal of a Young Chinese* (New York: Putnam, 1972); Liang Heng and Judith Shapiro, *Son of the Revolution* (New York: Random House, 1983); Yue Daiyun, with Carolyn Wakeman, *To the Storm: The Odyssey of a Revolutionary Chinese Woman* (Berkeley: University of California Press, 1985); Gao Yuan, *Born Red* (Stanford: Stanford University Press, 1987); Liu Binyan, *A Higher Kind of Loyalty: A Memoir by China's Foremost Journalist* (New York: Pantheon, 1990); Zhai Zhenhua, *Red Flower of China: An Autobiography* (New York: Soho, 1992).

5. On the resettlement campaign, see Thomas P. Bernstein, *Up to the Mountains and Down to the Villages: The Transfer of Youth from Urban to Rural China* (New Haven: Yale University Press, 1977).

6. Pioneering studies of labor in the Cultural Revolution include Lynn T. White, III, "Workers' Politics in Shanghai," *Journal of Asian Studies* 26, no. 1 (1976): 99–116; Raymond F. Wylie, "Shanghai Dockers in the Cultural Revolution," in Christopher Howe, ed., *Shanghai: Revolution and Development in an Asian Metropolis* (Cambridge: Cambridge University Press, 1981), 91–124; and Andrew G. Walder, "The Chinese Cultural Revolution in the Factories: Party-State Structures and Patterns of Conflict," in Elizabeth J. Perry, ed., *Putting Class in Its Place: Worker Identities in East Asia* (Berkeley: University of California Institute of East Asian Studies, 1996), 167–198.

Primary sources are from the Shanghai Municipal Archive.

7. For the French case see, for example, Richard Cobb, *The People's Armies* (New Haven: Yale University Press, 1987); and for China, see Susan Naquin, *Millenarian Rebellion in China: The Eight Trigrams Uprising of 1813* (New Haven: Yale University Press, 1976).

8. Charles Tilly, *From Mobilization to Revolution* (Reading, Mass.: Addison-Wesley, 1978; Sidney Tarrow, *Power in Movement: Social Movements, Collective Action, and Politics* (New York: Cambridge University Press, 1994).

9. The classic Marxian position can be found in Karl Marx and Friedrich Engels, *Manifesto of the Communist Party* (London, 1948); for psychological approaches, see Ted Robert Gurr, *Why Men Rebel* (Princeton: Princeton University Press, 1971); and James C. Davies, ed., *When Men Revolt and Why* (New York: Free Press, 1971).

10. Anthony Oberschall, *Social Conflict and Social Movements* (Englewood Cliffs, N.J.: Prentice-Hall, 1973); Tilly, *From Mobilization to Revolution;* Doug McAdam, *The Political Process and the Development of Black Insurgency* (Chicago: University of Chicago Press, 1982).

11. Mancur Olson, *The Logic of Collective Action* (Cambridge: Harvard University Press, 1965).

12. Alberto Melucci, *Nomads of the Present: Social Movements and Individual Needs in Contemporary Society* (Philadelphia: Temple University Press, 1989); Francois Furet and Mona Ozouf, eds., *The Transformation of Political Culture, 1789–1848* (Oxford: Pergamon, 1989); David E. Snow and Robert Benford, "Master Frames and Cycles of Protest," in Aldon Morris and Carol McClurg, eds., *Frontiers in Social Movement Theory* (New Haven: Yale University Press, 1992), 133–155; Sidney Tarrow, "Mentalities, Political Cultures, and Collective Action Frames: Constructing Meaning Through Action," in Morris and McClurg, *Frontiers in Social Movement Theory,* 174–202; James C. Scott, *Domination and the Arts of Resistance: Hidden Transcripts* (New Haven: Yale University Press, 1990).

13. See the sources cited in note 2. On the importance of class categories in Communist China, see especially Richard Kraus, *Class Conflict in Chinese Socialism* (New York: Columbia University Press, 1981). The recent work of Wang Shaoguang, although phrased in the language of rational choice theory, also stresses socioeconomic divisions, including class origins. See his *Failure of Charisma: The Cultural Revolution in Wuhan* (New York: Oxford University Press, 1995), esp. chap. 2.

14. Andrew G. Walder, *Communist Neo-Traditionalism: Work and Authority in Chinese Industry* (Berkeley: University of California Press, 1986); and "The Chinese Cultural Revolution in the Factories: Party-State Structures and Patterns of Conflict." Lynn White highlights both class labels (à la Lee et al.) and clientelist networks (à la Walder) and adds a third factor, campaigns, to account for the violence of the CR. See Lynn T. White, III, *Policies of Chaos: Organizational Causes of Violence in China's Cultural Revolution* (Princeton: Princeton University Press, 1989).

15. Lucian W. Pye, *The Dynamics of Chinese Politics* (Cambridge, Mass.: Oelgeschlager, Gunn, and Hain, 1981). For earlier discussions of the role of political culture in the Cultural Revolution, see Pye's *The Spirit of Chinese Politics: A Psychocultural Study of the Authority Crisis in Political Development* (Cambridge: MIT Press, 1968); and Richard H. Solomon, *Mao's Revolution and the Chinese Political Culture* (Berkeley: University of California Press, 1971). See also Alan P. L. Liu, *Political Culture and Group Conflict in Communist China* (Santa Barbara, Calif.: Clio Press, 1976); David M. Raddock, *Political Behavior of Adolescents in China: The Cultural Revolution in Kwangchow* (Tucson: University of Arizona Press, 1977); Anita Chan, *Children of Mao: Personality Development and Political Ac-*

tivism in the Red Guard Generation (Seattle: University of Washington Press, 1985); and Lowell Dittmer, "Political Culture and Political Symbolism," *World Politics* 29, no. 4 (July 1977): 552–584; and his *China's Continuous Revolution* (Berkeley: University of California Press, 1987), esp. chap. 4.

16. Stanley Karnow, *Mao and China: From Revolution to Revolution* (New York: Viking, 1972); Edward E. Rice, *Mao's Way* (Berkeley: University of California Press, 1972); Ahn Byung-joon, *Chinese Politics and the Cultural Revolution: The Dynamics of Policy Processes* (Seattle: University of Washington Press, 1976). The most useful overview in Chinese is clearly Wang Nianyi, *Da Dongluan de niandai* [Decade of great turmoil] (Zhengzhou: Henan People's Press, 1988). Other Chinese works include Jin Chunming, *Wenhua dageming lunxi* [Analysis of the Cultural Revolution] (Shanghai: Shanghai People's Press, 1985); Tan Zongji and Zheng Qian, eds., *Shinianhou de pingshuo—"wenhua dageming" shi lunji* [An evaluation ten years later: Collected essays on the history of the "Cultural Revolution"] (Beijing: Party History Materials Press, 1987); Li Ke and He Shengzhang, *Wenhua dageming zhong de renmin jiefangjun* [The People's Liberation Army in the Cultural Revolution] (Beijing: Party History Materials Press, 1989); Yang Jian, *Wenhua dageming zhong de dixia wenxue* [Underground literature during the Cultural Revolution] (Beijing: Chaohua Press, 1993); and Di Jiu and Zhi Wu, *Xie yu huo de jiaoxun—wenge zhongda wudou can'an jishi* [Lessons of blood and fire: Annals of large-scale CR battles and massacres] (Lanzhou: Xinjiang University Press, 1993).

17. Evelyn Anderson, "Shanghai: The Masses Unleashed," *Problems of Communism* (January–February 1968): 12–21; Gerald Tannenbaum, "The 1967 Shanghai January Revolution Recounted," *Eastern Horizon* (May–June 1968); Neale Hunter, *Shanghai Journal: An Eyewitness Account of the Cultural Revolution* (New York: Praeger, 1969); Vivienn B. Shue, "Shanghai After the January Storm," in *The Cultural Revolution in the Provinces* (Cambridge: Harvard East Asia Monographs, 1971), 66–93; Lynn T. White, III, "Shanghai's Polity in Cultural Revolution," in John W. Lewis, ed., *The City in Communist China* (Stanford: Stanford University Press, 1971), 325–370; Victor Nee, "Revolution and Bureaucracy: Shanghai in the Cultural Revolution," in Victor Nee and James Peck, eds., *China's Uninterrupted Revolution (From 1840 to the Present)* (New York: Pantheon Books, 1975); Andrew G. Walder, *Chang Ch'un-ch'iao and Shanghai's January Revolution* (Ann Arbor: Center for Chinese Studies of the University of Michigan, 1978); Parris Chang, "Shanghai and Chinese Politics: Before and After the Cultural Revolution," in Christopher Howe, ed., *Shanghai: Revolution and Development in an Asian Metropolis* (Cambridge: Cambridge University Press, 1981), 66–90; Nien Cheng, *Life and Death in Shanghai* (London: Collins, 1986); and White, *Policies of Chaos.* Chinese accounts include the historical novel by Hu Yuewei, *Fengkuang de Shanghai* [Crazed Shanghai] (Chengdu: Sichuan Cultural Press, 1986); and Chen Xianfa, *Minzu lei* [National tears] (Shanghai: Tongji University Press, 1988).

18. For recent scholarly elaborations of this position, see Daniel Kelliher, *Peasant Power in China: The Era of Rural Reform, 1979–1989* (New Haven: Yale University Press, 1992); and Xueguang Zhou, "Unorganized Interests and Collective Action in Communist China," *American Sociological Review* 58, no. 1 (February 1953): 54–73.

19. On class as caste, see Kraus, *Class Conflict in Chinese Socialism;* on party-state clientelism, see Walder, *Communist Neo-Traditionalism;* and Jean C. Oi, *State and Peasant in Contemporary China: The Political Economy of Village Government* (Berkeley: University of California Press, 1989); on rebel culture, see Lucian Pye, *The Mandarin and the Cadre:*

China's Political Cultures (Ann Arbor: University of Michigan Center for Chinese Studies, 1988); and Richard Madsen, *Morality and Power in a Chinese Village* (Berkeley: University of California Press, 1984).

Notes to Chapter 1

1. For further elaboration of this point, see Elizabeth J. Perry, "Shanghai's Strike Wave of 1957," *China Quarterly* (March 1994): 1–27.

2. See Jeffrey N. Wasserstrom, *Student Protest in Twentieth-Century China: The View from Shanghai* (Stanford: Stanford University Press, 1991); and Elizabeth J. Perry, *Shanghai on Strike: The Politics of Chinese Labor* (Stanford: Stanford University Press, 1993).

3. Descriptions of Jiang Qing's opera reforms and their political implications can be found in Roxane Witke, *Comrade Chiang Ch'ing* (Boston: Little and Brown, 1977); and Merle Goldman, *China's Intellectuals: Advise and Dissent* (Cambridge: Harvard University Press, 1981), chap. 3.

4. In December 1963, Ke Qingshi had staged an East China drama exhibition in tandem with Jiang Qing's announced opera reform in Beijing. The following year he mobilized a deputy-director of the East China Propaganda Department to pen a criticism of the traditional "ghost dramas" so disliked by Jiang. Ke died suddenly of illness in April 1965, just prior to the Cultural Revolution.

5. Shanghai Party Committee (SPC) CR Materials Small Group ed., *Shanghai "wenhua dageming" shihua* [Historical narrative of the "great Cultural Revolution" in Shanghai] (herafter *Shanghai shihua),* Shanghai, 1992. This multivolume internal-circulation report provides a detailed and authoritative history of the CR in Shanghai. Although published some years after the conclusion of the CR, it is based upon unrestricted access to archival sources, personal papers, and interviews with key participants.

6. The document, entitled "Transcript of a Military Art Symposium which Comrade Lin Biao Commissioned Jiang Qing to Convene," symbolized the new collaboration between Lin and Jiang.

7. For a recent analysis of the Hai Rui issue, see Tom Fisher, "'The Play's the Thing': Wu Han and Hai Rui Revisited," in Jonathan Unger, ed., *Using the Past to Serve the Present: Historiography and Politics in Contemporary China* (Armonk, N.Y.: M. E. Sharpe, 1993): 9–45.

8. On Yao's earlier career, see Lars Ragvald, *Yao Wen-yuan as Literary Critic and Theorist* (Stockholm: University of Sweden, 1978). On his role in the CR, see Goldman, *China's Intelluctuals,* chap. 5.

9. This was, however, not the first time that Mao had noticed either man. During the Anti-Rightist campaign of 1957, Yao had penned an essay extolling Mao Zedong Thought, which gained the chairman's personal approval. In 1958, an essay by Zhang Chunqiao advocating the introduction of supply systems to hasten China's transition to socialism had also elicited a favorable reaction from Mao. See Parris Chang, "Shanghai and Chinese Politics: Before and After the Cultural Revolution," in Christopher Howe, ed., *Shanghai: Revolution and Development in an Asian Metropolis* (Cambridge: Cambridge University Press, 1981), 71–72.

10. The Cultural Revolution Small Group was chaired by Chen Boda, with Kang Sheng as principal adviser. Zhang Chunqiao was made a special assistant to Vice-Chair Jiang

Qing, and Yao Wenyuan served as a regular member. Other members included Wang Renzhong, Liu Zhijian, Wang Li, and Guan Feng.

11. Yang Xiguang, then a member of the Shanghai Party Committee Standing Committee, was named vice-chair; Xu Jingxian, secretary of the party branch of the SPC Writers' Group, served along with Yao Wenyuan as the other regular member.

12. At the Shanghai branch of the Chinese Academy of Sciences, more than 300 posters went up during the three days from June 4 to June 7; a few days later the number had increased to more than 1800. At Shanghai's No. 1 Medical College, more than 5,000 were posted on June 5 alone. See *Shanghai shihua.*

13. In June, violent struggle sessions occurred at 191 of the 468 middle schools in Shanghai (about 40%). *Shanghai shihua.*

14. In particular, the SPC singled out eight targets for attack: Jia Luding, head of the Shanghai Music Conservatory; Zhou Xinfang, head of the Shanghai Drama Academy; Li Junmin, general editor of the Shanghai branch of the Zhonghua Publishing House; Ju Baiyin, film critic; Wang Xiyan, art critic; Zhou Gucheng, Zhou Yutong and Li Pingxin, historians and university professors. All had run afoul of Zhang Chunqiao or Yao Wenyuan in earlier encounters.

15. *Shanghai shihua.*

16. Cited in Wang Youqin, "1966: Xuesheng da laoshi de geming" [1966: The revolution in which students beat up teachers], *Ershiyi shiji shuangyuekan*, no. 31 (August 1995): 37.

17. *Shanghai shihua.*

18. *Zai wuchan jieji wenhua dageming zhong Cao Diqiu yanlunji* [Collected speeches and writings of Cao Diqiu during the Great Proletarian Cultural Revolution], handbill (February 1967).

19. Communist Youth League, ed., *Shanghai hongweibing dashiji* [Annals of the Shanghai Red Guards], Shanghai, 1983. The Shanghai Red Guards Third Headquarters, which had been founded on November 22, was limited to the Shanghai Drama Academy after the split-off of the Red Third Headquarters. Other prominent university Red Guard organizations included Jiaotong's "Struggle to the Finish," Tongji's "East is Red," the No. 2 Army Medical University's "Red Flag Batallion," and the Shanghai Drama Academy's "Revolutionary Tower" and "Crazy Brigade." Important middle school units included "Command Post of Red Guards in Shanghai's Southwest District" and "Command Post of Red Guards in Shanghai's Northeast District."

20. *Shanghai shihua.* The violent criticism had gained momentum even before the formal establishment of Red Guard organizations in Shanghai. Although the official media had printed nothing about Mao's August 1 letter supporting the Qinghua Red Guards, the news had been disseminated via private letters. On August 4, 194 teachers at Fudan University (11% of the entire faculty) were subjected to severe criticism. On August 8, ninety-five teachers (19% of the faculty) were criticized at the Shanghai Institute of Finance and Economics. At the Shanghai Institute of Physical Education, twenty-four teachers (60% of the faculty) were criticized on August 11. On August 12–13, 123 teachers at the Shanghai Medical College were criticized; later, ninety-seven had their homes ransacked by rampaging students. But the violence certainly increased after the formation of Red Guard units. Between September 1 and September 25, Red Guards at 361 of the 489 middle schools in the city (74%) were responsible for beating more than 10,000 people—eleven people died and 961 were severely injured.

21. Famous writer Ba Jin, translator Fu Lei, actor Zhao Dan, calligrapher Shen Yimo, and Beijing opera star Tong Zhilong were subjected to repeated ransackings. By October 10, more than 9,000 victims had been expelled to the countryside. *Shanghai shihua*. For an account of Red Guard attacks on religious buildings in Shanghai and an explanation of how the city's famous Jade Buddha Temple was spared destruction, see Li Lang, "Heshang yu hongweibing" [Monks and Red Guards], *Falu zixun* [Legal information] (September 1986): 9–12.

22. Shanghai Branch of the Bank of China, ed., *Jianguo yilai de Shanghai yinhang gongzuo* [Shanghai banking work since 1949], Shanghai, 1986.

23. Shanghai Federation of Trade Unions (SFTU) ed., *Gongzongsi da shiji* [Annals of the Workers' General Headquarters] (Shanghai, 1984). Red Guards from both the Bombard Headquarters and Jiaotong University's "Struggle to the Finish" organizations attended the planning meeting.

24. Our understanding of the *Liberation Daily* Incident differs substantially from the standard English-language account provided in Neale Hunter's *Shanghai Journal* (New York: Prager, 1969), chap. 8. Hunter characterizes the event as "the decisive engagement of the Cultural Revolution in Shanghai" (p. 162), which gave a "tremendous boost . . . to the revolutionary consciousness of the Rebel students and workers" (p. 165). Hunter's partisanship in favor of the Red Revolutionaries (which he candidly acknowledges in the new introduction to the 1988 edition of his book) may have inclined him to exaggerate the positive influence of this particular incident.

25. Cao Diqiu, "Wo de jiancha" [My self-criticism] (July 1967).

26. "Jiefang ribao shijian zhenxiang" [The true fact of the *Liberation Daily* Incident], handbill of employees at *Liberation Daily* (December 6, 1966).

27. Ibid.

28. Hunter, *Shanghai Journal*, 164.

29. SPC, ed., *"Quanmian duoquan" de fangeming naoju de qianzou* [Prelude to the counter-revolutionary drama of comprehensive power seizure], Shanghai, 1982.

30. *Shanghai shihua*.

31. *Shanghai gongren geming zaofan zongsilingbu wenxian huiji* [Compilation of documents of the Shanghai Workers' Revolutionary Rebels General Headquarters] (July 1967); *Sanxiang jueding* [Three-point resolution], handbill of the Red Revolutionaries (December 6, 1966).

32. Wang Zhichang (former member of the SPC Writers' Group), October 20, 1979, testimony.

33. Xu Jingxian, December 12, 1966, working notes.

34. Wang Zhichang, October 20, 1979, testimony.

35. *Shanghai shihua*.

36. Zhang Chunqiao, January 9, 1967, transcript of speech.

37. Xu Jingxian, January 4, 1967, working notes.

38. Zhu Yongjia et al., eds., *Shanghai yiyue geming dashiji* [Annals of Shanghai's January Revolution] (Shanghai, 1969).

39. Xu Jingxian, January 8, 1967, working notes; Zhang Chunqiao, January 9, 1967, speech.

40. Zhu et al. *Shanghai yiyue geming*.

41. Transcript of Wang Li's telephone call, January 15, 1967.

42. See Jin Qiu, "The Lin Biao Incident: A Study of Extra-Institutional Factors in the Cultural Revolution" (University of Hawaii, Ph.D. diss., 1995) for a discussion of the conflict between Jiang Qing and Lin Biao.

43. An Wenjiang (former leader of the Red Third Headquarters), informal memoir written after the Cultural Revolution.

44. The other rebel-worker leaders were Geng Jinzhang, Chen Ada, Huang Jinhai, Dai Liqing, and Ye Changming—whose brief biographies can be found in Chapter 2.

45. *Shanghai shihua*, 277.

46. Chen Ada, January 11, 1978, testimony; Geng Jinzhang, November 27, 1979, testimony; Huang Jinhai, December 12, 1978, testimony.

47. Later Zhang admitted that he had actually written the cable himself and then routed it through Beijing, but in any case the telegram was signed by the CRSG and had received its approval. "Zhongyang wenge xiaozu gei honggehui de teji dianbao" [Urgent cable from the CRSG to the Red Revolutionaries], Jiaotong University's "Struggle to the Finish" handbill (January 29, 1967).

48. Ye Changming, June 14, 1977, testimony.

49. *Shanghai shihua*.

50. Xu Jiangang, "Sirenbang pohai Shanghai ganbu qunzhong de sanchang yundong" [Three campaigns of the Gang of Four to harm Shanghai cadres and masses], *Shanghai dangshi* [Shanghai party history], no. 12 (1990).

51. Wang Shaoxi (member of the SPC Writers' Group), April 10, 1978, confession; Wang Zhichang (Writers' Group member), October 20, 1979, testimony.

52. The account of the *Morning Glow* affair is based primarily on Xu Guoliang's (member of the Writers' Group) April 10, 1978, confession; and Wang Zhichang's (Writers' Group member) October 20, 1979, testimony.

53. SFTU, ed., *Guanyu Wang Xiuzhen, Ye Changming liyong gongren lilun duiwu jinxing cuandang duoquan zui'e huodong de qingkuang* [Concerning the conditions of Wang Xiuzhen and Ye Changming's use of Workers' Theory Troops to further their dastardly activity of usurping party power], January 1978.

54. Ye Changming, June 14, 1977, testimony.

55. The case is drawn from an August 3, 1992, interview that Li Xun conducted with Lin Yaohua in Shanghai.

56. Further discussion of this phenomenon can be found in Elizabeth J. Perry and Li Xun, "Revolutionary Rudeness: The Language of Red Guards and Rebel Workers in China's Cultural Revolution," *Indiana East Asian Working Paper Series on Language and Politics in Modern China*, no. 2 (July 1993): 1–18.

57. The Writers' Group included only one member of working-class origin: Xiao Mu, a former railroad maintenance worker. As a worker-writer, Xiao's collection of short stories had received the praise of the renowned author Mao Dun. Ironically, however, once Xiao was transferred to the Writers' Group, he outdid those of intellectual background in assuming a cultivated, literati air.

Notes to Chapter 2

1. Hong Yung Lee, *The Politics of the Chinese Cultural Revolution* (Berkeley: University of California Press, 1978), 129.

2. Ibid. 340.

3. Discussions of the politics of the Gang of Four can be found in Parris Chang, "Shanghai and Chinese Politics: Before and After the Cultural Revolution," in Christopher Howe, ed., *Shanghai: Revolution and Development in an Asian Metropolis* (Cambridge: Cambridge University Press, 1981), 66–90; and Lowell Dittmer, "Bases of Power in Chinese Politics: A Theory and an Analysis of the Fall of the 'Gang of Four,'" *World Politics* 31, no. 1 (October 1978): 26–61.

4. For a general overview of this campaign, see Richard Baum and Frederick C. Teiwes, *Ssu-ch'ing: The Socialist Education Movement of 1962–1966* (Berkeley: Center for Chinese Studies, University of California, 1968).

5. Wang Nianyi, *Da dongluan de niandai* [Decade of great turmoil] (Zhengzhou: Henan People's Press, 1988), 27.

6. These were factories under the auspices of the First and Second Electronics Bureau and the Instruments Bureau.

7. This included factories under the bureaus of metals and chemical engineering.

8. These were the factories belonging to the bureaus of light industry, handicrafts, textiles, and materials.

9. Shanghai Party Committee (SPC) CR Materials Small Group, ed., *Shanghai "wenhua dageming" shihua* [Historical narrative of the "great Cultural Revolution" in Shanghai], (*hereafter Shanghai shihua*) Shanghai, 1992.

10. Ibid.

11. SPC, ed., *Guanyu dangqian gongye shengchan qingkuang de baogao* [Report on the current industrial production situation], (July 8, 1966).

12. Among the victims of worker criticism were the party committee secretary and factory director of the Zhonghua Shipyard. *Shanghai shihua.*

13. Christopher Howe, "Industrialization Under Conditions of Long-Run Population Stability: Shanghai's Achievement and Prospect," in Howe, *Shanghai* 178.

14. Chang, "Shanghai and Chinese Politics," 75.

15. *Shanghai shihua,* 139.

16. The seventeen representatives, all of whom became backbones of the new workers' rebel organization, were: Wang Hongwen, security cadre at the No. 17 Cotton Mill; Pan Guoping, worker at the Shanghai Glass Machinery Factory; Chen Ada, worker at the Lianggong Valve Factory; Ye Changming, worker at the Shanghai Hecheng Fiber Research Institute; Huang Jinhai, worker at the No. 31 Cotton Mill; Fan Zuodong, worker at the Shanghai No. 5 Thermos Factory; Huang Wenhai, worker at the Shanghai Lighting Factory; Dai Zuxiang, worker at the Shanghai No. 3 Steel Mill; Cen Qilin, technical staff at No. 822 Factory; Jiang Zhoufa, worker at the Shanghai Factory for Repairing Railway Cargo Machinery; Ding Defa, worker at the No. 51 Electronic Factory; Zhang Bosheng, worker at the People's Electronics Factory; Chen Jinxing, worker at the Shanghai No. 1 Dye Factory; Shi Meilong, worker at Shanghai's No. 147 Clothing Factory; Huang Hanqing, driver for the Jiangnan Metal Products Factory; Wang Xiangbo, technical staff at the Xinxin Instruments Factory; and Dai Zuda, clerk in the Xinshi Clothing Store. Others who attended the conference and became rebel activists, but who did not remain for the rest of the meeting, included: Xu Meiying (female), worker at Shanghai No. 147 Clothing Factory; Liao Zukang, student at the technical school of No. 17 Cotton Mill; Tao Guozheng, worker at the Jiangnan Metal Products Factory; and Xie Pengfei, worker at the Shanghai Factory to Repair Railway Cargo Machinery. (Ye Changming, April 5, 1977, testimony.)

17. WGH, ed., *Wuchan jieji wenhua dageming Shanghai gongren zaofanpai douzheng dashiji* [Annals of the struggles of Shanghai worker rebels in the Great Proletarian Cultural Revolution], Shanghai, February 1967; Chen Ada, December 12, 1978 testimony; Shanghai Federation of Trade Unions (SFTU), ed., *Gongzongsi dashiji* [Annals of the WGH], Shanghai, 1984.

18. Record of the WGH preparatory meeting of November 6, 1966 (recorded by No. 51 Electronics Factory worker Ding Defa).

19. On the expense involved in procuring cloth for turbans and sashes for a nineteenth-century rebellion, see Susan Naquin, *Millenarian Rebellion in China: The Eight Trigrams Uprising of 1813* (New Haven: Yale University Press, 1976), 151.

20. *Shanghai shihua*, 141.

21. "Anting fengbao" [Anting storm], *Gongren zaofan bao* [Worker rebel], May 19, 1967.

22. Cao Diqiu, "Wo de jiancha" [My self-criticism] (July 1967).

23. SPC, ed., "Tiegu zhengzheng—zhengqi haoran—ji Cao Diqiu tongzhi yu Jiang Qing yihuo de douzheng" [Iron bones clang—honest and forthright—a record of the struggle between Comrade Cao Diqiu and the Jiang Qing clique], *Zhibu shenghuo* [Party branch life], Shanghai, 1986.

24. SPC, ed. *Yiyue geming zhenxiang* [The true face of the January Revolution], Shanghai, 1982.

25. November 1966 working record of the Shanghai Railway Bureau control room.

26. See, for example, All-China Federation of Trade unions, ed., *Erqi dabagong ziliao xuanbian* [Compilation of materials about the great strike of February 7] (Beijing: Workers' Publishing House, 1983) on the history of the stoppage of 1923.

27. SPC, *Yiyue geming*.

28. "Chen Boda laidian" [Chen Boda's incoming telegram], Red Guard handbill during the Anting Incident (November 1966).

29. Shortly before his departure, Zhang Chunqiao was approached by CRSG adviser Tao Zhu, who asked him to persuade the workers to return to Shanghai so as to restore railway traffic as soon as possible. Tao emphasized that party central did not approve of workers establishing national or all-city types of mass organizations and, thus, that the Workers' General Headquarters could definitely not receive official recognition. (SPC, *Yiyue geming*.)

30. Ibid.

31. November 13, 1966, Workers' General Headquarters handbill.

32. Wang Nianyi, *Da Dongluan de niandai*, 131.

33. *Shanghai shihua*, 172.

34. In addition to seven functional divisions of the general office, an informal standing committee was established to perform general executive functions. There are different versions of who the seven members of the initial standing committee were. From the recollections of Ye Changming, Huang Jinhai, Dai Liqing, and Xu Meiying, as well as the November 21 work notes of Huang Jinhai, the core Small Group of the WGH included the following ten people: Wang Hongwen, Pan Guoping, Fan Zuodong, Huang Jinhai, Ye Changming, Chen Ada, Jiang Zhoufa, Dai Zuxiang, Xu Meiying, and Geng Jinzhang.

Later Xu Meiying recalled that among these people, she (as well as Dai and Geng) was just a nominal member who was seldom informed of headquarter meetings. The real core membership included only the original seven individuals. (Ye Changming, April 5, 1977, testimony; Xu Meiying, May 2, 1989, interview.)

35. Dai Liqing, August 26, 1981, testimony. According to Dai, the organizational structure was his idea. It was, however, remarkably similar to the functional divisions of autonomous Chinese unions since the Republican era.

36. Dai Liqing, August 26, 1981, testimony.

37. SFTU, ed., *Yijiuliuqinian gongzongsi zuzhi lingdao hexin ji qingcha qingkuang* [The 1967 WGH organizational leadership core and the cleansing situation], Shanghai, July 16, 1986. In December 1967, after the representative congress of the Shanghai worker rebels was convened, there was further change in the WGH administrative structure. According to an April 15, 1968, document of the WGH, it included the following division of labor: standing committee secretariat (with Pan Guoping as division chief and Ye Changming and Dai Liqing as deputy-chiefs) political propaganda (Wang Xiuzhen as chief and Xu Miaolin as deputy-chief), organization (Jin Zumin as chief, Wang Minglong as deputy-chief), administrative office (Huang Jinhai as chief, Cai Yunlong as deputy-chief), *Worker Rebel* (Ni Shuying and Wang Chenglong as responsible persons), and "Literary Offense Military Defense Command Post" (Zhang Baolin, Kang Zhengqin as responsible persons). Later, the "Literary Command Post" was changed in name to the "Militia Command Post," and in April 1971 the *Worker Rebel* ceased publication. (*Ge zushi fengong* [Division of labor among all divisions and offices], WGH archives).

38. In late 1966, following the expansion of the WGH, rebel groups set up bureau- , district- , county- and company-level "liaison posts," "command posts," or "branches," under the rubric of the WGH: e.g., "WGH x bureau liaison post." At the factory level, the typical rubric was "WGH x factory rebel brigade." In August 1968, the WGH issued a directive requesting all basic-level rebel brigades to amalgamate under the district, county, or bureau liaison post to which they belonged, thereby dissolving cross-unit rebel groups. WGH ed., *Guanyu tiaozheng qushu danwei lingdao guanxi de tongzhi* [Notice concerning adjustment of leadership relations in units under the district] (August 8, 1968).

39. This was true in other cities as well. Wang Shaoguang notes of Wuhan, "Rebel workers began to gain momentum in December, but in most cases they were still a minority in each unit." Wang Shaoguang, *Failure of Charisma: The Cultural Revolution in Wuhan* (New York: Oxford University Press, 1995), 90.

40. Ma Ji (former Scarlet Guard leader at the No. 17 Cotton Mill), July 6, 1989, interview with Li Xun; No. 17 Cotton Mill, ed. *Shangmian shiqichang wenhua geming shiji* [Annals of the CR at Shanghai's No. 17 Cotton Mill], Shanghai, 1975; WGH, ed., *Shanghai gongren tongjibiao* [Statistical tables on Shanghia workers], Shanghai, 1968.

41. WGH, ed., *Xin ganbu tongjibiao* [Statistical tables on new cadres], WGH, ed., Shanghai, December 1969. The units investigated included the liaison posts of the 10 districts and 20 bureaus, the 31 rebel brigades at the Clock and Watch Company under the Bureau of Light Industry, the 10 company liaison posts under the Light Industry Bureau, the 18 factories and research offices under the First Electronics Bureau, the 72 factory rebel brigades under the Machine Manufacturing Company of the First Electronics Bureau, and the liaison posts of 13 companies under the Textile Industrial Bureau.

42. Ibid.

43. Ibid.

44. Actually, there were a total of 44 WGH committee members in 1967, but age data are missing on the forms of three of the old rebels, and another three of the members were coopted labor models rather than old rebels.

45. Shanghai Statistical Bureau, ed., *1965nian Shanghai zhigong jiben qingkuang tongi* [Statistics on the basic conditions of the Shanghai workforce in 1965], Shanghai, 1966.

46. Ibid.

47. Ibid.

48. On the feisty proclivities of horn players in a very different cultural milieu, see Wynton Marsalis and Frank Stewart, *Sweet Swing Blues on the Road* (New York: W. W. Norton, 1994).

49. SPC Small Group to Investigate the Gang of Four case, ed., *Fandang fenzi Wang Hongwen zuixing nianbiao* [Chronology of criminal activities of anti-Party element Wang Hongwen], Shanghai, March 1977.

50. The forerunner of this factory was the Yufeng Cotton Mill, under Japanese management. With the conclusion of the war in 1945, Yufeng was nationalized and its name was changed to the No. 17 Cotton Mill of the Chinese Textile Construction Company. After 1949, it became the state-owned No. 17 Cotton Mill, and after the 1970s it was known as the Shanghai No. 17 Cotton Mill.

51. At that time, some 800,000 of Shanghai's industrial workforce of 1.4 million people were concentrated in Yangshupu.

52. Chen, former No. 17 Cotton Mill rebel, in a 1987 interview with Li Xun.

53. SPC Small Group to Investigate the Gang of Four case, ed., *Fandang fenzi Wang Hongwen.*

54. Ibid. Because of a cut-back in industrial production, the SPC decided to send 100,000 people to Chongming. Each factory assigned workers and cadres to participate.

55. Ibid.

56. Ibid.

57. No. 17 Cotton Mill *Shangmian 17chang*. In both content and style, Wang's poster was closely modeled upon the famous exemplar penned by Beijing University instructor Nie Yuanzi.

58. Ibid.

59. Ibid.

60. Ibid.

61. Tang Wenlan, May 17, 1992, interview with Li Xun.

62. Ma Ji, July 6, 1989, interview with Li Xun.

63. Wang Hongwen's followers at the No. 17 Mill numbered at most 100 to 200 workers (out of a workforce of more than 8,000) in summer 1966. By contrast, the conservative organization that formed in opposition to Wang's rebel initiatives enlisted between four and five thousand workers almost overnight. Ma Ji, July 6, 1989, interview.

64. Wang Hongwen, 1967 speech to the WGH Standing Committee.

65. No. 17 Cotton Mill, *Shangmian 17chang*.

66. Huang Jinhai, October 28, 1976, testimony.

67. Ibid.

68. Wang Xiuzhen, 1980 testimony; *Shanghai shihua.*

69. *Shanghai shihua.*

70. Wang Xiuzhen, 1980, testimony.

71. Women students were also known to be particularly feisty during the CR. On the violence of female Red Guards see, for example, Wang Youqin, "1966: xuesheng da laoshi de geming" [1966: The revolution in which students beat up teachers], *Ershiyi shiji shuangyuekan*, no. 31 (August 1995): 40.

72. *Guanyu erbingtuan fuzeren Geng Jinzhang juliu shencha de qingkuang baogao* [Situation report on the detention and interrogation of Second Regiment leader Geng Jinzhang] (April 11, 1967), Yangpu district office of the Shanghai Public Security Bureau (PSB).

73. Ibid.; Geng Jinzhang, November 27, 1979, testimony.

74. *Jingti hetushi de renwu Geng Jinzhang* [Be on guard against Krushchev-type person Geng Jinzhang], Shanghai Paper Pulp Mill rebel handbill (March 4, 1967).

75. Transcript of Shanghai Middle-Level Court roundtable concerning Geng Jinzhang at the Shanghai Paper Pulp Mill (December 1, 1979), Shanghai Middle-Level Court.

76. Geng Jinzhang, March 6, 1979, testimony.

77. Ibid.

78. Later, in spring 1966, the factory did agree to release him, but by this time the Cultural Revolution had already started and all specialized academies had stopped admitting new students. Liu Guande, 1987 interview with Li Xun. (Liu was a writer who undertook a lengthy interview with Pan Guoping after the latter's release from prison in 1987.)

79. Ibid.

80. Pan Guoping, April 24, 1979, testimony.

81. Pan Guoping, April 29, 1979, testimony.

82. Ibid.

83. Huang Jinhai, April 5, 1977, testimony.

84. Ibid., January 2, 1977, testimony.

85. Ibid., April 5, 1977.

86. Ibid.

87. Li Zhisui, *The Private Life of Chairman Mao* (New York: Random House, 1994), 93–94, 280, 345–346, 356, 479.

88. Wang Shaoguang, *Failure of Charisma*, 34.

89. Huang Jinhai, April 5, 1977, testimony. Up to 10% of the workforce was eligible for the status of "five-good worker," which was determined on the basis of productivity, political awareness, a cooperative attitude, etc.

90. Huang Jinhai, "Wo xuexile Zhonggong zhongyang shiyijie sanzhong quanhui gongbaohou de ganxiang" [My thoughts after reading the public report of the Third Plenum of the Eleventh Central Party Congress] (December 26, 1978).

91. Ibid., April 5, 1977.

92. Ibid.

93. Ibid., December 26, 1978, testimony.

94. Chen Ada, August 10, 1977, testimony.

95. Ibid., Ye Yonglie, *Wang Hongwen xingshuai lu* [The rise and fall of Wang Hongwen] (Changchun: Shidai Wenyi Chubanshe, 1989).

96. Chen Ada, August 10, 1977, testimony.

97. Chen asked another worker to give him a big-character-poster that was already written so he could claim it as his own, but the other worker refused. In 1967, when the Workers' General Headquarters sponsored an exhibition entitled "Long Live the Victory of the January Revolution," Chen, then a top leader in the WGH, finally commissioned someone to make a big-character-poster on his behalf. *Jiefang Ribao* [Liberation daily], November 20, 1977.

98. *Jianbao* [Bulletin], No. 46, WGH, March 22, 1968.

99. *Jiefang Ribao*, November 20, 1977.

100. *Shanghai shihua*, 135.

101. Ye Changming, August 26, 1977, testimony.

102. Ibid.

103. Ibid.

104. Ibid.

105. Shanghai Revolutionary Committee (SRC) Labor Liaison Group Materials Section, ed., *Qingkuang huibao* [Situation report] (April 18, 1977).

106. Ibid.

107. Indeed, Dai's most persistent demands during the course of his rebellion were to change his status from temporary to permanent worker and to bring his wife and children back from Lanzhou to Shanghai. Both wishes were granted before the end of the CR.

108. SRC Labor Liaison Group, *Qingkuang huibao.*

109. Dai Liqing, October 18, 1979, testimony.

110. Ibid.

111. Ibid., April 29, 1982, testimony.

112. Ma Zhenlong, April 28, 1982, interrogation notes.

113. Shanghai Enamelware Factory, ed., *Guanyu sirenbang heiganjiang Ma Zhenlong de zuixing cailiao huibian zhi er* [Second compilation of materials on the criminal activities of the Gang of Four black go-getter Ma Zhenlong] (November 1976).

114. Ibid.

115. WGH committee list.

116. Like most of the rebel leaders, Dai Zuxiang's difficulties predated the CR. During the Four Cleans, Dai's workshop party committee fingered him as overly ambitious and arrogant and demoted him from his cadre position. Later, Dai's roommates at the factory dormitory recalled that at the beginning of the CR Dai had excitedly shared with them a dream: "Last night, I had a great dream. I was the emperor's son-in-law, a big official. Ha, ha! If I can be a big official, you can all become officials." *Shanghai shihua*, 137. Although it was apparently recounted in jest, Dai's dream revealed an appetite for political office that put him in conflict with the party authorities at his factory.

117. Dai Zuxiang, "Zai Huai'entang dabianhuishang de fayan" [Speech at the Huai'entang debate], February 22, 1967, in Yangpu District Public Security Bureau of Shanghai Municipality.

118. Jiang Zhoufa, November 9, 1966, speech at the inaugural meeting of the WGH, Shanghai Municipal Museum.

119. Ibid.

120. Ibid.

121. Xu Meiying, May 2, 1989, interview with Li Xun.

122. Pan later insisted that, in attacking him, "the party committee was adopting the counterrevolutionary bourgeois line denounced by Mao Zedong; I therefore arose in rebellion." Pan Guoping, April 24, 1979, testimony.

123. Jin Zumin, August 1989, interview with Li Xun.

124. Recent work on the Tiananmen Uprising of 1989 also emphasizes the process of escalation. See Craig C. Calhoun, *Neither Gods Nor Emperors: Students and the Struggle for Democracy in China* (Berkeley: University of California Press, 1995); and Liu Xiaobo, "That Holy Word, 'Revolution,'" in Jeffrey N. Wasserstrom and Elizabeth J. Perry, eds., *Popular Protest and Political Culture in Modern China,* 2nd ed. (Boulder: Westview Press, 1994), 309–324.

125. Richard Cobb, *The People's Armies* (New Haven: Yale University Press, 1987), 142.

126. Kenneth Keniston, *Young Radicals: Notes on Committed Youth* (New York: Harcourt, Brace and World, 1969), 92.

127. See, especially, Richard Kagan and Norma Diamond, "Father, Son, and Holy Ghost: Pye, Solomon, and the 'Spirit of Chinese Politics,'" *Bulletin of Concerned Asian Scholars* 5, no. 1 (July 1973): 62–68.

128. Further discussion of this issue can be found in Elizabeth J. Perry, "Chinese Political Culture Revisited," in Jeffrey N. Wasserstrom and Elizabeth J. Perry, eds., *Popular Protest and Political Culture in Modern China*, (Boulder: Westview Press, 1994), 1–14.

129. Elizabeth J. Perry, *Shanghai on Strike: The Politics of Chinese Labor* (Stanford: Stanford University Press, 1993).

130. This conflict, a continuing theme in Shanghai politics since the establishment of the PRC, dated back to the earliest days of the Communist takeover. In a July 2, 1949, letter to All-China Federation of Trade Unions director, Li Lisan, Shanghai union leader Zhu Junxin noted that comrades from the old liberated areas in the north disagreed with the former underground leaders about how to organize in the factories. By his account, the northerners—lacking concrete knowledge of the local Shanghai scene—were easily prone to "subjectivist errors." The southerners, although familiar with local conditions, were less knowledgeable about general policy and thus more susceptible to "economistic errors." Shanghai Municipal Archives, C1–2–12.

131. Emily Honig, *Creating Chinese Ethnicity: Subei People in Shanghai, 1850–1980* (New Haven: Yale University Press, 1992), 109.

132. Gong Xiaoxia, who has interviewed a number of CR leaders in Guangzhou and other places, observes that "most rebel leaders I met had some peculiar hobby, such as photography, writing, painting, singing, etc. . . . which I did not see among the conservative leaders I know. . . . Evidence suggests that many early rebel organizations, especially at the work-unit level, were formed on the basis of such shared personalities." Personal communication, November 2, 1995.

Notes to Chapter 3

1. William Hinton, *Shenfan* (London: Picador Books, 1983), 611.

2. Initially, those who adopted a "conservative" stance were referred to as "royalists." The first use of royalist in conjunction with the Cultural Revolution appeared in a *People's Daily* editorial of June 5, 1966, which attacked Beijing University President, Lu Ping, as a "bourgeois royalist." Later, when the Red Guard movement got under way, Beijing's middle school students termed those who disagreed with their antiwork team position a "royalist faction" (*baohuang pai*) and referred to themselves as a "rebel faction" (*zaofan pai*). However, the term "royalist" was after all an alien one whose origins could be traced to the English and French Revolutions. Accordingly, Zhou Enlai, in a dialogue with a delegation of Red Guards, expressed his disapproval of this term and proposed instead that the rebels refer to their opponents as "conservatives" (*baoshou pai*). Zhou's admonition was immediately printed in handbills and disseminated widely. Later, the newspapers and Party Central documents also adopted this phrasing. Colloquially, the term was abbreviated as "old conserve" (*lao bao*). In some units and regions the conservatives were known at first simply as the "majority faction" (*duoshu pai*), inasmuch as initially they were everywhere the dominant social force. Carrying a less pejorative connotation—in contrast to the term "old

conserve"—the expression "majority faction" was favored by cadres who did not want to reveal any obvious bias. After the formation of revolutionary committees in 1967, the usage of both conservative faction and "old conserve" changed. Rather than being references to those who had misgivings about the Cultural Revolution's attack on the status quo, the appellations became terms of abuse used by one group to attack another. When it came time to decide which group should participate in the triple combination of local cadres, military cadres, and mass organizations in the formation of revolutionary committees, mass organizations accused one another of being "old conserves."

3. The two Red Guard organizations were the "Shanghai Red Guards General Headquarters" and the "Shanghai Municipal Red Guards Technical Institute General Headquarters."

4. The SPC actively supported this first Shanghai Red Guard organization, providing its members with an office, helping them to print up a tabloid, entitled *Red Guard*, and dispatching liaison personnel to give organizational and ideological guidance. But this assistance was not necessarily (as was later charged by the rebels) a ploy to manipulate the Red Guard movement for the purposes of self-preservation. The SPC supported the Shanghai Red Guard General Headquarters only after Mao Zedong had expressed his endorsement of the Red Guard movement. Moreover, in offering material aid and sending liaison officers, the SPC was continuing a seventeen-year practice of providing sponsorship and direction to a mass organization under its auspices.

5. Shanghai Federation of Trade Unions' (SFTU) "Writing Group on the History of the Scarlet Guards," *Zhongcheng yu dang de Shanghai gongren chiweidui* [Scarlet Guards: Shanghai workers loyal to the party] Shanghai, September 1983.

6. Ibid.

7. Ibid.

8. Ibid.

9. Andrew G. Walder, *Communist Neo-Traditionalism: Work and Authority in Chinese Industry* (Berkeley: University of California Press, 1986), 89.

10. Ma Ji not only worked at the same factory as Wang Hongwen, he was even employed in the same department. For a number of years prior to the Cultural Revolution, both men had been involved in security matters at the Number 17 Mill. Ma Ji interview with Li Xun, July 6, 1989.

11. Li Jianyu interview with Li Xun, July 3, 1992.

12. SFTU Writing Group, *Zhongcheng yu dang.*

13. Li Jianyu, July 3, 1992, interview.

14. WGH, ed., *Qingkuang huibao* [Situation bulletin], Shanghai, April 22, 1968.

15. Only two weeks after the formal inauguration of the Scarlet Guards, they already numbered 400,000; at their height they claimed twice that following. SFTU Writing Group, *Zhongcheng yu dang.*

16. At that time there were more than 8000 workers at the factory, including more than 700 party members. Li Jianyu, July 3, 1992, interview.

17. Ma Ji, July 6, 1989, interview.

18. SFTU Writing Group, *Zhongcheng yu dang.*

19. According to a report published in spring 1968 by the WGH: "At the 89 units investigated [in industry, city government, and transport], 110 [pre–Cultural Revolution] labor models and five-good workers were identified. These included 100 party members and 2 Communist Youth League members. Former Scarlet Guards among them numbered 31

people; of these, 9 people had served as top advisors." WGH, ed., *Qingkuang huibian* [Situation bulletin] (April 22, 1968). This particular survey included people who had been chosen as "five-good workers," a designation for which 10 percent of the workforce was eligible annually in the years 1962–1965. The criteria for election to this honor were fairly loose, in contrast to the labor models or advanced producers, who could compose no more than 0.1 percent of the workforce. If the survey had been confined to labor models, the proportion of Scarlet Guards would have been much higher.

20. "Shanghaishi 1968nian huoxue huoyong Mao Zedong sixiang jiji fenzi daibiao dahui fayangao" [Address at the 1968 Shanghai Representative Congress of Activists in flexibly studying and applying Mao Zedong Thought].

21. SFTU Writing Group, *Zhongcheng yu dang*.

22. On the restraining role of the trade unions, see Paul F. Harper, "The Party and the Unions in Communist China," *China Quarterly*, no. 37 (January 1969): 105–106. An exception was the Hundred Flowers period. See Elizabeth J. Perry, "Shanghai's Strike Wave of 1957," *China Quarterly* (March 1994): 1–27.

23. Li Jianyu, July 3, 1992, interview.

24. Ibid.

25. SFTU Writing Group, *Zhongcheng yu dang*.

26. WGH, ed., *Chouming zhaozhu de Shanghai chiweidui* [Notorious Shanghai Scarlet Guards], Shanghai, October 1968.

27. Ibid.

28. Ibid.

29. Ibid.

30. Ibid.

31. Ibid.

32. Ibid.

33. Ibid.

34. Ibid.

35. Ibid.

36. Li Jianyu, July 3, 1992, interview.

37. Ma Ji, July 6, 1989, interview.

38. "Shanghaishi 1968nian huoxue huoyong" (see note 20).

39. WGH, *Chouming zhaozhu de Shanghai chiweidui*.

40. Ibid.

41. SPC CR Materials Small Group, ed., *Shanghai "wenhua dageming" shihua* [Historical narrative of the "Great Cultural Revolution" in Shanghai], Shanghai, 1992.

42. Zhu Yongjia et al., eds., *Shanghai yiyue geming dashiji* [Annals of Shanghai's January Revolution], Shanghai, 1969.

43. Cao Diqiu, *Wo de shengming* [My announcement], handbill (December 25, 1966).

44. SPC, *Yiyue geming* (see Chapter 2, note 24).

45. Ibid.

46. Shanghai Revolutionary Committee (SRC) Political-Legal Command Post's "Special Investigation Group on the Scarlet Guards," ed., *Guanyu dui "chiweidui" zhuan'an shencha qingkuang de zonghe baogao* [Summary report on the investigation of the special case concerning the "Scarlet Guards"] (April 1, 1968).

47. Eventually, a five-point accord was reached in which the SPC gave its blessing to the Scarlet Guards' Beijing-bound protest. This agreement concluded the incident. SFTU Writing Group, *Zhongcheng yu dang*.

48. Yu Baonian (secretary to Chen Pixian during the Cultural Revolution), January 16, 1977, testimony; Yang Xiaobing (Red Guard of Jiaotong University's "Struggle to the Finish"), January 12, 1977, testimony.

49. SPC, *Yiyue geming* (see Chapter 2, note 24).

50. Li Jianyu, July 3, 1992, interview.

51. Ibid.

52. "Shanghaishi 1968nian huoxue huoyong" (see note 20).

53. Ibid.

54. Ibid.

55. June 23, 1970, WGH Standing Committee meeting record.

56. SRC, *Guanyu dui chiweidui* (see note 46).

57. Ma Ji, July 6, 1989, interview.

58. Shanghai Workers' Representative Conference, *Dui yuan chiweidui toutou biaoxian de diaocha baogao* [Investigation report on the *biaoxian* (performance) of former Scarlet Guard chiefs] (1974).

59. Ma Ji, July 6, 1989, interview.

60. Li Jianyu, July 3, 1992, interview.

61. WGH, *Qingkuang huibao.*

62. A December 1972 survey of 118 "influential" labor models and advanced producers in Shanghai found that forty-five (46%) had "good" attitudes and explained that "although some comrades had joined the wrong side [i.e., the Scarlet Guards] in the early period of the CR, with the help of the revolutionary rebels they quickly returned to the revolutionary line of Chairman Mao." WGH, ed., *Duiyu benshi youyingxiang de quanguo laodong mofan he shixianjin shengchanzhe de qingkuang fenxi* [Analysis of the situation of national labor models and municipal advanced producers who are influential in this city], Shanghai, December 20, 1972.

63. WGH, ed., *Youguan "laodong mofan" de yixie qingkuang* [Selected conditions of "labor models"], Shanghai, January 26, 1973.

64. Walder, *Communist Neo-Traditionalism*, 246–247.

65. On the legacy of the underground labor movement, see Elizabeth J. Perry, *Shanghai on Strike: The Politics of Chinese Labor* (Stanford: Stanford University Press, 1993).

66. CCP, *Zhongguo gongchandang zai Shanghai* [The Chinese Communist Party in Shanghai] (Shanghai: Shanghai People's Press, 1991), 561.

Notes to Chapter 4

1. Sidney Tarrow, *Power in Movement: Social Movements, Collective Action, and Politics* (Cambridge: Cambridge University Press, 1994), 7.

2. In some cases, these groups were extremely small and were engaged in rather suspect activities. For example, a "rebel headquarters," which specialized in robbery, actually consisted of a three-person family!

3. See Elizabeth J. Perry, "Shanghai's Strike Wave of 1957," *China Quarterly* (March 1994):1–27; and "Rural Violence in Socialist China," *China Quarterly* (September 1989):414–440 for earlier instances of popular protests in the city and countryside alike.

4. For a discussion of these inequalities, see Mark Selden, *The Political Economy of Chinese Development* (Armonk, N.Y.: M. E. Sharpe, 1993).

5. For a discussion of the impact of the household registration system, see T. J. Cheng and Mark Selden, "The Origins and Social Consequences of China's *Hukou* System," *China Quarterly*, no. 139 (September 1994): 644–668.

6. Shanghai Revolutionary Committee (SRC) Anti-Economism Liaison Headquarters, ed., *Wuchan jieji wenhua dageming zhong Shanghai fandui jingjizhuyi da shiji* [Annals of Shanghai's anti-economism during the Great Proletarian Cultural Revolution], Shanghai, March 17, 1967.

7. This organization was responsible for several million workers leaving their posts during the CR. Xiaoxia Gong, "Repressive Movements and the Politics of Victimization" (Harvard University Ph.D. diss., 1995), 259.

8. Wang Nianyi, *Da Dongluan de niandai* [Decade of great turmoil] (Zhengzhou: Henan People's Press, 1988), 155–156.

9. Shanghai People's Commune Anti-Economism Liaison Headquarters, ed., *Jixu qingshi de jige wenti* [Several issues in urgent need of instructions] (hereafter cited as *Jixu qingshi*) Shanghai, February 15, 1967.

10. For an overview of the changing policy concerning contract and temporary laborers and their role in the CR, see "Sources of Labor Discontent in China: The Worker-Peasant System," *Current Scene* 6, no. 5 (March 15, 1968).

11. Shen Jingbo, SFTU personnel, August 1989 interview with Li Xun.

12. Dai Liqing, July 16, 1980, testimony.

13. *Wuchanjieji . . . fandui jingjizhuyi* (see note 6).

14. Shanghai Statistical Bureau, ed., *Xin Shanghai 40 nian* [40 years of new Shanghai] (Beijing: China Statistics Publishing House, 1990).

15. *Jixu qingshi* (see note 9).

16. *Guanyu xianzai nongcun de jingjian zhigong de anzhi yijian* [Opinions concerning the settlement of streamlined workers now in the villages], a report of the Shanghai Labor and Wage Committee to the Shanghai Party Committee, with copies to Party Central and the East China Bureau (December 15, 1966).

17. Zhu Yongjia et al., *Shanghai yiyue geming dashiji* [Annals of the January Revolution in Shanghai], Shanghai, 1969.

18. *Jixu qingshi.*

19. CCP, *Zhongguo gongchandang zai Shanghai* [The Chinese Communist Party in Shanghai] (Shanghai: Shanghai People's Press, 1991), 504.

20. *Jixu qingshi.*

21. SPC, *Yiyue geming* (see Chapter 2, note 24).

22. *Jianjue fencui zibenzhuyi fubi niliu, chedi jiefa pipan "gelaosi" yixiaocuo bie you yongxin de toutou de zuixing* [Resolutely smash the capitalist restoration countercurrent, thoroughly expose and criticize the crimes of the ambitious heads of the "private entrepreneurs headquarters"], handbill, n.d.

23. *Wuchanjieji . . . fandui jingjizhuyi.*

24. *Jixu qingshi.*

25. *Wenge chuqi Shanghai gelei qunzhong zuzhi jiankuang* [Overview of various types of Shanghai mass organizations in the early period of the Cultural Revolution] (hereafter cited as *Wenge chuqi*), Shanghai Office to "Expose and Criticize the Gang of Four and Their Remnant Forces in Shanghai" (1982).

26. Telegram to Party Central, January 6, 1967.

27. *Wenge chuqi.*

28. *Wuchanjieji . . . fandui jingjizhuyi.*

29. Ibid.

30. Telegram to Party Central, Mao Zedong and Zhou Enlai from Small East Gate Branch of Shanghai People's Bank and Shanghai Nanshi District People's Bank's "Replete River Red Revolutionary Rebel League" (January 6, 1967).

31. *Wenge chuqi.*

32. SRC, *Yiyue geming.*

33. Rebel organizations were especially adept at securing such assistance. For example, on January 1, 1967, Chen Pixian signed an agreement to disburse 150,000 yuan in "living expenses" to the Second Regiment for a fleet of pedicabs, motorcycles, and bicycles. Zhu Yongjia et al., eds., *Shanghai yiyue geming dashiji* (see Chapter 3, note 42). According to an investigation in the four bureaus of industry, education, commerce, and labor: "These four bureaus have 297 mass organizations among them. From early November 1966 to the present (late February 1967), they received some 556,000 yuan in disbursements for Cultural Revolution activities." *Wuchanjieji . . . fandui jingjizhuyi.*

34. Telegram to Party Central, January 6, 1967.

35. *Guanyu gua jingjizhuyi yaofeng de qingkuang huibao* [Situation report on the blowing of the evil wind of economism], from Shanghai Number 2 Commercial Bureau to State Council's Ministry of Commerce (June 6, 1967).

36. SRC, *Yiyue geming.*

37. Shanghai Federation of Trade Unions (SFTU),*Guanyu jiti suoyouzhi gongchang qiye zhigong yaoqiu zuzhi gonghui de qingshi baogao* [Report requesting instructions concerning demands of workers at collectively owned factories to organize unions].

38. Shen Jingbo, August 1989, interview.

39. SPC, *Yiyue geming.*

40. This was also the case elsewhere in China. As Wang Shaoguang analyzes the tide of economism in Wuhan, "Although those economic demands were, almost without exception, made by the rebels, none of the major rebel organizations supported them. The leaders of the main rebel organizations cared more about the redistribution of political power." Wang Shaoguang, *Failure of Charisma: The Cultural Revolution in Wuhan* (New York: Oxford University Press, 1995), 169.

41. Ibid.

42. *Jingji tongling* [Emergency order], handbill of the WGH (January 7, 1967).

43. SRC and WGH, *Dui Xu Meiying de diaocha baogao* [Investigation report on Xu Meiying], (December 1968).

44. *Wen Hui Bao*, Shanghai, June 4, 1977.

45. SPC, *Yiyue geming.*

46. *Wuchan jieji . . . fandui jingjizhuyi.*

47. Document of the Shanghai Labor Bureau (December 2, 1966), no. 114.

48. Notice of the Shanghai Labor Bureau (December 2, 1966).

49. *Wuchan jieji . . . fandui jingjizhuyi.*

50. Document of the Shanghai Labor Wage Committee (November 24, 1966), no. 13.

51. *Guanyu xianzai nongcun* (see note 16).

52. Shanghai Labor Bureau, *Zaiyu qunzhong xieshang shi dui jige juti wenti de zhanxing chuli yijian* [Ideas for temporary handling of some concrete issues in negotiating with the masses] December 25, 1966.

53. SPC, *Yiyue geming.*

54. Ibid.

55. Ibid.

56. At the same time, they agreed upon two plans to supplement the five points: "Draft of preliminary opinions concerning job placement and livelihood questions of workers sent down to help agriculture, dismissed 'neighborhood workers' (i.e., workers at neighborhood factories), temporary workers, and unemployed personnel"; and "Preliminary opinions concerning some current wage and compensation issues." The next day these plans were disseminated to lower levels.

57. SRC, *Guanyu qingli jingjifeng shi suofa kuanxiang bing yaoqiu tuihuan de gongzuo qingkuang zongjie* [Situation summary on the work of accounting for and demanding the return of funds issued during the economism wind], (April 1967). In 1966, state enterprise workers received a total monthly wage of 141 million yuan. *Shanghaishi tongjiju guanyu Shanghai zhigong qingkuang de tongji ziliao* [Statistical materials from the Shanghai Statistical Bureau concerning the condition of Shanghai workers] (Beijing: China Statistical Publishing House, 1979). Another source notes, "From January 1 to January 7, in the space of one week the Shanghai branches of the People's Bank of China paid out 3.8 million yuan in supplemental wages, welfare and nutrition subsidies, bonuses, protective equipment, exchange revolutionary experiences fees, and the like." See SPC, *Yiyue geming*.

58. SPC, *Yiyue geming*.

59. Ibid.

60. Shanghai Frontline Command Post for Grasping Revolution and Raising Production, *Ge chanyeju huiyi jilu* [Record of the meeting of all bureaus of production](February 27, 1967).

61. *Guanyu gua jingjizhuyi yaofeng (see note 35)*.

62. Ibid.

63. Ibid.

64. The Red Workers and Private Entrepreneur Headquarters were banned during the January Revolution. At that time, the Support Agriculture Headquarters divided into two factions, both of which were required to send their members back to the countryside after social order was restored in 1969.

65. Shanghai Labor Bureau Revolutionary Committee, *Guanyu gongchang qiyezhong meiyou canjia gonghui de zhigong bingjia gongzi deng daiyu de tongzhi* [Notice concerning compensation for sick leave, etc., for factory and enterprise workers who have not joined the union] (1971); *Buchong tongzhi* [Supplementary notice] (June 21, 1971), in SFTU, ed., *Laodong gongzi zhengce huibian* [Compilation of policies of labor wages].

66. Hong Yung Lee, *The Politics of the Chinese Cultural Revolution: A Case Study* (Berkeley: University of California Press, 1978), 34.

Notes to Chapter 5

1. Shanghai Party Committee (SPC) CR Materials Small Group, ed., *Shanghai "wenhua dageming" shihua* [Historical narrative of the "Great Cultural Revolution" in Shanghai](hereafter cited as *Shanghai Shihua*), Shanghai, 1992, 306–307.

2. *Erbingtuan zai geming de baofeng liehuo zhong dansheng* [The Second Regiment, born in the storm of revolution], February 14, 1967, handbill of the Second Regiment.

3. Sun Yuxi, April 7, 1967, testimony.

4. Dai Zuxiang, April 1979, testimony.

5. Sun Yuxi, April 7, 1967, testimony.

6. Geng Jinzhang, March 6, 1979, testimony.

7. Ibid., March 5, 1967, testimony.

8. *Shanghai shihua*, 307.

9. Fang Jianhua (standing committee member of the Third Regiment), March 1970 exposé.

10. Geng Jinzhang, November 27, 1979, testimony.

11. *Shanghai shihua*, 308.

12. Zhu Yongjia et al., eds., *Shanghai yiyue geming dashiji* [Annals of the January Revolution in Shanghai] (Shanghai, 1969).

13. Huang Jinhai, September 6, 1979, testimony.

14. Chen Bin's notebook (1966).

15. Geng Jinzhang, June 25, 1979, testimony.

16. Wang Xiuzhen, January 23, 1978, testimony.

17. Wang Zhichang, December 12, 1977, testimony.

18. Geng Jinzhang, March 3, 1967, testimony.

19. *Beishang fanhu bingtuan de hongqi yongyuan budao* [The red flag on the regiment returned to Shanghai from Beijing will never fall], handbill of the First Regiment (January 1967).

20. Dai Zuxiang, "Zai Huaientang dabianhuishang de fayan" [Speech at the debate in Huaien Hall] (February 22, 1967).

21. Andrew G. Walder, *Chang Ch'un-ch'iao and Shanghai's January Revolution* (Ann Arbor: University of Michigan Center for Chinese Studies, 1977), 52.

22. Delegation of Shanghai Workers' Revolutionary Rebel United Command sent to Beijing to request instructions, *Xiang zhongyang wenge de huibao qingshi* [Request for instructions from the Cultural Revolution Small Group] (February 13, 1967).

23. Wang Minglong (representative of Wang Hongwen, founding member of the Shanghai People's Commune), December 7, 1979, testimony.

24. SPC, *Yiyue geming* (see Chapter 2, note 24); Geng Jinzhang, March 12, 1979, testimony.

25. SPC, *Yiyue geming*.

26. Transcript of talk between Xu Jingxian and Edgar Snow, 1970.

27. Parris Chang, "Shanghai and Chinese Politics: Before and After the Cultural Revolution," in Christopher Howe, ed., *Shanghai: Revolution and Development in an Asian Metropolis* (Cambridge: Cambridge University Press, 1981), 81–82.

28. *Fan renmin gongshe de niliu cong he er lai* [From whence came the reverse current against the People's Commune], handbill (Febuary 1967).

29. *Erbingtuan zai geming* (see note 2).

30. Geng Jinzhang, March 13, 1979, testimony.

31. Ye Changming, June 14, 1977, testimony.

32. Ibid., August 26, 1977, testimony.

33. Geng Jinzhang, March 6, 1967, testimony.

34. Sun Yuxi, April 7, 1967, testimony.

35. WGH proclamation, February 11, 1966.

36. *Shanghai shihua*, 308.

37. Ma Tianshui, April 8, 1978, testimony.

38. Huang Jinhai, June 19, 1977, testimony.

39. Fan Zuodong, April 25, 1989, interview with Li Xun.

40. Yangpu District Public Security Bureau, ed., *Geng Jinzhang, Sun Yuxi zhuyao cuowu shishi* [The truth of the major mistakes of Geng Jinzhang and Sun Yuxi] (March 26, 1967).

41. Wang Xiuzhen, January 23, 1978, testimony.

42. Geng Jinzhang, March 13, 1979, testimony.

43. Wang Xiuzhen, January 23, 1978, testimony.

44. Ibid.

45. Ye Changming, March 14, 1978, testimony.

46. Song Yongyi, June 13, 1989, interview with Li Xun. Song participated in the 1967 investigatory team of Red Guards stationed at Shanghai Diesel Engine Factory.

47. Chen Xianfa, *Minzu lei* [National tears] (Shanghai, 1988).

48. Ibid.

49. Song Yongyi, June 13, 1989, interview.

50. The "East is Red" was actually an amalgam of four anti-Zhu groups: the "East is Red Struggle Headquarters," the "Red Guard Command Post," the "Red Flag Revolutionary Rebel Regiment," and the "WGH Shanghai Diesel Brigade." *Guanyu Shangchai liansi de diaocha baogao* [Investigation report concerning Shanghai Diesel's Lian Si], handbill of the Red Flag General Headquarters of East China Chemical Engineering Institute (July 1967).

51. Lian Si comprised three pro-Zhu outfits: the "Exchange Experience Post," the "Red Guard Vanguard," and the "WGH Yangpu District Branch Brigade." Ibid.

52. On the relationship between the legacy of earlier political campaigns and the violence of the Cultural Revolution, see Lynn T. White, III, *Policies of Chaos: The Organizational Causes of Violence in China's Cultural Revolution* (Princeton: Princeton University Press, 1989).

53. Song Yongyi, June 13, 1989, interview.

54. Ibid.

55. Ibid.

56. *Guanyu Shangchai liansi* (see note 50).

57. The Security Police came from a rebel organization at the Public Security Bureau that was affiliated with the WGH.

58. *Shanghai shihua.*

59. Song Yongyi, June 13, 1989, interview.

60. Dai Zuda, "Wo weishemma yao 'zhilian,' fan gongzongsi" [Why I supported Lian Si and opposed the Workers' General Headquarters], *Gongren zaofanbao* (August 1967).

61. Chen Ada, October 13, 1978, testimony.

62. East China Chemical Engineering Institute, "Fan fubi" [Opposing restoration], handbill in *Chen Puchang de bufen yanlun zhailu* [Excerpts from Chen Puchang's speeches] (July 28, 1967).

63. Ibid.

64. Chen Ada, December 22, 1978, testimony.

65. Wang Chenglong, August 28, 1978, testimony.

66. Ibid.

67. On April 9, fierce battles between the "Production Army" and other factions of rebel organizations broke out in Sichuan Province's Chengdu, Zigong, Luzhou, Yibin, etc. Armed battles lasted in Sichuan until August 1969, with countless casualties. In June and

July 1967, in Wuhan, there was a large-scale armed battle between the Million Heroes and their rivals. In 1967 and the first half of 1968, 1,600 people were killed there. In June 1967, twenty people were killed in Harbin in similar battles. Di Jiu and Zhi Wu, *Xie yu huo de jiaoxun—wenge zhongda wudou can'an jishi* [Lessons of blood and fire: Annals of the major armed struggles and massacres of the Cultural Revolution] (Lanzhou: Xinjiang University Press, 1993).

68. As Christopher Howe notes, "Progress between 1965 and 1970 remained brisk in spite of Shanghai being a major centre of political activity during the Cultural Revolution." Christopher Howe, "Industrialization Under Conditions of Long-Run Population Stability: Shanghai's Achievement and Prospect," in Howe, ed., *Shanghai: Revolution and Development in an Asian Metropolis* (New York: Cambridge University Press, 1981), 178.

69. *Jiangjun juanjin xuanwo* [The general swept into the whirlpool] (Nanjing: Jiangsu Literary Arts Press, 1988).

70. *Fawang huihui, zuize nantao* [The arm of the law is extensive, criminal responsibility is hard to escape], *Gongren Ribao*, December 6, 1980. The official history of the CR published by the Shanghai Party Committee lists 650 injuries and one death, but other sources do not mention deaths.

71. For example, the May Eighth Regiment, which had participated in Geng Jinzhang's alliance, was smashed at this time.

72. Much additional research is required to explain the brutal torture, armed battles, and even cannibalism that occurred during the CR. Since Shanghai experienced an unusually low level of violence, this case study can shed little light on the causes of the more shocking manifestations of CR animosities. For a recent effort to deal with this complex subject, see Lu Xiuyuan, "A Step Toward Understanding Popular Violence in China's Cultural Revolution," *Pacific Affairs*, 67, no.4 (winter 1994–1995): 533–563.

73. Ye Changming, April 5, 1977, testimony.

74. Pan Guoping, 1977, testimony.

75. Ye Changming, April 5, 1977, testimony.

Notes to Chapter 6

1. Yao Wenyuan, "The Working Class Must Exercise Leadership in Everything," *Peking Review*, no. 35 (August 30, 1968): 3–6.

2. Mark Selden, "Labor Unrest in China, 1831–1990," *Review* 18, no. 1 (winter 1995): 78.

3. The forerunner of this organization was the "WGH Transport System Six Bureaus United Command Post," which had been formed in late December 1966 to counter Scarlet Guard strength in the six bureaus of the transport sector: railway, postal-telecommunications, shipping, transportation, Yangzi navigation, and port authority. Rebels in these six bureaus established a united organization so that they could mutually communicate and support each other in the face of Scarlet Guard opposition. Testimony of Gong Shigen, former staff at "Grasp Revolution, Promote Production Frontline Command Post" and rebel representative from the Shanghai Maritime Transport Bureau, February 2, 1978.

4. Wang Minglong, December 7, 1979, testimony.

5. Xie Pengfei, March 15, 1979, testimony.

6. Wang Minglong, December 7, 1979, testimony.

7. Ibid.

8. Shanghai Party Committee (SPC) CR Materials Small Group, ed., *Shanghai "wenhua dageming" shihua* [Historical narrative of the "Great Cultural Revolution" in Shanghai], Shanghai, 1992.

9. Ibid.

10. Ibid.

11. Ibid.

12. Ibid.

13. Ibid.

14. Zhu Yongjia et al., *Shanghai yiyue geming dashiji* [Annals of Shanghai's January Revolution] (Shanghai, 1969).

15. Ibid.

16. Wang Minglong, December 7, 1979, testimony.

17. WGH, ed., *Huanhu Shanghai renmin gongshe dansheng* [Welcoming the birth of the Shanghai People's Commune], February 5, 1967.

18. SFTU Small Group in the Movement to Expose the Gang of Four, ed., *Guanyu 'sirenbang' ji qi yudang tongguo Shanghaishi zonggonghui ancha qinxin, baobi huairen de qingcha qingkuang* (hereafter cited as *Guanyu 'sirenbang' ji qi yudang*) [Clarification of the situation concerning the Gang of Four and their remnants' use of the Shanghai Federation of Trade Unions to buttress their close associates and protect bad people], January 25, 1978.

19. SPC, *Zhongguo gongchandang Shanghaishi zuzhishi ziliao* [Materials on the organization history of the Shanghai Communist Party] (Shanghai: Shanghai People's Press, 1991).

20. The seven were Jin Zumin, Chen Ada, Ye Changming, Zhang Baolin, Jin Ai, Jin Chuande, and Huang Jinhai.

21. The four additions were Chen Xinfa, Huang Jinhai, Wang Chenglong, and Wang Xiangjun. SPC, *Shanghaishi zuzhishi ziliao* (see note 19).

22. Shanghai No. 1 Machine and Electriconics Bureau, ed., *Wenge dashiji zhuanti cailiao* [Special materials on the chronology of the CR], May 1984. Similarly, the revolutionary committee of the Shanghai Textile Bureau numbered 65 members in November 1968, of whom 47 were rebel workers. See Shanghai Revolutionary Committee Industrial-Transport Department, Shanghai WGH Investigation Team Stationed at the Textile Bureau, ed., *Guanyu fangzhiju geweihui, lianluozhan zuzhi gaikuang huibao* [Report on the condition of the Textile Bureau Revolutionary Committee, liaison post organizations], November 1968.

23. Shanghai SRC Industrial-Transport Dept., WGH Investigation Group at the Light Industrial Bureau, *Guanyu qinggongyeju geweihui, lianluozhan zuzhi gaikuang huibao* [Situation report concerning the revolutionary committee at the Bureau of Light Industry and liaison post organizations], November 1968.

24. WGH Standing Committee Secretariat, *Qingkuang huibao* [Situation report], November 26, 1968.

25. Of the fifteen core personnel in the working agencies of the four offices established by the revolutionary committee of the Textile Bureau in 1968, six were worker rebels. As in the Bureau of Light Industry, the others had all been cadres in the bureau. Among the five responsible persons in the bureau's revolutionary committee, one was a worker rebel, one a soldier, and three were cadres at the bureau. Among the 136 working personnel in the four offices, 25 were workers and 110 were former cadres. (WGH, ed., *Guanyu fangzhiju huibao*

[Situation report concerning the Textile Bureau], Shanghai, 1968.) In some cases, even the facade of worker representation was missing. When the Instruments Bureau first established its revolutionary committee, the four chairs and vice-chairs and the standing committee included no worker rebels, and all the working personnel were former cadres. (WGH, "Yibiaojunei de yiban fubi shili" [Restorationist forces inside the Instruments Bureau], *Jian Bao* [Brief report], May 8, 1968.)

26. SRC Industrial-Transport Department, WGH Investigation Team Stationed at the Handicraft Bureau, *Guanyu shougongyeju geweihui, lianluozhan zuzhi gaikuang de huibao* [Situation report concerning the Handicraft Bureau Revolutionary Committee Liaison Post Organization], November 27, 1968.

27. WGH Standing Committee Secretariat, *Qingkuang huibao* [Situation report], November 26, 1968.

28. Ibid., no. 19 (December 11, 1968).

29. WGH, "Guanyu jianyi gongzongsi suoshu geji zuzhi he tongji geweihui shixing 'yitao banzi liangkuai paizi' de baogao" [Report on implementing "one group, two signboards" in all organizations under the WGH and in revolutionary committees at the same level], WGH report to the SRC (December 31, 1968).

30. WGH, "Jixu fahui gongren geming qunzhong yingyou zuoyong de yige haobanfa—gongjiao xitong 13 geju shixing 'liangkuai paizi, yitao banzi' de qingkuang diaocha" [A good method for continuing to develop the rightful role of the worker revolutionary masses: Situation investigation of the implementation of "two signs, one group" in 13 bureaus of the industry-transport system], report of WGH to SRC (March 20, 1969).

31. WGH, "Xin ganbu qingkuang huizong tongjibiao" [Statistical tables summarizing the condition of new cadres], December 1969.

32. Ibid., July 1970.

33. *Shanghai shihua.*

34. Ibid.

35. WGH, "128ming gongdaibiao qingkuang huizongbiao" [Summary statistics on 128 worker representatives], 1968.

36. WGH, "128ming gongdaibiao qingkuang dengjibiao" [Registration forms of 128 worker representatives], 1968.

37. WGH, "128ming gongdaibiao fenpei qingkuang" [Allocation situation of 128 worker representatives], 1968.

38. On the operations of these special case groups, see Michael Schoenhals, "The Central Case Examination Group (1966–1979)," *China Quarterly* 145 (March 1996): 87–111.

39. Wang Chenglong, November 21, 1977, memoir.

40. The people co-opted by the rebel organization included: Wang Xiangjun (female), an old rebel worker, who later became Party Central Committee alternate and chair of the Shanghai Women's Federation; Xu Shiyu, a supervisor at the Wujing Chemical Engineering Factory, who later became one of the leaders of the SRC Organization Department; Su Guizhen (female), leader of the revolutionary committee at Shanghai's No. 7 Knitting Factory, who later became a core leader of the SRC Finance and Trade Department; Xu Chenghu, a supervisor at the Shanghai Diesel Engine Plant, who later became vice-chair of the party committee of the city Public Security Bureau; and Yang Yougen, leader of the revolutionary committee at the Shanghai Bicycle Factory, who later became a core leader of the SRC Finance and Trade Department. *Shanghai shihua.*

41. Hong Yung Lee, *The Politics of the Chinese Cultural Revolution* (Berkeley: University of California Press, 1978), 277–287.

42. Yao Wenyuan, "The Working Class Must Exercise Leadership."

43. Minutes of the August 16, 1968, enlarged meeting of the Shanghai Revolutionary Committee.

44. The distribution was as follows: more than 11,000 people were dispatched to universities, institutes, and academies; more than 22,000 to district-level middle and elementary schools; more than 20,000 to the sanitation system; more than 3,150 to the technology system (later, an additional 27,000 were added); more than 5,000 to district-level and street agencies; more than 4,000 to district-run units; more than 5,000 to the suburban counties; and more than 4,000 to the municipal party committee, municipal people's congress, and to agencies under the East China Bureau. *Shanghai shihua.*

45. Beginning in October 1968, the Numbers 1, 2, 3, 5, and 6 Offices of Worker Propaganda Teams were established under the Culture-Education Battlefront Office and Industry-Transport Battlefront Office of the WPT Leadership Small Group. The No. 1 Office, headed by Wang Xiuzhen, was in charge of WPTs for universities, institutes, newspapers, publishing, culture, and movies. The No. 2 Office, led by Zhang Baolin, handled middle and elementary schools and medical and sanitation WPTs. The No. 3 Office handled technology, transport, and basic construction and was led by Dai Liqing. The No. 5 Office, headed by Wang Minglong, took charge of suburban districts and counties. The No. 6 Office handled finance and trade systems and was led by Huang Jinhai. No No. 4 Office was established. According to conventional order, a No. 4 Office should have handled the industrial sector, but at that time Chen Ada was already in charge of the industrial department of the SRC. If one adds to that the fact that all of the WPT members were sent from the industry and transport system, it seemed that there was no need to send additional WPT members to that system; so no office was set up for the industrial system. The WGH General Office sent twenty-six people to take charge of these WPT offices, leaving only Ye Changming to mind the store. *Shanghai shihua.*

46. *Shanghai shihua.*

47. Ibid.

48. WGH, "Guanyu 10ge qu 'sangong' guanxi de qingkuang" [On the situation of "three workmen" in ten districts], no. 53 (August 8, 1969).

49. Ibid.

50. Wang Xiuzhen, June 30, 1978, testimony.

51. Ibid.

52. Ye Changming, September 1972 report to Wang Xiuzhen on the situation of the WPTs.

53. SFTU, *Sirenbang ji qi yudang tongguo Shanghaishi zonggonghui kongzhi gongxuandui jinxing cuandang duoquan yinmou huodong de qingcha qingkuang* [Investigation report on the plot by the Gang of Four and their remnants to go through the SFTU to control the WPTs and usurp party power], January 25, 1978.

54. Approximately 27% of the members were women.

55. SFTU, *Quanshi gongxuandui qingkuang* [Situation of Worker Propaganda Teams throughout the city], April 1974.

56. WGH, *Fahui pipan 'sirenbang' ji qi yudang kongzhi shangceng jianzhu da gao cuandang duoquan de yinmou huodong* [Develop criticism of the conspiracy by the Gang of Four and their remnants in control of the superstructure to usurp party power], June 1977.

57. *Shanghai shihua.*

58. Ibid.

59. WGH, *Jian Bao* [Brief report], November 29, 1969.

60. Ibid.

61. *Shanghai shihua.*

62. Ibid.

63. Ibid.

64. Ibid.

65. Ibid.

66. Huang Jinhai, July 26, 1977, testimony.

67. People were killed, however, in smaller-scale conflicts that erupted on the outskirts of the city. The bloodiest was the Battle of Qingpu, which resulted in twenty-three deaths. Virtually all battles of any size in which workers were involved were connected with the WGH.

68. Jiang's slogan was proposed after the July 1967 Wuhan Incident (in which emissaries from Beijing were kidnapped by local conservatives). Concerning that event, see Thomas W. Robinson, "The Wuhan Incident: Local Strife and Provincial Rebellion During the Cultural Revolution," *China Quarterly*, no. 47 (July–September 1971): 413–418.

69. PLA Shanghai Garrison, ed., *Sirenbang zai Shanghai jingying dier wuzhuang shimo* [The saga of the Gang of Four's management of a second military force in Shanghai], 1988.

70. Ibid.; *Shanghai minbing gongzuo jingyan xuanbian* [Compilation of Shanghai militia work experience], 1973–1974. Our thanks to Michael Schoenhaels for supplying the latter source.

71. Ye Changming, April 5, 1977, testimony.

72. Ibid.

73. Ibid., June 14, 1977, testimony.

74. Ibid.

75. Ibid.

76. Ibid.

77. Ibid.

78. Wang Xiuzhen, June 30, 1978, testimony.

79. Ye Changming, June 14, 1977.

80. Wang Xiuzhen, June 30, 1978.

81. Ye Changming, June 14, 1977.

82. Ibid.

83. Ibid.

84. Ibid.

85. Wang Xiuzhen, November 25, 1976, testimony.

86. Additionally, some frequent participants in the brainstorming sessions were Zhou Hongbao, core leader of the State Council Ministry of Education after 1974; Wang Chenglong, leader of the SRC Culture-Education Department; Wang Minglong, chair of the Machine-Electric No. 1 Bureau; Wang Xiangjun, chair of the Shanghai Women's Federation; Shi Shangying, head of the Shanghai Militia Command Post; Jin Zumin, SRC Organization Department head, who had already accepted the assignment of going to Beijing to restore the national trade union; Wang Richu, head of the Shanghai Party Committee Organization Department (who had been sent from the PLA to help direct the WGH); and SRC Security Department chief, Kang Ningyi (who also had been sent by the PLA to the WGH).

Occasionally, Wang Xiuzhen also asked old cadre Shen Han, who served as vice-chair of the union, to participate in the sessions.

87. Wang Xiuzhen, June 15, 1978, testimony.

88. Ibid., June 30, 1978.

89. Ye Changming, April 5, 1977.

90. Ma Tianshui, October 14, 1977, testimony.

91. Xu Jingxian, August 11, 1977, testimony.

92. Wang Xiuzhen, March 23, 1974, work notes.

93. Ibid., March 3, 1980 testimony.

94. *Guangming Ribao,* November 30, 1976.

95. Wang Xiuzhen, August 11, 1977, testimony.

96. Xu Jingxian, August 11, 1977.

97. Shanghai Party Committee (SPC), The ten who did assume such positions were distributed in the State Council's Ministry of Education, Post and Telecommunications Ministry, Construction Ministry, Ministry of Public Health, Ministry of Culture, Ministry of Public Security, No. 6 Ministry of Machine Industry, as well as in the All-China Federation of Trade Unions and Communist Youth League. Nine of the ten had been ordinary factory workers before the CR. The only exception was Yu Jinyong, who became minister of culture, and who had been an instructor at the Shanghai Conservatory of Music prior to the CR. "Guanyu sirenbang fangeming jituan zhongyao chengyuan Ma Tianshui, Xu Jingxian, Wang Xiuzhen dengren de shencha baogao" [Investigation report on important members of the Gang of Four counter-revolutionary clique, Ma Tianshui, Xu Jingxian, Wang Xiuzhen, etc.], December 26, 1980.

98. SPC, "Guanyu 'gongren dashi' 'zuge' shifou lieru qisushu de jizhong yijian" [Some opinions on whether or not the "worker ambassadors" and "zuge" should be included in the indictment], 1980.

99. Ibid.

100. Wang Xiuzhen's speech in July 1974 at the SFTU organizational work meeting.

101. Those investigated were directors, vice-directors and members of standing committees in the ten districts and fifteen industrial bureau liaison posts under WGH command.

102. The problems were classified as follows: (1) serious shortcomings in one's political history; (2) bad leadership style, requiring detention; (3) acting as a gangster chief (*liumang afei touzi*), calling for labor reform; (4) a counterrevolutionary family background; (5) a spouse who was a petty entrepreneur or capitalist boss; (6) "thoroughly reactionary" thinking; (7) speculation and profiteering or graft and embezzlement; (8) illicit sexual relations; (9) major foreign connections among one's friends and relatives; (10) complicated social relations; and (11) others. "Zhuan'an diaocha qingkuang huibao" [Situation report on the special case investigation], January 1968.

103. WGH, "Guanyu yuan gezu, xian, ju lianluozhan yishang changwei bei juliu, daibu de qingkuang baogao" [Situation report on detentions and arrests of standing committees at district, county, bureau liaison posts, and above], April 19, 1969.

104. Xu Jiangang, "Sirenbang pohai Shanghai ganbu qunzhong de sanchang yundong" [Three campaigns of the Gang of Four to harm Shanghai cadres and masses], *Shanghai dangshi* [Shanghai party history], No. 12 (1990).

105. Ibid. Among scientists, those who remained in Shanghai in 1949, rather than fleeing the country for Taiwan, Hong Kong, or other foreign locations, were castigated as "hid-

den secret agents." Those who had returned from stints abroad were said to be "deployed secret agents," and those who had graduated from Chinese universities were "newly cultivated secret agents." The Shanghai Academy of Natural Sciences of the Japanese Occupation era and the Academia Sinica of the KMT era were dubbed the "two fronts." When the KMT retreated, scientific personnel at Academia Sinica founded a "safe reception committee" to protect facilities, equipment, books, materials, etc. during the transition. This incident was now investigated under the rubric of the "two fronts–one committee case"; it touched 14 scientific units and 639 scientists—of whom 239 were illegally incarcerated, two were inadvertently beaten to death, four were persecuted to death, and ten were purposely beaten to death. Within the literary world, writers and artists of the sixth rank or higher were virtually all attacked, and, in special cases, more than 80% were interrogated. Even in the suburbs, some 45,600 people were subjected to various degrees of persecution, and 2,922 were killed.

106. Wang Hongwen, August 10, 1968, report at the Conference to Hold High the Red Banner of Mao Zedong Thought.

107. WGH, ed., *Qingkuang huibao* [Situation report], May 28, 1969.

108. Ibid., March 11, 1969.

109. Ibid., March 28, 1969.

110. WGH, ed., *Jian Bao* [Brief report], July 1968.

111. *Qingkuang huibao*, November 26, 1968.

112. Ibid., February 28, 1969.

113. Ibid., March 24, 1969.

114. Wang Hongwen, April 11, 1968, speech at WGH expanded conference.

115. Ibid.

116. Shortly after the launching of the One Strike, Three-Antis campaign, another draconian sweep was initiated: the "Cleanse May Sixteenth" movement. The latter campaign began on March 27, 1970, after Party Central issued a proclamation against a so-called May Sixteenth Conspiracy. Although the alleged conspiracy was fictitious, the search for culprits lasted until 1973. The main targets were former Red Guards and rebels from the literary and art worlds. In Shanghai, the campaign was a pretext to seek out those who had participated in the bombardment of Zhang Chunqiao. In May 1971, the SRC established a special agency, which fingered more than 2,500 people around the country for involvement in the bombardment. Xu Jiangang (see note 104).

117. SRC, ed., *Guanyu qingdui yida sanfan zhong dingxing chuli luoshi zhengce de jiben qingkuang* [The basic situation concerning definitions and policy implementation during the Cleansing of Ranks and One Strike, Three-Antis (campaigns)], 1974.

118. Ibid. Even the Red Guards of Bombard Headquarters were not spared. A Workers' Propaganda Team at Fudan University fabricated a "Hu Shoujun counter-revolutionary clique case"; in connection with this case, the WPT held some 40 people and implicated more than 100 others, some of whom were sentenced to jail terms. Xu Jiangang (see note 104).

119. WGH, "Xiaqu renyuan tongjibiao" [Statistics on sent-down personnel], 1970.

120. WGH, "Zhongbiao gongsi zaofanpai xin ganbu qingkuang tongji" [Statistics on new cadres of rebels in the Watch Company], November 1972.

121. WGH, "Xin ganbu fenxi qingkuang tongjibiao" [Statistics analyzing the condition of new cadres], February 23, 1971.

122. WGH, "Zai dang de yiyuanhua lingdao xia jiaqiang xinganbu duiwu he gongdaihui de jianshe" [Establishment of worker representative congresses and strengthening of new cadre ranks under the unified leadership of the party], March 1972.

123. SFTU, "Zhu Shanghaishi wenjiao xitong gongxuanduiyuan qingkuang tongjibiao" [Statistics on WPTs in Shanghai's industry-transport system], January 1974. Of the 1,548 WPT members sent to 18 universities, 453 had an elementary school education, 1,042 a middle or high school education, and 53 (3.4%) a university education. The same investigation noted that of the 935 WPT members sent to movie theaters, broadcast stations, the Cultural Bureau, the Publishing Bureau, *Liberation Daily*, *Wenhui Bao*, the Education Bureau and the Public Health Bureau, 312 had an elementary school education, 588 a middle and high school education, and 35 (3.7%) a university education. Of the 15 WPT members who occupied *Wenhui Bao*, for example, only one had a university education.

124. WGH, "Guanyu gongxuandui jinzhu shangceng jianzhu lingdao doupigai de yixie qingkuang" [Concerning the condition of WPTs occupying upper echelons of leadership] 1974.

125. At Shanghai Science and Technology University there were about 2,500 students and faculty, and WPT members numbered 27 people, a ratio of 92 to 1. At the Shanghai Railways Institute, students and faculty numbered 1,800, and WPT members numbered 29, a ratio of 60 to 1. At Tongji University, there were 97 WPT members, but the campus had 104 party branches and research and teaching offices, so there were not even enough WPT members to send one to each division. At the elementary schools, the number of WPT members was even smaller—an average of 1.8 WPT member per school. Ibid.

126. For example, at the Shanghai Drama Academy, 28 out of 47 WPT members (60%) were former cadres. At the No. 1 Medical College, of 76 WPT members 42 (55%) were former cadres.

127. SFTU, "Zhu Shanghaishi wenjiao."

128. SFTU, 1974 Situation Report on WPTs (see note 55).

129. Ibid.

130. Wang Xiuzhen, June 30, 1978, testimony.

131. Maurice Meisner, *Mao's China and After* (New York: Free Press, 1977), 413.

132. The participants included Ye Changming, Chen Ada, Jin Zumin, Huang Jinhai, and Dai Liqing, as well as Kang Ningyi and Wang Richu, military representatives to the union.

133. The ninth struggle was the criticism of Liu Shaoqi and the tenth struggle was the criticism of Lin Biao.

134. Wang Xiuzhen, Feburary 24, 1977, testimony.

135. For example, on February 3 the Shanghai Construction Bureau Union convened a meeting, on February 4 the Shanghai No. 1 Machinery/Electronics Union convened a meeting, on February 7 the Yangpu District Union convened one, etc. There were several thousand people at all of these meetings. At the meetings, cadres were criticized for being "restorationists," "Confucians," "detractors of newborn things," "right-wing conservatives," "oppressors of new forces," etc. *Shanghai shihua*.

136. Ye Changming, June 14, 1977, testimony.

137. Zhang Chunqiao, February 1974 letter to Ma Tianshui. Mao had advocated a cultural revolution every seven or eight years.

138. For example, during February and March of 1974, the No. 1 Machine-Electric Bureau uncovered 186 units with "two denials" problems (45% of the total number of units

under bureau supervision). More than 1,000 people were targeted, of whom 103 were top-level cadres in the factories. Similarly, in the Textile Bureau, every level from bureau to company to factory chose "rightist restorationist representatives," and in several months, 510 cadres were dismissed or set aside; a total of 157 units were affected. *Shanghai shihua.*

139. Ibid.

140. Ibid.

141. Ibid.

142. SFTU 1974 work report.

143. Ye Changming, June 14, 1977.

144. *Shanghai shihua,* 694–695.

145. Ibid.

146. Ibid.

147. Huang Jinhai, June 9, 1977, testimony.

148. SFTU, ed., *1974nian gongzuo qingkuang he 1975nian gongzuo yijian de baogao* [Report on the 1974 work situation and work plans for 1975], 1974, second draft.

149. Wang Nianyi, *Da dongluan de niandai* [Years of great chaos] (Kaifeng: Henan People's Press, 1988).

150. On symbolic scapegoats during the CR, see Lowell Dittmer, *Liu Shao-ch'i and the Chinese Cultural Revolution: The Politics of Mass Criticism* (Berkeley: University of California Press, 1974).

151. Wang Xiuzhen, December 26, 1980, testimony.

152. Ibid.

153. Ibid.

154. Actually, the list—which was compiled in haste—contained 186 names, but five turned out to be redundant; only 181 people were identified for rehabilitation. SFTU Small Group, *Guanyu 'sirenbang' ji qi yudang* (see note 18).

155. Ibid. Also included under this rubric were several early WGH leaders: Xu Meiying, Huang Wenhai, Jiang Zhoufa, Jiang Zuodong, and Chen Jinxing.

156. Ibid. This category included WGH leaders Ding Defa, Cen Qilin, Zhang Bosheng, and Xie Pengfei; WGH Yangpu District Liaison Post leader Cheng Lin, etc.

157. Ibid.

158. Wang Xiuzhen, December 29, 1980, testimony.

159. SFTU Small Group, ed., *Guanyu 'sirenbang' ji qi yudang.* After the conclusion of the CR, the 181 people who had been slated for rehabilitation were subjected to yet another round of investigations. In January 1978, thirty of them were imprisoned.

160. Sebastian Heilmann, "The Social Context of Mobilization in China: Factions, Work Units, and Activists During the 1976 April Fifth Movement," *China Information* 8, no. 3 (winter 1993–94): 1–19.

161. *Shanghai shihua,* 906–907. Although Shanghai saw little action at the time of the April Clear and Bright Festival, the city had witnessed a mass demonstration in honor of Zhou on January 15, a week after the premier's death. See *Shanghai shihua,* 899–900.

162. PLA Shanghai Garrison, ed., *Sirenbang zai Shanghai jingying dier wuzhuang shimo* [The saga of the Gang of Four's management of a second military force in Shanghai], 1988.

163. Ibid.

164. *Shanghai shihua,* chap. 36.

165. Ibid.

166. "Dog-beating brigades" (*dagou dui*) had been established by the Communists in the 1920s and 1930s to deal harshly with scabs and other opponents of the radical labor movement. See Elizabeth J. Perry, *Shanghai on Strike: The Politics of Chinese Labor* (Stanford: Stanford University Press, 1993), p. 84 footnote.

167. *Shanghai shihua*, chap. 36.

168. Ibid.

169. Ibid.

170. Xiaoxia Gong concludes in her study of the CR, "Different authority groups manipulated the various mass movements to victimize different groups of people." Xiaoxia Gong, "Repressive Movements and the Politics of Victimization" (Harvard University, Ph.D. diss., 1995), 278.

171. Continuing rebel influence was not unique to Shanghai, however. Keith Forster credits leaders of rebel organizations in Zhejiang Province with considerable "organizational achievements" between 1973 and 1976. See Keith Forster, *Rebellion and Factionalism in a Chinese Province: Zhejiang, 1966–1976* (Armonk, N.Y.: M. E. Sharpe, 1990), 252.

172. Stephen Andors, *China's Industrial Revolution: Politics, Planning, and Management, 1949 to the Present* (New York: Pantheon, 1977), 213.

173. Wang Shaoguang notes of the worker rebels in Wuhan, "The rebel faction leaders wanted to be in power, not so much because they needed power to realize noble goals such as reforming the existing system as because they wanted power as such." Wang Shaoguang, *Failure of Charisma: The Cultural Revolution in Wuhan* (New York: Oxford University Press, 1995), 170.

174. *Shanghai gongyun zhi* [Shanghai labor movement gazetteer], pt. 2, chap. 21 (Shanghai, 1996).

175. Lowell Dittmer, *China's Continuous Revolution: The Post-Liberation Epoch, 1949–1981* (Berkeley: University of California Press, 1987), 165. Keith Forster, in a more detailed study of the Hangzhou Incident, attributes the strikes primarily to political factionalism. Forster, *Rebellion and Factionalism*, 224–228.

176. Ibid., 166.

Notes to Chapter 7

1. See especially Michel Oksenberg, "Occupational Groups in Chinese Society and the Cultural Revolution," in Oksenberg, *The Cultural Revolution: 1967 in Review* (Ann Arbor: University of Michigan Center for Chinese Studies, 1968); David S. G. Goodman, ed., *Groups in the People's Republic of China* (Armonk, N.Y.: M. E. Sharpe, Inc., 1984); and Victor C. Falkenheim, ed., *Citizens and Groups in Contemporary China* (Ann Arbor: University of Michigan Center for Chinese Studies, 1987).

2. Andrew G. Walder, "Communist Social Structure and Workers' Politics in China," in Falkenheim, *Citizens and Groups*, p. 82.

3. See, especially, Steffen W. Schmidt, James C. Scott, Carl Lande, and Laura Guasti, eds., *Friends, Followers, and Factions: A Reader in Political Clientelism* (Berkeley: University of California Press, 1977).

4. Lucian Pye and Richard Solomon have portrayed the Cultural Revolution as a crisis in political development reflective of an age-old Chinese desire for greater authority. As

Pye puts it, "In the Great Proletarian Cultural Revolution . . . we see the same themes be-deviling the Chinese. . . . The demand of the revolutionaries is for a more complete disci-plining of life." (Lucian W. Pye, *The Spirit of Chinese Politics: A Psychocultural Study of the Authority Crisis in Political Development* [Cambridge: MIT Press, 1968], 10.) For Solomon, Mao's Cultural Revolution was essentially a (futile) one-man crusade to over-come the dependent character of China's traditional political culture: "Mao might be said to be an 'anal' leader seeking to transform an 'oral' society." (Richard H. Solomon, *Mao's Revolution and the Chinese Political Culture* [Berkeley: University of California Press, 1971], 521.)

5. Harold Lasswell, *Psychopathology and Politics* (New York: Viking Press 1960).

6. The notion of a "rebel personality" has attracted substantial interest among Western students of revolution, but the terms of the analysis have usually been Freudian in inspira-tion. See, for example, Erik H. Erickson, *Young Man Luther: A Study in Psychoanalysis and History* (New York: Norton, 1958); Bertram David Wolfe, *Three Who Made a Revolution* (New York: Dell, 1964); E. Victor Wolfenstein, *The Revolutionary Personality* (Princeton: Princeton University Press, 1967). If it is unclear that an exploration of the "Oedipal com-plex" has taught us much about Western revolutionaries, the approach seems even less ap-plicable in the Chinese cultural context.

7. Yang Dongping, *Chengshi jifeng* [Urban monsoon] (Beijing: Dongfang Press, 1994), 296, 303.

8. Emily Honig's pioneering work on native-place divisions in Shanghai is an important contribution to our understanding of "ethnic" influences among the working class, even after the establishment of the People's Republic. See her *Creating Chinese Ethnicity* (New Haven: Yale University Press, 1992), esp. chap. 7. On the culture of the shantytowns of Shanghai, see Nai Peichun's drama entitled *Dushili cunzhuang* [Village within a city].

9. In his more recent writings, Lucian Pye has acknowledged the existence of two politi-cal cultures in Communist China: a Maoist rebel culture, which he identifies with the het-erodoxy of Daoism, Buddhism, and folk religion in imperial days; and a Dengist restraint, which he identifies with the orthodoxy of Confucianism. See *The Mandarin and the Cadre: China's Political Cultures* (Ann Arbor: University of Michigan Center for Chinese Studies, 1988), esp. chap. 2. Unfortunately, Pye does not provide a convincing explanation for the origins and operations of these competing cultural tendencies in the contemporary con-text.

Anita Chan's (1985) use of the "authoritarian personality" concept to explain student rebels during the CR also offers little help in understanding rebel leadership among work-ers. Chan's interviews with student Red Guards led her to highlight the centrality of the school socialization process, a factor that does not figure significantly in workers' accounts of their turn to rebellion. A similar problem applies to David Raddock's (1977) interpreta-tion of Red Guard activism in terms of adolescent hostility. Raddock's emphasis on the re-lationship between father and (teen-age) son is of limited utility in explaining the behavior of the much older worker rebels.

10. Tang Wenlan, May 17, 1992, interview.

11. Concerning rebel culture, see Elizabeth J. Perry and Li Xun, "Revolutionary Rude-ness: The Language of Red Guards and Rebel Workers in China's Cultural Revolution," *In-diana East Asian Working Paper Series on Language and Politics in Modern China*, no. 2 (July 1993): 1–18. For the influence of this cultural style on the uprising of 1989, see Vera

Schwarcz, "Memory and Commemoration: The Chinese Search for a Livable Past," in Jeffrey N. Wasserstrom and Elizabeth J. Perry, eds., *Popular Protest and Political Culture in Modern China.* 2nd ed. (Boulder: Westview Press, 1994), 170–183; and Liu Xiaobo, "That Holy Word, 'Revolution,'" in Ibid., 309–324.

12. In these cases, military representatives had been present in the factories *before* the CR to provide technical direction.

13. On political opportunity structure, see Bert Klandermans, Hanspeter Kriesi, and Sidney Tarrow, eds., *From Structure to Action* (Greenwich: JAI Press 1988).

14. Yang Dongping, *Chengshi jifeng,* 309 (see note 7).

15. See Elizabeth J. Perry, "To Rebel is Justified: Maoist Influences on Popular Protest in Contemporary China," *Hong Kong Journal of Social Sciences* (forthcoming, 1996).

16. Solomon, *Mao's Revolution and Chinese Political Culture.*

17. Walder, *Communist Neotraditionalism.* For a critique of Walder's work that proposes the term "work unit socialism" as a substitute for the "neotraditionalism" of Walder (following Ken Jowitt), see Brantly Womack, "Transfigured Community: Neo-Traditionalism and Work Unit Socialism in China," *China Quarterly,* no. 126 (July 1991): 324–332.

18. Gail E. Henderson and Myron S. Cohen, *The Chinese Hospital: A Socialist Work Unit* (New Haven: Yale University Press, 1984), 140. An additional study of a *danwei* is found in Marc J. Blecher and Gordon White, *Micropolitics in Contemporary China: A Technical Unit During and After the Cultural Revolution* (Armonk, N.Y.: M. E. Sharpe, 1979).

19. The point is developed in Elizabeth J. Perry, "From Native-Place to Workplace: Labor Origins and Outcomes of China's *Danwei* System," in William Kirby, ed., *China's Mid-Century Transitions,* (Cambridge: Harvard University Press, forthcoming).

20. For a case study of worker activism during the Hundred Flowers, campaign, see Elizabeth J. Perry, "Shanghai's Strike Wave of 1957," *China Quarterly* (March 1994): 1–27. On the Tiananmen Incident of 1976, see Sebastian Heilmann, "The Social Context of Mobilization in China: Factions, Work Units, and Activists During the April Fifth Movement in 1976," *China Information* (1994); and on the 1989 uprising see Andrew G. Walder and Gong Xiaoxia, "Workers in the Tiananmen Protests: The Politics of the Beijing Workers' Autonomous Federation," *The Australian Journal of Chinese Affairs,* no. 29 (January 1993): 1–29. An elaboration of this argument can be found in Elizabeth J. Perry, "Labor's Battle for Political Space: The Role of Worker Associations in Contemporary China," chap. 11 in Deborah Davis, Richard C. Kraus, Barry Naughton, and Elizabeth J. Perry, eds., *Urban Spaces in Contemporary China: The Potential for Autonomy and Community in Post-Mao China* (New York: Cambridge University Press, 1995).

21. Dietrich Rueschemeyer, Evelyne Huber Stephens, and John D. Stephens, *Capitalist Development and Democracy* (Chicago: University of Chicago Press, 1992); Ruth Berins Collier, *The Contradictory Alliance: State-Labor Relations and Regime Change in Mexico* (Berkeley: International and Area Studies, University of California, Berkeley, 1992); Ruth Berins Collier and David Collier, *Shaping the Political Arena: Critical Junctures, the Labor Movement, and Regime Dynamics in Latin America* (Princeton: Princeton University Press, 1991).

22. Xueguang Zhou, "Unorganized Interests and Collective Action in Communist China," *American Sociological Review,* vol. 58, no. 1 (February 1993): p. 58.

23. Ibid., 59.

24. Daniel Kelliher, *Peasant Power in China: The Era of Rural Reform, 1979–1989* (New Haven: Yale University Press, 1992), 31.

25. Ibid., 103.

26. Zhou, "Unorganized Interests," 55.

27. Ibid., p. 54.

28. A recent dissertation categorizes the CR as a species of "repressive movement," which is defined as "a social movement manipulated from above, where the role of the state authorities is essential." Xiaoxia Gong, "Repressive Movements and the Politics of Victimization: Patronage and Persecution During the Cultural Revolution" (Harvard University, Ph.D. diss., 1995), 9.

Selected Bibliography

Ahn Byung-joon. *Chinese Politics and the Cultural Revolution: The Dynamics of Policy Processes.* Seattle: University of Washington Press, 1976.

Anderson, Evelyn. "Shanghai: The Masses Unleashed." *Problems of Communism* 17 (January–February 1968): 12–21.

Andors, Stephen. *China's Industrial Revolution: Politics, Planning, and Management, 1949 to the Present.* New York: Pantheon, 1977.

Baum, Richard, and Frederick C. Teiwes. *Ssu-ch'ing: The Socialist Education Movement of 1962–1966.* Berkeley: Center for Chinese Studies, University of California, 1968.

Bennett, Gordon A., and Ronald N. Montaperto. *Red Guard: The Political Biography of Dai Hsiao-ai.* Garden City NJ: Doubleday, 1972.

Bernstein, Thomas P. *Up to the Mountains and Down to the Villages: The Transfer of Youth from Urban to Rural China.* New Haven: Yale University Press, 1977.

Blecher, Marc J., and Gordon White. *Micropolitics in Contemporary China: A Technical Unit During and After the Cultural Revolution.* Armonk, NY: M. E. Sharpe, 1979.

Calhoun, Craig C. *Neither Gods Nor Emperors: Students and the Struggle for Democracy in China.* Berkeley: University of California Press, 1995.

Chan, Anita. *Children of Mao: Personality Development and Political Activism in the Red Guard Generation.* Seattle: University of Washington Press, 1985.

Chan, Anita, et al. "Students and Class Warfare: The Social Roots of the Red Guard Conflict in Guangzhou (Canton)" *China Quarterly* 83 (September 1980): 397–446.

Chang, Parris. "Shanghai and Chinese Politics: Before and After the Cultural Revolution," pp. 66–90. In Christopher Howe, ed., *Shanghai: Revolution and Development in an Asian Metropolis.* Cambridge: Cambridge University Press, 1981.

Chen Xianfa. *Minzu lei* [National tears]. Shanghai: Tongji University Press, 1988.

Cheng, Nien. *Life and Death in Shanghai.* London: Collins, 1986.

Cheng, T. J., and Mark Selden. "The Origins and Social Consequences of China's *Hukou* System." *China Quarterly* 139 (September 1994): 644–668.

Cobb, Richard. *The People's Armies.* New Haven: Yale University Press, 1987.

Collier, Ruth Berins. *The Contradictory Alliance: State-Labor Relations and Regime Change in Mexico.* Berkeley: International and Area Studies, University of California, Berkeley, 1992.

Collier, Ruth Berins, and David Collier. *Shaping the Political Arena: Critical Junctures, the Labor Movement, and Regime Dynamics in Latin America.* Princeton: Princeton University Press, 1991.

Communist Youth League, ed. *Shanghai hongweibing dashiji* [Annals of the Shanghai Red Guards]. Shanghai, 1983.

Davies, James C., ed. *When Men Revolt and Why.* New York: Free Press, 1971.

Davis, Deborah, et al., eds. *Urban Spaces in Contemporary China: The Potential for Autonomy and Community in Post-Mao China.* New York: Cambridge University Press, 1995.

Di Jiu and Zhi Wu. *Xie yu huo de jiaoxun—wenge zhongda wudou can'an jishi* [Lessons of blood and fire: Annals of large-scale Cultural Revolution battles and massacres]. Lanzhou: Xinjiang University Press, 1993.

Dittmer, Lowell. *Liu Shao-ch'i and the Chinese Cultural Revolution: The Politics of Mass Criticism.* Berkeley: University of California Press, 1974.

———. "Political Culture and Political Symbolism." *World Politics* 29, no. 4 (July 1977): 552–584.

———. "Bases of Power in Chinese Politics: A Theory and an Analysis of the Fall of the 'Gang of Four.'" *World Politics* 31, no. 1 (October 1978): 26–61.

———. *China's Continuous Revolution: The Post-Liberation Epoch, 1949–1981.* Berkeley: University of California Press, 1987.

Erickson, Erik H. *Young Man Luther: A Study in Psychoanalysis and History.* New York: Norton, 1958.

Erqi dabagong ziliao xuanbian [Compilation of materials about the great strike of February 7]. Beijing: Workers' Publishing House, 1983.

Falkenheim, Victor C., ed. *Citizens and Groups in Contemporary China.* Ann Arbor: University of Michigan Center for Chinese Studies, 1987.

Fisher, Tom. "'The Play's the Thing': Wu Han and Hai Rui Revisited," pp. 9–45. In Jonathan Unger, ed., *Using the Past to Serve the Present: Historiography and Politics in Contemporary China.* Armonk, NY: M. E. Sharpe, 1993.

Forster, Keith. *Rebellion and Factionalism in a Chinese Province: Zhejiang, 1966–1976.* Armonk, NY: M. E. Sharpe, 1990.

Gao Yuan, *Born Red.* Stanford: Stanford University Press, 1987.

Goldman, Merle. *China's Intellectuals: Advise and Dissent.* Cambridge, MA: Harvard University Press, 1981.

Gong, Xiaoxia. "Repressive Movements and the Politics of Victimization." Ph.D. diss., Harvard University, 1995.

Goodman, David S. G., ed. *Groups in the People's Republic of China.* Armonk, NY: M. E. Sharpe, 1984.

Gurr, Ted Robert. *Why Men Rebel.* Princeton: Princeton University Press, 1971.

Harper, Paul F. "The Party and the Unions in Communist China." *China Quarterly* 37 (January 1969).

Heilmann, Sebastian. "The Social Context of Mobilization in China: Factions, Work Units and Activists during the 1976 April Fifth Movement." *China Information* 8, no. 3 (Winter 1993–1994): 1–19.

Henderson, Gail E., and Myron S. Cohen. *The Chinese Hospital: A Socialist Work Unit.* New Haven: Yale University Press, 1984.

Hinton, William. *Shenfan.* London: Picador Books, 1983.

Honig, Emily. *Creating Chinese Ethnicity: Subei People in Shanghai, 1850–1980.* New Haven: Yale University Press, 1992.

Howe, Christopher. "Industrialization Under Conditions of Long-Run Population Stability: Shanghai's Achievement and Prospect." In Christopher Howe, ed., *Shanghai: Revolution and Development in an Asian Metropolis.* Cambridge: Cambridge University Press, 1981.

———, ed. *Shanghai: Revolution and Development in an Asian Metropolis.* Cambridge: Cambridge University Press, 1981.

Hunter, Neale. *Shanghai Journal: An Eyewitness Account of the Cultural Revolution*. New York: Praeger, 1969.

Hu Yuewei. *Fengkuang de Shanghai* [Crazed Shanghai]. Chengdu: Sichuan Cultural Press, 1986.

Jiangjun juanjin xuanwo [The general swept into the whirlpool]. Nanjing: Jiangsu Literary Arts Press, 1988.

Jin Chunming. *Wenhua dageming lunxi* [Analysis of the Cultural Revolution]. Shanghai: Shanghai People's Press, 1985.

Jin, Qiu. "The Lin Biao Incident: A Study of Extra-Institutional Factors in the Cultural Revolution." Ph.D. diss., University of Hawaii, 1995.

Kagan, Richard, and Norma Diamond. "Father, Son, and Holy Ghost: Pye, Solomon, and the 'Spirit of Chinese Politics.'" *Bulletin of Concerned Asian Scholars* 5, no. 1 (July 1973): 62–68.

Karnow, Stanley. *Mao and China: From Revolution to Revolution*. New York: Viking, 1972.

Kelliher, Daniel. *Peasant Power in China: The Era of Rural Reform, 1979–1989*. New Haven: Yale University Press, 1992.

Keniston, Kenneth. *Young Radicals: Notes on Committed Youth*. New York: Hartcourt, Brace and World, Inc., 1969.

Kirby, William, ed. *China's Mid-Century Transitions*. Cambridge, MA: Harvard University Press, forthcoming.

Klandermans, Bert, et al., eds. *From Structure to Action: Comparing Social Movement Research Across Cultures*. Greenwich, CT: JAI, 1988.

Kraus, Richard. *Class Conflict in Chinese Socialism*. New York: Columbia University Press, 1981.

Lasswell, Harold. *Psychopathology and Politics*. New York: Viking, 1960.

Lee, Hong Yung. *The Politics of the Chinese Cultural Revolution: A Case Study*. Berkeley: University of California Press, 1978.

Lewis, John W., ed. *The City in Communist China*. Stanford: Stanford University Press, 1971.

Liang Heng and Judith Shapiro, *Son of the Revolution*. New York: Random House, 1983.

Li Ke and He Shengzhang. *Wenhua dageming zhong de renmin jiefangjun* [The People's Liberation Army in the Cultural Revolution]. Beijing: Party History Materials Press, 1989.

Li Lang. "Heshang yu hongweibing" [Monks and Red Guards]. *Falu zixun* [Legal Information]. (September 1986).

Li Zhisui. *The Private Life of Chairman Mao*. New York: Random House, 1994.

Ling, Ken. *The Revenge of Heaven: Journal of a Young Chinese*. New York: Putnam, 1972.

Liu, Alan P. L. *Political Culture and Group Conflict in Communist China*. Santa Barbara: Clio Press, 1976.

Liu Binyan. *A Higher Kind of Loyalty: A Memoir by China's Foremost Journalist*. New York: Pantheon, 1990.

Liu Xiaobo. "That Holy Word, 'Revolution,'" pp. 309–324. In Jeffrey N. Wasserstrom and Elizabeth J. Perry, eds., *Popular Protest and Political Culture in Modern China*. 2d ed. Boulder: Westview Press, 1994.

Lu Xiuyuan. "A Step Toward Understanding Popular Violence in China's Cultural Revolution." *Pacific Affairs* 67, no. 4 (winter 1994–95): 533–563.

MacFarquhar, Roderick. *The Origins of the Cultural Revolution*. Vol.1, *Contradictions Among the People, 1956–1957*. New York: Columbia University Press, 1974.

Madsen, Richard. *Morality and Power in a Chinese Village*. Berkeley: University of California, 1984.

Marsalis, Wynton, and Frank Stewart. *Sweet Swing Blues on the Road*. New York: W. W. Norton, 1994.

Marx, Karl, and Friedrich Engels. *Manifesto of the Communist Party*. London, 1948.

McAdam, Doug. *The Political Process and the Development of Black Insurgency*. Chicago: University of Chicago Press, 1982.

Meisner, Maurice. *Mao's China and After*. New York: Free Press, 1977.

Melucci, Alberto. *Nomads of the Present: Social Movements and Individual Needs in Contemporary Society*. Philadelphia: Temple University Press, 1989.

Morris, Aldon, and Carol McClurg, eds. *Frontiers in Social Movement Theory*. New Haven: Yale University Press, 1992.

Naquin, Susan. *Millenarian Rebellion in China: The Eight Trigrams Uprising of 1813*. New Haven: Yale University Press, 1976.

Nee, Victor. "Revolution and Bureaucracy: Shanghai in the Cultural Revolution." In Victor Nee and James Peck, eds., *China's Uninterrupted Revolution (From 1840 to the Present)*. New York: Pantheon Books, 1975.

Nee, Victor, and James Peck, eds. *China's Uninterrupted Revolution (From 1840 to the Present)*. New York: Pantheon Books, 1975.

Oberschall, Anthony. *Social Conflict and Social Movements*. Englewood Cliffs, NJ: Prentice-Hall, 1973.

Oi, Jean C. *State and Peasant in Contemporary China: The Political Economy of Village Government*. Berkeley: University of California Press, 1989.

Oksenberg, Michel. *The Cultural Revolution: 1967 in Review*. Ann Arbor: University of Michigan Center for Chinese Studies, 1968.

——————. "Occupational Groups in Chinese Society and the Cultural Revolution." In *The Cultural Revolution: 1967 in Review*. Ann Arbor: University of Michigan Center for Chinese Studies, 1968.

Olson, Mancur. *The Logic of Collective Action*. Cambridge: Harvard University Press, 1965.

Perry, Elizabeth J. "Rural Violence in Socialist China." *China Quarterly* 119 (September 1989).

——————. *Shanghai on Strike: The Politics of Chinese Labor*. Stanford: Stanford University Press, 1993.

——————. "Chinese Political Culture Revisited," pp. 1–14. In Jeffrey N. Wasserstrom and Elizabeth J. Perry, eds., *Popular Protest and Political Culture in Modern China*. 2d ed. Boulder: Westview Press, 1994: 1–27.

——————. "Shanghai's Strike Wave of 1957." *China Quarterly* 137 (March 1994).

——————. "Labor's Battle for Political Space: The Role of Worker Associations in Contemporary China." In Deborah Davis, Richard C. Kraus, Barry Naughton, and Elizabeth J. Perry, eds., *Urban Spaces in Contemporary China: The Potential for Autonomy and Community in Post-Mao China*. New York: Cambridge University Press, 1995.

——————, ed. *Putting Class in Its Place: Worker Identities in East Asia*. Berkeley: University of California Institute of East Asian Studies, 1996.

——————. "From Native-place to Workplace: Labor Origins and Outcomes of China's *Danwei* System." In William Kirby, ed. *China's Mid-Century Transitions*, Cambridge, MA: Harvard University Press, forthcoming.

―――. "To Rebel is Justified: Maoist Influences on Popular Protest in Contemporary China." *Hong Kong Journal of Social Sciences* (forthcoming, 1996).

Perry, Elizabeth J., and Li Xun. "Revolutionary Rudeness: The Language of Red Guards and Rebel Workers in China's Cultural Revolution." *Indiana East-Asian Working Paper Series on Language and Politics in Modern China*, no. 2 (July 1993): 1–18.

Pye, Lucian W. *The Spirit of Chinese Politics: A Psychocultural Study of the Authority Crisis in Political Development*. Cambridge, MA: MIT Press, 1968.

―――. *The Dynamics of Chinese Politics*. Cambridge, MA: Oelgeschlager, Gunn and Hain, 1981.

―――. *The Mandarin and the Cadre: China's Political Cultures*. Ann Arbor: University of Michigan Center for Chinese Studies, 1988.

Raddock, David M. *Political Behavior of Adolescents in China: The Cultural Revolution in Kwangchow*. Tucson: University of Arizona Press, 1977.

Ragvald, Lars. *Yao Wen-yuan as Literary Critic and Theorist*. Stockholm: University of Sweden, 1978.

Rice, Edward E. *Mao's Way*. Berkeley: University of California Press, 1972.

Robinson, Thomas W. "The Wuhan Incident: Local Strife and Provincial Rebellion During the Cultural Revolution." *China Quarterly* 47 (July-September 1971): 413–418.

Rosen, Stanley. *Red Guard Factionalism and the Cultural Revolution in Guangzhou (Canton)*. Boulder: Westview Press, 1982.

Rueschemeyer, Dietrich, et al. *Capitalist Development and Democracy*. Chicago: University of Chicago Press, 1992.

Schmidt, Steffen W., et al., eds. *Friends, Followers, and Factions: A Reader in Political Clientelism*. Berkeley: University of California Press, 1977.

Schoenhals, Michael. "The Central Case Examination Group, 1966–79," *China Quarterly* 145 (March 1996): 87–111.

Schurmann, Franz. *Ideology and Organization in Communist China*. Berkeley: University of California Press, 1968.

Schwarcz, Vera. "Memory and Commemoration: The Chinese Search for a Livable Past." In Jeffrey N. Wasserstrom and Elizabeth J. Perry, eds., *Popular Protest and Political Culture in Modern China*. 2d ed. Boulder: Westview Press, 1994.

Scott, James C. *Domination and the Arts of Resistance: Hidden Transcripts*. New Haven: Yale University Press, 1990.

Selden, Mark. *The Political Economy of Chinese Development*. Armonk, NY: M. E. Sharpe, 1993.

―――. "Labor Unrest in China, 1831–1990." *Review* 18, no. 1 (winter 1995).

Shanghai Branch of Bank of China, ed. *Jianguo yilai de Shanghai yinhang gongzuo* [Shanghai banking work since 1949]. Shanghai, 1986.

Shanghai Federation of Trade Unions, ed. *Gongzongsi da shiji* [Annals of the Workers' General Headquarters]. Shanghai, 1984.

Shanghai gongyun zhi [Shanghai labor movement gazetteer]. Shanghai, 1996.

Shanghai Party Committee Cultural Revolution Materials Small Group, ed. *Shanghai "wenhua dageming" shihua* [Historical narrative of the "Great Cultural Revolution" in Shanghai]. Shanghai, 1992.

Shanghai Revolutionary Committee, ed. *Guanyu qingdui yida sanfan zhong dingxing chuli luoshi zhengce de jiben qingkuang* [The basic situation concerning definitions and policy implementation during the cleansing of ranks and one strike, three antis]. Shanghai, 1974.

Shanghaishi tongjiju guanyu Shanghai zhigong qingkuang de tongji ziliao [Statistical materials from the Shanghai Statistical Bureau concerning the condition of Shanghai workers]. Beijing: China Statistical Publishing House, 1979.

Shanghai Statistical Bureau, ed. *1965nian Shanghai zhigong jiben qingkuang tongi* [Statistics on the basic conditions of the Shanghai workforce in 1965]. Shanghai, 1966.

———, ed. *Xin Shanghai 40 nian* [40 years of new Shanghai]. Beijing: China Statistics Publishing House, 1990.

Shue, Vivienne B. "Shanghai After the January Storm," pp. 66–93. In *The Cultural Revolution in the Provinces*. Cambridge, MA: Harvard East Asia Monographs, 1971.

Snow, David E., and Robert Benford. "Master Frames and Cycles of Protest," pp. 133–155. In Aldon Morris and Carol McClurg, eds., *Frontiers in Social Movement Theory*. New Haven: Yale University Press, 1992.

Solomon, Richard H. *Mao's Revolution and the Chinese Political Culture*. Berkeley: University of California Press, 1971.

"Sources of Labor Discontent in China: The Worker-Peasant System." *Current Scene* 6, no. 5 (15 March 1968).

Tannenbaum, Gerald. "The 1967 Shanghai January Revolution Recounted." *Eastern Horizon* (May-June 1968).

Tan Zongji and Zheng Qian, eds. *Shinianhou de pingshuo—"wenhua dageming" shi lunji* [An evaluation ten years later: Collected essays on the history of the "Cultural Revolution"]. Beijing: Party History Materials Press, 1987.

Tarrow, Sidney. "Mentalities, Political Cultures, and Collective Action Frames: Constructing Meaning Through Action," pp. 174–202. In Aldon Morris and Carol McClurg, eds., *Frontiers in Social Movement Theory*. New Haven: Yale University Press, 1992.

———. *Power in Movement: Social Movements, Collective Action, and Politics*. New York: Cambridge University Press, 1994.

Tilly, Charles. *From Mobilization to Revolution*. Reading, MA: Addison-Wesley, 1978.

Unger, Jonathan, ed. *Using the Past to Serve the Present: Historiography and Politics in Contemporary China*. Armonk NY: M. E. Sharpe, 1993.

Walder, Andrew G. *Chang Ch'un-ch'iao and Shanghai's January Revolution*. Ann Arbor: Center for Chinese Studies of the University of Michigan, 1978.

———. *Communist Neo-Traditionalism: Work and Authority in Chinese Industry*. Berkeley: University of California Press, 1986.

———. "Communist Social Structure and Workers' Politics in China." In Victor C. Falkenheim, ed., *Citizens and Groups in Contemporary China*. Ann Arbor: University of Michigan Center for Chinese Studies, 1987.

———. "The Chinese Cultural Revolution in the Factories: Party-State Structures and Patterns of Conflict." In Elizabeth J. Perry, ed., *Putting Class in Its Place: Worker Identities in East Asia*. Berkeley: University of California Institute of East Asian Studies, 1996.

Walder, Andrew G., and Gong Xiaoxia. "Workers in the Tiananmen Protests: The Politics of the Beijing Workers' Autonomous Federation." *Australian Journal of Chinese Affairs* 29 (January 1993).

Wang Nianyi. *Da Dongluan de niandai* [Decade of great turmoil]. Zhengzhou: Henan People's Press, 1988.

Wang Shaoguang. *Failure of Charisma: The Cultural Revolution in Wuhan.* New York: Oxford University Press, 1995.

Wang Youqin. "1966: Xuesheng da laoshi de geming" [1966: The revolution in which students beat up teachers]. *Ershiyi shiji shuangyuekan* 31 (August 1995).

Wasserstrom, Jeffrey N. *Student Protest in Twentieth-Century China: The View from Shanghai.* Stanford: Stanford University Press, 1991.

Wasserstrom, Jeffrey N., and Elizabeth J. Perry, eds. *Popular Protest and Political Culture in Modern China.* 2d ed. Boulder: Westview Press, 1994.

White, Lynn T., III. "Shanghai's Polity in Cultural Revolution," pp. 325–70. In John W. Lewis, ed., *The City in Communist China.* Stanford: Stanford University Press, 1971.

———. "Workers' Politics in Shanghai." *Journal of Asian Studies* 26, no. 1 (1976).

———. *Policies of Chaos: Organizational Causes of Violence in China's Cultural Revolution.* Princeton: Princeton University Press, 1989.

Witke, Roxane. *Comrade Chiang Ch'ing.* Boston: Little and Brown, 1977.

Wolfe, Bertram David. *Three Who Made a Revolution.* New York: Dell, 1964.

Wolfenstein, E. Victor. *The Revolutionary Personality.* Princeton: Princeton University Press, 1967.

Womack, Brantly. "Transfigured Community: Neo-Traditionalism and Work Unit Socialism in China." *China Quarterly* 126 (July 1991): 324–332.

Wylie, Raymond F. "Shanghai Dockers in the Cultural Revolution," pp. 91–124. In Christopher Howe, ed., *Shanghai: Revolution and Development in an Asian Metropolis.* Cambridge: Cambridge University Press, 1981.

Yang Dongping. *Chengshi jifeng* [Urban monsoon]. Beijing: Dongfang Press, 1994.

Yang Jian. *Wenhua dageming zhong de dixia wenxue* [Underground literature during the Cultural Revolution]. Beijing: Chaohua Press, 1993.

Yao Wenyuan. "The Working Class Must Exercise Leadership in Everything." *Peking Review* 35 (30 August 1968).

Ye Yonglie. *Wang Hongwen xingshuai lu* [The rise and fall of Wang Hongwen]. Changchun: Shidai Wenyi Chubanshe, 1989.

Yue Daiyun, with Carolyn Wakeman. *To the Storm: The Odyssey of a Revolutionary Chinese Woman.* Berkeley: University of California Press, 1985.

Zhai Zhenhua. *Red Flower of China: An Autobiography.* New York: Soho, 1992.

Zhongguo gongchandang zai Shanghai [The Chinese Communist Party in Shanghai]. Shanghai, Shanghai People's Press, 1991.

Zhou Xueguang. "Unorganized Interests and Collective Action in Communist China." *American Sociological Review* 58, no. 1 (February 1953): 54–73.

Zhu Yongjia, et. al., eds. *Shanghai yiyue geming dashiji* [Annals of Shanghai's January Revolution]. Shanghai, 1969.

About the Book
and Authors

This pathbreaking book offers the first in-depth study of Chinese labor activism during the momentous upheaval of the Cultural Revolution. The authors explore three distinctive forms of working-class protest: rebellion, conservatism and economism. Labor, they argue, was working at cross-purposes through these three modes of militancy promoted by different types of leaders with differing agendas and motivations. Drawing upon a wealth of heretofore inaccessible archival sources, the authors probe the divergent political, psycho-cultural, and socioeconomic strains within the Shanghai labor movement. As they convincingly illustrate, the multiplicity of worker responses to the Cultural Revolution cautions against a one-dimensional portrait of working-class politics in contemporary China.

Elizabeth J. Perry is Robson Professor of Political Science at the University of California at Berkeley. **Li Xun** is a visiting researcher in the Institute of East Asian Studies, University of California at Berkeley.

Index